"For half a century this wise professor-scholar, ~~counsel~~ deeply dedicated practitioner, and icon of genuine diversity has taught Buddha Dharma. The beautiful fruit of her work is visible here."
—Jack Kornfield, PhD, author of *A Path with Heart*

"Jan Willis has practiced, reflected, and taught at one of the most important crossroads of American Buddhist life—the intersection of the activism of the Civil Rights movement and feminism, of Buddhist meditation with authentic Tibetan masters, and of the academic translation of Buddhism. This collection of her pioneering essays reveals her at once as a brilliant visionary, a pristine scholar, a heartfelt Vajrayāna practitioner, and an incisive social commentator in the twenty-first century. What ties these together is her wise heart."
—Judith Simmer-Brown, Distinguished Professor of Contemplative and Religious Studies, Naropa University, and author of *Dakini's Warm Breath: The Feminine Principle in Tibetan Buddhism*

"Wisdom flows from every page of Jan Willis's *Dharma Matters*. Her clarity of thought and insight remarkably expands the academic discourse of Buddhism into sacred conversations about gender, Buddhism, and race. Her art of storytelling and her voice bring Buddhism to life in a new way that offers hope for the present day and keeps the tradition alive for practitioners across the planet. Her scholarship sings with a deep resonance that rocks the soul and awakens the heart-mind. This powerful collection of essays is a cherished gift reflective of an incredible life of scholarship, spiritual activism, and devoted practice."
—Melanie L. Harris, American Council of Education Fellow and Professor of Religion and Ethics at Texas Christian University, author of *Gifts of Virtue, Alice Walker, and Womanist Ethics*

"This new book by Dr. Jan Willis is not only a must-read for all Buddhists interested in an unbiased inside look at gender issues in Buddhism; it is a delightful read that jumps off the page."
—Glenn Mullin, author of twenty-five books on Tibetan Buddhism

"This wonderful collection of essays and studies testifies not only to Professor Willis's achievements as a scholar with multiple interests but also, in the more personal essays, to her dedication to teaching and her role as a pioneering African American Buddhist whose call for greater inclusiveness in American Buddhism is always enfolded in love, compassion, and plain human decency."
—Ven. Bhikkhu Bodhi, translator and scholar

"For longtime fans of Jan Willis such as myself, it is a treat to have these essays gathered in one place. Her style of fine scholarship coupled with her unique personal touch and lifelong experiences will also delight new readers. There are important and even urgent issues discussed in these pages; the section on Buddhism and race is a rare contribution to a field with far too few resources for concerned practitioners and researchers."
—Sarah Harding, Tibetan translator and author of *Machik's Complete Explanation*

"In *Dharma Matters*, Dr. Willis weaves together personal, historical, cultural, religious, and universal wisdom, eloquently and tenderly offering a textured tapestry of intelligence and transformation. In this heartwarming and sagacious book, we are invited to recognize the green and golden threads of women and race wrapped in the warmth and timeless wisdom of the Dharma."
—Ruth King, author of *Mindful of Race: Transforming Racism from the Inside Out*

"Jan Willis—beloved teacher, learned scholar, pioneering practitioner-translator, cultural activist—is a national living treasure. With magisterial grace, wit, insight, wisdom, and compassion, she ranges in these eighteen diverse essays over vitally important topics of gender, Dharma, race, tantra, and liberation. In a rare yet inclusive achievement, she has kept faith with all her ancestors."
—Gaylon Ferguson, PhD, Acharya and Core Faculty in Religious Studies, Naropa University

Dharma Matters

❧ ❧

Women, Race, and Tantra

Collected Essays by Jan Willis

Forewords by Charles Johnson
and Janet Gyatso

Wisdom Publications
199 Elm Street
Somerville, MA 02144 USA
wisdomexperience.org

Library of Congress Cataloging-in-Publication Data
Names: Willis, Janet Dean, author.
Title: Dharma matters: women, race, and tantra: collected essays by Jan Willis.
Description: Somerville, MA, USA: Wisdom Publications, 2020. |
    Includes bibliographical references and index.
Identifiers: LCCN 2019044562 (print) | LCCN 2019044563 (ebook) |
    ISBN 9781614295686 (paperback) | ISBN 9781614295938 (ebook)
Subjects: LCSH: Buddhism.
Classification: LCC BQ126.W552 E87 2020 (print) | LCC BQ126.W552 (ebook) |
    DDC 294.5/48—dc23
LC record available at https://lccn.loc.gov/2019044562
LC ebook record available at https://lccn.loc.gov/2019044563

ISBN 9781614295686   ebook ISBN 9781614295938

24 23 22 21 20   5 4 3 2 1

Cover design by Jess Morphew. Interior design by Tony Lulek. Set in DGP 11.75/15..
Cover artwork: Green Tara courtesy of the Rubin Museum of Art

Contents

❦

Foreword by Charles Johnson

❧ ⟡ ❧

Jan Willis is an intellectual and spiritual pioneer. Her beautiful and important memoir, *Dreaming Me: Black, Baptist, and Buddhist—One Woman's Spiritual Journey*, is, as I wrote when I reviewed it for *Tricycle*, a twenty-first-century slave narrative rendered in Buddhist terms. In other words, it is something new and groundbreaking in the literature of black America. I have referred often to this remarkable, very influential woman in my essays, and sometimes I wondered if we were separated at birth—we were born the same year, earned advanced degrees in philosophy, survived the racially turbulent late 1960s when we were college students, and found refuge in the Buddhadharma—she in the Tibetan lineage and me in the Soto Zen tradition. But oh, how I wish I had—after twenty-two years of study—her mastery of Sanskrit and Eastern languages!

I feel honored to be able to call Jan Willis a friend, my beloved sister in the Dharma, but even more important, I see her as being one of my cherished teachers because, as she writes in this book's introduction, "teaching has been, and continues to be, the central focus of my life." In the eighteen essays that comprise *Dharma Matters*, she indeed teaches with lucidity and *upāyakauśalya*, "skillful means." And in her life, her daily practice, she models for all of us *metta*, or lovingkindness, as a scholar, educator, writer, and person with much earned wisdom.

Her own teacher, Lama Thubten Yeshe, understood her importance in the buddhaverse. In a delicious story Willis tells in *Dreaming Me*, when she and Yeshe were in Nepal, they noticed from the upper deck of his Kopan monastery a group of Western students in the courtyard below them. "Suddenly," writes Willis, "Lama Yeshe grabbed my arm and began calling out to all of them below. In a booming voice, he called, 'Look, all of you! Look! Look! You want to see women's liberation? *This* is'—pointing at me and patting me on the shoulders—'This *is* women's liberation! *This is* women's liberation!'"

This is so true. So true! But I would add to Lama Yeshe's enthusiasm that Jan Willis represents the human liberation that awaits all of us, regardless of race or gender, or whether we live in the East or West. In nondualistic fashion, hers is not a spirit of *either/or* but one of *both/ and*, as when she says, "I can use *Buddhist* methods to realize *Baptist* ideals." Willis knows all phenomenon are interdependent and interconnected, or as a writer whose name I've forgotten once said, *Whatever it is, it's you.*

If black America has a defining historical essence (*eidos*) or meaning that carries through the colonial era to the post-civil-rights period, it must be the quest for freedom. Willis's life and works deepen our understanding of what it means to be free. Truly free. She is a reliable guide into the brave new world of being black and Buddhist, and *Dharma Matters* is a book we can trust.

CHARLES JOHNSON is professor of English emeritus at the University of Washington in Seattle, a MacArthur fellow, and a renowned writer whose fiction includes *Night Hawks, Dr. King's Refrigerator, Dreamer, Oxherding Tale, Faith and the Good Thing,* and *Middle Passage,* for which he won the National Book Award.

Foreword by Janet Gyatso

❧ ❧

Jan Willis is one of our outstanding American pioneers of Buddhist studies. By that I mean both the field of Buddhist studies in America and what might be called "American Buddhist studies." On the first, she was already influential back in the 1970s, when she served as one of the critical advocates for the field to be recognized and allowed panels at the American Academy of Religion annual conventions. Jan Willis had in any case begun to demonstrate in her own work what the range of that field could and should be, starting with traditional doctrinal/philological study of Yogācāra Buddhism but quickly moving into things like the study of women in Buddhism, the concurrent use of secular and normative sources to complement each other, an interest in vernacular genres like biography, and even the importance of material culture to the study of Buddhism before that became a thing. In all of this work, Jan Willis evinces a fine and nuanced sense of the issues, raised widely in the social sciences, around the impossibility of pure objectivity in academic scholarship, not to mention the complexities around identity and advocacy, especially in the study of religion.

Just as much, Jan Willis's work has been a model for what we might call "American Buddhist studies." By that I mean learned and careful work that can speak to contemporary issues of importance to people in America, not only specialist scholars—issues especially related to race, class, and gender, all of which continue to trouble both theory and practice in religion today. It is amazing how much this side of Jan Willis's work remains at the current cutting edge of American Buddhist studies. She is not only one of the first to deploy feminist criticism in her study of Buddhism. She is also one of the first to explore openly the problems around race and the discomfort of people of color in American Buddhist communities. The latter writings, some of which are included in this volume, are still fresh and relevant around a problem that one would think could have been, and would have been, eliminated long ago! But in fact the problem is very much still with us today—Buddhist inclusiveness and compassion notwithstanding. We all have very much to learn from Willis's judicious reporting on this discouraging state of affairs and her accompanying thoughtful and balanced insights. Her work has, moreover, a great relevance for the recent womanist intersectionality with Buddhism. But again, Willis was writing about these things before they were named as such in larger academic circles.

This is also to say that Jan Willis's scholarship can readily be said in particular to instantiate what we might call "African-American Buddhist studies," even if the precise meaning of such category has yet to be defined. It may still be early in the development of any such orientation to pinpoint exactly what it is in Willis's ways of thinking about Buddhism past and present—what she notices, what she highlights, how she tells her stories—that can be connected specifically to the traumatic social memory, on the one hand, and the rich intellectual and cultural heritage, on the other, that she is heir to from her family and upbringing in Alabama in the 1950s. This question will best be left to those who have expertise in the history and nature of that memory and that heritage. But for starters we can propose that Willis's distinctive take on her work in Buddhist studies has everything to do with her own unflagging concern for social justice and her insistence on placing that concern on the moral horizon of all of her writing and research.

What we have in the present volume is a full range of Willis's expansive perspectives and concerns. With the exception of her scholarship in Yogācāra doctrine, which is not included here, the reader will be treated to important samples of her thinking on topics from Buddhist sociology, history, scripture, and doctrine to candid reflections on a slew of intractable matters around race, gender, religious identity, and the conundrums of being simultaneously a scholar, teacher, and practitioner, including her own personal investment therein. In the essays reproduced here Jan Willis gives us extremely useful historical studies and overviews of the situation of nuns in a religion that has not always been egalitarian with respect to gender, itself still a very live issue in the Buddhist community worldwide. She provides us with an overview both of the transition of Buddhist scriptures out of misogyny into inclusivity and what can be gleaned of the social facts on the ground about Buddhist female patrons and practitioners. We get a wonderful essay filled with astounding stories about the playfully brilliant figure of the ḍākinī, that famous Buddhist female angel/trickster/teacher. We get broad insights and information about the practice of telling and writing life stories of Buddhist masters in Tibet. But despite their erudition and scholarly gravity, in these essays we can also always tell that Jan Willis is pursuing such topics in light of questions close to her own heart.

For me, there is something about Jan's writing voice that perhaps is most impressive of all. Jan Willis does not stint on critique where it is called for, but she also finds creative ways forward with a generous hermeneutic that has at least one eye on the future. Her voice is kind. It is kind to her readers, providing accessible explanations and food for thought, patient and methodical, but without ever pandering or going light. Many of the essays in the volume deal specifically with Willis's own personal experiences. This includes her interviews with living examples of whatever concerns her in the essay at hand, from the nuns of Ladakh, to fellow African Americans feeling adrift or uncomfortable in a range of Buddhist contexts, to inspiring and highly accomplished African American teachers in that same American Buddhist world. And while the interview mode already opens up the personal and real-life dimensions of the topic under discussion for both author and reader, Jan Willis is never shy to go even further and use her own self as an example too, and to write candidly, for example, out of her own experience of the perils of the Western Buddhist saṅgha for a person of color.

Many of the essays reference Willis's struggles with issues around her identity, including most of all the question of being Baptist and

Buddhist at the same time, as well as all the complexity around being African American in Buddhist settings. Yet another issue for Willis, and I dare say many other scholars, especially the younger generation in the academic field of Buddhist studies, is the conundrum around being not only a scholar and practitioner at the same time but also feeling frustrated at the potentials of teaching from a Buddhist perspective while being constrained from so doing in a liberal arts setting. Such a question about engaged scholarship and pedagogy is in fact resonant with some of the central issues raised in womanist thought. Willis may not solve all of these conundrums, but she has many ideas to share and the courage to lay them out. In this she is continuing on a path she first opened up for herself when she came out as a Buddhist practitioner in her earlier book *Dreaming Me*. But perhaps most inspiring for me in all of this is simply the tenor of an authorial voice that is comfortable with hyphens. Jan Willis has never shied at crossing boundaries, be these intellectual or spiritual.

I would add that these essays have been really useful to me myself as a reader, both in thinking through the hyphens in my own identity and my own experiences of negotiating boundaries between history and normative discourse as a scholar and teacher. Willis finds a way to inch us forward in resolving some of these tensions, even providing in one of the chapters here a veritable manual, with bibliographical detail, of how to teach Buddhism in the academy in a way that does justice to the richness of the tradition for both the study of religion and for religious life going forward.

I would personally also like to mention with considerable gratitude that it was Jan Willis who got me started on my own academic path. When I was floundering after finishing my doctoral dissertation, Jan offered me a chance to teach twice for her in the wonderful Religion Department at Wesleyan University when she went on sabbatical. It was an honor to step briefly into her shoes, and I think my sense of her greatness of spirit and vision helped shaped my own trajectory and sense of what is possible, and desirable, in being a teacher and scholar of Tibetan Buddhism.

Let me close with my gratitude for this lovely new collection, and for its many rich and delightful passages. For example, it is highly interesting—and I dare say, useful and instructive—to read her accounts of several near-death experiences and how she just spontaneously—and very naturally—burst into both Buddhist and Christian songs and prayers in her moments of panic and confusion. And why not? Look out too for an astonishing, if not entirely anguish-free, vignette in this book, where you will find Jan Willis staring down a black Buddha in Bangkok, Thailand, in 1981. And then there is a great account of the eminent Lama Yeshe hearing Angela Davis speak and then expressing his high admiration for her. Talk about beautiful intersectionality! And just one more—you will meet in these pages a wonderful Buddhist nun who tells Jan Willis, "If I could practice higher thoughts and teachings, that would be better, but just saying *Oṃ maṇi padme hūṃ* is enough for me."

Well this book, with its panoply of knowledge, experience, wisdom, and kindness, is more than enough for me—not to mention chanting the mantra of compassion, *Oṃ maṇi padme hūṃ*, as much as I can.

JANET GYATSO is the Hershey Professor of Buddhist Studies at the Harvard Divinity School. She was elected a member of the American Academy of Arts and Sciences in 2018. Her books include *In the Mirror of Memory: Reflections on Mindfulness and Remembrance in Indian and Tibetan Buddhism* (1992), *Apparitions of the Self: The Secret Autobiographies of a Tibetan Visionary* (1998), *Women of Tibet* (coedited, 2005), and *Being Human in a Buddhist World: An Intellectual History of Medicine in Early Modern Tibet* (2015). Her research focuses on Tibetan and South Asian cultural and intellectual history; she has written on the topics of sex and gender in Buddhist monasticism; visionary revelation in Buddhism; lineage, memory, and authorship; the philosophy of experience; autobiographical writing in Tibet; and science and religion in Tibet. Her current writing focuses on subjectivity and animal ethics for our posthuman future.

Introduction

❧∞❧

The eighteen essays you have in your hands were written over the span of some thirty-five years, the earliest here going back to 1983—just a few years into my career in academia. They focus on four seemingly disparate areas, to wit: women and Buddhism, Buddhism and race, tantric Buddhism and saints' lives, and Buddhist and Christian comparative reflections. I say "seemingly disparate" because, in my mind and heart, they are all connected—through me. I am an African American woman who was raised Baptist in the Jim Crow South until I went off to Ivy League universities in the North, and my academic life has been lived as one who studies, practices, and teaches Buddhism, especially Tibetan Buddhism. The specific subjects focused on here have attracted my attention owing to those particular set of facts.

There *is* certainly a sense that the African American part of me predominates. How could it not? I have lived my entire life in a black, female body in these United States.

I remember well the very first public lecture I gave at my first academic position, at the University of California, Santa Cruz, in 1974. I had titled my talk "An Introduction to Buddhism" and fashioned it, I thought, to be a broad-enough presentation of the Buddha's life and the basic points of his teachings for a general audience. I had initially been nervous—as I still am before presentations—but managed to give what I considered a fairly energetic and engaging talk. When I finished, many students jumped to their feet in applause. Some even cheered. Smiling then, I invited questions. The very first question brought an abrupt end to my feelings of relief. It came from a slim black student who sat in the front row. He had been slumped for most of the talk, and as he spoke, he adjusted a long walking stick or cane that rested on his shoulder. "Okay," he began slowly, "so what does this Buddha guy and his Buddhism *have to do with me?*"

Whatever satisfaction I had momentarily enjoyed prior to that question quickly vanished. Thoughts started to race: Had I not pitched the lecture correctly? Had it been too technical? The young man's question appeared to be a challenge, though there was no actual combativeness in his tone. In response, and in an attempt to get my own bearings, I began anew, rehearsing again a few of my key points. These remarks seemed to appease the young man, and finally he said, "Okay. Thanks."

The very next day, a new friend I'd made in the university's Supportive Services said to me, "Oh, Dr. Jan. You're a perfectionist!" She told me that that student was simply trying to relate with me and so he'd asked a question. *I* was the one, she suggested, giving it too much weight. She proposed that I try to be kinder and gentler to myself. She was, of course, right. I learned later, in fact, that that particular student, in trying to "relate" with me, had done something that he seldom did: he had engaged. I had caused him to listen; I had piqued his interest.

But for me, his question was much larger and much deeper. In many respects, it has been the driving force, and the challenge, of most of my life's work, whether as a person of color or as a woman, or indeed as a human being who shares this planet with more than seven billion others. It was the question I have been trying to answer for myself and others for the entirety of my adult life: *So what does this Buddha guy and his Buddhism have to do with me?*

❧

No one could have told you—and especially not me!—that the little black girl called Deanie Pie (Dean is my middle name) who was raised in a segregated coal-mining camp outside of Birmingham, Alabama, would grow up to become a teacher and scholar of Tibetan Buddhism.

That she would travel to India at age nineteen and be greeted and embraced by refugee Tibetans in Sarnath, a place where the Buddha some twenty-five hundred years before had given his famed "First Sermon." I mean . . . how do those kinds of things happen?

Perhaps, as Buddhists might say, it is simply a matter of karma: *This one life is not all there is, and countless lifetimes had gone before this one. And in* this *one, she was born a little black girl! Thus, finding her way back to Buddhism was a story written long before this particular birth.* Some Tibetans have told me this very thing and even added details that tell me exactly who they think I actually was centuries ago. And so, for them, that previous life explains who I am now and why I am attracted to and so at home with Tibetans. The great Tulshig Rinpoché (a revered lama of the Nyingma school) once explained to monks gathered around him that—because of the spot of blonde in my hair—I had surely been one of the builders of the great Samyé (the "Inconceivable") Monastery, the very first Buddhist monastery in Tibet.

While I have no memory or vague recollection of a previous life, or even a close feeling about this particular hypothesis, I do know that I have experienced great joy from the deep connections I have shared with certain Tibetans during this life. This was especially the case with the man who became my primary, or root, teacher back in 1969: Lama Thubten Yeshe. Becoming his student, and as Tibetans say, "being held dear" by him, undoubtedly changed the entire course of my life, and I am grateful to him beyond measure. (I have written about this more spiritual side of my life in my memoir *Dreaming Me: Black, Baptist, and Buddhist.*)

❧ ❧

I consider myself very fortunate to have been born at the particular historical moment that I was. It meant, for example, that even while I was forced to suffer the indignities of painful segregation in the South— the signs marked "white" and "colored" posted above water fountains, the poorly stocked schools and libraries assigned to black children even after the Brown vs. Board of Education decision of 1954 (the year I entered first grade)—I got the chance to march, as a fifteen-year-old tenth-grader, with Dr. King and others during the 1963 Birmingham Civil Rights Campaign. As a result, the seeds of nonviolent activism were born in me.

The particular historical moment also meant that I was among that early group of counterculture Western hippie types who traveled to India and other places in the East in the late 1960s and early '70s, a time when encountering recently exiled Tibetans was a fairly easy and ordinary happening. During my 1967–68 junior-year-abroad study in Banaras, India, I met early, and engaged often, with Tibetans in nearby Sarnath. I visited Nepal at the end of that year and a year later, after graduating from Cornell University, I traveled back to Nepal to stay in a Tibetan monastery and study among sixty monks (no other women and no other Westerners). During that time, I traveled a short distance out of the valley and met, at Kopan, Lama Thubten Yeshe. He introduced me to Tibetan Buddhist meditation, both its theory (which he later explained so wonderfully in his book *Introduction to Tantra*) and its daily, inner practice. And in one fell swoop, I had found both my spiritual and my academic home.

And because of that particular moment of history during which I encountered the Tibetans (and also most assuredly because of Lama Yeshe's blessings), I was able to meet with many of the most renowned Tibetan teachers of the day—those still alive after their exile from Tibet in 1959—and to receive blessings from them. Thus, beginning in 1970 in Dharamsala, India, I met personally with His Holiness the Dalai Lama and with his two tutors, Ling Rinpoché and Trijang Rinpoché, and with Geshé Rabten. I met in Sarnath with the terrifyingly wonderful Zong Rinpoché and, later, in Leh Ladakh with the renowned Mongolian teacher Bakula Rinpoché. In Nepal, I met Tulshig Rinpoché and shared three intense days face-to-face learning from the great Khunu Lama Rinpoché. I met many of the greatest teachers of other Tibetan traditions as well. For example, I met in Boudhanath with Dilgo Khyentse Rinpoché and with Khetsun Sangpo Rinpoché. And in the United States, with Sonam Kazi in New York City and Deshung

Rinpoché in Seattle. In Toronto and Berkeley, I met the wondrous Kalu Rinpoché. I knew in New York Rato Kyongla Rinpoché and Lama Pema. In Charlottesville, Geshé Thardö and Lati Rinpoché befriended me. Even today, I continue to participate in events and on panels with great teacher-practitioners such as Tsoknyi Rinpoché, Chökyi Nyima Rinpoché, and the all-knowing Lama Zopa Rinpoche.

I have been blessed indeed by these great scholar-practitioners, and for their blessings, I am extremely grateful.

❧ ❧

What I want to do here—as an introduction to this group of essays—is to provide an overview of the varied kinds of academic work I have engaged in as a result of meeting the Tibetans and to offer an account of the sources, and costs, of those endeavors.

I must first say that I am extremely happy that Wisdom Publications agreed to work with me to bring out this collection. That they thought it a worthy project was gratifying indeed, and having worked with them before, I was certain that they would do a stellar job of it. My sincerest thanks go to Daniel Aitken and Laura Cunningham, who initially took on the task of doing this project, and to Mary Petrusewicz, the superb editor who painstakingly brought it to its conclusion, as well as to all the others at Wisdom whose efforts helped to make the idea of this collection a reality—and the process a great pleasure.

Some of these essays are scholarly, others are more popular. Some were first published in India, others at American or British university presses, and still others in Buddhist journals or Buddhist-linked publications. The pieces span both time and distance. Some are still available—online even!—but some are, even in this age of the internet, hard to find outside of graduate university libraries. I am therefore all the more pleased that Wisdom has brought them together here for the first time in one place.

As mentioned above, these essays focus on women and Buddhism, Buddhism and race, tantric Buddhism and saints' lives, and

Buddhist-Christian reflections. Within each grouping, the individual pieces are arranged generally, though not always, in chronological order. This was done not so much to show how my thinking *evolved* on a particular topic (though that has certainly sometimes been the case) but to demonstrate the various *ways* I chose to approach a single issue. For example, with regard to women and Buddhism, I have asked: Should we look at Buddhist women solely through orthodox texts, or use secular histories as well? Would our knowledge benefit if we also included material artifacts? Can we tell much about *women* in a given culture by looking at *one* woman, in depth? Can the stories of women ancestors empower modern-day women? And, if so, since "lineage" is about inspiration, why can't we women fashion our own lineage outside of and apart from the patriarchal traditions?

My writing on Buddhism and race has operated in the same way: Does one's race or ethnicity make a difference in Western Buddhist settings? Should it? Are there black Buddhists in America? Why or why not? Let's actually meet some black Buddhists and ask them how it feels to practice in American Buddhist centers. Do "convert Buddhists" tell the real history of Buddhism in America? Is anything left out in their narrations? Can Buddhist Dharma in America teach both the "dominant" group and the "subordinate" group how to be free?

With the tantric Buddhist narratives, I wanted to both explore the sacred life story in its traditional and formulaic forms as well as introduce readers to living, breathing human beings, then and now. The first essay in this grouping introduces a man who was a recognized and highly regarded *tulku* (or reincarnation) in Tibet. When I met him, in 1982, he was a refugee, having fled Tibet without robes or status. When he told me his life story, he included the formulaic "miracles" of traditional saints' lives as well as the details of his capture and brutal treatment at the hands of the Chinese as part of one flowing narrative. How does one make sense of such incongruities when sitting face-to-face with the narrator? (I don't answer this question in the piece, but I hope I have raised it well enough.)

I go on in the other essays in this grouping to discuss the nature and meanings of "life story" in the Tibetan Buddhist tradition and to show

how the narratives are structured using a three-tiered model common to other forms of tantric ritual and text. It is in this section that I also discuss the manifold and pregnant meanings of the ubiquitous and famed tantric feminine *dakini* principle. I am delighted to say that, even after all these years, I still consider "Dakini: Some Comments on Its Nature and Meaning" to be one of my best essays.

In the Buddhist-Christian reflections, I mainly seek to draw out how, and in what forms, both these traditions speak of the universal principle of love. Here, whether through the Buddhist notions of "interdependence" and "nonharm" or through Dr. Martin Luther King Jr.'s examination of the parable of the Good Samaritan, I draw on my Baptist and Buddhist education, instincts, and experience to explain the most striking parallels.

Toward the book's end, two essays have been added on teaching Buddhism in academia—"A Teacher's Dilemma" and "Teaching Buddhism in the Western Academy." The reason is simple: teaching has been, and continues to be, the central focus of my life. However, teaching a religious tradition for which one also has some affinity is never an easy path. One is sometimes viewed with suspicion; looking back, this has certainly been my cross to bear. I could not hide—or could not always hide well enough, even if I wished to—the fact that I, myself, found these teachings compelling. The line between "engaging, enthusiastic, and energetic teacher who cares about her students' well-being" and one who "might be too close to the subject matter to be objective enough about it" is sometimes judged to be a thin one. Though I always strove not to use the classroom, or any other venue, for conversion, I always did want to help my students to contact their true, naturally good and loving, best human selves. I am guilty of trying to encourage them to discover that truth.

Finally, there is a chapter from my memoir here that tries to describe the deep sources of my dual identity as a Baptist-Buddhist. It seems clear to me that I am culturally an African American but spiritually both a Baptist and a Buddhist.

❧⃟ ❧⃟

Of course, the pieces gathered here don't represent the entirety of my academic endeavors. Prior to this collection, I had written five books: *The Diamond Light: An Introduction to Tibetan Buddhist Meditation* (1972); *On Knowing Reality: The Tattvartha Chapter of Asanga's Bodhisattvabhumi* (1979); an edited collection of essays focusing on women in Tibetan Buddhism called *Feminine Ground* (1989); a group of translations I did of the *namthar*, or sacred biographies, of certain renowned Tibetan Gelukpa teachers and practitioners titled *Enlightened Beings* (1995); and my memoir, *Dreaming Me: Black, Baptist, and Buddhist*, which came out in 2001 and was reissued by Wisdom Publications in 2008. Of these works, the translation from Sanskrit of Asanga's "Chapter on Reality" in *On Knowing Reality* and the translations from Tibetan of the life stories in *Enlightened Beings* best represent my scholarly endeavors.

The collection of meditations published before I undertook graduate studies at Columbia University and the collection of essays on women in Tibetan Buddhism were intended for a more general audience. The memoir was my first—and only, I dare say—"trade book," sought after by a number of publishers who thought it made for, in the words of one Doubleday acquiring editor, "a pretty good story."

In the meantime, I have taught full-time for just over forty-one years—including thirty-six years at Wesleyan University, a challenging teaching job that I loved. I had also initially taught for three and a half years at UCSC (I loved that job as well), and in the mid-1980s I spent a year teaching at the University of Virginia. During those years of teaching, I also wrote and presented more than 180 invited talks and lectures at various universities and Buddhist venues in the United States, Europe, and Asia. Some of these talks became essays, and a few of them are here.

It should also be noted that I had the opportunity to serve our larger "guild" as well. Though it is little known, I was commissioned in the 1970s by Dr. John Wiggins of the American Academy of Religion (AAR) to evaluate whether Buddhist studies constituted a valid area of study to be added to the academy. I did research, interviewed Buddhist scholars, and wrote a fifteen-page report that concluded, "Yes, it was"—and Buddhist studies was subsequently admitted. I can truly say that I have enjoyed a bountiful and gratifying academic career, one blessed by compassionate Buddhist teachers, excellent colleagues, and brilliantly engaged and energetic students.

Looking back, I am grateful that I chose to teach at the undergraduate level. Had I not done so, my intellectual and academic foci would undoubtedly have been much more limited and circumscribed. At undergraduate campuses, especially those like UC Santa Cruz and, later, Wesleyan, I felt freer to branch out and to investigate broader subject areas. Topics of inquiry could be more holistic in nature: ones that speak not only to an undergraduate audience but to a more general audience as well. Additionally, I have always enjoyed getting in touch with young people at this stage of their intellectual journey, to aid and gently nudge them as they come to discover their unique intellectual callings and to help introduce them to the tools they will need in order to get at the answers they seek. I am therefore grateful for the courage to stay in undergraduate teaching and to turn down the seeming advancement to graduate university teaching. I hope that former students of mine will enjoy reading these pieces as much as I enjoyed being a mentor to them.

❦ ❦

As a last comment—and something my students know well—I am passionate about stories and I am, myself, an avid storyteller. I think knowledge comes alive through this medium above all others. As I reviewed these eighteen essays, I noted once again how storytelling has both influenced and fueled my teaching and writing throughout my life. Thus, these essays are filled with stories. I noted also that, though written years ago, the main foci of these pieces—whether on women and gender, race, or interfaith dialogue—still matter and have relevance for our lives right now. In this sense, I hope you'll agree, they are not dry discourses intended only for the dusty shelves of old libraries but rather essays to be read, pondered, and discussed within the ongoing and ever-evolving conversations happening right now. With that said, dear reader, I give them over to you.

Part I
Women and Buddhism

❧ ❧

I

Nuns and Benefactresses: The Role of Women in the Development of Buddhism

❧❧❧

Recently a number of studies have appeared which address the issue of the portrayal of women in Buddhist literature.[1] Such studies are valuable and timely to be sure, since they begin to provide us with an entrée into the relatively neglected area of Buddhism's relationship to, and view of, women. They have sought to investigate the complex and changing status of women in relationship to Buddhist doctrine and practice and to paint a picture of women's place and standing within the Buddhist fold over time. To date, however, in order to present such a picture, all the studies have relied exclusively on data supplied by the Buddhist scriptures themselves, viewed in isolation. Of course, such an approach ultimately proves to be too limiting. While the texts certainly inform us about the various orthodox Buddhist views regarding women, they cannot themselves be expected to tell us how such views were received or acted on by the women—and men—who have throughout Buddhist history called themselves "Buddhists."[2]

It is now time, in my opinion, to attempt to go beyond reliance solely on the sacred scriptures of Buddhism; to attempt to fill out, if possible, the contours of what may be called an actual social history of Buddhism, using the issue of women as a base. For such a social history, two pools of information have to be used together: (1) the Buddhist scriptures which address the issue of women, and (2) secular histories of the periods relevant to the composition and dissemination of those scriptures.

Granted, the attempt to fashion a social history of Buddhism as it relates to women is no easy task. The main source of difficulty is the very nature of the two primary pools of information related to this issue. On the one hand, we have the Buddhist texts themselves. These evidence a wide typology of diverging images and views regarding the female and the feminine, ranging from quite negative (even clearly misogynous) ones early on, to "acceptable" and more positive ones over time. Dating of the texts, moreover, often is problematic, making it difficult to correlate a particular composition with a specific historical period. The authors of the texts in all cases were men,[3] monk-scholars, often with various agendas of their own. Finally, in many cases it is difficult to gauge the size and makeup of the audience of a given text and consequently to assess its impact and influence on the larger community.

On the other hand, when we look to the purely historical studies (that is, secular histories as opposed to religious histories or scriptural examples) we come upon the perennial problem that history is indeed most often "his-story," and thus the depiction of the participation of women (as well as other "minority" groups) in affecting events and change is conspicuously absent. Still, we must do the best we can.

Having noted these drawbacks, what I wish to do here is focus on women and the Buddhist tradition, on both those women who served the cause as nuns and those who, as laywomen, served in the important capacity of benefactresses of the Dharma. In short, I wish at least to begin the discussion of Buddhism's impact on women and their impact in turn on it. I do so, first, by tracing some of the images of women (and of the feminine) presented in a number of Buddhist texts, from the early Theravada period through the crown-jewel representatives of the developed Mahayana tradition;[4] and second, by mentioning some of the known historical facts regarding how certain women, notably certain laywomen, were impacting Buddhism at the time some of those texts were enjoying a good deal of popularity. While this is only a preliminary study, I think it can be adequately demonstrated that women played a key role in supporting and literally "maintaining" Buddhism in India and beyond.

❧ ❧

During the last forty-five years of his life, Siddhartha Gautama (563–483 BC), the "Buddha," the "Path-shower" and founder of Buddhism, instructed monks, nuns, laymen, and laywomen. Like so many other teachers of his time, however, his primary aim, at least initially, had been to establish a monastic organization—an order of celibate monks—for the propagation of his teachings. Women, therefore, played no pivotal role in the formation or formulation of the early Buddhist tradition. Or so it would seem.

Given the social and cultural context of sixth-century BC India and the importance of celibacy to the early Buddhist monastic organization, it is not surprising that women *qua* women would have been devalued in some of the early literature. In India, as in China, women were subservient to three masters: to their parents when young, to their husbands when mature, and to their children when old. They were helpmates at best and burdens at worst, but always they were viewed as being inferior, second-class citizens.

In spite of such cultural bias, however, some five years' after establishing his male *sangha*, or order, the Buddha did something quite radical. Along with the Mahavira (founder of Jainism, and an older contemporary of Siddhartha), the Buddha attacked the caste system of the Brahmans; he condemned the outmoded language of the Vedas together with the Vedic practice of ritual animal sacrifice; *and* he allowed for the "going forth" of women from home into the homeless life. He admitted women into the community of his enrobed religious practitioners.

The monk Ananda, perhaps the Buddha's favorite disciple, is shown in the scriptures to be a chief advocate for women;[6] and honor falls to him for having pushed for the admission of women into the order. According to the early scriptures, the woman destined to become the first Buddhist nun was Mahaprajapati, the Buddha's aunt and the

woman who had raised him since he was seven days old.[7] The *Cullavagga's*[8] account of Prajapati's admission into the order begins as follows:

> At one time the Awakened One, the Lord, was staying among
> the Sakyans at Kapilavatthu in the Banyan monastery. Then
> the Gotamid, Pajāpatī the Great, approached the Lord;
> having approached, having greeted the Lord, she stood at a
> respectful distance. As she was standing at a respectful dis-
> tance, the Gotamid, Pajapati the Great, spoke thus to the
> Lord: "Lord, it were well that women should obtain the
> going forth from home into homelessness in this *Dhamma*
> and discipline proclaimed by the Truth-finder." "Be careful,
> Gotami, of the going forth of women from home into home-
> lessness in this *Dhamma* and discipline proclaimed by the
> Truth-finder." And a second time.... And a third time did the
> Gotamid, Pajāpatī the Great, speak thus to the Lord: "Lord,
> it were well. . . ." "Be careful, Gotami, of the going forth of
> women from home into homelessness in this *Dhamma* and
> discipline proclaimed by the Truth-finder."
>   Then the Gotamid, Pajāpatī the Great, thinking: "The Lord
> does not allow women to go forth from home into homeless-
> ness in the *Dhamma* and discipline proclaimed by the Truth-
> finder," afflicted, grieved, with a tearful face and crying, having
> greeted the Lord, departed keeping her right side toward him.

Later, speaking to the Buddha on Mahaprajapati's behalf, Ananda
queried, "Are women competent, Revered Sir . . . to attain the fruit of
once-returning . . . of never returning, to attain arhatship?"[9] The Buddha did not deny their competence but predicted that, as a result of
the founding of a women's order, his doctrine would not abide long
in India.[10] Moreover, the Buddha declared "eight weighty regulations"[11]
which had to be accepted by Mahaprajapati prior to her admission.
These eight special regulations for women served to make clear the
nuns' separate and inferior status compared to the monks'. According
to F. Wilson's[12] translation, the eight rules were as follows:

(1) In the presence of monks, O Ānanda, women are expected to
request ordination to go forth as nuns. I announce this as the
first important rule for women to overcome the obstructions
so that instruction can be maintained throughout life.

(2) In the presence of monks, O Ānanda, a nun must seek the
teaching and instructions every half month. I announce this
as the second important rule. . . .

(3) No nun may spend a rainy season, O Ānanda, in a place where
no monks are resident. This, O Ānanda, is the third important rule. . . .

(4) After the rainy season a nun must have both orders [monks
and nuns] perform the "end of the rainy season" ceremony
for her with reference to the seeing, hearing, or suspicion [of
faults committed by her]. This is the fourth important rule . . .

(5) It is forbidden that a nun, Ānanda, accuse or warn a monk
about transgression in morality, heretical views, conduct, or
livelihood. It is not forbidden for a monk to accuse or warn
a nun about morality, heretical views, conduct, or livelihood.
This is the fifth important rule I announce. . . .

(6) A nun, Ananda, should not scold or be angry with or admon-
ish a monk. I announce this as the sixth important rule for
women. . . .

(7) When a nun violates important rules, O Ānanda, penance
must be performed every half month. This I declare as the seventh important rule. . . .

(8) A nun of one hundred years of age shall perform the correct
duties to a monk. She shall, with her hands folded in prayerful
attitude, rise to greet him and then bow down to him. This
will be done with appropriate words of salutation. I declare
this as the eighth important rule. . . .

"If, O Ānanda, Mahāprajāpatī Gautamī will observe these
important rules as a religious duty, then she shall go forth
from a home life, take ordination, and become a nun."

Mahaprajapati is said to have gladly accepted the "eight rules," and taking them as "a garland of lotus flowers,"[13] she placed them upon her head, swearing never to transgress them. Moreover, the "five-hundred Sakyan women"[14] accompanying her are said to have done likewise.

Once the door was opened to them, women flocked into the order of nuns.[15] To be sure, one can imagine that the addition of a nuns' order would have caused problems. Early on, there were no permanent structures—no monasteries, or *viharas*—to house either the monks or nuns.[16] The religious life was physically hard and rugged. In the eyes of contemporary onlookers, no doubt, a dangerous situation prevailed with monks and nuns living in close proximity to each other; and undoubtedly the Buddha himself knew as well that many of his monk converts had but recently abandoned the worldly life with all its ties to womenfolk. Now these very women had entered the monastic confines.

Perhaps this new situation accounted for the prediction the Buddha reportedly voiced to Ananda immediately after allowing Mahaprajapati to enter the order. Again, the *Cullavagga*[17] records:

> If, Ānanda, women had not obtained the going forth from home into homelessness in the *dhamma* and discipline pro- claimed by the Truth-finder, the Brahma-faring, Ānanda, would have lasted long, true *dhamma* would have endured for a thousand years. But since, Ānanda, women have gone forth . . . in the *dhamma* and discipline proclaimed by the Truth-finder, now, Ānanda, the Brahma-faring will not last long, true *dhamma* will endure only for five hundred years.
>
> Even, Ānanda, as those households which have many women and few men easily fall a prey to robbers, to pot- thieves, even so, Ānanda, in whatever *dhamma* and discipline women obtain the going forth from home into homelessness, that Brahma-faring will not last long.

But the Buddha did allow women to take the robes, and, having been admitted, they lost no time in proving their capacity and ability to cope with the rigors and to scale the heights of the religious life. Many became widely renowned as teachers of the Buddha's Dharma,[18] and a number of nuns attained the ultimate fruit of nirvana itself. Their *annas*, or "songs of triumph," are recorded in the text known as the *Therīgāthā*, or *Psalms of the Sisters*.[19] (It should be added that while individual nuns are praised as great teachers, they are always depicted as imparting teachings only to other women; and that while some may have possessed an individualized style or unique delivery, their teachings did not depart from the standard message as articulated by the Buddha himself.)

Even though the scriptures show that there were problems associated with the women's order,[20] it was not the nuns who presented the major problems. These women were at least confined and controlled under the "rules" of the order. Instead those who posed the greatest threat to the early Buddhist enterprise were the nonrobed, unconfined women: women in their "natural" state. As with all monastic organizations, a precarious tension prevailed. Having deliberately chosen the life apart and isolated from worldly domestic realms, the enrobed community yet remained dependent on that domestic realm for its very existence and maintenance. The sangha depended on gifts from the laity. Moreover, monks who had recently left mothers, wives, children, and sweethearts were forced daily to interact with them in order to collect their very food. An early scripture records the following exchange between Ānanda and the Buddha:[21]

"Master," says Ānanda, "how shall we behave before women?"
"You should shun their gaze, Ānanda."
"But if we see them, master, what then are we to do?"
"Not speak to them, Ānanda."
"But if we do speak to them, what then?"
"Then you must watch over yourselves, Ānanda."

That woman is the monk's most dreaded threat is attested to by many scriptures of the Theravada. Representing everything that is the antithesis of his quest for ultimate salvation, she becomes a symbol for all that he wishes to escape from. Entangled in family life and reproduction, in some texts woman is made a veritable synonym for samsara[22] itself. I cite a few examples of such negative imagery:

The Anguttara Nikāya states:

> Monks, I know of no other single form, sound, scent, savour, and touch by which a woman's heart is so enslaved as it is by the form, sound, scent, savour, and touch of a man. Monks, a woman's heart is obsessed by these things.[23]

(As Paul has pointed out, "the passage immediately prior to this citation discusses the equivalent obsession men have for women."[24]) Three other passages may also be cited from the Anguttara collection. Thus i, 11, I, 72 records:

> Monks, womenfolk end their life unsated and unreplete with two things. What two? Sexual intercourse and childbirth. These are the two things.[25]

At Anguttara Nikāya, xxiii, 6, III, 190, the following is said:

> Monks, there are these five disadvantages to a monk who visits families and lives in their company too much. What five? He often sees womenfolk; from seeing them, companionship comes; from companionship, intimacy; from intimacy, amorousness; when the heart is inflamed, this may be expected: Either Joyless he will live the godly life, or he will commit some foul offense or he will give up the training and return to the lower life. Verily, monks, these are the five disadvantages...[26]

And, again, at vi, 5, III, 56:

> Monks, a woman, even when going along, will stop to ensnare the heart of a man; whether standing, sitting, or lying down,

laughing, talking, or singing, weeping, stricken, or dying, a woman will stop to ensnare the heart of a man. Monks, if ever one would rightly say: "It is wholly a snare of Mara, verily, speaking rightly, one may say of womanhood: It is wholly a snare of Mara."[27]

Another corpus of early texts, referred to collectively as the Jatakas, or Previous-birth stories of the Buddha, also contain numerous accounts "designed to point the moral of feminine iniquity."[28] Coomaraswamy summarizes the Jatakas' contents as follows:

"Unfathomably deep, like a fish's course in the water," they say, "is the character of women, robbers with many artifices, with whom truth is hard to find, to whom a lie is like the truth and the truth is like a lie. . . . No heed should be paid either to their likes or to their dislikes."[29]

And the *Kunalajataka* (verses 24–25) records:

No man who is not possessed should trust women, for they are base, fickle, ungrateful, and deceitful. They are ungrateful and do not act as they ought to; they do not care for their parents or brother. They are mean and immoral and do only their own will.[30]

Clearly, the passages cited above—far from accurately describing the female's nature—betray the fear of women felt by some of the early writers. That sword of fear was double-edged. Coomaraswamy notes, "for of all the snares of the senses which Ignorance sets before the unwary, the most insidious, the most dangerous, the most attractive, is woman."[31] Such fear produced a thoroughly misogynist polemic even in a text which later found its way into an early Mahayana collection known as the *Maharatnakuta (Collection of Jewels).*[32] I quote a number of verses translated by Paul from "The Tale of King Udayana of Vatsa."[33]

Fools
lust for women
like dogs in heat,
they do not know abstinence.

They are also like flies
who see vomited food.
Like a herd of hogs,
they greedily seek manure.

Women can ruin
the precepts of purity.
They can also ignore
honor and virtue.

Causing one to go to hell,
they prevent rebirth in heaven.
Why should the wise
delight in them? . . . .

If one listens
to what I have said
they can be reborn, separated
from women.

Then theirs will be
the majestically pure heaven
and they will attain
supreme Enlightenment. . . .

Those who are not wise,
act like animals,
racing toward female forms
like hogs toward mud.

Fools cannot see
the vice in desires
and ignorantly focus on them
like blind men . . . .

Because of their ignorance
they are bewildered by women who,
like profit seekers in the market place,
deceive those who come near.

Foolish men close to desire
enter a realm of demons.
Like maggots
they are addicted to filth . . . .

Ornaments on women
show off their beauty.
But within them there is great evil
as in the body there is air.

With a piece of bright silk
one conceals a sharp knife.
The ornaments on a woman
have a similar end.

So much for one (tormented!) man's view of women.

When we come to the scriptures proper of the Mahayana—with its more universal outlook and appeal, its emphasis on compassion and "self-lessness," its "more sympathetic [attitude] to the existential concerns of the laity,"[34] and its recognition of its growing dependency on the laity (resulting in the concomitant elevation of all members of the laity, both male and female)—we would expect to find less explicit disparagement of women. Happily, this is generally the case. However, the specific means to this end were not direct, but proceeded in stages. That is, while the Mahayana conceded that women might attain to ultimate enlightenment, some of its early texts required that women first change their sex.[35] For example, an early Mahayana text, the *Lotus Sutra*,[36] recorded:

> If a woman, hearing this Chapter of the Former Affairs of the Bodhisattva Medicine King, can accept and keep it, she shall put an end to her female body, and shall never again receive one.[37]

In another famed passage of the *Lotus*, we find the following episode recounted:

> At that moment, the venerable Sāriputra spoke to the daughter of Sāgara, the Nāga king: "Good daughter, you have certainly not wavered in awakening to the thought of enlightenment, and have immeasurable wisdom. However, the state of Supreme, Perfect Enlightenment is difficult to realize. Good daughter, even a woman who does not falter in diligence for many hundreds of eras and performs meritorious acts for many thousands of eras, completely fulfilling the six perfections, still does not realize Buddhahood. Why? Because a woman still does not realize five types of status. What are the five types? (1) The status of Brahma, (2) the status of Sakra (Indra), (3) the status of a great king, (4) the status of an emperor, and (5) the status of an irreversible Bodhisattva."[38]

It should be pointed out that in the scenario which immediately follows the one just cited above, the eight-year-old Naga princess, after offering her priceless Naga-jewel to the Buddha, magically transforms her "sexual" self, changing first into a male bodhisattva and then into a buddha possessing the "thirty-two major marks."[39] She thereby demonstrates that her sexual transformation is performed out of compassion for the still-ignorant Prajnakuta and Shariputra, and in full accordance with *her* realization of the ultimate teachings of *shunyata* (that is, voidness of inherent self-existence). Still, the bias against the female sex per se remained in a number of Mahayana works.

This bias is also evidenced in some noncanonical (that is, nonsutra) Mahayana works. A key example is provided by the famed *Bodhisattvabhumi,* composed in the fourth century AD by the renowned philosopher Asanga. In the "Chapter on Enlightenment" (*Bodhipatalam*), Asanga writes:

> All buddhas are exactly the same (in respect to their spiritual attainments). However, they may be distinguished according to four factors: with regard to (1) length of life (*ayur*), (2) name (*nama*), (3) family (*kula*), and (4) body (*kaya*)....
> Completely perfected buddhas are not women. And why? Precisely because a bodhisattva [i.e., one on his way to complete enlightenment], from the time he has passed beyond the first incalculable age (of his career), has completely abandoned the woman's estate (*stribhavam*). Ascending (thereafter) to the most excellent throne of enlightenment, he is never again reborn as a woman. All women are by nature full of defilement and of weak intelligence. And not by one who is by nature full of defilement and of weak intelligence is completely perfected buddhahood attained.[40]

Fortunately, a number of Mahayana texts seek to put an end to such disparagement of the female sex. They do so by building on the all-important philosophical theory of *shunyata* (that is, voidness), and by carrying this theory to its logical conclusion. Thus a number of the *Prajnaparamita* sutras,[41] or "Perfection of Wisdom" texts, challenge head-on the ill-conceived idea that distinctions of sex or gender can have any bearing whatsoever on a being's attainment of ultimate enlightenment. Thus, in one *Prajnaparamita* text,[42] the Buddha is reported to have said:

> Those who by my form did see me,
> and those who followed me by voice
> wrong the efforts they engaged in,
> me those people will not see.

From the Dharma should one see the Buddhas,
from the Dharmabodies comes their guidance.
Yet Dharma's true nature cannot be discerned,
and no one can be conscious of it as an object.[43]

When the Buddha is made to say that those who saw him by his form
(that is, by his body, bearing the "thirty-two major marks") did not see
him in truth, the argument is made against the notion that maleness (or
femaleness) has any bearing on enlightenment. Firmly based on "voidness," it forcefully asserts that questions of sexuality are irrelevant to the
spiritual quest.

But perhaps the two Mahayana sutras which best exemplify the spirit
of "voidness" as it pertains to the issue of women and Buddhist practice
and attainment are the *Vimalakirtinirdesha Sutra*[44] and the *Shrimala
Sutra*.[45] Importantly, both of these sūtras are addressed to and focus on
the laity, as opposed to the monastic community, and both portray the
former as possessing higher insight.

In the *Vimalakirtinirdesha Sutra*, a goddess who lives in the house of
the layman Vimalakirti instructs Shariputra (who here represents the
old conservatism of the Theravada monastic community) that a female
form is no hindrance to comprehending the ultimate, void, nature of
reality. The thrust of the passage is that reality transcends all distinctions, including those associated with a given sex. It reads:

> *Shariputra:* Goddess, what prevents you from transforming
>   yourself out of your female state?
> *Goddess:* Although I have sought my "female state" for these
>   twelve years, I have not yet found it. Reverend Sharipu-
>   tra, if a magician were to incarnate a woman by magic,
>   would you ask her, "What prevents you from transform-
>   ing yourself out of your female state?"
> *Shariputra:* No! Such a woman would not really exist, so
>   what would there be to transform?
> *Goddess:* Just so, reverend Shariputra, all things do not really
>   exist.[46]

Lastly, the *Shrimala Sutra* must be cited. Its chief protagonist is the Queen Shrimala, who is characterized as having "roared the lion's roar" of the Buddha's doctrine. The text was composed in the Andhra region of South India in the third century AD. It enjoyed immediate popularity in India, and later became influential in China as well, particularly during the reign of the famed T'ang empress, Wu Tse-t'ien. In the *Shrimala*, one sees the full flowering of female capability. I quote Paul's summary of this unique text:[47]

The sutra of *Queen Śrīmālā Who Had the Lion's Roar* is an exceptional text in several distinctive ways. (1) The assembly of those who listen to Queen Śrīmālā consists entirely of laymen and laywomen who are the attendants and citizens in Queen Śrīmālā's court and kingdom. The religious community of monks and nuns are [*sic*] absent. (2) Queen Śrīmālā is the central figure, preempting even the Buddha, with regard to the length and content of the speeches. No other Bodhisattvas share the center stage with Śrīmālā, which was not the case in other texts depicting female Bodhisattvas. (3) The entire exposition is addressed to both the good sons and daughters who love and accept the true Dharma, teaching all other living beings to do likewise. These good sons and daughters are compared to a great rain cloud pouring forth countless benefits and rewards, reminiscent of the parable in the *Lotus Sūtra*. They are also compared to the great earth which carries the weight of the sea, mountains, vegetation, and sentient life, bestowing compassion like a great Dharma mother of the world. At no time is there a hierarchical pattern of the division of labor in which good sons are the administrators and teachers while good daughters are the assistants. (4) After the discourse, the order of the conversion of the citizens in Queen Śrīmālā's kingdom is extraordinary. First, the women of the city seven years of age and older are converted; then Queen Śrīmālā's husband, and finally the men of the city who were seven years of age and older. The

preeminence of women over men in the order of conversion
may either suggest a concession for the sake of the narration
since Queen Śrīmālā is the central figure, or it may suggest
that there was either a prominent woman in the ruling class
at that time or that women could ideally have such a societal
and religious position in a Buddhist community.

There shall be occasion to speak of the *Shrimala Sutra* again, but for
now I must close off the discussion of images of women in Buddhist
literature.[48]

∽ ∾

Let me now shift briefly to what may be called a more socio-historical
account of Buddhism's relationship to women. As Buddhism developed, and especially as the Mahayana took shape (ca. 100 BC–200 AD),
ties to the laity of necessity had to be strengthened. Not only was there
the question of dependency in terms of simple daily alms; now the laity's
support was necessary to fund the construction of more permanent and
ever-larger monastic complexes as the number of clerics increased, and
to fund the construction of *stupas*,[49] or reliquary structures for public
worship, as the number of lay followers increased.

Responding to the needs of the increasing number of lay devotees,
the Mahayana proclaimed that the bodhisattva's course was open to all,
regardless of whether one was a cleric or not and, as we have seen, regardless of whether one was a man or a woman. In place of the great emphasis on *shila* (discipline and restraint) advocated by the early Theravada
monastic community, the Mahayana gave primacy to *dana*, or giving.
Indeed, *dana* was made first in the list of the Mahayana's so-called "six
perfections" (or *paramitas*) of practice, this formulation replacing the
Theravada's "threefold training" (*tri-shiksapada*)—in monastic discipline, meditation, and insight. If one did not have the good karmic fruit
of being able to practice the monastic life, one could still practice Buddhism, gain merit through giving, and mount the successive stages of

the bodhisattva to finally reach enlightenment. Naturally, such a doctrine appealed to popular religious sentiments and aspirations.

During his own lifetime, owing to his birthright (he was the son of the Shakyan king, Shuddhodana), the Buddha moved freely in well-to-do circles.[50] He consorted with royalty, merchants, and other wealthy laypersons. Many of these people were converted to his religious cause. Others at least remained loyal supporters. Such support did not disappear following the Buddha's passing.

It is not accidental that Romila Thapar, in her *History of India*, discusses both Buddhism and Jainism in the chapter "The Rise of the Mercantile Community (ca. 200 BC–AD 300)." Thapar notes:

> The occupation of north-western India by non-Indian peoples was advantageous to the merchant, since it led to trade with regions which had as yet been untapped. The Indo-Greek kings encouraged contact with western Asia and the Mediterranean world. The Shakas, Parthians, and Kushanas brought central Asia into the orbit of the Indian merchant and this in turn led to trade with China. The Roman demand for spices and similar luxuries took Indian traders to southeast Asia and brought Roman traders to southern and western India. Through all India the merchant community prospered, as is evident from inscriptions, from their donations to charities, and from the literature of the time. Not surprisingly, the religions supported by the merchants, Buddhism and Jainism, saw their heyday during these centuries.[51]

And Robinson, speaking specifically of Buddhism, remarks:

> Throughout its history, Buddhism has appealed particularly to the merchant class, especially those engaged in the caravan trade and in large-scale finance. Mercantile ideas of accountability and responsibility underlie the doctrines of merit and karma. A world view in which fortune is rational, the regular result of specific acts, appeals to enterprising men who

would rather shape their destiny than just let fate happen to them. And the doctrine of the conservation of virtue reassures them that even if they fail in business they can succeed in religion.[52]

But let us return to the issue of women. While the Buddha may have been reluctant to found the order of nuns, early scriptural accounts attest to the fact that he did not disdain to accept gifts (often quite elaborate and expensive ones) from devout (and often quite wealthy) laywomen followers. It is, I suggest, in regard to female lay patronage that we may begin to formulate answers to the question of the role of women in the formation and development of Buddhism in India and other countries.[53]

It appears in fact that from his earliest days as a teacher, the Buddha was patronized[54] by a number of wealthy women—by women merchants, wealthy courtesans, and royal queens. Moreover, it may be argued that such material support from women not only embellished but actually sustained the continuance of Buddhism in India right up to its final "disappearance" from the subcontinent.

In one of the early scriptures, the woman Visakha, "a rich citizen commoner of Śrāvastī," is described by the Buddha as his "chief benefactress."[55] Further described as "the mother of many blooming children [she is reported to have had ten sons and ten daughters], and the grandmother of countless grandchildren [said to have numbered 8,400],"[56] she is portrayed as having lavished gifts on the Buddhist order and as having generously catered to its every need. Having tried surreptitiously to donate her jewels, valued at "ninety millions," she instead donated money to the sangha at three times their value. Visakha made a gift of treasured property at Shravasti,[57] built a monastery on the site, and single-handedly provided for the needs of the order whenever its members resided there. Her story is long and cannot be recounted here in detail. Instead, I quote a passage from the text, which summarizes her donations:

For four months did Visākhā give alms in her monastery to the Buddha and to the congregation which followed him;

and at the end of that time she presented the congregation of the priests with stuff for robes, and even that received by the novices was worth a thousand pieces of money. And of medicines, she gave the fill of every man's bowl. Ninety millions were spent in this donation. Thus ninety millions went for the site of the monastery, ninety for the construction of the monastery, and ninety for the festival at the opening of the monastery, making two hundred and seventy millions in all that were expended by her on the religion of the Buddha. No other woman in the world was as liberal as this one who lived in the house of a heretic.[58]

The last sentence of this passage is quite interesting, for history shows that it was often the case that the husbands of the Buddha's wealthy benefactresses were followers of some other religious tradition.[59]

The benefactresses of the Buddha's order were not limited to the "respectable" classes. The wealthy courtesan Ambapali,[60] who later became a nun under the Buddha's charge, is lauded in the scriptures as having been, while still a lay follower, "one of the most loyal and generous supporters of the order."[61] An account of her life is found in the *Therigatha*,[62] but Coomaraswamy has summarized the occasion of her chief offering to the Buddha—a *vihara* on her mango grove in Vesali—as follows:

Then the Master proceeded to Vesālī. At this time, also, there was dwelling in the town of Vesālī a beautiful and wealthy courtesan whose name was Ambapālī, the Mango-girl. It was reported to her that the Blessed One had come to Vesālī and was halting at her mango grove. Immediately she ordered her carriages and set out for the grove, attended by all her train; and as soon as she reached the place where the Blessed One was, she went up toward him on foot, and stood respectfully aside; and the Blessed One instructed and gladdened her with religious discourse. And she, being thus instructed and gladdened, addressed the Blessed One and said: "May

the Master do me the honour to take his meal with all the
Brethren at my house tomorrow." And the Blessed One gave
consent by silence. Ambapālī bowed down before him and
went her way . . . .

The next day Ambapālī served the Lord and all the Brethren with her own hands, and when they would eat no more
she called for a low stool and sat down beside the Master
and said: "Lord, I make a gift of this mansion to the order
of which thou art the chief." And the Blessed One accepted
the gift; and after instructing and gladdening Ambapālī with
religious discourse, he rose from his seat and went his way.[63]

The intricate and intimate connections between the medieval Indian
courtesans and the royalty of that day make for a fascinating story. The
Therigatha, for example, tells us that four famous courtesans became
nuns under the Buddha. Ambapali has just been mentioned. The three
others were Vimala, Addhakasi, and the monk Abhaya's mother, Padumavati. The latter had been known as "the town-belle of Ujjeni," and
"her boy, Abhaya, was King Bimbisāra's son."[64] (It can also be noted here
that one of the actual wives of Bimbisara, Queen Kṣema, was converted
and became a prominent nun under the Buddha.[65])

While mention has been made of women from the merchant class
and of wealthy courtesans, undoubtedly the most important women
supporters of Buddhism were the queens of the various historical periods. This fact becomes ever more evident as one traces the later development of Buddhism in India and in the countries to which it spread.

That Buddhism prospered in India under the beneficence of wealthy
queens is well attested to by a close reading of historical studies. The
phenomenon seems to have occurred in both the southern and northern centers of Buddhism and to have continued from the second and
third centuries AD up through the twelfth century. In connection with
a key example of this situation in southern India, I ask you to think
once again about the *Shrimala Sutra*. Recall that this sutra was written
in South India in the third century AD. What was the historical situation? Following the fall of the South Indian Satavahana empire around

220 AD, the region was partitioned into several kingdoms, the Andhra region coming to be ruled by the Ikshvakus. Nilakanta Sastri describes this royal house as follows:

> The reign of [Siri Chāntamūla's] son Vīrapurisadāta formed a glorious epoch in the history of Buddhism and in diplomatic relations. He took a queen from the Śaka family of Ujjain and gave his daughter in marriage to a Chutu prince. Almost all the royal ladies were Buddhists: an aunt of Vīrapurisadāta built a big stupa at Nāgārjunikonda for the relics of the great teacher, besides apsidal temples, *vihāras,* and *mandapas.* Her example was followed by other women of the royal family and by women generally, as we know from a reference to one Bodhisiri, a woman citizen.[66]

The Waymans suggest that by "taking these facts into consideration, one may postulate that the *Śrī-Mālā* was composed partly to honor the eminent Buddhist ladies who were so responsible for this glorious period of South Indian Buddhism."[67]

Nor should we fail to mention that a few centuries later, in China, the *Shrimala Sutra* enjoyed increased popularity and prestige when Empress Wu liberally patronized Buddhism there (in exchange, one might add, for the propaganda campaign carried out on her behalf by her Buddhist supporters!).[68]

To return to India, what was true in South India was true in the north as well. Historical records show that particularly for the important northwestern center of Buddhism, that is, the regions around Kashmir, the Tradition enjoyed the continuous support of the queens of the period. Buddhism having fallen on hard times following the fall of the Kushana empire,[69] its revival in the north is partly—if not wholly—attributable to certain notable queens. Thus, Nalinaksha Dutt provides the following glimpses into the history of the Mahayana's development in the north:

> Meghavāhana, a descendant of Yudhiṣṭhira I, was brought by the people from Gandhāra and placed on the throne.

He had a soft corner for Buddhism, hailing, as he did, from
Gandhāra, a predominantly Buddhistic country. His queen
Amṛtaprabhā of Prāgjyotisa is said to have built for the use
of Buddhist monks a lofty vihāra called Amṛtabhavana. . . .

During the reign of Raṇāditya, one of his queens called
Amṛtaprabhā placed a fine statue of Buddha in the vihāra
built by a queen of Meghavāhana. Raṇāditya was succeeded
by his son Vikramāditya, who was a devotee of Śiva. His
minister Galuna had a vihāra built in the name of his wife,
Ratnāvali. . . .

Bālāditya [mid-eighth century CE] was succeeded by
his son-in-law, Durlabhavardhana, whose queen set up the
Anaṅgabha-vana-vihāra, referred to by Ou K'ong as Ānanda
or Ānaṅga vihāra. The king himself, as also his successors,
were mostly Viṣṇu-worshippers. . . .

Jayamatī, queen of Uccala, built two monasteries, one of
which was in honor of her sister Sullā. This, it is said, was completed by King Jayasiṃha, the illustrious ruler, who succeeded
Uccala. King Jayasiṃha patronised literary men, and there was
once more a revival of learning in Kashmir. He looked after the
Maṭhas and Vihāras, the first of which that attracted his attention was the one built by his queen Ratnādevī. His chief minister Rilhaṇa was also very pious. He showed his veneration to
both Śiva and Buddha, and erected a monastery in memory
of his deceased wife Sussalā. Sussalā must have been a great
devotee of Buddha, as she erected [a vihāra] on the site of the
famous Caṅkuna-Vihāra, which had been destroyed. It had
a magnificent establishment for the Buddhist monks. Cintā,
wife of Jayasiṃha's commander Udaya, adorned the bank of
the Vitastā by a monastery consisting of five buildings, and
Dhanya, one of the ministers, commenced the construction
of a vihāra in honour of his late wife. Evidently, therefore, the
reigning period of Jayasiṃha [1128–49 CE] marked a revival of
the Buddhist faith in Kashmir.[70]

CONCLUSION

When we attempt to arrive at an accurate picture of the role played by women in the formation and subsequent development of Buddhism, two main sources of material are available. One is the vast corpus of Buddhist literature itself. Such scriptures present a variety of images of women, of the female, and of the feminine, with such portrayals generally getting more positive as we advance from the early to later texts. It can be noted that women were elevated, presented more positively, and granted more esteem in the texts *at the same time* that such elevation and esteem were accorded to the laity in general. Still, if only the texts are relied on, a one-sided picture emerges in which women as a whole are most often portrayed as being reacted to (or, against) rather than as being active participants in their own right.

The other major source is the information provided in secular (as distinct from religious) histories. A close reading of this material shows women as independent and active in the world, and as capable of affecting and, in some cases, even of shaping the development of the Buddhist tradition. Contrary to the Buddha's prediction that his doctrine would not long abide in India because he now admitted women to his order, history shows that women's support at least in some cases may actually have been responsible for the tradition's flourishing on the subcontinent for as long as it did.

Both pools of information must be used together. The women who became followers of the Buddha served him as nuns and as lay benefactresses. While neither group can be said to have actively influenced the early teachings per se, both groups of women proved that by practicing them they could attain spiritual heights equal to those of their male counterparts. Moreover, though the order of nuns did not remain a strong factor in Buddhism's historical development in India, laywomen supporters there did play a significant role in nourishing and sustaining the growth and development of the tradition.

2

The *Chomos* of Ladakh:
From Servants to Practitioners

❧ ⚬⚬

In 1995 Jan Willis traveled to Ladakh to attend a Sakyadhita conference of Buddhist women. Recently she returned and found that a movement started at that conference has dramatically improved the lives of Ladakhi nuns.

❧ ⚬⚬

Tucked away on a high plateau in the far northwest of India lies the dry and windswept region of Ladakh, one of the most beautiful and remote outposts in the Buddhist world. To the east it is bordered by the Himalayas. To the west lies war-troubled Kashmir and Pakistan. From the fifth to the fifteenth century Ladakh was an independent Tibetan kingdom and many Buddhist monasteries were established there.

Modern-day Ladakh—whose population of 160,000 is about evenly divided between Buddhists and Muslims—is still home to many monks and nuns, but for generations nuns have held a grossly inferior position. I first traveled to Ladakh in 1995 to attend the Sakyadhita Conference of Buddhist Women held in its capital city, Leh. I was astounded by the appalling conditions of Ladakh's nuns, who seemed to be mere helpers for the monks, with no status and no attention being paid to their spiritual path. But on a return visit in July 2003, I was able to see how the work of the Ladakh Nuns Association in the intervening eight years had made it possible for many of Ladakh's nuns to move away from servitude and toward becoming true spiritual practitioners.

In her book *Servants of the Buddha*, Anna Grimshaw chronicled a winter's stay during the 1970s among the nuns of Chulichan, the nunnery subsumed under the grand monastery of Rizong, which is a favorite tourist destination.[11] Grimshaw bemoaned the sad circumstances of the nuns there, who, in her eyes, were little more than servants to the Rizong monks and didn't receive so much as a thank you in return. When I visited Chulichan in 1995, only four of the eleven nuns Grimshaw had lived with remained. The four elderly nuns worked at growing, harvesting, and preparing for sale the apricots that give the nunnery its name. They were living in the dilapidated courtyard of the nunnery—not only because it was summer when I visited but because there was not a single room in the crumbling structure without a leaking roof.

Buddhist nuns in general do not command the respect that Buddhist monks do, but the situation of nuns in Ladakh has, until quite recently, been a case unique unto itself. In a real sense, the decline in the nuns' fortunes began with the perceptions of them held by Ladakhi monks and laypeople, for in Ladakh a girl may wear the robes of a nun even though she may have taken only the five precepts prescribed for an *upasika*, or lay practitioner. Historically, this practice is said to have originated in the nineteenth century when a rinpoché of Rizong monastery first granted a group of young girls the right to don the robes, provided they vow to take the ten higher precepts (of novice monastics) when they reached the age of eighteen. Apparently, few of them did so. The wearing of robes was meant to be a sign that these young women were serious, but that altruistic intent clearly backfired. Since any enrobed nun encountered in Ladakh today may be "only" an *upasika*, no special—let alone revered—status is accorded to her at all. Instead, she is given menial jobs by her family or is hired out to villagers or work projects with no guarantee that she will ever be free to join a spiritual community or even enjoy the free time to hear Dharma teachings.

Even after the recent reforms, it is still not unusual to see a lone Lada-khi nun herding goats, tilling the fields, or even working on a road gang. Road work in particular is not only labor-intensive but often dangerous as well, since roads cut through mountain passes that surge upwards of 14,000 feet. Such grueling work allows little time for communal liv-ing or spiritual practice. In her talk at the 1995 conference, Dr. Tsering Palmo, who would go on to found the Ladakh Nuns Association the following year, spoke eloquently about the need to improve the living and studying conditions of the nuns there. Explaining the conditions that led the nuns to have so little spiritual training, Dr. Palmo said:

> Due to the lack of financial support, from generation to gen-eration, nuns in Ladakh have not been able to educate them-selves. The only alternative left to them is to stay with the family and help it to earn a living. In return, the family may help the nun by supporting a retreat for one or two months of the year or by financially supporting a long pilgrimage out of Ladakh. In reality, nuns have to depend on their families for any religious activities they wish to do.
>
> Those who manage to enter a nunnery, with great aspira-tions and hopes, soon have their dreams shattered by lack of proper monastic and secular educational programs. By 1994, the pious traditions of Buddhist nuns and nunneries had so far declined that they very nearly reached the point of extinction.

It is clear from my recent visit that by founding the Ladakh Nuns Association, Dr. Palmo has managed to bring a genuine nuns' tradition back from the brink of extinction and to make dramatic improvements in the nuns' lives and livelihoods. Accordingly, the number of nuns has tripled since 1995 to just over 900. While 790 of these women live within the three major districts of Leh, Kargil, and Chang Thang, another 120 are now engaged in higher studies outside Ladakh in various locations throughout India, such as Dharamsala, Darjeeling, Mungod, and Vara-nasi. These Ladakhi nuns have come a long way from road work.

One measure of the nuns' progress can be seen by comparing the current situation of the Chulichan nuns with that described by Grimshaw in *Servants of the Buddha*. Whereas in 1995 I had seen only four elderly nuns living in the courtyard and working as farmhands, in 2003 I saw that the nunnery at Chulichan was being completely rebuilt, with a slate of new rooms being constructed with solar panels outside. The number of Chulichan nuns had now grown to 20 and most were in their mid-twenties. These new nuns no longer harvest the fields; they have a resident *geshe* (scholar-teacher) and time for their own spiritual practices. And all of this takes place with the blessings of the current Rizong abbot.

Within Ladakh today, the nuns' community is growing at a strong pace while the number of monks, in fact, is decreasing. Tsering Samphel, president of the Ladakh Buddhist Association, gave three reasons for the monks' decline. The first is that the Indian military—whose presence is felt everywhere throughout this region—has stepped up its campaign to recruit eligible young men. The second is that young men, being generally more educated, are more mobile than young females, lay or ordained. Finally, the overall Buddhist population in the area is decreasing, because, Samphel said, "Buddhists take the family-planning guidelines to heart. Our Muslim neighbors do not. Hence, we are on the verge of becoming a minority in our own country."

One of the main factors that accounts for the rise in the number of nuns is the promise of receiving an education. Nuns and education were not related in the minds of Ladakhis in the past. In fact, almost all nuns were illiterate. (Even today, with reforms, only 20 percent are literate.) Without sufficient nunneries or teachers to staff them, few nuns entered communities or were instructed in the vinaya (disciplinary rules) governing their lifestyle. Those few fortunate enough to secure a place in a nunnery were still unable to gain access to qualified Dharma teachers willing to invest time in them.

The 1995 Sakyadhita Conference marked a turning point in the nuns' fortunes. It was at that point that how the nuns viewed themselves and how they were viewed by others began to change. The Ladakhi nuns in attendance were encouraged to see that there were others in the

THE CHOMOS OF LADAKH   41

world—Buddhists and non-Buddhists alike—who were concerned about their plight. Dr. Palmo's eloquent presentation at the conference pushed her to the forefront of the struggle to improve the living and studying conditions of the nuns, and this ultimately led her to found the Ladakh Nuns Association. Though not present at the conference, the Dalai Lama sent an inspirational letter to the attendees encouraging the nuns to persevere and to educate themselves. His Holiness's Office in Dharamsala later made a donation to the nuns association that it earmarked for education. And, perhaps most importantly, particularly with regard to their own self-esteem, the Ladakhi nuns democratically and unanimously decided to cast off the outmoded and derogatory Tibetan term *ani* by which they had formerly been known. In Tibetan, *ani* literally means "aunt," but it also connotes and conjures the image of a servant. The Buddhist nuns of Ladakh decided that they wanted henceforth to be called *chomos*, "female religious practitioners"; nothing more, and nothing less!

In ancient times in India, Mahāprajāpatī, the Buddha's aunt and the first Buddhist nun, declared:

I have been mother, son, father, brother, and grandmother.
Knowing nothing of the truth, I journeyed on.
But I have seen the Blessed One, and this is my last body.
I will not go from birth to birth again.

Her testament, recorded in the *Therigatha*, has become the chomos' anthem.

Since 1996, Dr. Palmo's nuns association has acted as the most inclusive umbrella organization for the overall improvement of the nuns' situation in Ladakh. The association, working closely with the now twenty-seven nunneries in the region, has set clear priorities, including helping existing nunneries become self-reliant and self-sufficient, seeking ways to provide training opportunities in both monastic and secular education to the nuns, and renovating old nunneries and establishing new ones. The association has sponsored study tours as well as Dharma teachings by eminent teachers for the nuns, and it has secured places for nuns in schools, both secular and Buddhist. It also seeks to help nuns develop skills in Tibetan medicine so they can take more responsibility for their own and others' health care. This latter priority has grown directly out of Dr. Palmo's own experience. She was the first Ladakhi woman to earn a degree in traditional Tibetan medicine from the Chokpori Medical College in Dharamsala.

As I witnessed—and marveled at—the tremendous shift of energy taking place for the nuns of this remote, barren, and yet breathtaking region, I couldn't help but reflect on the lost opportunities for former generations of nuns and for those now quite elderly nuns who had spent almost their entire lives working as the servants of various worldly masters, instead of becoming servants of the Dharma. Then, as if by magic, early one morning a jeep arrived at my guest house door. I and three other colleagues were being summoned to attend a special groundbreaking ceremony for the new nunnery to be run under the auspices and blessings of the renowned Thiksey Monastery.

The 500-year-old Thiksey Monastery, perched high on a hill above the Indus River, roughly ten miles south of Leh, is home to 120 monks. Because it also houses one of the largest statues of Maitreya, the future Buddha, whose form rises majestically through two stories of its main gompa, Thiksey is on every foreign visitor's must-see list. At Thiksey, Khenpo Nawang Jamyang Chamba and a gentle and unassuming geshé named Tsultrim Tharchin have taken His Holiness's words to heart and become nuns' activists. The rinpoché spearheaded a drive to have his monastery donate the land for the nunnery; Geshé Tharchin has been offering classes in the Thiksey village town hall in reading, writing, and ritual skills for the past two years to the 26 Thiksey area nuns. The youngest of these nuns is forty-three; the oldest eighty-seven. Though enrobed, most of the nuns have never lived together with any other nuns. Instead, they have spent thirty to fifty years working on road construction. Geshé-la's classes are the first they have ever had.

The jeep raced past the imposing Thiksey buildings and continued on a few miles south. It then turned off at a sign that declared the entrance to Nyerma. Nyerma is dotted by melted-away stūpas designed by none other than Rinchen Zangpo himself, the celebrated tenth-century Tibetan translator and redactor of the Tibetan Buddhist canon. This land was the site of Zangpo's very first monastic seat; it will now become the site of Thiksey's first-ever nunnery and home for these 26 nuns and a few others.

The nuns gathered here—aged and wrinkled, the years of hard labor showing on their faces—were wearing their robes and beaming. Even as they chanted with all the soft sweetness of their mature voices, most dreamt of the time when they would feel educated, practiced, and hence qualified enough to take the vows of higher ordination. For them, Thiksey Nunnery will become the place where they can devote themselves to their spiritual practices, where they can study and truly become chomos.

Of Ladakh's 900 enrobed women, these 26 will—in a few years—have a place for their communal life of spiritual practice. For other young girls and women, there is only hopeful waiting. At present, just over 500 nuns actually reside in such communities, and some of these communities carry on in spite of less-than-ideal living conditions. Roughly 250 nuns are enrobed in Ladakh but are still forced to live on their own and to practice in whatever free time they can manage to secure. Many positive changes have occurred for some of the nuns in a relatively short period of time. In this respect, one can say that Ladakh's chomos are on the rise. But they were coming from a pretty low place. If Buddhism is to remain and flourish in this region so close to the sky, and to sustain and strengthen its followers, much more work remains to be done.

To learn more about the Ladakhi nuns visit
www.ladakhnunsassociation.com.

3

Tibetan Anis: The Nun's Life in Tibet

❧ ❧

I.

I am a woman—I have little power to resist danger.
Because of my inferior birth, everyone attacks me.
If I go as a beggar, dogs attack me.
If I have wealth and food, bandits attack me.
If I do a great deal, the locals attack me.
If I do nothing, gossips attack me.
If anything goes wrong, they all attack me.
Whatever I do, I have no chance for happiness.
Because I am a woman, it is hard to follow the Dharma.
It is hard even to stay alive![72]

These words were spoken by Yeshé Tsogyal (Ye shes mtsho rgyal), one of the two chief tantric consorts of "Guru Rinpoché"—that is, Padmasambhava, the Indian *siddha* (tantric master) credited with having "established" Buddhism in Tibet.[73] The quote is taken from Tsogyal's *namthar*, or "complete liberation life story" (in many respects an equivalent of hagiographies, or sacred biographies, in the West).[74]

Now, though she may sound in the passage above a bit *burdened* by the female form, in an episode just prior to this one, her tantric accomplishments have been publicly praised by the guru in words like the following:

> Wonderful yoginī, practitioner of the secret teachings!
> The basis for realizing enlightenment is a human body.
> Male or female—there is no great difference.
> But if she develops the mind bent on enlightenment,
> the woman's body is better.
> From beginningless time,
> you have accumulated merit and wisdom.
> Now your good qualities are flawless—
> what an excellent woman you have become, a true Bodhisattma!
> Are you not the embodiment of bliss?
> Now that you have achieved what you wanted for yourself,
> strive for the benefit of others.[75]

Recently a number of studies have begun to appear which address the issue of women as religious practitioners in both Western and non-Western cultures.[76] Women's place within Buddhism has proven to be a fertile area of investigation, and several treatments have appeared which discuss the various portrayals of women in Buddhist literature.[77] However, analyses limited solely to the literary sphere invariably neglect a good deal of what constituted, or constitutes, the day-to-day world of religious practice.[78]

The topic of women and Tibetan Buddhism and of women's place within Tibetan Buddhist religious life has received considerably less attention and remains to be explored in full. While there are—in the vast corpus of Tibetan scriptural literature—examples of perhaps a dozen or so women who have risen to eminence within the tradition (and about whom namthar have thus been composed),[79] the religious life of the far larger group of unsung ordinary women practitioners has received little or no attention at all. And yet it is precisely these "unspoken worlds" of the uncelebrated Tibetan women practitioners that offer the most potential for revealing religious life as actually lived and practiced in Tibet. It is hoped that the present article, which focuses on the lives of five Tibetan Buddhist nuns, will help to illumine that religious life a bit better.

In Tibet, prior to 1959, there existed a number of different types of women *chöpa* (*chos pa*),[80] or religious practitioners. There were women *lhakhas* and *pawo* (*dpa' mo*, i.e., "spirit mediums");[81] there were female religious bards called *manipas*; and—representing what may be viewed as the two poles of Buddhist practice—there were the tantric adepts (like Yeshé Tsogyal) and the *anis*, or Buddhist nuns. To be sure, the type of women lauded in the sacred annals are the accomplished tantric practitioners: women like Niguma, "wife" of the Indian siddha Naropa, who developed and taught her own system of the famed six yogas. There is Dagmema (Bdag med ma), Marpa's accomplished wife; and Machik Lapdrönma, Phadampa Sangyé's chief consort and fashioner of the advanced meditative Chö (Gcod) rite.

Though there are fewer sacred biographies of women tantric adepts than of their male counterparts, such biographies do nevertheless exist and they evidence that the Tantras were, and remain, effective for producing enlightened beings regardless of sex. But these women are the rare and fabulous examples. They are all tantric masters, having left society's constraints to follow the treacherous path conducive only for a chosen few. And all these women are *mudras*, or "consorts" (to male tantric practitioners). Some are referred to simply as *yoginis*; others are called human *dakinis*—that is, incarnations of the feminine principle of insight and wisdom itself. They are not your ordinary everyday Tibetan women practitioners.

On the other end of the spectrum there are the Tibetan Buddhist nuns, women who have quietly, and often with great difficulties, continued to practice in accordance with the monastic rules laid down at Buddhism's very inception in India, circa sixth century BC. About this type of enrobed female practitioner the texts do not speak and very little information is presently available. No indigenous Tibetan literature, of whatever historical period, focuses on them. Moreover, only the most scant attention has been paid to them in the very recent past. Yet the *ani* tradition has managed to survive.[82]

In what follows I wish to look more closely at the *ani* tradition in Tibet. And so, leaving aside the fabulous women of the namthar, my aim here is to focus on a set of life histories of five Tibetan *anis* of the twentieth century. Two of these *anis* were well-known figures in Tibet. The other three, including Ani Drölkar (Sgrol dkar), whom I personally interviewed in Nepal in 1980, are simple practitioners to whom little or no attention has been paid previously. I believe that the lives of these *anis* can shed a great deal of light on how Buddhism functioned in the lives of Tibetans (both men and women), and on how it was actually practiced by them. Again, the issue of women serves as an entrée into the larger question of the social world of religious practice.

2.

Before proceeding to describe the case histories themselves, some general—though often overlooked or misconstrued—features of the Tibetan religious landscape need to be noted. In the past, the failure of many Western explorers and scholars to accurately depict and weigh certain geographic, demographic, and linguistic features of Tibet has resulted in a quite distorted picture of Tibetan religious life.

Because Tibet (or Khawachen, the "Abode of Snows") is situated virtually at the top of the world and is fortified on three sides by many of the highest mountains on Earth, the country itself until very recently was famed for its very remoteness and inaccessibility. Those few travelers and explorers who managed to reach Lhasa, Tibet's capital city (the name means "Dwelling Place of the Gods")—men like Heinrich Harrer, Marco Pallis, and even Lowell Thomas, Jr.—told of its magic and mysteries in a grandiose and idealized fashion. Tibet was depicted as a type of Shangri-la—a country where the sheer vastness and stark beauty of nature itself caused heightened awareness, where peace reigned eternally, where the Buddhist religion permeated all facets of life at all times, where celibate monks and nuns were prized above all other citizens, and where such clerics—by the thousands—chose to live a life apart in cloistered enclaves continually engaged in religious endeavors. Such descriptions are a bit too idyllic and much too idealized. They present a static, capital-centered view of Tibetan life. A truer picture of Tibetan Buddhism, Tibetan monasticism, and Tibetan religious life would show it to be much more dynamic, bustling, diverse, and fluid.

Most Western accounts seem unaware of Tibet's actual demography, of its distinction between town and village hamlet, and of the quite striking fact that only one seventy-fifth of Tibet's pre-1959 population was urban. No accurate census was ever taken of Tibet's three chief regions (Chölkha Sum, chol kha gsum) prior to 1959, but estimates put the overall population figure at between 4.5 million and 6 million. Basing his analysis on the 6 million figure, Shakabpa[83] has suggested that of this number, 48 percent of ethnic Tibetans were nomads, 32 percent were traders and agriculturalists, and 20 percent were clerics. His estimates are that 18 percent of these latter were monks and 2 percent were nuns. (This would mean that in Tibet some 1,080,000 men were monks as compared to 120,000 nuns—or roughly 9 monks to every nun.)[84]

As Shakabpa also notes, there were only four large cities, or towns, in all of Tibet:[85] Lhasa, the capital, with a population that ranged normally between 35,000 and 40,000 but expanded to as many as 70,000 or 80,000 during the Tibetan New Year, when clerics and pilgrims converged for the Great Prayer Festival (*mönlam*); Shigatse, with a population ranging between 13,000 and 20,000; Chamdo, with a population of between 9,000 and 12,000; and Gyantse (for which Shakabpa gives no figures). By Tibetan standards these were bustling cities, to be sure, and they were also the sites of some of the largest and most celebrated monastic institutions. But their combined population figures would only count some 57,000 to 72,000 (say 80,000 counting Gyantse) ethnic Tibetans to be urban city dwellers—or roughly 1 in 75 of all Tibetans. The rest of the population lived (and carried on their religious lives) in much smaller towns and village hamlets, scattered throughout the vast 1.5 million square miles of the country.

In another important respect, Western capital-centered views of Tibet have resulted in distortion of Tibetan religious life. Namely, such accounts have misconstrued the nature and degree of celibacy among the various Buddhist sects. There are four major schools or sects of Tibetan Buddhism—the Nyingmapa, the Sakyapa, the Kagyüpa, and the Gelukpa. In modern times (actually, since the seventeenth century), the Gelukpa have enjoyed political dominance, the Dalai Lamas all being trained in this "reformed" tradition. Of the four schools, only the Gelukpa enjoins strict celibacy, and then only on its religious elite. While lamas (or venerated teachers) in the other three "nonreformed" sects *may* be celibate, a life of strict chastity is nowhere enjoined on all religious practitioners, and the ideals of the noncelibate tantric *yogin* are always upheld. Early Western travelers to Lhasa saw the three massive Geluk monastic complexes built nearby: Drepung, Sera, and Ganden. With monk populations of 9,000, 7,000, and 3,000–5,000, respectively, these *densa sum* ("three great sees") gave the impression no doubt that Tibet was a land of celibate monks and monasteries. But just as Lhasa was not representative of all of Tibet, this capital-centered view told only part of the story.

Lastly, even the language used by Western scholars to describe the central institution around which much of Tibetan religious life revolves has suffered distortion. Thus the word *gönpa*, usually translated as "monastery," in Tibetan means "any solitary place where meditative practice can be carried on."[86] The term is used both with reference to an isolated retreat spot or to any settlement where men or women have gathered together to practice the religious life. Among the "unreformed" sects, there are countless so-called *serkhyim gönpa*, that is, religious communities composed of married clerics. Such *serkhyim* members are tantric practitioners and ritual experts who, while performing priestly duties and being affiliated with a gönpa, still live as householders. Such an arrangement probably would appear odd to outsiders who have other notions about what a monastery or convent means.

Even when primarily celibate establishments, most gönpa were not usually designated or distinguished as being strictly either monasteries or nunneries, though one sometimes comes across the designation *ani gönpa* ("nunnery").[87] The more common arrangement seems to have been a joint venture wherein groups of nuns were appendaged to monasteries or inhabited a given area of a monastic compound.

Because most gönpa in Tibet were small rural establishments, close ties existed between village and gönpa. Speaking of this relationship, Snellgrove has remarked:

Apart from a number of very large monasteries . . . and some medium sized monasteries with five hundred monks or so, other Tibetan monasteries were comparatively small with fifty to two hundred monks, and often far less. These small communities possessed little or no land and depended for their existence mainly on the families whose members were actually monks. Thus most monasteries developed in close relationship with nearby villages, providing for the religious, educational and in large part the cultural needs of the community. Monks and layfolk lived in such close association, joining in so many activities together, that it completely falsifies the real nature of Tibetan society if one sets monks in opposition to layfolk.[88]

For the majority of Tibetans, these close ties and close distances accounted for fairly continuous movement back and forth between village and *gönpa*. A palpable connection existed between the secular and the religious life. Indeed for most Tibetan *chöpa* (i.e., *religieux*), to separate them completely would have been not only impractical, but a falsification of the actual workings of their religious practice.

Holding all the various types of religious communities together was the lama, or teacher. He or she was the center and cement of the community. Yet the styles of teachers were as diverse and individualistic as the teachers themselves. There is an old Tibetan saying which goes: "Every ten *li* (Chinese, "three miles"), heaven is different. Each district has its way of speaking; each lama his way of teaching." The lama set the tone for a particular religious community and area; and his or her distinctiveness was mirrored by the members of the community. What Barbara Aziz has noted for the inhabitants of Dingri could easily be applied more broadly. She writes:

Paralleling the range of life styles exhibited by their *la-ma*, D'ing-ri novices make a choice as to how they will proceed. The religious life is one that symbolizes free choice and so there is no one to dictate a religious style to the new initiate.

Each therefore begins life as a *ch'o-pa* according to individual circumstances. An *a-ni* may remain with her family for many years (if she gets on well with her brother's *na-ma*); or immediately after her ordination she may go on a major pilgrimage to parts beyond D'ing-ri where she had never been before. She may opt to live with a kinswoman in a *gonpa* or she may become an itinerant and avoid any permanent home for years. Such a range of possibilities is also open to the new *dr'a'-pa* [i.e., a male *chospa*]. And after following any one for a time, it is not unusual for the devotee to shift to another style.[89]

Indeed a great deal of religious freedom seems to have been the norm in Tibet. But the freedom to choose one's own course of religious practice did not mean—and should not be equated with—material ease and comfort. The life of the Tibetan *ani* in particular was not an easy one.[90]

It may be argued that the nun's order was never a strong component of Buddhism's development at any time or in any country.[91] Tibet was no exception. While the earliest ordination of Tibetan monks (a solemn ceremony in which the Indian Acharya Shantiraksita ordained the first seven indigenous Tibetans at Samyé [Bsam yas] Monastery in the late eighth century AD) is an event well documented and much lauded in the major religious annals of the country, I have been unable to find a single reference to the earliest ordination of Tibetan nuns. There were, however, *ani* in Tibet; and, though very few in number, there were even some *ani khenpos* (*a ni mkhan pos*), or abbesses. Thus for some Tibetan women, the life of a nun, even with all its hardships, offered a viable, even attractive, means by which to practice their faith.

3.

Having presented the foregoing comments for reflection and clarification, I now turn to the specific case histories. As mentioned, I will here briefly summarize five different examples of nun's lives.

1. The Abbess of Samding Gönpa (Bsam sding dgon pa)

Samding was the state nunnery of Tibet and its abbess was regarded as the incarnation of the deity Dorjé Phakmo (Rdo rje phag mo; Skt. Vajravārāhī). Situated 70 miles southwest of Lhasa, on a slip of land some 14,512 feet high and overlooking the famed Yamdrok (Yar 'brog) Lake, the gönpa was a most impressive sight. Waddell mused that Samding was "noteworthy as a monastery of monks as well as nuns, presided over by a female abbot."[92] He continued his description as follows:

> This august woman is known throughout Tibet as Dorje-P'ag-mo [Dorjé Phakmo], or "the diamond sow"; the abbesses of Samding being held to be successive appearances in mortal form of the Indian goddess, Vajravarahi. The present incarnation of this goddess is thirty-three years old (in 1889); and is described as being a clever and capable woman, with some claim to good looks, and of noble birth. She bears the name of Nag-dban Rin-ch'en Kun-bzan-mo dbAn-mo [Ngawang Rinchen Kunsangmo Wangmo], signifying "The most precious power of speech, the female energy of all good." Under this lady the reputation which Samding has long enjoyed for the good morals of both monks and nuns has been well maintained.[93]

Tucci's expedition briefly visited Samding in 1948. In *To Lhasa and Beyond,* he comments:

> I could not leave the place without seeing the Samding monastery, built by Potopa Chogle Namgyal (P'yogs las rnam rgyal). That convent is famous on account of the incarnation of the goddess Dorjepamo (rDorje p'ag mo [Dorjé Phakmo]), "the hog-headed One" supposed to dwell there uninterruptedly, changing [only] her mortal form. Never fear: the goddess' mortal mirror does not look that dreadful and was, at the time, a pretty girl of 13.[94]

The early nineteenth-century Tibetan work *The Geography of Tibet*
mentions Samding Gönpa and terms the abbess a *rikma* (*rig ma*, a "wisdom being"; also a synonym for *mudra*).[95] Both Taring[96] and Waddell[97]
attribute the abbess's high esteem to the fact that during the 1719 invasion of Tibet by the Dzungar Tartars she miraculously transformed
herself and her followers into "a large herd of pigs,"[98] the sight of which
caused the Dzungars to flee in disgust. The convent was chiefly affiliated with the Nyingma sect, but its abbess is the only woman in Tibet
venerated on a par with and "accorded privileges shared only by" the
Panchen and Dalai Lamas.[99]

2. Ani Lochen

In her wonderfully interesting autobiography, *Daughter of Tibet*,
Rinchen Dölma Taring briefly mentions a saintly woman who com-
manded the respect of all the religious sects. This woman was called
Ani Lochen. Sometimes a fuller title was given: Shuksep Jetsun Lochen
Rinpoché. Shuksep (*shugs gseb*, "juniper forest") named the location of
Ani Lochen's nunnery, some 30 miles outside Lhasa. The titles Jetsun
(*rje btsun*) and Rinpoché are honorific ones, reserved for Tibet's most
accomplished and treasured teachers.

Taring describes Ani Lochen as being the reincarnation[100] of Machik
Lapdrönma (mentioned previously),[101] and as also being affiliated pri-
marily with the Nyingmapa sect. As a summary of Ani Lochen's life,
Taring writes the following:

> She had been born in India in about 1820 at Tsopadma
> Rawalsar in the district of Mandi of a Nepalese mother
> and Tibetan father. From the age of six she preached, with
> a *thang-ka*, by singing of religion in a wonderfully melodi-
> ous voice, and whoever heard her found their hearts coming
> closer to religion. As a child she had a little goat to ride, and
> when in her youth she went along the streets of Lhasa with
> her *thang-ka*, preaching from door to door, she caught the
> hearts of many Lhasa girls, who became nuns and followed
> her. She was known as "Ani Lochen." . . . At the age of about

forty Ani Lochen promised her mother that she would always stay in the mountains and meditate; later she found a place near Lhasa called Shuksep, where there was a cave in which Gyalwa Longchen Rabjampa had meditated. . . . Many nuns also came, and there was a little nunnery nearby for about eighty women. People regularly visited Ani Lochen, for her cave was near Lhasa and she had many worshippers—lamas, monks, officials and women. Sometimes nuns would leave their nunnery to marry, but Ani Lochen always said, "Never mind—even if they have been nuns for only a week they will be different forever afterwards."[102]

There are differing accounts of this accomplished woman's age at death. At one place in *Daughter of Tibet*, Taring provides a photograph of Ani Lochen. Next to it the caption reads: "Shuksep Jetsun Lochen Rinpoché, a saint. She died in 1950, aged over 130 years."[103] To my knowledge the only other source in English for information on Ani Lochen comes from Lobsang Lhalungpa.[104] Lhalungpa's comments regarding Ani Lochen are found in two separate sources. One says she died at age 115; the other says 113.

In an interview for *Parabola* magazine, Lhalungpa was asked about his own teachers. I give below excerpts of his response:

Fortunately I have had quite a number of teachers. I was admitted to a monastery but my father wouldn't allow me to stay there; he wanted me to stay with him and study privately under great lamas. This I did. It proved to be very effective and beneficial to me. Some of them are still alive in India.

I had a woman lama in Tibet, an extraordinary woman. Her name was Jetsun Lochen Rinpoché. She had very close connections with my family. Two of my cousins became nuns at her nunnery. It wasn't a nunnery in the strict sense of the word, but a kind of institution where old or young women—anyone—could go and spend time with her for different teachings, and then stay at the establishment and carry on

their practices. There were many nuns and lay people as well.
She belonged to the order known in the West as the Red Hat
sect, the *Nyingmapa* order, but actually she was eclectic. In
giving teachings to students or disciples, she would always
speak in comparative terms and encourage them to develop
understanding of every teaching of the different schools
and traditions. She herself was certainly respected by all the
great monasteries in Tibet; she was one of the most widely
respected women teachers that have lived in Tibet.

She lived to one hundred and fifteen years of age and had
a tremendous following throughout the country. She never
travelled very widely, but people came to her at her mountain
retreat. An extraordinary woman! Not so much in terms of
deep learning; while she knew a good deal about Buddhism
itself, it was her own inner development, inner experience
and attainment that was so great. A lot of people who didn't
actually study with her still received from her directly. Just
being present there in front of her, they seemed to experience
some deep sort of change. . . .

She never actually slept. She trained herself in that way.
She was always in a high meditational state of mind—very
alert. I was able to spend a good deal of time listening to her
and she really gave me many things.

I have had many great teachers, but this woman lama, Jetsun Lochen Rinpoché, gave me tremendous insight into the
spiritual life.[105]

In his introductory "chronicle" to the 1983 publication of *Tibet, the
Sacred Realm: Photographs 1880–1950*, Lhalungpa again speaks of Ani
Lochen. In a section entitled "Teachings of the Great Lamas," he speaks
of his education under Ling and Trijang Rinpochés (the two chief
tutors of the present Dalai Lama),[106] under Gonsartse Rinpoché, and
lastly under Ani Lochen. In a sensitive portrayal, he states:

Not long after that I went to visit a holy woman mystic

named Jetsun Lochen at her nunnery in the Juniper Forest, thirty miles from Lhasa, in order to receive from her the highest esoteric teachings and initiations of the Nyingmapa order, known as Atiyoga. Her religious center was situated on the high slope of Mount Gangri Thokar (Whitehead Mountain), one of the most sacred places in Tibet. The only daughter of poor parents, Jetsun Lochen had shaped her own destiny in childhood. Showing intense interest in religious songs and studies, she had risen to the eminence of a revered lama. Long before I went to her, my family had been among her ardent followers. Some of my close relatives were nuns at the nunnery.

During my first two-week visit I met with Jetsun Lochen for several hours a day, sometimes in the company of her main disciples. She was an extraordinary woman, small in stature, with a serene face radiating compassion and sensitivity. Only her white hair betrayed her age: she died a few years later at the age of one hundred thirteen. In her presence we felt an awesome power that permeated our whole stream-being. Her teachings and blessings have given me inner strength and inspiration ever since. To me she was the personification of the great woman teachers of Tibet.[107]

Taring notes that "Ani Lochen died in 1950, at the age of a hundred and thirty, and her reincarnation was born to Jigme's brother, Chime Dorjé, in 1955. He was a fine little boy who remembered his prayers and many of his disciples, and he had just been recognized by the Dalai Lama as the true reincarnation when the uprising [of 1959] took place."[108] (I do not know what has become of him.)

3. and 4. Two Anis of Dingri
In the course of her description of Dingri society (an area close to the Nepal-Tibet border where over a quarter of the hamlets are Serkhyim Gönpa [ser khyimdgon pa]), Barbara Aziz gives brief portraits of two contemporary nuns. One is an "itinerant" nun named Ani Chödrön,

and the other a sort of hermit nun named Ani Drölma. I present these case histories as examples of living practitioners. Apart from my own oral history of Ani Drölkar, Aziz's cases are the only published studies I have come across. Taken altogether, these three life histories vividly demonstrate the great flexibility of Tibetan religious and monastic life, the close ties and continual movement between village and *göngpa*, and, importantly, the great varieties of religious practice that were common-place and acceptable in pre-1959 Tibet.

Aziz introduces her account of Ani Chödrön with the following general assessment:

> The escape from the hamlet to the *gon-pa* is usually the begin-ning of a new life for the refugee in one form or another. Those who realize they cannot remain in the *gon-pa* launch into an itinerant life from which they may never emerge. D'ing-ri is full of itinerants like Ani Chödrön and her son Zang-po. The son, now over fifty, only joined Ani Chödrön wandering around D'ing-ri after he broke his vow of celibacy and had to leave Dza-rong.[109]

Aziz's summary of Ani Chödrön's life is described as follows:

> Chodron's pursuit began with the decisions she had to make after a poorly contracted marriage. "My family arranged it. They sent me far away to a house and village where I knew no one, not even my husband. And alone I had to bear the beat-ings his sister inflicted on my body. Because a baby started to grow inside my stomach, I stayed on to wait for this little companion. But two weeks after its arrival, the baby died," Chodron abruptly concluded, "and I went back to D'ing-ri."
>
> She described the first few years of her wanderings around D'ing-ri. Months were spent in the company of a band of itinerants—men and women who studied the texts and prayed together in abandoned retreats and moved through the mountains from one holy site to another. She confided

that it only happened once that she lay with one of her companions. After that she returned home to the family of her brother, for she was pregnant with Zangpo. Until he was born Chodron lived on with her relatives. As soon as the boy was old enough to travel, the young mother took him with her back to the hermitages and pilgrims' paths.[110]

Introducing the case history of the retreatant nun Ani Drölma, Aziz writes:

Many small *gon-pa* around D'ing-ri are *a-nii-gon-pa*, annexes of the Tr'i-pon and Dza-rong systems. Here we find *a-ni* who prefer to remain near their home village and in touch with their kin. These local retreats also serve the aged members of the hamlets when they retire from domestic life and are too old to undergo any systematic training . . . . A-ni Drol-ma's history . . . is another example of how one family's needs weave into the monastic and other religious life styles.[111]

And summarizing Ani Drölma's life, Aziz writes:

Drol-ma had never wanted to marry, so before her approaching betrothal she had insisted on visiting Dzarong and beginning her religious studies. Since her father's sister, Nam-drol, was already living at Dzarong, this was easy to arrange. So Drol-ma, at the age of nineteen, went to live with her vestal aunt. She stayed at Dza-rong for a year until taking her own vestal vows to become what is known as a *rab-j'ang-a'ni*. Ani Drol-ma thereupon left Dza-rong to return to Kura village. For the next ten years she passed her time alternating between her home and the nearby sanctuary of J'ang-ding, an *an-nii-gon-pa* annex of Dza-rong. Drol-ma says she had liked living with her brothers and their *na-ma*. She had also felt welcome there, and had not minded helping with domestic chores. The time came, however, when she found

the growing children irritating, and Drol-ma left the house
in preference for the quiet of the small *gon-pa*. It was a major
move even though the retreat was not more than forty-five
minutes away.

Drol-ma took her youngest sister, then seventeen, with her
to J'ang-ding . . . . Drol-ma became the girl's mentor [and]
some months later they journeyed together to Dza-rong in
order that the younger woman be ordained. So it was now
two vowed nuns who returned to J'ang-ding to live. They
continued for two years, until the young nun became pregnant. This had happened when the girl was in Gang-gar visiting a married sister there. It was her sister's husband who had
impregnated her—a stroke of luck for the family since the
married sister had proved to be barren. That infertility was
a greater shame than the young nun's apostasy. Therefore, as
soon as the pregnant girl had made her amends to her *la-ma*
and her other sister, she was welcomed as the junior wife in
the Gang-gar house.

Meanwhile Drol-ma stayed on at J'ang-ding but it was not
long before she built a hut at Dza-rong, making it her permanent home, and only returning to J'ang-ding during the
unpleasant winters.[112]

5. Ani Drölkar (Sgrol dkar)

Ani Losang Drölkar is her religious ordination name. She considered
telling me her given name prior to ordination, but then told me that
she preferred if I "wrote down" only her religious name; that was sufficient and most important. I had spoken briefly with Ani Drölkar a few
times before showing up at her residence with my Uher tape recorder
to interview her. She lived in a room of her own, in the house of her
brother and his family.

She set the stage and tone of the interview by announcing that *before*
we began, she would like to tell me why she had chosen to become a
nun. She said:

My parents gave me out in marriage to others and I gave birth to four children: two sons and two daughters. My first child, a son, was born when I was eighteen years old. He did not survive. I later had three other children—four altogether—but none of them lived. [Each of her children had died before reaching the age of two.] Then I prayed to Gönpo (Mgon po) [i.e., Mahākāla] and asked many lamas about my fate; and I was told that "religion is very deep."

Apparently, it was at this time that Ani Drölkar had inquired about becoming a nun, for she next commented:

They [or he] said, "You think hard before becoming a nun. It is not an easy life. Think about whether you really want to do it. You have had no peace as a householder. You have suffered much. So, if you think you can really do it, becoming a nun is very good."

She then asked her husband, who gave his approval. Her husband was already a sick man. She said that she had told him, "If (or, as long as) you need me, I won't become a nun. When you don't need me, then I will become a nun!" "But then," she continued, "he died within a few months."

Ani Drölkar was from Kyirong in southwestern Tibet. Her "root guru" (Tib. *tsawai lama*) was one Chö Sangyé (Chos sans rgyas) Rinpoché, a Kagyüpa hermit who preferred to do long retreats at the places in that area that were famed owing to their connection with Tibet's great yogi, Milarepa. Chö Sangyé practiced meditation in caves and other isolated areas where Milarepa had practiced. Apparently, it was owing to Chö Sangyé Rinpoché that Ani Drölkar decided to become ordained. Since the Rinpoché had no monastery of his own, he suggested that she take ordination at the nearest monastic establishment so that the requisite quota of fully ordained monks could be assembled to administer to her the vows. The monastery happened to be a Gelukpa one named Samten Ling Gönpa (Bsam gtan gling dgon pa).[113] Unlike the portrayals of rigid distinctions between the sects found in many Western accounts of Tibetan religious life, the blending of traditions did not seem a problem for either Ani Drölkar or her guru.

Further describing her teacher's advice, Drölkar said:

> He told me not to enter the nunnery [there] since I had to take care of the children [i.e., her siblings, her father and mother having died since her marriage, and she being the eldest of their six children], but to go into retreat from time to time whenever I could. So I did whatever he advised me to do; no deviation from that!

Once ordained, Ani Drölkar studied for a while at Samten Ling before returning home and later resuming her studies with Chö Sangyé Rinpoché. Though she could not read, she described some of the teachings she had received orally. During her early tenure at Samten Ling she had had two teachers: Khensur Tenzin Dhondrup and Gelong Losang Tenpa. (Later in Tibet, Nepal, and India, she had taken teachings from the Dalai Lama and from both of his two chief tutors: Ling Rinpoché and Trijang Rinpoché. She had also studied with Rato, Tsenshap, and Kyabjé Zong Rinpoché. She said it was impossible to list all her teachers.)

As for practicing, she had done many solitary retreats. She had managed to construct a small retreat hut for herself in relative nearness to her root guru. During such retreats, she had completed the *ngöndro* practices (100,000 prostrations and refuges, 100,000 *maṇḍala* offerings, 100,000 Vajrasattva mantra recitations, etc.). "Actually," she added, "I completed 200,000 of each of these; and I did more after coming to Nepal. In Tibet, because I had to take care of my brothers, I couldn't practice religion all the time; I had to stay home a lot. Since coming out of Tibet the kids have all grown up and I have no work [they now support her], so I keep on saying *mani*. But in Tibet, I would finish one *ngöndro* retreat, then return home to check on the family. Then another *ngöndro* retreat, then return home to check on the family. Then another *ngöndro* retreat, and then home again." Again, the fluid and continuous movement between domestic life and solitary religious practice was echoed in Ani Drölkar's remarks.

When I suggested to Ani Drölkar that there seemed to be far fewer nuns now than there had been in former times, she responded with a fascinating and somewhat curious—if not distorted(!)—account of the history of the nun's order. She said:

> Yes, very few, even when the Buddha himself was alive. It is said that Kungawa (Kun dga' ba; Skt. Ānanda) asked the Buddha to ordain a nun, so he ordained one. But because of this it is said that the Buddha's Dharma suffered much. Then Jé Rinpoché [i.e., Tsongkhapa, the founder of the Geluk tradition into which Ani Drölkar was ordained] offered a rite to the Buddha and "healed" the Buddha Dharma [in Tibet?]. So it is said.

I told her that some texts had said it was necessary to have a man's body in order to attain full enlightenment, and asked her opinion. She responded, "No one has a choice about his or her birth [or bodily] form. That may have been said during the Buddha's time, but now of course anyone can practice. It is only that we Tibetans are in other people's countries. It is difficult when one doesn't have freedom.[114] In Tibet there were thirty-eight nuns [belonging to the same group as those now in Yulmo, Nepal],[115] but only ten could come out. Some have [since] died; some couldn't earn a living, etc. Women can get spoiled more easily than men, so in a way the Buddha had predicted [correctly] that women wouldn't be able to practice all of his teachings. So many times even his *gelongma* (*dge slong ma*) had to be restricted."

"But did that happen in Tibet as well?" I queried. "Weren't there *gelongma* in Tibet?"

"That I don't know for sure. Probably not—there were some only during the Buddha's time."

Ani Drölkar's final assessment of her religious career was stated as follows: "If I could practice higher thoughts and teachings, that would be better, but just saying *Om maṇi padme hum* is enough for me. Even though I didn't learn how to read the scriptures and now have to content myself with simply reciting *mani*, by the grace of the Triple Gem [i.e., Buddha, Dharma, and Sangha], my mind is happy."

⤞ ⤝

The nuns' lives recounted above mirrored the lives of hundreds, even thousands, like themselves in Tibet. They moved in a dynamic and vital religious world both extraordinary and commonplace. In terms of religious practice they chose and changed courses until a balance was found that suited their own individual needs, abilities, and aspirations. Such flexibility and dynamism is missed (or worse, condemned) by Westerners who approach Tibetan Buddhism with preconceived and static ideas about what constitutes the sanctity of the religious life.

In closing, let me again quote a few passages from Aziz. In *Tibetan Frontier Families*, characterizing both the day-to-day happenings in a Tibetan dgonpa and the flexible nature of Tibetan Buddhist religious life in general, she wrote:

> In *Views from the Monastery Kitchen* (1976) I make a point of illustrating the open, accommodating and flexible atmosphere of the Tibetan dgon-pa. One meets here several individuals, lay and cleric, men and women, each of whom is a distinctive personality with a role in the community suited to them. There are few ch'o-pa who live in a silent retreat meditating, reading and writing for months and years on end.
>
> Most ch'o-pa I have met are not so inspired, or so disciplined, or so economically independent. They begin their religious training learning simple vocal and bodily exercises, performing simple rituals and reading. For many this is the extent of their religious education. The few inclined to scholarship, debate and liturgy are brought into the inner circle of gon-pa offices and given the most rigorous training. The rest

keep employed in numerous menial tasks around the gon-pa kitchen performing those minimal but useful religious exercises.[116]

And again:

> A peculiarity of this system is its ability to develop the indi-vidual rather than simply mould him into a member of a rigid community. I have been surprised to find that the dgon-pa does not subsume the needs of the individual. Here more than in the hamlet one finds men and women leading rich, individualistic lives. If one has the opportunity to meet and talk with ch'o-pa one quickly realizes that each is a different person who interprets his religion in a particular way and expects of it something unique.[117]

In Tibet, as in all other countries and historical periods, people prac-tice religion; and whether monks or nuns, people are as varied as any other species. Perhaps with more communication and dialogue with Tibetans we in the West can come nearer to an understanding of the varied features of Tibetan religious life, as practiced and lived, and to an appreciation of the benefits of its "open and accommodating atmo-sphere." Perhaps we shall even ourselves become more open and accom-modating by virtue of the attempt.

4

Tibetan Buddhist Women Practitioners, Past and Present: A Garland to Delight Those Wishing Inspiration

❧ ❦

The renowned teacher Kalu Rinpoché, who was one of the greatest meditation masters of the twentieth century, had this to say about women and the Dharma:

> Regardless of whether you are a man or a woman, regardless of your particular situation in this life, if you have faith, confidence, and diligence, if you have compassion and wisdom, you can become enlightened. If you are merely caught up in your emotional confusion and continue to let that dominate your life, no matter whether you are a man or a woman, enlightenment will be difficult to attain. But if you have the necessary qualities for Dharma practice, the kind of body you have makes no difference at all.[118]

Similar assessments have been voiced by other great Tibetan lamas, including my own precious guru, Lama Thubten Yeshe. Lama Surya Das, in *The Snow Lion's Turquoise Mane*, relates that "Namkhai Norbu Rinpoché says that women are more likely than men to attain, through Dzogchen practice, the Rainbow Light Body of perfect enlightenment;

he claims to quote Garab Dorjé, the first Dzogchen patriarch, in that vein." And "Padma Sambhava, the second Buddha, said, 'Male, female: no great difference. But when she develops the aspiration for enlightenment, to be a woman is greater.'"[119] Still, when modern-day women look to the Tibetan tradition, they seem to find few examples of realized women practitioners.[120] Without such models, their faith and determination to practice remains hindered and dissatisfied.

I remember reading a book review written in 1987 by Anna Grimshaw, who several years ago spent four months at Julichang Nunnery in Ladakh and published a book about her stay there called *Servants of the Buddha: Winter in a Himalayan Convent.*[121] Grimshaw's review was of the "coffee-table book" *The World of Buddhism*, by Heinz Bechert and Richard Gombrich. In her critique of the work, Grimshaw noted that "a serious weakness" of the book was that although "the subtitle of the volume is: 'Buddhist monks and nuns in society and culture,' reference to, let alone discussion of, Buddhist nuns is almost nonexistent."[122] Happily, such is not the case today. Rather, today there is a persistent interest in, and a desire to learn more about, Buddhist women practitioners— both monastic or lay—of all traditions and of all historical periods and geographic spaces.

It seems to me that over the last few decades, particularly since 1990, many new publications have sought at least to take notice of women practitioners. A few have even appeared that focus exclusively on exemplary women practitioners. Slowly, then, a library of works is appearing that addresses the issues of women's place, status, and importance within Buddhism. This development is to be applauded, I believe, and encouraged.

My suggestion is that we now begin to fashion for ourselves a "special lineage of renowned women practitioners." As a model for how this might be done, here I will: (1) fashion such a lineage of Tibetan Buddhist women practitioners who have been inspirational for me personally, and (2) briefly narrate some of the details of the life stories of a few of these women. In an important way, what a listing like this does is show us that such exemplary women have existed and do now live. This provides encouragement to women to practice as they did. In a sense, as stated above, this is like creating a "special lineage" of women practitioners—not women of one particular sect or school, not merely a listing of important nuns, but an enumeration of women practitioners who can inspire us, whether they be Buddhist *yoginis* or *tantrikas*, nuns or laywomen.

When I first attempted to formulate such a list, I came up with only six or seven names. Having talked with friends, scanned my personal library, and reflected on the matter, I came up with a few more. And soon, I could see that about thirty or so women, in my opinion, clearly belonged in such a special women's lineage. Whom did I list, and whom should we list?

A special lineage of Tibetan Buddhist women practitioners—in addition to renowned women like Yeshé Tsogyal, Machig Labdron, and Dakmedma—ought to, it seems to me, extend back to India, especially since so many famed Tibetan women practitioners are said to be reincarnations of certain Indian women saints. It would include such inspirational women as Mahamaya, the Buddha's mother; Mahaprajapati, his aunt and the woman who became the first Buddha nun; many of the renowned early Indian teacher-nuns; as well as tantrikas like Niguma, wife and partner of Naropa, herself the author (with Sukhasiddhi) of the practice tradition transmitted until today in the Shangpa Kagyüpa. The great practitioner Gelongma Palmo, fashioner of the fasting ritual associated with the thousand-armed, eleven-headed form of Avalokiteshvara,[123] also belongs in such a lineage.

Such a special women's lineage would actually begin with the two chief female representatives of practice, namely, the great goddesses Vajrayogini and Tara. Added to this would be a listing of eminent women practitioners starting from India at the time of the Buddha, including Mahamaya, Mahaprajapati, the early *theris* (female elders), Mandarava, Niguma, Sukhasiddhi, and Gelongma Palmo. Crossing over into Tibet, we would certainly want to include such early exemplary practitioners as Yeshé Tsogyal, Machig Labdron (1055–1149), Dakmedma (consort of Marpa, 1012–96), Rechungma, and Paldar Bum. The latter two were Milarepa's most renowned women disciples. Skipping through several centuries, the list might continue by noting the life and inspirational practice of Ahkon Lhamo. The latter was instrumental in maintaining a number of Nyingmapa practice lineages, as well as Mindröling Monastery itself and a host of Nyingmapa nunneries.

The latter half of the nineteenth century and the early twentieth century saw a number of revered Tibetan women practitioners, such as the abbesses of Samding, the state nunnery of Tibet; Jetsun Ani Lochen (1852–1953); Delog Dawa Drölma; Drigung Khandro (the reincarnation of Achi Chökyi Drölma, also called "Grandmother Tara");[124] Ayu Khandro;[125] Doljin Khandro Suren (the great Mongolian *chod* master);[126] Jetsun Kushog; Ani Pelu and Ani Rilu, the latter two being Sogyal Rinpoché's two great-aunts;[127] the Abbess of Chimé Lung Gönpa (of whom Lama Thubten Yeshé was the reincarnation); the mother of Lama Thubten Zopa Rinpoche; Khandro Chenmo Rinpoché;[128] Ani Tsen-la; other accomplished nuns in Tibet, many of whom suffer greatly under Chinese rule; and other female Tibetan Buddhist practitioners who are especially inspiring to you.

But not all inspirational Tibetan women were nuns or *tantrikas*. Many have made important contributions as lay devotees. Among these women, I would list Rinchen Dölma Taring,[129] Ama Adhe,[130] Ama Dölma,[131] and many, many others. In this way, I personally would fashion a lineage of more than thirty-two exemplary and inspirational women practitioners. In doing so, one can readily recognize the many Tibetan (as well as Indian and other) women Buddhist practitioners who are worthy of being included in a special lineage of inspirational women practitioners. I see no reason why similar lineages of women practitioners cannot be created to serve as models for Buddhist women in other geographic areas or cultural traditions, and I encourage all women who desire such inspiration to do just that.

LIVES OF EXEMPLARY TIBETAN BUDDHIST WOMEN PRACTITIONERS

In what follows, I will briefly discuss the lives of some of the women I have listed above. My comments will focus, cursorily, on eight of these thirty-two, namely: Gelongma Palmo, Yeshé Tsogyal, Machig Labdron,

Dakmedma, Ahkon Lhamo, Jetsun Ani Lochen, Delog Dawa Drölma, and Rinchen Taring.

Gelongma Palmo

Before the spread of Buddhism into Tibet, there lived a young princess in India. She was known for her intelligence and, of course, for her beauty. However, when she was a young woman, she contracted a dreaded disease, similar to leprosy, that was particularly virulent and contagious. Afflicted by this disease, she became ugly and disgusting to look at. For the sake of her parents' happiness, she decided to leave the kingdom, to go far away from home and become a nun. After being a nun for some time, she came upon a teacher who was deeply moved by her situation. He taught her the method of Avalokiteshvara, the Buddha of Compassion. For several years she made this her main practice. Even so, during this time her disease got worse and worse. Her body was covered with sores and it became very painful for her to sit or lie down. Still, she persisted with the practice.

After several years, she had a dream in which she saw a being dressed in brilliant white. That being came into her room holding a vase that was filled with a pure liquid. In her vision she saw this being pour this pure substance all over her body from head to toe, and in the dream she felt as though her body was completely liberated from the disease. The next morning when she awoke she found that her dream had been actualized: her body was completely renewed, as though nothing had ever been wrong with it. In that moment she was completely filled with intense devotion to Avalokiteshvara. When she saw her healed body, she thought first of this Buddha, and just then she had a completely clear vision of thousand-armed Avalokiteshvara, who approached and dissolved into her. From that time on, Gelongma Palmo not only made Avalokiteshvara meditation her chief practice, but she developed a complete system for doing so and she conjoined it with a ritual of fasting. The particular form of practice she developed has come down to us today as the practice method known as *nyung nas*. In fact, the tradition of *nyung nas*, which is so popular in all Tibetan nunneries today, is known as the "tradition of Gelongma Palmo."[132]

Yeshé Tsogyal

There are two fairly recent translations of the life story (Tib. *namthar*) of Yeshé Tsogyal: one by Tarthang Tulku, entitled *Mother of Knowledge: The Enlightenment of Yeshe Tsogyal*,[133] and one by Keith Dowman, called *Sky Dancer: The Secret Life and Songs of the Lady Yeshe Tsogyel*.[134] Rita Gross has produced a very thoughtful essay about Yeshé Tsogyal, based on these two translations.[135]

In brief, Yeshé Tsogyal was Padmasambhava's chief female Tibetan disciple and his tantric partner. (His other chief tantric consort was the Indian disciple Mandarava.) In addition to her many individual accomplishments, we owe our gratitude to Yeshé Tsogyal for preserving for us both the life story of Padmasambhava himself[136] and for preserving a number of his important works, such as *The Tibetan Book of the Dead*.[137]

Machig Labdron

The life story of Machig Labdron has been mentioned or partially translated by a number of Tibetologists. For example, she is mentioned in Gö Lotsawa's *The Blue Annals*,[138] and in Tsultrim Allione's *Women of Wisdom*, which gives an abbreviated version of her life.[139] It is especially wonderful that a complete version of Machig's life history is now available in English translation.[140] A brief but succinct summation of Machig's life is given by Keith Dowman in his *The Power-Places of Central Tibet*. It reads as follows:

> Machik Labchi Dronma (1055–1149) settled at Karmar late in her life. She was ordained by Drapa Ngonshe in her youth and became fluent in the *prajnaparamita sutras*. Later she met her root Guru, the Indian yogin Padampa Sangye, at Tingri, and received the entire transmission of the *choyul* tradition, becoming the principal exemplar of this practice. Through exposure to charnel-ground demons in *choyul*, this yoga is particularly efficacious in inducing awareness of the pure nature of all emotion and the empty essence of all kinds of mental obstruction, including disease, which is all reduced to psychosomatic functions. Machik then cohabited with

the yogin Topa Bhadra, but scorned as a *samaya* breaker she
left Tingri to begin an itinerant existence in eastern Tibet.
She gave birth to three boys and two girls. Then she came
to Sangri alone, and re-ordained, she spent several years in
retreat here.[141]

But Machig is really known in the Tibetan tradition for two other
great accomplishments. Early on in her meditations, her chief practice
had been Amitayus, the Buddha of Long Life, and this method reached
Tibet because Machig taught it to Rechungpa, Milarepa's famous disciple. She accomplished the practice of Amitayus and thus was able to
pass on that tradition to subsequent practitioners of the Kagyüpa sect
of Tibetan Buddhism.

Her second great accomplishment was that she designed a completely new method of tantric practice known as *chod*. If you look at
Western sources and get an abstract philosophical description of *chod*
practice—namely, a method of cutting through or severing the clinging
to ego—one might get the impression that it is a violent sort of meditative practice. But in fact, when among those who practice *chod*, who are
inside the practice, one learns that the method involves a great deal of
singing, playing of musical instruments, dancing, and even specific gaits
in walking. It is particularly significant that this meditative technique,
which is so unusual and unique, was designed by a woman practitioner.
No other tantric method I know of exhibits *chod*'s unique features.

Dakmedma

Dakmedma, whose name means "nonself" or "selflessness" (Tib. *bdag
med ma*; Skt. *anatman*), was wife and partner to the famed Tibetan
translator Marpa Lotsawa. In the life story of Milarepa, Tibet's most
famous yogi and the renowned disciple of Marpa, Dakmedma is portrayed as the embodiment of compassion, acting as mother and com-
forter to Milarepa throughout his ordeals. But, like other women in that
text, her motherliness is interpreted as a sign of attachment and therefore actually impedes Mila's obtaining the teachings and realizations he
seeks. Quite another picture of Dakmedma emerges in other accounts,

such as *The Life of Marpa*,[142] where she appears as an accomplished practitioner of Tantra in her own right, almost as advanced as Marpa himself. Indeed, in one important episode, it is only Dakmedma—and not Marpa—who can impart the necessary instructions to the couple's dying son. Marpa is shown as too overwhelmed with remorse. Dakmedma, on the other hand, is shown as having the necessary skills to instruct her son, and as having always been a guru to him.

Ahkon Lhamo

The present-day Nyingmapa Buddhist Center in Poolesville, Maryland (Kunzang Odsal Palyul Changchub Choling, KPC), is headed by the American-born former housewife Catharine Burroughs, who, in 1987, was recognized as being the reincarnation of Genyenma Ahkon Lhamo, a famed Tibetan *yoginī* of the seventeenth century. In 1988 Penor Rinpoché formally enthroned Burroughs.[143] I wanted to learn more about the *yoginī* whom Burroughs reincarnates. To do so, I spoke with Rick Finney, a good friend and former member of KPC.[144] Rick reported that in late 1994, Terton Kusum Lingpa had visited KPC and had spoken at length about the many previous lives of Ahkon Lhamo. A complete transcript of his talks was made and plans are underway to have these stories printed.[145]

In brief, the story of Ahkon Lhamo's seventeenth-century life is as follows. She was born the sister of the founder of the Payul monastic tradition. She was recognized very early on as being the reincarnation of White Tara, Niguma, and Mandarava. Later it was said that she also embodied Vajravarahi and Queen Akara Tsaldrung, and that she was the spiritual "daughter of Machig." She spent her life in strict meditative retreats and became known as a great *yoginī*. Being a perpetual cave-dweller, she always appeared unkempt, yet people flocked to her various cave retreats to receive her blessings. She said nothing to them, but simply touched their heads. (The present-day reincarnation says she has "very strong *tactile* memories of touching hundreds and thousands of greasy heads"!) At Ahkon Lhamo's cremation, it is said, her skull flew out of the fire and traveled in the air for about a mile, finally falling at the feet of her brother. The skull landed intact and bore the Tibetan letter *ah*. This relic has been preserved; it was brought to the United States by Penor Rinpoché and presented to the present incarnation.

Jetsun Ani Lochen Rinpoché

A brief presentation of the life story of Jetsun Ani Lochen appeared in my essay in *Feminine Ground*.[146] Tibetan authors have also written about her. These include Rinchen Taring in *Daughter of Tibet*,[147] and Lobsang Lhalungpa, both in an interview about his own gurus published in *Parabola* magazine[148] and in his introductory "chronicle" to *Tibet, the Sacred Realm: Photographs 1880–1950*.[149] A few years ago a page-long recounting of Ani Lochen's life story appeared in a Snow Lion Publications newsletter;[150] and in the special "Year of Tibet" edition of *Chö Yang*,[151] a more complete version of her life story appears, along with line drawings of key episodes.

The life stories of famed women practitioners tell us very clearly that it does not matter where we started or how many hardships we have faced, women can still become accomplished practitioners. Ani Lochen's story is particularly relevant in making this point. Lochen was born near Tsopadme. Both of her parents had been married formerly. Her father, Dondrup Namgyal, had been an alcoholic most of his life. He was also known as being a quarrelsome type. Later in life, he got a job with a Bhutanese lama named Kalwar Lama. That lama later died, leaving a young wife, Tsentsar Pemba Dölma, who had originally hailed from Nepal. The couple had had no children. Dölma then hired Dondrup (who was to become Lochen's father) as a companion to accompany her as she went on a religious pilgrimage. After some time spent like this, the couple decided to get married.

They both wanted to have a son. In order to bring this about, Dölma asked all the women in the villages through which they traveled for advice on how to have a son. They advised her to collect large stones from all the sacred sites they visited and to carry them on her back until auspicious signs appeared. After some months of doing this, Dölma had a dream that she took to mean that she had conceived a male child. Dondrup was very pleased. But when the child was born, it was a little girl, and this made Dondrup furious. They named the child Lochen.

Their home life was not happy; especially after Lochen's birth, Dondrup drank much more and was quite abusive to Dölma.

Once, when Lochen was about four years old, Dondrup came home drunk and told his wife he was leaving her. Then he proposed that since they had only one daughter, they should cut her in half and each take a half. Little Lochen overheard this and ran away. She hid under some thorny bushes. Before she knew it, a week had passed while the villagers searched for her. Even her father showed some concern. But Lochen had been experiencing visions of deities and had been feeling very light and blissful, so she was completely unaware of the time that had passed. When she finally emerged, she was greeted by some village children. On the spot, she asked them to sit down and began teaching them the mantra of Avalokiteshvara, *Om mani padme hum*. Many of the adults in the village had a hard time with this, calling the young girl arrogant. Some even said she was possessed by demons.

When Lochen was about six, she began to give teachings in public to crowds. Slowly her fame started to spread and people made offerings to her. She took a special liking to one such offering, a small goat, which she began to ride around throughout the western areas of Tibet, giving teachings. One day an aged male *manipa* (master storyteller) showed up in the area, and after questioning Lochen, he announced to the villagers that she was very knowledgeable in what she was teaching. The *manipa* gave Lochen further teachings and she continued to teach for some time.

When Lochen was thirteen, she met a lama named Pema Gyatso who was to become her root guru. Pema Gyatso was a Kadampa lama, and he told her that if she were willing to observe the ascetic precepts known as the "Ten Innermost Jewels of Kadam," he would accept her as his disciple. She decided right then and there that whatever this lama asked, she would do. If ever she failed to understand completely the lama's teaching, she cried and wailed, so great was her earnest desire to learn the Dharma. However, another monk at Pema Gyatso's monastery came to him complaining that the girl received more offerings than he or any of the other monks received. He also accused her of teaching things beyond her comprehension. When Lochen next saw her lama, the lama refused her entrance into the monastery and, instead, threw his shoes down on her. Thus, she was abused by her guru as well as by the monks. Still, much like Milarepa's devotion for his guru Marpa, Lochen persisted with complete faith in her guru, Pema Gyatso. Even so, it was a long time before he agreed to give her any further teachings.

On one occasion, in an attempt to humiliate Lochen, Pema Gyatso asked her to strike a boulder with his walking stick. She did so and excrement poured forth from the boulder. Then he took the staff and struck the boulder in the same place. A natural image of Avalokiteshvara's mantra appeared. It is said that this is when she realized that her lama was clairvoyant. Sometime later, Lochen entered a three-year retreat under his guidance. After that, for some time she, Pema Gyatso, and some of his other disciples went on extended pilgrimages throughout most of Tibet. For a while Lochen, Pema Gyatso, and the others stayed in Lhasa. One day during that time, Pema Gyatso became extremely ill, and although Lochen nursed him, he never recovered. Lochen remembers seeing many rainbows overhead when the lama died. After his death, Lochen stopped wandering and decided to take up residence in a cave called Sangyé Drak. She stayed there during the winters, and in the summers she moved to Shungseb. This is the place where Lochen's nunnery was later established.

Lochen performed a number of extended meditative retreats. During some of these, she "died" and traveled to other realms. Her fame as an accomplished meditator spread throughout all regions of Tibet. From her nunnery at Shungseb, she gave advanced meditation instructions to some of Tibet's highest lamas.[152]

Rinchen Dölma Taring's account says that Ani Lochen lived to be 130 years old. Lobsang Lhalungpa, who was proud to have studied with her, claimed that she lived to be 115. The *Chö Yang* says that she lived to be 101, giving as her dates 1852–1953.[153] More important than the actual age at which she died is that this wondrous woman practitioner is recognized by all Tibetan Buddhist traditions as having been one of the most accomplished teachers of the century.

Delog Dawa Drölma

A wonderful book that appeared in 1995 narrates the life story of Delog Dawa Drölma, the renowned teacher and medium, who was the mother of Chagdud Rinpoché, now a well-known teacher in the United States. This book, called *Delog: Journey to Realms Beyond Death*,[154] contains Delog Dawa Drölma's five-day-long deathlike "journey," at age sixteen, to the various realms beyond death. No other narration of after-death experiences is comparable to Dawa Drölma's own richly detailed account, which deserves to be read in its entirety.

Rinchen Dölma Taring

Daughter of Tibet[155] is a familiar, truly classic autobiographical account written by Rinchen Dölma Taring, an aristocratic member of pre-1959 Tibetan society. Valuable firsthand information on the life of women in the society of that time is recounted there. Ms. Taring is still going strong, living in Rajpur, India, and, at the age of eighty-five, continues to carry on an energetic life of service and teaching, setting an inspiring example. Another book that recounts the stories of Tibetan women from various walks of life, including Taring, is *One Hundred Voices of Tara: A Spiritual Journey Among Tibetan Women*, which will appear in 1999.[156] The author, Canyon Sam, met Ms. Taring in Rajpur in 1994 and stayed in her home for a week of extended discussions.

From the beginning, at the request of His Holiness the Dalai Lama, Taring was a tireless contributor to the well-being and education of the newly exiled Tibetan community. Abandoning her former sense of class superiority, she selflessly plunged in to help establish the Tibetan Homes project, to found the Tibetan Central Schools, and to spearhead several other desperately needed institutions. Having benefited from a European-style education as a young aristocrat, Taring became the consummate teacher. Even while still in Tibet prior to 1959, she had been recruited by the Chinese to teach Tibetan to more than seven hundred Chinese students. Her talent for teaching English was especially in demand following the Tibetans' flight from the Chinese in 1959. One of Mrs. Taring's first tasks, after the exile, was to teach English to His Holiness's bodyguards.

Taring now lives with her grand- and great-grandchildren. Highly educated herself, she is very much concerned with proper elocution. One of her sons is married to a Muslim woman from Tibet, and during Canyon Sam's visit, Taring continued daily English lessons with the young wife. Although Taring sometimes complains of sore arms and legs, she remains a vigorous woman. Once after missing a bus, Taring suggested that the two of them *walk* into town, and Sam says that it was only with great difficulty that she herself managed to keep up!

Sam describes two brief but inspiring encounters that occurred during their walk into town. She observed that whenever they passed people—whether business folk or beggars, at work or just sitting—all the town's people without exception stood and bowed as Taring passed. This reverence was shown because Taring had been so instrumental in helping each one of them according to their individual, specific needs. For one she had found an ophthamologist, for another she had arranged a child's higher education, and so forth. One man ran and addressed her in Hindi, repeatedly pointing in the direction of her house. As it turned out, even after thirty-five years of living in India and speaking Hindi daily, Taring continues to take Hindi lessons from the man one day each week. Thus she also remains the consummate student. This particular characteristic—of never ceasing to both teach and study—reminds me of my own precious guru, and so I find it especially inspiring. I would therefore definitely include Ms. Taring in my special lineage of Tibetan women practitioners.

The stories of great women practitioners are endless. So I hope that others will be added to this lineage and that others will create their own special lineages of Buddhist women practitioners. Such special lineages, I believe, are truly garlands to delight those wishing inspiration.

5

Female Patronage in Indian Buddhism

❧ ❦

It has long been my opinion that it is impossible to arrive at an accurate estimation of the socio-religious world of early Buddhism by looking solely to the sacred scriptures. This is especially true if one's concern is to focus upon the place, standing, and practices of women in the early world of Buddhism. While a number of studies have recently appeared that address the issue of the various portrayals of women in Buddhist literature (and which attempt thereby to plot the complex and changing status of women in relationship to Buddhist doctrine and practice), since their approach has been solely textual, they have ultimately proved to be too limiting. While the texts certainly may inform us about the various "orthodox" Buddhist views regarding women, they cannot in themselves be relied upon to tell us how such views were received or acted upon by the women—and men—who have throughout Buddhist history called themselves "Buddhists."

What then are we to do if we wish to get at a more adequate, or at least a fuller, picture of early Buddhism and of women's place in it? In an article entitled "Nuns and Benefactresses: The Role of Women in the Development of Buddhism,"[157] I suggested that Buddhist scriptures which focused on women ought at least to be read together with secular histories. Here I broaden this earlier suggestion by investigating three separate pools of data, namely: (1) the Buddhist scriptures which address the issue of women, (2) secular histories of the periods relevant to the composition and dissemination of those scriptures, and (3) the information which is provided by the "material culture" produced during such periods.

Focusing on patronage provides the opportunity both to test the value of this latter pool of information and to see if and how making material culture central may change our reading of the texts. That is, by allowing for the inclusion of source materials related directly to concrete practices and concrete structures, such a forum provides the chance to take a new view of early Buddhism. Moreover, this new vantage point may provide, for future studies, a fuller backdrop against which to test the purely literary approaches.

Almost no one would argue with the fact that Buddhism might never have blossomed into the full-scale religion it became had its chief audience remained solely a forest-dwelling band of mendicants. That it grew to become a major religious tradition is certainly due in part to its finding a way to involve the population at large by developing ways in which that wider population—without becoming celibate clerics— could still participate in the faith. At the heart of such participation stands the notion of *dana*, or "giving," and its fruits.

As Buddhism developed—and especially as the Mahayana took shape (ca. 100 BC to CE 200)—ties to the laity, of necessity, had to be strengthened. Not only was there the question of the mendicant's dependency in terms of simple daily alms, but the laity's support was necessary now to fund the construction of more permanent, and ever-larger, monastic complexes as the number of clerics increased, and to fund the construction of *stupas*[158] (or reliquaries), lecture halls, and other structures for public worship as the number of lay followers increased.

Giving (*dāna*) was not a new creation of the Mahayāna—its virtues having already been lauded in some of the early Theravadin literature, e.g., in the Jatakas and in numerous tales comprising the *avadana* literature—but in the Mahayana this particular activity became central. Responding to the needs of the increasing number of lay devotees, the Mahayana proclaimed that the bodhisattva's course (i.e., the course of service) was open to all—regardless of whether one was a cleric or not and, importantly, regardless of whether one was a man or a woman. In place of the great emphasis on *shila* (i.e., moral discipline and restraint) advocated by the early Theravada monastic community, the Mahayana gave primacy to *dana*. Indeed, *dana* was ranked first in the list of the Mahayana's so-called six perfections (or *paramitas*) of practice, this formulation replacing the Theravada's "threefold training" (*tri-shiksapada*) in monastic discipline, meditation, and insight. If one did not have the good karmic fruit of being able to practice the monastic life, one could still practice Buddhism, gain merit through giving, and mount the successive stages of the bodhisattva to finally reach enlightenment. Naturally, such a doctrine appealed to popular religious sentiments and aspirations.

Generally speaking, the virtuous activity of *dana* (which is further glossed as "generosity" or "liberality"; an alternate term is *caga*) is viewed as involving two distinct types of offerings: (1) material offerings of various sorts, and (2) instruction in the Dharma. The latter activity of giving is, of course, most often reserved for the Buddha himself, though a few of his most esteemed disciples—some of them women—were enabled also to make this offering. With respect to the first form of *dana*—i.e., that of giving material offerings—all Buddhist followers could participate. Some of the *avadāna* stories, for example, tell of the marvelous store of merit that accrues from the simple offering of flowers, incense, or salutation to a Buddha. Great benefits are said to be the fruit of making certain material offerings to the sangha, namely, any of the four so-called requisite objects: robes, food, medicine, and bedding. Even more positive fruits, we are told, accrue for those who construct, repair, or whitewash a stupa or other religious monument. In the words of W. G. Weeraratne: "The construction of stūpas and worshipping them, etc., are extolled as yielding rich harvests to such an extent that the importance of pursuing a moral life is relegated to the background."[159]

If we look to all three sources indicated above—that is, to the scriptural accounts, to the material culture of Indian Buddhism, and to the later secular histories—it is safe to say that women participated fully in the virtuous activity of giving and did so both as nuns and as laywomen.

EARLY SCRIPTURAL ACCOUNTS

About women and *dana*, the early texts tell us two things. Firstly, they indicate that the Buddha was reluctant, or hesitant initially, to found a female order, even though they also affirm that the nuns later proved themselves capable of scaling the heights of rigorous ascetic practice and of winning the fruit of nirvana. (Their songs of triumph are recorded in an exceptional record known as the *Therigatha*.[160]) Some of these early nuns became famed as teachers of the Buddha's doctrine in their own right, though the *vinaya* rules of the order enjoined that they impart such teachings only to other women. Secondly, the texts show that, during his lifetime, the Buddha had several important laywomen benefactresses and that female lay patronage was extremely important to the establishment of the religion.

It appears in fact that from his earliest days as a teacher, the Buddha was supported by a number of wealthy women—by women merchants, wealthy courtesans, and queens. (Moreover, it may be argued that material support from such women not only embellished but actually sustained the continuance of Buddhism in India right up to its final "disappearance" from the subcontinent.) Two examples of such lay benefactresses, from early scriptural sources, warrant special mention.

In one of the early scriptures, the woman Visakha, "a rich citizen commoner of Shravasti," is described by the Buddha as his "chief benefactress."[161] Further described as "the mother of many blooming children [she is reported to have had ten sons and ten daughters], and the grandmother of countless grandchildren [said to have numbered 8,400],"[162] she is portrayed as having lavished gifts on the Buddhist order, and as having generously catered to its every need. Having tried surreptitiously to donate her jewels, valued at "ninety millions," she instead donated money to the sangha at three times their value. Visakha made a gift to the Buddha of a treasured piece of property at Shravasti,[163] built a monastery on the site, and single-handedly provided for the needs of the order whenever its members resided there. Her story is too long to be recounted here in detail. Instead, I quote a passage from the text which summarizes her donations:

For four months did Visākhā give alms in her monastery to
the Buddha and to the congregation which followed him;
and at the end of that time she presented the congregation
of the priests with stuff for robes, and even that received by
the novices was worth a thousand pieces of money. And of
medicines, she gave the fill of every man's bowl. Ninety millions were spent in this donation. Thus ninety millions went
for the site of the monastery, ninety for the construction of
the monastery, and ninety for the festival at the opening of
the monastery, making two hundred and seventy millions in
all that were expended by her on the religion of the Buddha.
No other woman in the world was as liberal as this one who
lived in the house of a heretic.[164]

(The last sentence of this passage is quite interesting, for history shows
that it was often the case that the husbands of the Buddha's wealthy
benefactresses were followers of some other religious tradition. Usually
they were Hindu, and worshippers of either Viṣṇu or Shiva.)

The lay benefactresses of the Buddha's order were not limited to
the "respectable" classes. The wealthy courtesan Ambapali, who later
became a nun under the Buddha's charge, is lauded in the scriptures
as having been, while still a lay follower, "one of the most loyal and
generous supporters of the order." An account of her life is found in the
Therigatha, but Coomaraswamy has summarized the occasion of her
chief offering to the Buddha—a *vihara* on her mango grove in Vesali—
as follows:

Then the Master proceeded to Vesālī. At this time, also, there
was dwelling in the town of Vesālī a beautiful and wealthy
courtesan whose name was Ambapālī, the Mango-girl. It was
reported to her that the Blessed One had come to Vesālī and
was halting at her mango grove. Immediately she ordered her
carriages and set out for the grove, attended by all her train;
and as soon as she reached the place where the Blessed One
was, she went up toward him on foot, and stood respectfully

aside; and the Blessed One instructed and gladdened her with religious discourse. And she, being thus instructed and gladdened, addressed the Blessed One and said: "May the Master do me the honour to take his meal with all the Brethren at my house tomorrow." And the Blessed One gave consent by silence. Ambapālī bowed down before him and went her way. . . .

The next day Ambapālī served the Lord and all the Brethren with her own hands, and when they would eat no more she called for a low stool and sat down beside the Master and said: "Lord, I make a gift of this mansion to the order of which thou art the chief." And the Blessed One accepted the gift; and after instructing and gladdening Ambapālī with religious discourse, he rose from his seat and went his way.[165]

Secular histories of Buddhism's later development in India tell us about other important female lay supporters of the religion.

WOMEN AND EARLY BUDDHIST MATERIAL CULTURE

The scriptures are almost completely silent about women's participation as donors—whether as nuns or lay benefactresses—during the centuries when Buddhism became a significant religious force throughout the subcontinent (i.e., between the second century BC and the third century CE). Indeed, if one relied solely on scripture for an accounting of women's activities within the Buddhist fold during these centuries, one might conclude that it was nonexistent. If, however, one looks to other *kinds* of historical testimony—and here I have reference to the numerous inscriptions found in association with certain monuments of this period—quite another view emerges. For example, as Nancy Falk has noted, such inscriptions "provide evidence of a thriving nuns' community in virtually all areas where the men's order is also well attested to. Especially in the south, the nuns seem to have been both numerous and wealthy. Their names are found in inscriptions in numbers almost equal to the monks' and they were able to offer generous gifts themselves as well as to receive donations."[166] Once again, women were, in fact, active participants.

Examples of this type of female support can be gleaned from the art historical studies of scholars such as Burgess, Cunningham, Coomaraswamy,[167] and others. Here, I simply list some of the donations made by individual women to three of the major religious monuments of the period, namely: the Sanci, Bharhut, and Amaravati stupas. The main artistic activities of the first mentioned two compounds belong roughly to the third century BC; the third, roughly to the second and third centuries CE. The dates of their respective construction neatly encompass the very period during which the scriptural sources are almost silent regarding women.

A woman named "Buddhā" donated a railing pillar to the Sanci stupa. A Buddhist nun called "Buddhapalita" made a donation to the same structure, and the donation is recorded in an inscription found on the southern gateway of the stupa. Another woman, called only "Bura," likewise was the donor of a railing pillar at the Sanci compound. The gift of a railing pillar to the stupa at Bharhut is recorded in an inscription found there. It names as its donor a nun called "Buddharaksita." Regarding the great stupa compound at Amaravati, one learns that the principal donor of all the subsidiary structures associated with that famed South Indian compound was one Camtasiri, the sister of king Camtamula and mother-in-law of King Siri Virapurisadata. These are but a few examples of women's significant and continued support. Others could also be enumerated.

SECULAR HISTORIES

While mention has now been made of nuns (acting both as teachers and as material donors) and of various types of women lay supporters (whether of the merchant class or wealthy courtesans), undoubtedly the most important benefactresses were the royal queens of the age. This fact becomes ever more evident as one traces the later development of Buddhism in India (i.e., from the third to the twelfth century CE). That Buddhism prospered in India under the beneficence of wealthy queens is well attested to by a close reading of the secular histories which address this time period.

There is also the interesting case where Buddhist sacred and secular histories merge. For example, the *Shrimala Sutra* (wherein a queen named Shrimala preaches the central discourse, in place of the Buddha) was written in South India in the third century CE. If we look to the secular histories for an indication of the type of environment which produced such a scripture, we find, in Nilakanta Shastri's words, the following description:

> The reign of [Siri Chāntamūla's] son, Vīrapuriṣadāta, formed a glorious epoch in the history of Buddhism and in diplomatic relations. He took a queen from the Śaka family of Ujjain and gave his daughter in marriage to a Chutu prince. Almost all the royal ladies were Buddhists: an aunt of Vīrapuriṣadāta built a big stūpa at Nāgārjunikoṇḍa for the relics of the great teacher, besides apsidal temples, *vihāras*, and *mandapas*. Her example was followed by other women of the royal family and by women generally. . . . [168]

The translators of the *Shrimala Sutra* suggest that "taking these facts into consideration, one may postulate that the *Shrimala* was composed partly to honour the eminent Buddhist ladies who were so responsible for this glorious period of South Indian Buddhism." [169]

What was true in South India was true in the north as well. Historical records show that particularly for the important northwestern center of Buddhism—that is, the regions around Kashmir—the tradition enjoyed the continuous support of the queens of the period. Having fallen on hard times following the collapse of the Kushana empire, the revival of Buddhism in the north was partly—if not wholly—attributable to certain notable queens. For example, Nalinaksha Dutt records the following glimpses into the history of the Mahayana's development in the north:

> Meghavāhana, a descendant of Yudhiṣṭhira I, was brought by the people from Gandhāra and placed on the throne.

He had a soft corner for Buddhism, hailing, as he did, from Gandhāra, a predominantly Buddhistic country. His queen Amṛtaprabhā of Prāgjyotisa is said to have built for the use of Buddhist monks a lofty vihāra called Amṛtabhavana . . . During the reign of Raṇāditya, one of his queens called Amṛtaprabhā placed a fine statue of Buddha in the vihāra built by a queen of Meghavāhana . . . Balāditya [mid-eighth century CE] was succeeded by his son-in-law . . . whose queen set up the Anaṅgabhavana-vihāra. . . . The king himself as also his successors were mostly Viṣṇu-worshippers. . . .[170]

And, lastly,

Jayamatī, queen of Uccala, built two monasteries, one of which was in honor of her sister Sullā. This, it is said, was completed by King Jayasiṃha, the illustrious ruler, who succeeded Uccala. King Jayasiṃha patronised literary men and there was once more a revival of learning in Kashmir. He looked after the Maṭhas and Vihāras, the first of which that attracted his attention was the one built by his queen Ratnādevī. His chief minister Rilhaṇa was also very pious. He showed his veneration to both Śiva and Buddha, and erected a monastery in memory of his deceased wife Sussalā. Sussalā must have been a great devotee of Buddha, as she erected [a *vihara*] on the site of the famous Caṅkuna-Vihāra, which had been destroyed. It had a magnificent establishment for the Buddhist monks. Cintā, wife of Jayasiṃha's commander Udaya, adorned the bank of the Vitastā by a monastery consisting of five buildings, and Dhanya, one of the ministers, commenced the construction of a vihāra in honour of his late wife. Evidently, therefore, the reigning period of Jayasiṃha [1128–49 CE] marked a revival of the Buddhist faith in Kashmir.[171]

In the above discussion I have tried to suggest that a fuller view of woman's participation within the religious and social world of Indian Buddhism—especially as this regards her role as donor—can be achieved if we are willing to read together data from at least three separate pools. Reliance upon the sacred scriptures of Buddhism alone is insufficient—not only because they often present purely stereotypical models and imaging of women, but also because for certain time periods the texts are almost completely silent about women's activities.

A social history of Buddhism may be ultimately impossible to achieve. Nevertheless, focusing upon a specific group of Buddhists (in this case, women) engaged in a specific activity (in this case, *dana*, or giving) provides a starting point. Combining a reading of the scriptures together with a reading of secular histories *and* other kinds of historical testimonies such as that provided by Buddhist monuments, monasteries, and other material culture productions enables us to broaden our vision and to begin to imagine what the lived world of Indian Buddhist women was like. As a result, we begin to see such women as independent and active in the world; as being capable of affecting—and in some cases, even of shaping—the development of the Buddhist tradition. In contradistinction to the Buddha's prediction that his doctrine would not abide long in India as a result of his admitting women to his order, historical evidence shows that women's support may actually have been responsible for the tradition's flourishing on the subcontinent for as long as it did.

Part II
Buddhism and Race

꿈 꿈

6

Buddhism and Race: An African American Baptist-Buddhist Perspective

❧ ❧

I've called myself a "Baptist-Buddhist" not because I intend to take up explicitly the subject of how these two faiths come together. Nor do I mean, necessarily, to contend with writers like Rodger Kamenetz, for example, who in his widely selling book *The Jew in the Lotus*[172] bemoans the idea that so many young people of Jewish background seem to have "gone over" to Buddhism—though perhaps my particular heritage and background would form a sort of rebuttal to that idea.

I've headed my essay this way simply because it is *descriptive* of who I am. Actually, I think of myself as being more an "African American Buddhist" really; when I seek to make sense of things or to analyze a particular situation, I am more likely to draw on Buddhist principles than Baptist ones. But . . . if it seems as though the plane I'm on might actually go down (and such has been, frighteningly, the case), I call on both traditions! It is a deep response.

I have often been asked over the years—by friends as well as colleagues—whether or not I feel a "gap," a kind of disjuncture, between what I do and who I am. By this, I take it that they mean a disjuncture between the facts that I am an African American who has studied and taught Tibetan Buddhism for many years. I admit that I may be somewhat of an anomaly. I don't myself know of another African American who teaches Tibetan Buddhism, or any Buddhism for that matter, at the university level. But it hasn't *seemed* anomalous to *me*; it is, after all, *my life*. It is me and it is what I do.

Only recently have I begun contemplating what particular benefit might come from my *making a point* of this "unusual" or "anomalous" combination of circumstances. But, a benefit for whom? One obvious answer, I have come to believe, is that my doing so might be of some benefit for other African Americans, and other people of color, generally. Moreover, in adding my voice to such discussions as those in this book, it might well be the case that there is some benefit for "American Buddhists" and for Western Buddhists more broadly.

❧ ❧

Over the years, it has certainly been the case that other persons of color have come up to me in various Buddhist gatherings and told me, "I was *so glad* to look around and see *you* here!" It is a way of validating their own choice to be there, a way of not being pulled under or dismissed by being "the other," a way of finding sanity in the scene. White Americans don't yet seem to get the point that, given the history of societally marginalized people in this country, whenever we find ourselves in spaces where we are clearly in the minority, we have a natural tendency to be fearful, guarded, and mistrusting.

Whether at Buddhist centers, at meditative retreats, or at large gatherings at which His Holiness the Dalai Lama is speaking, there are simply *not* many blacks to be found. (When His Holiness spoke in Boston in September 1995 there were exactly *three* in a crowd of several hundred: a wonderful African American Buddhist monk, once known by the nickname "Yogi," but now called Venerable Jampa Kunchog; an African American woman named Loyse who'd just returned from India after journeying there following a car accident during which a vision and voice had told her to journey East (!); and myself.) Those "others" of us in the crowd always seem to find one another. I, too, notice the composition of the audiences. Most times, however, I am the only

African American (and the only person of color) attending or teaching at a Buddhist retreat.

I should say that I am aware of a few other African Americans who have taken to the various traditions of Asian Buddhism. In the San Francisco Bay Area, for example, there are not only groups of women Buddhist practitioners but also at least one separate group of African American Buddhists. One man wrote a letter, published in *Tricycle*, that said in part: "As an African American Buddhist practitioner, I am astounded at the number of seemingly well-meaning white Buddhists who simply 'do not get it.' Some assumptions that I am greeted with would be laughable, if they were not so hurtful. Many Asian practitioners that I know and love have suffered similar experiences. Here in the Bay Area a number of African American men have formed our own sangha to create a safe haven within which we may learn from the Dharma. The cultural dismissal that we have individually encountered in the Bay Area is sad, but we are collectively hopeful. . . ."[173]

The African American monk Reverend Suhita, according to another *Tricycle* piece, "prides himself on being 'the first Afro-American ordained in all three traditions of Buddhism'" (Theravada, Mahayana, and Vajrayana).[174] Rev. Suhita founded a small temple of his own, the Metta Vihara in Richmond, California. Rev. Suhita's center has become a haven for the homeless and for those infected with the HIV virus or already suffering from AIDS. His is "engaged Buddhism" in practice.

I know of at least three African Americans who are serious Buddhist students and practitioners living in Hawai'i: Lori Pierce is an African American woman completing her PhD at the University of Hawai'i with a dissertation on American Buddhism. An African American monk-priest of Jodo Buddhism also resides there, as well as an African American woman, Leslie Robinson, currently on a three-year retreat. Readers familiar with Patricia Bell-Scott's anthology, *Life Notes*, will already have come to know about Faith Adiele, who became the first black woman to live as a nun in the Thamtong Temple nunnery in northern Thailand.[175]

When I taught at the University of California, Santa Cruz, in the mid-1970s I was somewhat surprised when a group of African American students taking my large lecture course "Introduction to Buddhism" asked if I would lead them once a week in "a meditation session that was just their own." Although we didn't form a group, we did meet throughout the quarter, separately. Some of these students still maintain an interest in and connection with Buddhist Dharma. Still, these folk only account for a smattering of the slightly more than 500,000 "American Buddhists" in this country.

That Buddhist centers in this country have not exactly had an "open-door policy" toward people of color is a fact so well known that it is almost taken for granted. Some people have been noting the absence of people of color for some years now. In 1988 Sandy Boucher put the matter quite bluntly when, in *Turning the Wheel*, she characterized the number of North American–born people committed to Buddhism as being "overwhelmingly white and middle or upper middle class."[176] Yet there seems to be little open discussion of why this is so or of how the situation might be changed.

Again, after noting that the only school of Buddhism in America able to boast comparatively large numbers of people of color is Nichiren Shoshu of America (NSA), Boucher stated:

> Many people in the world of American Buddhists are leery of Nichiren Shoshu, seeing it as a pseudoreligion in which people "chant to get a Cadillac," and they are repelled by Nichiren's aggressive recruiting tactics. It is also said that Nichiren is "'political' in some ill-defined but presumably sinister way . . . People in Nichiren do chant to get a car, a house, a job, a better life. It is also true that the majority of people in this country practicing the other forms of Buddhism already have access to those things and so can comfortably choose to renounce them."[177]

I am neither a member of nor an advocate for NSA Buddhism. I do, however, think that their success in attracting people of color into their groups makes them worthy of study, and in some respects, perhaps even worthy models. NSA organizations have done two things in particular that impact on their having a more diverse community of members: (1) NSA centers are located in large urban areas, and they draw a more diverse following; and (2) the ritual practices that are enjoined on members are simple. Apart from the mandatory recitation of the *Nam myoho renge kyo* mantra, the scriptures and prayers are recited in English.

More recently, the Korean Zen Master Samu Sunim remarked in an interview:

> We Buddhist teachers—those of us who came from Asia— are like transplanted lotuses. Many of us are refugees. Here we find ourselves in the marketplace—as Dharma peddlers, you might say. I am concerned with the Zen movement becoming more accessible to ordinary common people.

The Venerable Sunim went on to say:

> It was largely the intellectuals who were attracted to Zen Buddhism in the beginning. Even today most Zen Buddhists are college-educated, liberal-minded—they're mostly white baby-boomers who couldn't make it back to their own childhood religions. We have failed to attract people from African-American communities. And we also have this attitude: if you cannot sit properly on the mat and cushion, then you cannot practice Zen meditation. That's not very inclusive.[178]

It is worth noting that, as far as I know, it has always been either women or "ethnic," that is, Asian, Buddhists who have noted the non-inclusiveness of the various Buddhisms in Western societies. Western men haven't seemed to notice. That, in itself, may say something. Whenever I've brought up the subject, I've been told: "But Buddhists don't proselytize! They never have." Historically, though, this isn't exactly true. Except for the three-month "rainy season," the earliest Buddhist mendicants were told to travel continuously and spread the faith.

ॐ ॐ

When certain people ask me whether I feel a "gap" between who I am and what I do, it seems to me that they are really asking, "What does Buddhism offer to *any* African American?" That is a legitimate question, and one that I feel is worthy of real consideration. To answer most simply, I believe that Buddhism offers us a methodology for enhancing our confidence. This is especially true of the various forms of tantric Buddhism, since tantric Buddhism aims at nothing less than the complete transformation of our ordinary and limited perception of who we are as human beings.

I was very fortunate to have been a close student of Lama Thubten Yeshe. We met in Nepal in fall 1969. Lama Yeshe kindly accepted me as his student, and I was honored that he chose to call me his "daughter." When I look back on the fifteen years that Lama Yeshe was my teacher, I see *confidence* as his main teaching—not only to me but to countless others who over the years came to him for guidance. Indeed, when Lama Yeshe discussed the essential teachings of tantric Buddhism—as he did so simply, so eloquently, and so profoundly in his *Introduction to Tantra*—he stated this idea quite explicitly. Here, I provide only a few examples:

> According to Buddhist tantra, we remain trapped within a circle of dissatisfaction because our view of reality is narrow and suffocating. We hold onto a very limited and limiting view of who we are and what we can become, with the result that our self-image remains oppressively low and negative, and we feel quite inadequate and hopeless. As long as our opinion of ourselves is so miserable, our life will remain meaningless.[179]

> One of the essential practices at all levels of tantra is to dissolve our ordinary conceptions of ourselves and then, from the empty space into which these concepts have disappeared,

arise in the glorious light body of a deity: a manifestation of the essential clarity of our deepest being. The more we train to see ourselves as such a meditational deity, the less bound we feel by life's ordinary disappointments and frustrations. This divine self-visualization empowers us to take control of our life and create for ourselves a pure environment in which our deepest nature can be expressed. . . . It is a simple truth that if we identify ourselves as being fundamentally pure, strong, and capable we will actually develop these qualities, but if we continue to think of ourselves as dull and foolish, *that* is what we will become.[180]

The health of body and mind is primarily a question of our self-image. Those people who think badly of themselves, for whatever reasons, become and then remain miserable, while those who can recognize and draw on their inner resources can overcome even the most difficult situations. Deity-yoga is one of the most profound ways of lifting our self-image, and that is why tantra is such a quick and powerful method for achieving the fulfilment of our tremendous potential.[181]

This is not just my interpretation of Lama Yeshe's view. Once, when Lama Yeshe was visiting California, I took him to hear a lecture given by Angela Davis. She spoke one afternoon in the quarry on the University of California, Santa Cruz, campus. Lama Yeshe was visibly excited to see and to listen to Davis speak. Several times during her talk, with clenched fist, he said aloud, "*This* is how one ought to be: strong and confident like this lady!"

Still, none of the great benefits that tantric meditative practice offers can be experienced and realized by "ordinary, common people" if those people don't hear about it and don't have a chance to try it for themselves—in short, if the teachings are not *accessible.* And as long as Buddhist practice is viewed and packaged as a commodity—like so many other commodities in the West—it will remain inaccessible to a great many people. And here, it seems clear that the question of accessibility is one of *class*, not—at least not *necessarily*—one of race. In order to study and to practice Buddhism in America, two requisites are absolutely essential: money and leisure time.

I met Tibetan lamas because I was able to travel to India (on a fully paid scholarship) for my junior year of college. I was part of that late 1960s phenomenon of Western students traveling to the mysterious East; part of the infamous '60s counterculture. I would not have met the Tibetans had I not been able to travel East. Neither would I now be able to attend or to afford Buddhist meditation retreats were it not that I have the kind of job I do, both in terms of the financial security and the ample vacation time and break periods it affords.

The Tibetans took me in instantly and I saw in them a welcoming family of compassionate and skilled people who, as I viewed myself, were refugees. I soon learned that the Tibetans possessed the type of knowledge and wisdom I longed for—knowledge of methods for dealing with frustrations, disappointments, and anger, and of developing genuine compassion. Indeed, their very beings reflected this. They had suffered untold hardships, had even been forced to flee their country. We shared, it seemed to me, the experience of a profound historical trauma. Yet they coped quite well, seeming to possess a sort of spiritual armor that I felt lacking in myself. Lama Yeshe's personal example inspired me, and his compassion led him to entrust some of the tantric teachings to me. Having come personally to see the benefits of such teachings, I would like to see them disseminated much more widely than they are at present.

Once Lama Yeshe looked at me piercingly and then remarked, "Living with pride and humility in equal proportion is very difficult!" In that moment, it seemed to me, he had put his finger on one of the deepest issues confronting all African Americans: the great difficulty of having gone through the experience of 250 years of slavery, during which one's very humanness was challenged and degraded at every turn, and yet through it all, to have maintained a strong sense of humanness and the desire to stand tall, with dignity and love of self, to count oneself a human being equal with all others.

It is the trauma of slavery that haunts African Americans in the deepest recesses of their souls. This is the chief issue for us. It needs to be dealt with, head-on—not denied, not forgotten, not suppressed. Indeed, its suppression and denial only hurts us more deeply, causing us to accept a limited, disparaging, and even repugnant view of ourselves. We cannot move forward until we have grappled in a serious way with all the negative effects of this trauma. Tantric Buddhism offers us some tools to help accomplish this task, since it shows us both how to get at those deep inner wounds and how to heal them.

But again, none of Buddhist tantra's benefits can be recognized if more African Americans and more people of color generally don't have access to it. So the question remains: How do we remedy this situation? As international Buddhist leaders and their American counterparts continue to mount extensive dialogues and conferences that focus on "Buddhism and Science," "Buddhism and Psychology," "Buddhism and Christianity," and so on, they would do well, it seems to me, to devote efforts toward trying to make Buddhism in all its forms more readily available and accessible to a wider cross-section of the American population. Indeed, such efforts would go a long way toward helping a truly "American" Buddhism to emerge.

In the end, the question of what Buddhism has to offer African Americans and other people of color may not be as important as what such people have to offer Buddhism in America. For even when African Americans deny, out of shame and embarrassment, the horrors of slavery, they carry the deep knowledge of that experience in their very bones. Amiri Baraka, in his classic text on African American blues and jazz, *Blues People*, expressed this well, I think, when he wrote:

> The poor Negro always remembered himself as an ex-slave and used this as the basis of any dealings with the mainstream of American society. The middle-class black man bases his whole existence on the hopeless hypothesis that no one is

supposed to remember that for almost three hundred years there was slavery in America, that the white man was a master, the black man a slave. This knowledge, however, is at the root of the legitimate black culture of this country. It is this knowledge, with its attendant muses of self-division, self-hatred, stoicism, and finally quixotic optimism, that informs the most meaningful of Afro-American music.[182]

This deep knowledge of trying to hold on to humanness in a world firmly committed to destroying it adds a kind of spiritual reservoir of strength at the same time that it is so burdensome. The spiritual resilience of black folk has something to offer us all.

The First Noble Truth of Buddhism asks us to "understand" the noble truth of suffering. Apart from the newness, exoticism, and aesthetic attractiveness of the various traditions of Buddhism now existent on American soil, in the end, it is the sobering and realistic recognition of our individual and collective suffering that marks the true beginning of the Buddhist path. The physical presence of more dark faces in Buddhist centers will serve both to focus the issue of what makes us *all* "Americans" and, hopefully, allow a freer American expression of Buddhism to emerge.

The atmosphere of a lot of Buddhist centers may be peaceful to most of their regular followers, but it is off-putting to some "outsiders" who find the sweetness and tender voices of the *pujas* and other ceremonies disingenuous. It's as though certain center members have just exchanged one pretense for another. I remember well the admonition from the great Kalu Rinpoché never to engage in such pretense. And I will never forget hearing Alice "Turiya" Coltrane at a birthday celebration for her teacher, the venerable Hindu guru Satchidananda. She began a hymn to Krishna by striking up her harmonium and singing, "*I said, ah,* Om Bhagawata. . ." with all the strength and power of an African American Baptist choir! My own heart rejoiced as I thought, *Now,* this *is truly the Dharma coming West!* There is clearly a sense in which more diverse membership in centers will stir changes in ritual and, perhaps, more straightforward and honest behavior.

❧ ☙

I do not intend any of what I've discussed here either to glorify vic-timization or to vilify current Buddhist practitioners in America. My intention was to make needed suggestions about how changes might be begun. There is the perception that there is a disjuncture between what Buddhists in America preach and what they practice. One of these perceived disjunctures revolves around the issue of the non-inclusion of persons of color in the events and memberships of Buddhist organiza-tions in this country. Clearly, if centers act as though people of color are anomalies within their precincts, then people of color will certainly become so. It would seem to me that changing such perceptions (and the actions that foster them) ought to lie at the heart of what genuine Buddhists are all about: in a word, openness. In other words, equanim-ity and compassion toward all.

Just as Buddhism in America has begun to undergo transformations to find its American identity—which is really a way of saying "finding itself" in this social and geographic space—to the extent that it has seen the disproportionately greater number of women teachers of the Dharma emerge here, so it will change for the better and become more itself when its overall audience is more representative of *all* Americans. That is, when the various forms of Buddhism are offered freely to Amer-icans of all racial and economic backgrounds.

7

Diversity and Race: New Koans for American Buddhism

On a hot summer's day in 1981, I stood in the inner courtyard of a large Buddhist monastery in central Bangkok. The courtyard, showcasing the "Thousand Buddhas," was ringed by hundreds of life-sized Buddha statues, each one gilded and lightly draped with a delicate saffron shawl. Yet even amid so many Buddha figures I found myself gravitating, ever so slowly, toward the sole statue there that still sat awaiting its new gold leaf. In its as yet unrefurbished state, it sat peacefully, peering out from a body as black as soot. I had spent the previous year and a half in Nepal and had studied and taught Buddhism back in America for more than a decade. Buddha statues were no novelty to me. But this one in particular drew my attention because of its blackness. I was irresistibly drawn to it, pulled forward, I believe, by the urge to see myself reflected there. I asked a friend to take a photo of me staring back into this black Buddha's face. It seemed obvious that this Buddha was for me. It spoke to me because it mirrored me, physically and viscerally. I hoped to find others along my way. And upon my return to the United States, I hoped to find other Buddhists who shared not only my interest in Buddhism but my racial background, my color, as well.

For many years after that I did not find other African Americans in the centers and circles of Buddhism in which I orbited back in the

States. There seemed to be very few African Americans with either the time for or the interest in matters Buddhist. Of course I had occasions to teach African Americans in my university classes on Buddhism, but in most Buddhist venues outside the classroom our numbers seemed almost inconsequential.

In 1996 I wrote an essay about Buddhism and race and about African Americans and Buddhism for an anthology called *Buddhist Women on the Edge: Contemporary Perspectives from the Western Frontier.*[183] It was no accident that the anthology focused on Buddhism as experienced and perceived by women. For throughout Buddhism's time in the United States, it has been mainly women who have challenged, and raised questions about, Buddhism at the institutional level.[184] Virtually all other books published on the subject of Buddhism in America have focused almost exclusively on meditation and on the tradition(s) of Buddhism as a spiritual path and practice.[185]

From that day when I stood in the wat of a Thousand Buddhas, more than seventeen years would pass before I picked up a Buddhist magazine in 1998 and read the following advertisement:

> Why doesn't Buddhism attract more people of African-American, Latino, and other ethnic backgrounds? A group of practitioners in the Bay area have formed the Buddhism and Racism Working Group, and in November they'll host a conference to address this question. "It is our hope that by addressing issues of race and diversity, our sanghas may become more welcoming and responsive to people from all backgrounds," says Working Group member Rosa Zubizarreta.... "Healing Racism in Our Sanghas," November 7 in Berkeley, will provide an opportunity for Buddhists from a variety of cultures and traditions to explore how their attitudes toward people of other races affect both themselves and their communities. The conference is co-sponsored by the Buddhist Peace Fellowship.[186]

Yet even before seeing this advertisement, I had managed—on my own—to find other African American Buddhists. In this essay I aim to introduce some of them and allow readers to hear our views—as African American students, teachers, and practitioners of Buddhism in America. Of course, this does not mean that we share a single view. Our experiences are as varied as we, as unique individuals, are ourselves. I must admit, however, that I chose these particular African Americans on purpose because I knew them to be serious, thoughtful, and extremely articulate individuals. (I also knew that they were industrious and compassionate enough to respond in relative haste to my request for their views.) Aiming to represent diverse Buddhist traditions, I contacted five individuals, four of whom responded in full. One is a Zen practitioner, another a Tibetan Buddhist lama, another a Theravada *vipassana* practitioner, and the last is an academic student of Buddhism in America. I myself am a professor of Indic and Tibetan Buddhism.

For the most part, I have tried to allow each to speak for him- or herself. However, I first devised a questionnaire in order to give coherence to the project. I asked them questions about their respective backgrounds, their earliest encounters with Buddhism, and their teachers. I asked whether, in fact, they considered themselves to be Buddhists, and I asked them to speak about their own experiences at Buddhist centers here in America—whether they found them to be open and welcoming spaces, and whether they had ever personally experienced any forms of discrimination in them. Lastly, I asked them if they had any specific advice for other African Americans, or for persons of color in general, who might be considering beginning Buddhist practice, and I asked them to share any specific recommendations for improving the current situation.

THEIR BACKGROUNDS

Lori Pierce comes from a comfortable, upper-middle-class religious family in Chicago, where her father is a surgeon. She was raised in the Catholic schools and church of the area, and was active in the church through high school and Lake Forest College, where her interests broadened to include world and comparative religions. Her first exposure to Buddhism, she writes, was academic.

> Reading Herman Hesse's *Siddhartha* was probably my introduction . . . . Through classes and casual reading I eventually began to read Shunryu Suzuki, D. T. Suzuki, Philip Kapleau, Robert Aiken, Eido Shimano, Alan Watts, etc. Sometimes it came in a "new age" package, but I came to Buddhism like many Americans—by way of the dregs of the countercultural movement. There was nothing systematic about it; we knew next to nothing about the complex intercultural movements that distinguished Japanese Rinzai Zen from Tibetan Buddhism. We read what was available and, as newly mature adults, believed that we were free to believe what we liked and be what we wanted to be.

After college, Lori went to California and for a time worked in the poor black neighborhood of West Oakland for the Jesuit Volunteer Corps, an organization she describes as "a kind of Catholic urban Peace Corps." Referring to that experience as her first prolonged exposure to black people since leaving the mainly white surroundings of her Chicago life, Lori determined that the question of religion and the question of race ought not to be separated. After studying a bit about Buddhism in the Bay Area, she entered the World Religions program at Harvard Divinity School. Of her California ventures into Buddhism, Lori writes, "I was sitting randomly on my own, studying tai chi, and running. It didn't occur to me to go to find an organization with which to get involved. And in the Bay Area in the early 1980s, there was just too much choice." Lori now lives in Hawai'i with her husband and six-year-old daughter. She is currently completing her doctoral dissertation for the University of Hawai'i on the racial dynamic of the religious encounter between European Americans and Japanese Americans in Hawai'i during the years before World War II.

Lama Thupten Gyalsten Dorjé (Jerry Gardner) writes of his early life, "I was born on Guam to a military couple and then adopted by a different military couple. I was raised as an only child." His family moved around a lot in the United States, living in Alabama, Texas, Washington, North Carolina, New York City, and Oklahoma. It was in Alabama that, with his grandmother, he attended Baptist services. "I remember the preacher yelling and shouting. It seemed surrealistic to me as a young child." In his early years, Gardner became obsessed with death. "Even though I wasn't Catholic, I used to sleep with a rosary." When he was twelve years old, he began his lifelong practice of the martial arts. This practice included meditation, and he found he liked the discipline of learning to discipline his mind. Martial arts also helped him to become less fearful of death.

In 1968, in New York City, he met his first Buddhist teacher, Master Ronald Takanashi, a Pure Land Buddhist priest. Takanashi was the first to introduce him to a more formal meditation practice—for example, how to practice, and how to set up a shrine. Jerry began to search out books and teachers to guide him "to the mastery of self," and then determined to go to the East. "In 1970 I sold my belongings and was ready to travel to India or Tibet to search for a teacher." However, a series of "seemingly unfortunate" events occurred that forced him to cancel his trip. As a result, he met Lama Sonam Kazi in New York, and was accepted as his student. Commenting on this turn of events, he says, "I find it interesting that instead of going to the mountains of Tibet to find a teacher, I went to the highrises of New York City!"

Then, while living again in Guam in 1988, the opportunity arose for Jerry to travel to Kathmandu, Nepal. He remarks, "I went there without having any knowledge of what might occur or who I might meet, but my goal was to have a direct experience of Buddhism in a place where it was lived as part of the ongoing fiber of the society." In Nepal, Jerry met Chökyi Nyima Rinpoché, who sent him to his father, Tulku Urgyen Rinpoché. The latter became his root teacher. In the past ten years, he has traveled to Nepal two or three times each year. Most recently, he has been receiving teachings from Khenpo Kunchok Molam Rinpoché, and writes that "it was Khenpo Kunchok Molam Rinpoché who was so kind as to ordain me as Lama Thupten Gyalsten Dorjé."

In 1994, after moving to Salt Lake City, Utah, Lama Dorjé and his

wife established the nonprofit Urgyen Samten Ling Meditation Center, in the "Nyingma, Dzogchen, Long Chen Nying Thig" lineage.
Lama Dorjé is the center's resident teacher. He also continues, now as a
teacher, his martial arts—in the form of tai chi, kung fu, and mime—at
the Red Lotus School of Movement, which he owns and directs.

Lewis Woods describes himself as "an African American man who has
lived his whole life in the post-civil-rights-movement United States,"
and goes on to note:

> By the time I was five years old, my family had moved to
> Berkeley, California. This was in 1968, the heyday of student
> activism and radical social change. Though I was relatively
> sheltered from the events taking place across town, the atmo-
> sphere of liberalism, openness to change, and the questioning
> of authority and tradition was my native cultural landscape,
> if you will, reaching me through my teachers and my par-
> ents who very much chose to live in Berkeley because of this
> atmosphere.

Commenting on the religious life of his family, Lewis writes, "If our
family had a religion, it was atheism. Both of my parents had rejected
the religions of their youth by the time I was born . . . . At present I am
the only person in my immediate family who is at all religious." At the
age of eighteen, Lewis "became a born-again Christian and remained
within that evangelical, mixed race, doctrinally conservative church for
four years." But at the age of twenty-two, he "made a decisive break
with Christianity and began studying Judaism." In fact, after a three-
year period of study which included becoming conversant in modern
Hebrew and two prolonged visits to Israel and the occupied territories,
Lewis formally converted to orthodox Judaism.

Lewis first encountered Buddhism through the books of Alan Watts
and Suzuki Roshi, though, he confides, "initially, I was more interested
in Taoism than Buddhism." In the end, it was the Buddhist Dharma
that impressed Lewis most. "For so long the *only* Buddhists I knew were
in books. I didn't meet a 'real' Buddhist until well after I had become

convinced of the merits of Buddhism." Although Lewis began by mainly sitting Zen in the Bay Area, he later took Buddhist refuge and lay vows with Geshe Michael Roach. He describes his daily practice as being "pretty idiosyncratic," saying that he draws "most on Tibetan and Theravada traditions, though my background in Zen is never far below the surface." Lewis remains one of the main anchors of the Berkeley headquarters of the Buddhist Peace Fellowship.

Ralph Steele was born on Pawleys Island, one of the sixteen islands along the coast of South Carolina that stretch out for 160 miles between Myrtle Beach and Charleston. When Ralph was five years old, his father died, and so he describes his mom as being a single parent. "I was raised mostly by my grandparents," Ralph says. "Everyone called my grandmother 'Sister Mary'; and everybody called my grandfather 'Baba James.' My great-grandfather was called, by everyone, simply 'Father.'" Ralph's family members were very religious and were strong supporters of the African Methodist Episcopal Church, "for more than 110 years supplying ministers, deacons, treasurers, and bookkeepers to the church."

When Ralph's mother remarried a military man, the family left Pawleys Island and began traveling, moving first to Montgomery, Alabama, then to Bakersfield, California, and then on to Japan, where Ralph went to high school. There, he encountered a Japanese martial arts master and began studying seriously with him.

> Even though I was only thirteen or fourteen years old, eventually I ended up in his class, the only student who was not in the military. And I learned a lot from him. I began to understand the concepts of Buddhism from a practitioner's perspective through the eyes of martial arts. And I began to go into temples at an early age and to get some understanding of what was going on there.

Before entering college, Ralph enlisted in the military and served a tour in Vietnam. He found himself in "very heated situations" and he saw many of his friends die. "I had to call on my own deep, deep inner self and what my martial arts teacher and Sister Mary and Baba James had taught me in order to keep my sanity and survive."

After returning from Vietnam, Ralph became a student at the University of California, Santa Cruz, and later did graduate work at Santa Clara University. In both locations, and in other places, he found Buddhist teachers: Zen master Kobun Chino, the eclectic Steven Levine, the Tibetans Kalu Rinpoché and Sogyal Rinpoché among them. But, eventually, Ralph found his primary teacher in Jack Kornfield, and in Theravāda *vipassana* meditation he found his main practice. Ralph is now a therapist living in Santa Fe, New Mexico. Specializing in combining psychotherapy and Dharma practice for pain and grief management, his office group is called "Life Transition Therapy, Inc." Having led *vipassana* groups himself, Ralph is in training to become a *vipassana* teacher. He is currently doing intensive meditation retreats in Burma and Thailand. For some years, he has also been writing his memoir, which is entitled *Tending the Fire*.[87]

Jan Willis was born in Birmingham, Alabama, and raised until college in a coal mining camp just outside the city limits. "Both my parents were active in the Baptist Church, my father being one of the youngest deacons of his church. Although my own baptism was a wonderfully expansive and spiritually liberating experience, I was not much attracted to the Baptist faith. As a high school student, I took an active part in the civil rights movement and marched with King and others during the Birmingham campaign of 1963. Always good at mathematics, I won a number of scholarships for college and selected Cornell University, where, initially, I majored in physics. It was at Cornell that I became interested in Buddhism, in large part because of observing Buddhist monks and nuns immolate themselves protesting against the Vietnam war. I read works mostly by Alan Watts and D. T. Suzuki and determined to study and meditate in Japan. I was able to spend my junior year in India on a University of Wisconsin Year in India program scholarship, and, while studying in Banaras, I met Tibetans living in Sarnath. I was immediately captivated by the Tibetans and was warmly received by them. Consequently, during that first year I never got east of India. In 1969, in Nepal, I met Lama Thubten Yeshe, who became my main teacher for the next fifteen years until his death in 1984. Back in the United States, I finished a BA and an MA in philosophy at Cornell, and then enrolled at Columbia, where I earned my PhD in Indic and Buddhist Studies in 1976. In 1996 I was asked to write about my personal journey from the Jim Crow South to Tibetan Buddhism and I did so by writing the memoir titled *Dreaming Me: An African American Woman's Spiritual Journey* (Riverhead Books, 2001). In 2008 Wisdom Publications issued a new edition of the memoir titled *Dreaming Me: Black, Baptist, and Buddhist: One Woman's Spiritual Journey.*"

FIVE AFRICAN AMERICANS ON BUDDHISM IN AMERICA

In my 1996 essay on African Americans and Buddhism, I described myself as a "Baptist-Buddhist," remarking that I found the hyphenated description most genuine. I wrote then:

> I've headed my essay this way simply because it is *descriptive* of who I am. Actually, I think of myself as being more an "African American Buddhist" really; when I seek to make sense of things or to analyze a particular situation, I am more likely to draw on Buddhist principles than Baptist ones. But . . . if it seems as though the plane I'm on might actually go down (and such has been, frighteningly, the case), I call on both traditions! It is a deep response.[188]

Not surprisingly, then, the questionnaire I sent for the present essay included the following questions: *Do you consider yourself to be a Buddhist? Do you ever find yourself qualifying or hyphenating this appellation?* The answers I received were straightforward and varied.

Lori: "I see [taking Buddhist refuge] as something akin to being rebaptized. I figured if you're going to take refuge, to take on a teacher, you had better be pretty ready, pretty committed to this path, at least committed to the teacher. I still am not-sure enough to want to do that. When people ask me if I am a Buddhist, I assume . . . they mean: Have you taken refuge? Do you have a teacher? What is your practice? This to me is not something to be taken lightly .... Maybe I'm like a divorced person after having left the Catholic Church; I'm not that anxious to make the mistake again. I've been known to say that I would be willing to entertain returning to the liberal American Catholic Church when it breaks from Rome, ordains married people, accepts homosexuals, and acknowledges its role in the perpetuation of patriarchy, sexism, and racism. I don't want too much, do I?"

Lama Dorjé: "I am Buddhist. I follow the Buddhadharma. For me, the mixing and matching [hyphenating] does not work. The Buddhist tradition is complete. If one has truly embraced the teachings of the Buddha, there is no need to add or mix anything else."

Lewis: "I definitely consider myself a Buddhist, especially now that I have taken the five lifetime lay vows. I seldom feel a need to hyphenate that appellation except under certain circumstances. Adding 'African American' to the term 'Buddhist' is important at times, but it really doesn't modify the term 'Buddhist' in the same way that calling myself a Theravada Buddhist, a Vajrayana Buddhist, or an eclectic Buddhist does. Calling myself a Northern California Buddhist or, better, a Berkeley Buddhist probably says a bit more about my approach to the Dharma. But even that doesn't explain enough to make it worth mentioning.... When I'm feeling confident enough to follow my own path, I think of myself as a 'critical Buddhist,' as one whose approach to the Dharma is rooted in an attempt to take seriously the problems posed for Buddhism by modem, pluralistic social conditions and by contemporary philosophy and science. It is also based on an endeavor to remain responsibly open to criticism regardless of the quarter from which it arises. I also like to call myself an 'engaged Buddhist' to make it clear that I do not think that attention to social problems is tangential to the practice of awakening."

Ralph: "Of course I'm a Buddhist, from head to toe! Also, I'm a Hindu, a bigtime *bhakti* [devotional] man. It's pretty hard for an Afro-American to run around saying he's Hindu in this culture ... but, a Buddhist? Yes, I am. A Buddhist from head to toe. I've taken vows many, many, many times; and any time the string falls off I put one on again. So, that's who I am. And—what can I say?—the practice keeps my sanity."

Jan: "In an odd way, I have always found myself feeling especially 'at home' when I am with Tibetans in Nepal or India. I attempted to comment on this feeling of welcomeness in my 1996 essay by saying:

> The Tibetans took me in instantly and I saw in them a welcoming family of compassionate and skilled people who, as I viewed myself, were refugees. I soon learned that the Tibetans possessed a type of knowledge and wisdom I longed for—knowledge of methods for dealing with frustrations, disappointments, and anger, and of developing genuine compassion. Indeed, their very beings reflected this. They had suffered untold hardships, had even been forced to flee their country. We shared, it seemed to me, the experience of a profound historical trauma. Yet they coped quite well, seeming to possess a sort of spiritual armor that I felt lacking in myself."[189]

When I asked whether, in their experiences, these four African Americans had ever noticed or felt discrimination or prejudice toward them in Asia from Asians, most of them skipped the question, giving, on my subsequent inquiry, the uniform response "No." Like me, they found their Asia experience to be most welcoming. Lama Dorjé was quite specific on this point, saying, "When I visit Nepal, I generate a fair amount of curiosity from Nepalese and Tibetans, as I *truly* am a stranger in a strange land. If anything, my differences tend to draw people to me. Personally, I feel more comfortable walking the streets of Kathmandu than the streets of America!"

However, when I asked, *Do you find Buddhist centers in the United States "open" places for you and other people of color? Do you see yourself represented in them?* all four respondents had comments.

Lori: "Going to the Cambridge Buddhist Association was my first experience with *zendo* culture, and I have to say I found it a bit off-putting. I liked Maurine;[190] she was like a stern but loving grandmother, but . . . what, I wondered, was the point of schlepping all the way over there (a forty-five minute walk from our house) if, after sitting, chanting, and walking, you just went home? Where was the fellowship? Where were the tea and cookies? What was the point of a sangha if you didn't know anyone's name? The whole thing felt so formal and distant, I never really warmed up to it."

Lama Dorjé: "The Buddhist centers I have visited have been accepting of me as a person of color. But, then again, I don't walk in the door with the concern, 'Am I going to be accepted?' My feeling is that the Buddha taught all people, and his teachings are for all persons. The Buddha himself was a person of color. At this point in time, people of color are not well represented in the American Buddhist tradition. . . . In general, Buddhism has limited exposure in the black communities, so even if someone of color had an interest in Buddhism, the resources may not be as apparent. Obviously, Buddhist centers are not as common as mainstream American religious organizations. An individual really has to make an effort to seek the Buddhist resources out. But I think these same dynamics are also found in many communities, regardless of color."

Lewis: "I have found the predominantly White Buddhist center that I have been involved with open but not especially welcoming. I've never been overtly discouraged from participating in a Buddhist event. However, I have felt marginalized, not seen, and at times not just misunderstood but written off as all but inscrutable. In just about every Buddhist setting I have ever found myself, my being African American has meant that my concerns are second-class, that my experience insofar as it is conditioned by my ethnic identity is seldom addressed directly, that I have to do a lot of translating in order to apply the teaching to the social situation in which I find myself, and that not infrequently I have to endure the ever-so-unpleasant experience of having to listen to a White person talk about how much further we have to go in this society toward achieving true equality for African Americans."

Ralph: "All Buddhist centers are 'open,' as far as I know. It's just a question of whether you're bold enough to walk through the doors. Of course, for any person of color who walks through any Buddhist center's door, it's just like walking through the doors of any European church where people of color don't normally go: you will be on stage. People of color need to understand that. The main concept of Buddhism is seeing things as they are; but it's the human nature in those Buddhist centers that manifests. Some people will be surprised and they'll be taken aback, but they won't close the doors on you. Still, until the people in those centers, the practitioners in this country, deal with the fire inside themselves—the rejection, the hate, the anger, the racism—there will always be a conditioning in the fabric of those places. So, don't walk through the doors of temples in this country without expecting some subtly unintentional action coming toward you. Don't be offended by that, because the practitioners [at those centers] themselves are not totally enlightened people. Who is? It takes time. This is a big process; a big subject matter here."

Jan: "All too often I find myself one of only a handful of people of color in Buddhist venues, whether retreats or large public lectures by prominent Asian Buddhist teachers. Yet there seems to be little open and frank discussion of either why this is the case or of how the situation might be changed. That is a discussion that needs to take place."

Ralph's response to the former question made it seem only natural to consider the last set of queries on my questionnaire at this point. I had asked respondents, *What advice would you give to African Americans or other persons of color who are considering beginning Buddhist practice?* Ralph wanted to forewarn people of color not to expect Buddhist centers to be any different than other institutions in this country. How could they be? Lori chose not to give a more specific answer to this particular question. She had, after all, already given focused and quite serious attention to it in her essay "Outside In: Buddhism in America." I give below the comments offered by Lama Dorjé, Lewis Woods, Ralph Steele, and myself to this specific query.

Lama Dorjé: "Typically, it's not part of the Buddhist tradition to proselytize, but rather to let people come to the teachings and teachers on their own. But as Buddhism progresses in America, it may be a good idea to take a more engaged approach and create a better means of visibility that would allow easier access to the Buddhist practice for individuals who are interested. Speaking directly to people of color, if they see that there are Buddhist practitioners and teachers of color, this might be encouragement that they, too, have a place in this age-old religion that was started in a land that was infused with people of color. I'm interested in being instrumental in broadening the base of Buddhism in America to include people of color. If there is any way I can assist in this goal, please let me know."

Lewis: "At this point in time I would probably caution African Americans or other people of color who are considering beginning Buddhist practice at a predominantly White center to be prepared for racism. I would also make it clear that I think that, up to a point, the Dharma is worth it. I would also suggest that they join with others for support, and I express the hope that we all take responsibility for those who will come after us and do what we can to make sure that others will have an easier time in the future."

Ralph: "I'd say, 'I'm a person of color, and I hope to see you at some of my retreats.' Don't look to the practitioners at any center to teach you about racism. Don't expect the practitioners themselves not to be biased, at least unintentionally. One thing to remember is it's not the practitioners or the teacher, any teacher. It's the teachings, the Dharma itself, that is important. That doesn't change. That's what is over 2,500 years old. That doesn't change. And that's what has saved me and kept me in this practice. I'm sitting in this room with two hundred people, la-di-da, and I'm the only person of color. So what? It's no big thing. Because I know my practice. And I can sit here and do my practice and do my thing. And that's what's so wonderful about this practice: it's about direct experience. And you don't need anybody to hold your hand, or anything of that nature. That's why I'm still in this practice. Because if I needed someone to hold my hand, or if I needed to believe in something, I wouldn't be in this practice."

Jan: "There are many valuable insights to be gleaned from Buddhist teachings. These insights are as meaningful, and as potentially healing, for persons of color as for any other human being. Therefore, I would encourage all people of color who have a desire to learn more about Buddhism to do so, through books, lectures, and visits to Buddhist centers and retreats. A well-known saying among African Americans is 'Keep your eyes on the prize.' After carefully investigating and choosing a Buddhist teacher and organization or center, people of color should be willing to give the teachings and the practice a try."

I asked these articulate African American Buddhists, *Are there specific recommendations for helping to make Buddhist centers more receptive and accessible for people of color?* Both Lama Dorjé and Ralph Steele suggested that when people of color could *see themselves* represented in centers, they might come. Both said that becoming teachers themselves in their respective Buddhist traditions was part of their personal attempt to help provide such representation. (As I read their responses, I felt myself back in that monastery in Thailand.)

Jan: "In this regard, I am in complete agreement with Lama Dorjé and Ralph. If we, as people of color, prepare ourselves to become and continue to be *teachers* in Buddhist venues, whether in Buddhist centers or in universities, we will have an impact. I also believe that Buddhist centers throughout America ought to mount more concerted efforts to make themselves more open and accessible places. Hosting 'open houses' is a good way of breaking down even invisible barriers. For longer retreats, center-sponsored scholarships and work-study programs may serve to help alleviate conflicts in choosing between one's job and time for meditation."

Lewis Woods and Lori Pierce had more theoretically based recommendations.

Lewis: "Because racism and White supremacy are not going to end within Buddhist centers very much before they end in society—and at the rate things are going many Buddhist communities are lagging behind even the corporate world—the Buddhist community as a whole has a Dharmic responsibility to take affirmative action. Such action should at least include supporting the creation of alternative pathways (separate retreats, classes, and even separate centers) to the Dharma for African Americans and other people of color. For these alternatives to be truly Buddhist they must be based on a recognition of the impermanent, unsatisfactory, and no-self nature of racial and ethnic identity. In practice, this means not only that they must acknowledge that the day will come when such separate institutions are no longer necessary, but that they will actively look forward to it.

"Secondly, such action should also include acknowledging the contradiction in speaking of 'American Buddhism' when so many Americans are underrepresented, if not functionally unwelcome, in Buddhist communities.

"Thirdly, I hope that Buddhist teachers and leaders will not just acknowledge the racism that plays a role in the culture of their centers, but take responsibility for it and make every effort to include outgrowing it as part of the practice of Buddhism."

Lori shares her analysis and recommendations with people interested in these issues, in the classroom and through her published works. Since 1995, she has been writing and lecturing about "how institutional racism works to undermine discussions of race in religious groups."

RACE AND GENDER

Before concluding this multivocal discussion, it seems only appropriate, given the context of the present anthology, to ask one additional question, namely, *Would/Does gender make a difference?* Although my original questionnaire did not ask this specific question, Lori Pierce and I do have some comments to make on this important concern.

Jan: "Yes. Gender makes a profound difference. For most of my early life, it seemed that the specter and concomitant hindrances of racism far outweighed those of sexism, even though, of course, the two worked very closely together. The question was, how was I as a black girl going to be able to succeed in the world? For black boys, there were some avenues open; but for black girls, the possibilities seemed much more limited. Today, as an adult woman Buddhist scholar, the links between racially-based and gender-based discrimination seem all the more obvious. Although I have managed to forge a career in an academic field that I find personally very rewarding, it is still a field that is disproportionately dominated by men. While some women are now assuming leadership roles in Buddhist centers throughout America, very few of these women are persons of color. Even fewer women of color are instructors of Buddhism within academia. As long as this is the case, Buddhism in America will continue to mirror the hierarchical and patriarchal institutions it has maintained throughout its long history in Asia. If genuine progress is to be made, the issues of race, class, gender, and sexuality need to be addressed much more seriously than they have been thus far. Only then will the tantalizing promises of Buddhist philosophical notions like 'selflessness,' 'interdependence,' 'inclusiveness,' and, ultimately, 'insight' and 'compassion' become real possibilities."

Describing the aftermath of a lecture she had delivered at a conference on Buddhist diversity, Lori remarked, "I left there thinking that the Buddhist community needs a forum for an extended discussion of all aspects of race and gender, diversity and discrimination. I was encouraged by Rosa,[191] who suggested to me that we must somehow make diversity a central practice. We always wonder what is 'American' about 'American Buddhism,' and Rosa suggested to me that diversity might be it. What might make American Buddhism distinctive is the challenge to think through problems of racial ideologies. To sit with them. How would you make that not just part of your practice but the center of your practice?"

And on this matter, I think that Lori's remarks should be the final word. In Rinzai Zen practice, for example, one makes a koan the center of one's practice. One "sits" with it. A koan is a riddle, a puzzle, a question that cannot be "solved" by linear, discursive reasoning. Yet as countless generations of Zen practitioners have demonstrated, koans can be resolved. Again in Lori's words, "a koan is *unsolvable*, but *resolvable*." So what if Buddhists in America made "diversity" and "race" and "gender" their koans? I say, go ahead, American Buddhists. Please try these new koans on!

8

Dharma Has No Color

At the closing session of the 2002 African American Buddhist Retreat and Conference held at Spirit Rock, a young black woman asked me, "Was there anything that was *left out* as Buddhism made its way here?" She had prefaced her question by saying that the books she'd read seemed to present a neatly uniform picture of Buddhism coming to the West, and she wondered whether this idyllic picture was true, or even if it was the *only* story. She was asking me because I was one of only two academics among the fourteen teachers gathered at the conference.

I paused before responding, realizing the true profundity of the inquiry. It seemed clear to me that, in fact, the question contained and suggested many other questions left unspoken. After hesitating, I then gave a somewhat rambling and long-winded answer about the Dharma's being for everyone, even though I thought we people of color had a sort of head start given the prominence of Buddhism's discussions of suffering. I hoped that some of what I said might be of use. The young woman was kindhearted and, nodding as I answered, let me off the hook. In the months since the conference, I have often thought about that question and about the varied implications and unvoiced experiences that may have lain behind it. What I want to do here is attempt a clearer response. This means that I will first attempt to draw out some of the other questions latent within that pregnant one that was uttered.

When the woman asked if there was anything that was *left out* when the varied traditions of Buddhism were brought here, I heard another related question—namely, is there anything in the Buddhist traditions in Asia that has *not* been brought here? In a way, I hear this question as asking, Have we been given the *whole* picture, told the whole truth? I hear it as a question that bears a bit of skepticism as well as suspicion. I believe that the skepticism at least is well-founded.

It is certainly true that if you walk into any bookstore or library or visit any number of internet sites of cyber-Dharma, you'll come away with the sense that Buddhism is all about only one thing: *meditation*. But is this all or even most of what Asian Buddhists do? I think that the true answer is absolutely not. American or other Western convert Buddhists like to pick and choose. They like to take this element or practice from this Buddhist tradition, and this other element from this other tradition. This is understandable since most of us in the West live in and with a supermarket mentality, and since we, as unique individuals, like to fashion what will be uniquely ours. If we now add to this propensity the fact that most early convert Buddhists went to Asia in the 1970s to get away from religious traditions they found to be overly devotional and hence stifling, we can understand that their initial desire was to find a so-called pure religious practice that was uncluttered by any elements that smacked of devotionalism.

We can imagine them saying, *Just give me the pith without any fluff!* Of course, this demand was, and remains, unrealistic. In Asia, as anywhere else in the world, religion and religious practice comes wrapped in the trappings and paraphernalia of the particular culture. Yet, seemingly unaware of this, those early counterculture Westerners—myself included—were fed up with the trappings of religion. Encountering and being attracted to Buddhism, we thought we could isolate its essence. And that essence was assuredly meditation. At this point, however, picking and choosing became not just a process of selection but also a process of subtraction. So, many things, in fact, *were* left out.

On the one hand, Buddhist traditions that seem to smack of the old devotional and worshipful stances from which we were fleeing were the last traditions to make their way here. It has only been recently that we in the West have heard much about Pure Land or Jodo Shinshu Buddhism, traditions of Buddhism that extol *tariki*, or reliance on other-power in addition to reliance on self-power alone. A form of Buddhist practice that actually enjoins prayer to the buddhas and rituals of repeating the names of buddhas appears threatening and un-Buddhist to some. It's too close to the stuff many of us were trying to get away from. But in Asia—even in those seemingly more spare traditions, like Japanese Zen or Thai vipassana—there are still Buddha statues, and altars, and water bowls, and incense burning, and prayers, and bowing. These practices are different from what we normally think of as purely meditation.

On the other hand, most Asian Buddhists didn't—and still don't—have the time to devote all of their time to meditation. Though we may tend to think that *all Buddhists meditate all the time*, for most Buddhists in the world, meditation is not the sole or even the main activity. It is a cherished activity, to be sure, but not the only one. For most Asian lay Buddhist followers, the majority of their time must be devoted to the tasks of living. However, even among monastics, meditation is not the sole activity. My teacher, Lama Yeshe, had been a monk at the renowned Sera Jé Monastery just outside of Lhasa. One of the three main Gelukpa sees, Sera housed thousands of monks. But according to Lama Yeshe, only about fifty of the Sera Jé monks were revered as great meditators and so were allowed to be absent from group rituals. The great majority of monks busied themselves with the day-to-day chores of running such an institution, whether as cooks, gardeners, teachers, managers, and so forth. The idea that all Buddhists do is meditate is an invention of Westerners; it does not give a true picture of Buddhism as actually practiced in Asian countries.

Another question behind, or internal to, the one the young woman asked is this: "Is this a teaching that *I* can really use?" My answer was and is: "Absolutely." The Buddha's teachings of love, compassion, kindness, and insight are available to all of us here and now, and all of us, it seems to me, are in clear need of them. They can help us to see the roots of our pain, dissatisfaction, and anguish and they can help us to methodically work to overcome them. Twenty-six hundred years of heart and mind science has come up with some pretty good answers.

Even so, unlike most of the world's religious traditions, Buddhism does not ask us to accept uncritically a set of dogmas or principles. Rather, Buddhism calls on us simply to check up! One of the core aspects of Buddhism is, in fact, its call to *experience*. Urging his followers to come and see for themselves, the Buddha cautioned them against accepting as fact anything that did not accord with their own experiences.

The most foundational teachings recorded in the Buddha's first sermon, the Four Noble Truths, are not taught as dogma to be accepted and believed with blind faith. Rather, for each of the truths, there is a specific action required on our part, which is geared to lead us to a type of certainty regarding the truth and veracity of that truth. Not until that action has been carried out and tested against our own experience should we embrace it as a guiding principle. We cannot take the teachings for granted; we have to come and see for ourselves.

The First Noble Truth says that there is suffering. The specific action enjoined on us in connection with this truth is that we must *understand* it (that is, suffering). With respect to the Second Noble Truth—that there is a cause of suffering which is, most palpably, desire, but on a deeper level, ignorance—we are to *eliminate* the cause. With respect to the Third Truth—that there is the cessation of suffering—we are told that we must *realize* that cessation directly, by experiencing it. And, lastly, with respect to the Fourth Noble Truth—that there is a path leading to the cessation of suffering—we are asked to follow and *cultivate* that path. Of course, all this is easier said than done.

For the time being, I want to concentrate on the First Noble Truth and the specific injunction to *understand* it. "Understanding" here means more than just grasping the idea intellectually. I have taught many intelligent students over the past three decades. These students certainly grasp the meanings of the Sanskrit term *duhkha*, which is usually translated as "suffering." The best students have no trouble in grasping the further Buddhist subdivision of duhkha into three kinds—namely, suffering plain and simple, suffering caused by change, and suffering that is inherent in the cycle of birth and death that is called *samsara*. Yet even appreciating the three kinds of suffering is not the same as understanding suffering. I believe that people of color—because of our experience of the great and wrenching historical trauma of slavery—understand suffering in a way that our white brothers and sisters do not, and, moreover, that this understanding is closer to what is meant by the Buddhist injunction. Hence, I believe that—in this regard, and without putting suffering on a scale—we people of color are actually already one up on other convert Buddhist practitioners. We come to the practice with this deeper understanding. And this understanding, I believe, makes it *easier* for us to actually get it when we're told that we need to *understand* the Noble Truth of *suffering*.

Now, there is another question in the one uttered by the young black woman. It is a question that is pressing for blacks and other people of color who see something of value in Buddhist teachings. That question, simply stated, is this: "In order to practice Buddhism, do I have to abandon the tradition of faith in which I was raised?" Often this question is asked explicitly of me in private moments. Since I have publicly referred to myself as a Baptist-Buddhist, I get the question a lot. I believe that the answer to this question is, most assuredly, "No." Buddhism does not demand blind allegiance from us. Usually, however, our own faith tradition is not so open.

I once gave a reading at the only state women's prison in Connecticut. As I reached the conclusion of my talk, a very tall, slender, and muscular black woman stood up and began waving a pocket-sized Bible in the air. She then yelled out, "I have all the help with overcoming my problems right here, in this book!" I was clearly being challenged. On this one, I had no hesitation. I responded, "I am very happy for you, then. However, I couldn't find the answers there—at least not when I needed them. I needed to know how to love my neighbors when my neighbors—some of them Klan members—didn't care much for me. I liked the sentiment, Love thy neighbor, but I didn't know how to put it into practice. I needed another method. And *I* found those methods in Buddhism." She seemed to hear me. The point is that I can use *Buddhist* methods to help me practice *Baptist* ideals. I can use Buddhist meditations to help me to transform negative emotions and perceptions into more positive ones. In a well-known Buddhist parable, the Buddha tells his followers to use his teachings like a raft. If they are helpful, use them.

But, afterward, you needn't hold on to them or carry them around with you. I'll quote a bit of this parable here, as translated by the Venerable Walpola Rahula. It goes like so:

> "O bhikkhus, a man is on a journey. He comes to a vast stretch of water. On this side the shore is dangerous, but on the other it is safe and without danger. No boat goes to the other shore . . . nor is there any bridge for crossing over. He says to himself: '. . . It would be good if I would gather grass, wood, branches and leaves to make a raft, and with the help of the raft cross over safely to the other side, exerting myself with my hands and feet.' He does this and safely crosses to the other shore. Having crossed over to the other side, he thinks: 'This raft was of great help to me. With its aid I have crossed safely over to this side. . . . It would be good if I carry this raft on my head or on my back wherever I go.' What do you think, O bhikkhus, if he acted in this way would that man be acting properly with regard to the raft?"
>
> "No, Sir" (the monks respond).
>
> "In which way then would he be acting properly with regard to the raft? . . . Suppose that man should think: 'This raft was a great help to me. . . . It would be good if I beached this raft . . . or moored it and left it afloat, and then went on my way.' . . . Acting in this way would that man act properly with regard to the raft. *In the same manner*, O bhikkhus, I have taught a doctrine similar to a raft—it is for crossing over, and not for carrying."[192]

Practicing Buddhist meditation does not require that one abandon one's original faith tradition. I can find many virtuous ideals in biblical scriptures but still need to work on developing compassion and fearlessness with specific meditations from the Buddhist traditions that are aimed at helping these qualities to grow and blossom within me. At least so far, this strategy has proven beneficial for me.[193]

Perhaps when the young black woman at the people of color retreat was asking her question she was thinking of the very special nature of the retreat we had all just shared, and which was fast coming to an end. In this case, the question also entailed the recognition that such retreats were indeed a rarity. *To what extent,* she may have been pondering, *are the teachings of Buddhism truly accessible to me, and to us people of color generally, when we leave these grounds?* I have written about this particular issue before. There is little doubt that convert Buddhism in America is largely a white, and upper-middle-class, affair. This is so not only because those 1970s counterculture folk who went to Asia and brought back a fervent interest in Buddhism were from this economic background, but also because of the way American Buddhist institutions have been organized and developed here. In short, there are two essential requirements necessary for doing a Buddhist retreat here: money and leisure time. Most working-class people and many people of color do not have a great quantity of either. This situation calls for creative solutions worked out between those white convert Buddhists and people of color with a sincere interest in Buddhist Dharma.

The Dharma itself is colorless. It is not limited by the sex, gender, race, class, sexual orientation, or church affiliation of the person studying or practicing it. The *Diamond Sutra,* an early Mahayana wisdom text, said this like so:

> Those who by my form did see me,
> and those who followed me by my voice,
> wrong the efforts they engaged in,
> me those people will not see.[194]

When the Buddha says in this text that those who saw him by his physical form did not see him in truth, an end is posited to questions of discrimination based on categories like those mentioned above. None of these categories has any bearing on enlightenment. Therefore, the answer to the question of accessibility, like the Buddhist notion of the "two truths"—that is, conventional, or relative truth on the one hand, and ultimate truth on the other[195]—is twofold: on the ultimate level, the answer is, "Of course, Buddhist Dharma is accessible and available to all sentient beings, without exception, and, since every sentient being already possesses buddha-nature, all without exception have the capacity and potential of becoming fully enlightened beings." On the conventional or relative level, however—where we all exist until we are enlightened—we need to work together to insure that diversity is a reality in all Buddhist communities.

A last question—though not a final one—inherent in the query voiced by the young woman might be this: *Is there really value for us in the Buddhist teachings?* I think the answer here is, "Yes, there is much of value." But that is my personal opinion and one that I have verified for myself through trial and experience. I cannot speak in the name of others here. We might, however, for a moment consider the question of value as it was posed by a very distinguished black intellectual. In a speech delivered in 1923, W. E. B. Du Bois asked us, as a people, to consider the question of value in the following way: "What do we want? What is the thing that we're after? If you suddenly should become full-fledged Americans, if your color faded or the color line . . . was miraculously forgotten, what would you want? What would you immediately seek? Would you buy the most powerful of motorcars? Would you buy the most elaborate estate?"[196]

Clearly these are important questions for people of color to ponder. Yet they are also important questions for everyone who lives and breathes and shares this planet. Buddhists answer the question of what do we want like this: *we all wish happiness and we all wish to avoid suffering.*[197] It is our most common denominator as living beings. Therefore, if we have heard about a tradition which might offer us genuine help in accomplishing this most basic of goals, wouldn't it be prudent to check it out, to come and see for ourselves?

9

Yes, We're Buddhists, Too!

෴ ෴

On occasion, people have said to me, "Oh, I didn't know that there were African American Buddhists!" Mostly my reaction is demure, but I sometimes want to respond with the question, "Why shouldn't there be?" After all, African Americans are human beings who think and breathe and experience suffering just as other human beings do.

More than 2,500 years ago, at the very end of his life, the Buddha declared, "In all these years, I have taught only two things: suffering and its cessation." What a marvelous statement! And, given the end of the declaration, pretty good news. Who, having heard and reflected on such teachings, would not wish to undertake and practice them? As the Dalai Lama often says today, "All beings wish to have happiness and to avoid suffering. In this regard, we are all exactly alike, exactly the same." It should come as no surprise, then, that at this historic time in Buddhist history—when almost all the world's traditions of Buddhism are found together in one geographic space, the United States—that African Americans too would find Buddhist teachings attractive.

Many African Americans of my generation who later inclined toward Buddhism had already heard similar teachings in the words of Martin Luther King Jr. Striving to move this country closer to being a more just society, King and others had built the nonviolent civil rights movement around the principles of love, forgiveness, and interdependence.

Hearing these same principles and practices extolled in Buddhist teachings was like coming home.

When we learned the details of the Buddha's life, he became even more of an inspiration. Here was a man who actually, in practice, rejected the systemic oppression of his country's people by denouncing the caste, or *varna*, system of the Aryans (originally founded on color discrimination) and allowing all castes and women to enter his community of practitioners. Both actions were extremely radical—even revolutionary—for his time. Because of the Buddha's teachings and because of his own life example, many African American children of the civil rights movement have been finding their way to Buddhism.

Yet, as has so often been the case, we have been doing this without much fanfare or even recognition, once again being made almost invisible. Why is this the case? And, why is it important? We should, it seems to me, explore these issues.

According to a number of recent essays and reports, Buddhism is now one of the fastest-growing religions in the United States. In terms of adherents, it is said to rank either third or fourth behind Christianity, Judaism, and the "nonreligious," and has grown at a rate of 170 percent since 2000. The Pew Religious Landscape Survey published in 2008 said that people in the United States who say they are Buddhist account for about 0.7 percent of the total population (which translates into around 2 million followers), but a study by Wuthnow and Cadge suggests that at least 12 percent of the U.S. population—"as many as 25–30 million people—believe they have had some contact with Buddhists or with Buddhist teachings and thus have had the opportunity to be influenced by Buddhism."[198] Clearly, Buddhist ideas have affected many Americans, and some of them are African Americans.

In many ways, the history of Buddhism in America is a distorted and racialized one, with one group of people being extolled while other groups are disparaged or ignored. When we trace the roots of Buddhism's introduction to the United States only to the 1893 World Parliament of Religions, we ignore the fact that there were Chinese and Japanese Buddhists in this country decades before that event. The first groups of Buddhists were actually the Chinese who came to the West

Coast as menial laborers in the mines and on the railroads. In 1860, the California census showed that one out of ten California residents was Chinese. Around this time the Japanese also came to Hawaii and other West Coast states, bringing with them their respective forms of Buddhism. While these different forms caught the attention of some Euro-Americans, the Chinese and Japanese Buddhists themselves were not so warmly welcomed here. As Paul Numrich points out in *Buddhists, Hindus, and Sikhs in America*, "America's encounter with Buddhism began with a mixture of fascination and hostility."[199]

Contemporary discussions of American Buddhism still employ the outmoded "two-Buddhisms" model wherein a distinction is drawn between "Asian immigrant Buddhists" on the one hand and "American convert Buddhists" on the other. There is often said to be a gap between these two, each serving their respective, and different, religious constituents and goals.

Clearly, this model is too simplistic to account for who actually is an "American Buddhist." Moreover, there is a type of racism and essentializing at work here—one which sees all Asians as being alike, with no understanding of, or appreciation for, the great variety of distinctive cultures subsumed under this term or whether such immigrants derive from East, South, or Southeast Asia. It also sees no diversity within the convert Buddhists in America, who are generally characterized as being either Euro-American, elite, or white Buddhists. As an African American Buddhist, I do not see myself reflected here. While it is certainly true that a large majority of convert Buddhists in this country are homogeneously white, middle to upper-middle class, well educated, and, generally, liberal, there are some African Americans (as well as Hispanics and other so-called minorities) who are Buddhists too!

For some, thinking about African Americans and Buddhism may seem odd because they think that all African Americans are surely ardent members of Christian denominations. Such membership is cemented by the legacy of slavery and the spiritual and social uplift offered by the transformative message of antebellum evangelical Christianity. Some scholars have even suggested that the quiet meditative styles of Buddhist services are too sedate for people coming from such an exuberant background as the Black Church. However, having embraced the virtues of both traditions, I happily call myself a "Baptist-Buddhist."

For others, when African Americans and Buddhism are mentioned in the same breath they immediately conjure up the movie *What's Love Got to Do With It?* in which the singer Tina Turner's life is saved when she begins the chanting practices of Nichiren Buddhism through the Soka Gakkai organization. For these folk, Turner, and perhaps Herbie Hancock, are the only African American Buddhists they have likely ever heard about. Interestingly, however, when American convert Buddhist organizations and centers are mentioned, it is only this one, the Soka Gakkai, that is left out. For example, Don Morreale's *The Complete Guide to Buddhist America*, which lists well over one thousand Buddhist centers and groups, makes no mention of it at all. I believe we must ask ourselves why the sole Buddhist group in America with the most diverse makeup of practitioners is precisely the one that is not counted?

While I do not personally know any African Americans who are members of Soka Gakkai, I do know quite a number of African Americans who practice in and with a wide variety of other Buddhist traditions and sanghas in America. We African Americans have come to Buddhism—like other hyphenated Americans—because of books and education, because of movies, because, in some cases, of psychedelics, because of travel, because of the martial arts. We have come seeking spiritual wisdom, healing, and liberation from suffering. Some of us follow Tibetan traditions; some of us are Zen roshis. Some of us are Tibetan lamas; some vipassana teachers. Some of us wear robes and are ordained. Some of us are called "acharyas." Some of us teach at universities; others offer workshops at prisons, record music, or head dojos. Some have founded separate, African American–only meditation groups; some work at peace organizations. Recently, it seems, a number of us have taken to writing memoirs. We are in many ways as diverse as the different traditions of Buddhism that have made their way to the United States in the past 150 years.

As of yet, there are no studies that focus exclusively on African American Buddhists. No sociologist of religion has looked at the issue.

There are, however, individual African American Buddhists themselves who are writing about and speaking about their own journeys to, and with, the path of Dharma. In my memoir, *Dreaming Me: Black, Baptist and Buddhist*, for example, I write about my own story—from being raised in the Jim Crow South, to marching with King during the Birmingham civil rights campaign, to discovering Buddhism in college and meeting Tibetan Buddhists in India and Nepal. It is a book about crossing boundaries, finding methods that work, and returning home as a Baptist-Buddhist. Other African American Buddhists—like Charles Johnson, bell hooks, Alice Walker, angel Kyodo williams, Bhante Suhita Dharma, Lewis Woods, Jules Harris, Lori Pierce, Gaylon Ferguson, Earthlyn Manuel, Faith Adele, and Sister Jewel—have also written about Buddhism and the value of its teachings. At least two incarcerated African American men, Jarvis Jay Masters and Calvin Malone, have written powerful accounts of finding the Dharma while in prison.

And there are a good number of essays addressing the particular challenges presented by trying to practice Buddhism within the present structure of mostly white convert Buddhist centers as they've been established in the United States. The issues that are addressed in these writings are well worth reading about.

Since Buddhist practice offers us the chance to "sit" with our sufferings and to look deeply, we must begin with the recognition that, here in the United States, we sit in a country and within a society that is racially diverse and heterogeneous but which was founded by whites who received and thrived on power that was built on, and undergirded by, a system of slave labor. Recognizing this as fact, how do we who were harmed forgive and go forward? Conversely, how do we who were privileged by such circumstances recognize this and go forward? We need to find ways to allow our meditations to help us with this foundational, existential suffering and to move beyond it.

Given the history of this country and the development of convert Buddhist organizational structures here, we need to find ways to nurture more racially integrated sanghas. A steppingstone to this may be, ironically, having retreats of our own. Since 2000, a number of Buddhist retreats have been held which have been limited to people of color. I was invited to serve as a teacher at one such retreat, the 2002 African American Buddhist Retreat held at Spirit Rock Meditation Center in California. On the first day of the retreat, seated on the raised dais in front of seventy-five African American students, fourteen African American Buddhist teachers were introduced. Just as the introductions concluded, a woman who was also a teacher stood in a far corner of the meditation hall and sang, soulfully, the moving strains of "Amazing Grace." It was, indeed, a stirring welcoming of Buddhism coming to African Americans, coming home and taking root.

At this retreat I mentored a young African American woman who initially felt troubled that practicing Buddhist meditation might mean she was abandoning the Methodist tradition of her upbringing. At the end of the retreat, however, she informed me that she now believed Christian prayer was asking God for something, while Buddhist meditation helped one to hear His answer. Not bad!

The best way to make African Americans, and people of color generally, less anomalous in convert Buddhist centers throughout America is clearly to have more African Americans and people of color present and visible, and the best way to do this is to have African American teachers present. Ralph Steele, an African American psychologist in New Mexico and a vipassana teacher, has been saying this for a while. Many others agree with him.

In a recent interview, an African American woman and Nichiren priest, Myokei Caine-Barrett, spoke openly and directly about what's required to make Buddhism in America more inclusive. "I think outreach has to happen. Centers that are predominantly white need to become more educated about the challenges facing people of color. As a person of color, I've always faced people telling me that race is not an issue, or that I'm overreacting," she said. "It would help a great deal for sanghas to become educated about unaware racism, institutionalized racism, and internalized racism" so that no one's experience is negated simply because it isn't common to the entire community.

"Any community that wants to welcome diversity has to make sure diversity goes throughout the entire community—including teachers and administrators of color. It has to look like there's no difference;

YES, WE'RE BUDDHISTS, TOO!   137

and the reality has to be that there is no difference," she said. "If I truly believe that Buddhism is for everyone, then I have to act that way."

The issue of accessibility is the one that I worry most about. Given the way centers are set up here, getting the chance to study and practice with a bona fide lineage teacher requires leisure time and money. Working-class people don't have much of either to spare. So if Dharma centers really want to encourage diversity in their communities, they will have to put in the effort and the generosity required to invite and encourage people of color and working-class people to come in. Having found Buddhist teachings to be so helpful for me personally, and seeing their amazing potential to help suffering sentient beings everywhere—whatever their color—I want everyone to have access to them. The Buddha taught to all, equally. I'd like to see equal-access Dharma become the norm here in the States.

Part III
Tantric Buddhism and
Buddhist Saints' Lives

ন৵৽ ৵৽

The Life of Kyongru Tulku: An Example of Contemporary Tibetan Hagiography

❧ ❧

The child born in a small village in Khams, Tibet, in the late 1930s and given the name "Döndrup Tsering" was destined to be the eighth holding the title "Kyongru Tulku" (Skyong ru sprul sku; pronounced in the dialect of Khams, "Chong-ru Tulku"). As a Khampa, Döndrup is proud of his prestigious military heritage. Even his religious office and title echoed and exemplified this ideal: *kyong* (*skyong*) is the Tibetan equivalent of the Sanskrit term *pāla*, meaning "protector." As the Kyongru Tulku, Döndrup considered this role of protector the primary and sacred duty of his life. Indeed, it was in order to defend and protect more effectively the people of his area that he studied the Buddhist Dharma, concentrating on the tantras, medicine, and various rites of exorcism. Prior to his capture by the Chinese in 1959 and his subsequent imprisonment and torture, Döndrup La[200] saw himself as a religious warrior and as a protector of the downtrodden. I believe that he still does.

In 1980, at the age of forty-three, Döndrup no longer wore religious robes; nor did he enjoy the status and wealth associated with being a recognized tulku.[201] He escaped from the Chinese in 1964, but owing to certain events of his imprisonment had refused, once freed, to take up a strict monastic life again—on religious and moral grounds. When

I met him in Nepal in July 1980, however, his bearing was still striking. He remained eloquent, cultured, fun-loving, gentle, rugged, and strong. I spent several weeks with Döndrup recording the details of his remarkable life; and it is this "life" which serves as the central focus of this paper.

I.

Historians of religion have long been concerned with the study of what are termed the "sacred biographies" of the founders of religious traditions, and with the so-called hagiographies of lesser religious figures. Interest thus far has centered exclusively on ancient and classical written accounts of the lives of "holy" ones, and consequently the primary tools for such study have remained confined to the areas of text-critical research and other religio-historical methodologies. However, owing to the availability of a growing number of more or less "confessional" biographies now being narrated by contemporary religious figures—Eastern and Western—it seems clear that hagiographical studies must be broadened and that new methodologies must be either created or incorporated from other disciplines in order to address adequately the material of these contemporary biographical forms.

The academic study of "biography" per se, while relatively new, is still not a stranger to the fields of literature, history, psychology, and anthropology—though the focus for these disciplines is most often on secular rather than religious lives. Anthropological studies in particular have given us two important methodological approaches to biography—termed the "cultural models" approach and the "life history" approach, which in turn have exerted great influence on the way biography is dealt with in modern literary, historical, and psychoanalytic studies. The "cultural models" approach to biography views "lives" as expressions of a given culture's understanding of itself and as vehicles for portraying a culture's "ideal." The assumption here is that through a careful analysis of a given life, an inside view of a given culture can be gained. Thus Clifford Geertz, in a study of two Islamic leaders, could write: "These men are metaphors. Whatever they originally were or did as actual persons has long since been dissolved into an image of what Indonesians or Moroccans regard to be true spiritually."[202] And, taking the "cultural models" approach to its extreme, W. E. H. Stanner has suggested that among-so-called primitive peoples, life is often understood as a "one-possibility thing"[203] with little room for variation. Gregory Bateson provided a dramatic example of the latter position when he discussed what had occurred when he questioned a young New Guinean informant about his life. "The young Iatmul, aged seventeen, on being asked to describe his life, started with birth, went through childhood, adolescence, manhood and his advanced years, without indicating any awareness of his actual age. What the young man described was the prescribed course of his life, the life of man in a specific culture."[204]

The "cultural models" theory of biography has generated a number of other new approaches—for example, the search for the "primal myths" that nourish a given biographical tradition;[205] studies in recurring mythic and heroic patterns;[206] and the suggestion that some biographical patterns, being primarily psychological in nature, may be in fact transcultural.[207]

The second anthropological methodology mentioned above, the "life history" approach, has also added to our means of grappling with biographical forms.[208] In contrast with the "cultural models" approach, the "life history" approach emphasizes and highlights the diversity and individuality of biographies. In searching to reveal the uniqueness of an individual personality, it poses the problem of how one determines what is cultural pattern and what is true individual history. In its juxtaposing of culture and personality, the "life history" approach has carried over into psychoanalytic studies, notably those studies of deviance[209] and of genius.[210]

A man who did much to bridge the gap between these two models offered by anthropology was the psychoanalyst Ernst Kris, who, in his *Psychoanalytic Explorations in Art*, saw biography as "a literary category having a social function."[211] Kris's work focused on certain medieval and Renaissance biographies of artists and noted *both* (1) that there was an older biographical pattern/model that served as the basis for those biographies (which he called "enacted biographies"), *and* (2) that, owing to specific socio-historical phenomena, the pattern itself under-goes changes and developments. In short, he argued that "once the biographical pattern becomes known, younger would-be artists begin self-consciously to pattern their lives according to the biographical model. Thus, the pattern becomes constitutive of human life and not merely its consequence. However, as the pattern becomes constitutive, it also undergoes changes. . . ,"[212] in some cases assuming new depth, in others becoming trivialized. Historians of religion, I believe, would be well advised to keep Kris's work in mind as they attempt to bridge the transition from the classical written hagiographies to the contemporary narrations of religious personalities.

II.

From November 1979 until September 1980, supported by an NEH fellowship, I conducted research in Nepal on what may generally be called "sacred biography in the Tibetan Buddhist tradition." My work centered on two specific forms of such biography: first, a set of writ-ten accounts called in Tibetan *namthar* (an abbreviated form, meaning "complete liberation life-stories"), which describe the lives of six mid-fourteenth to mid-seventeenth-century Gelukpa tantric practitioners and, at the same time, sets forth for future practitioners the very course to enlightenment itself; and second, a set of six oral histories of con-temporary religious practitioners that I recorded on tape. This paper focuses on one of these contemporary oral accounts.

A brief overview of the other five contemporary informants may be helpful here:

(1) Pasang Tsering, a young shopkeeper in Bodhanath, aged twenty-four in 1980. Pasang's father was a Newari trader who had married a Tibetan woman from Chamdo and settled in Tibet. The family lived near the famed Ramoché (Ra mo che) Monastery on the outskirts of Lhasa. Because of its dual-citizenship, the family maintained relative freedom of movement, even following the events of 1959, and relocated in Nepal only in the early 1970s. I had met Pasang on a previous visit to Nepal in 1974. It was he who introduced me to Döndrup La and who

served as admiring (i.e., of Döndrup) and enthusiastic translator during my sessions with the latter.

(2) Ani-la Drölkar, an elderly nun. In 1980 she was sixty-two, having become a nun in Tibet at the age of twenty-seven. Ani Drölkar had left Tibet in 1954 at the urging of other family members then living in Nepal. Not connected with a nunnery in Nepal (there are only two active Tibetan Buddhist nunneries in the country, both with rapidly declining memberships), she lived in a room of her own with her brother's son and his family, near Asan Tol in Kathmandu. She wore the religious robes and continued her practices faithfully.

(3) Thubten Sonam, a forty-one year old monk at the Ganden Chöpal Ling (Dga' ldan Chos dpal gling) Monastery in Bodhanath. Originally from the region of Sakya, Sonam had taken part in the relocation of the entire monastery from Tibet to Nepal in 1959. Sonam had held many posts at the monastery. (He had been the cook there when I first met him in 1969, and, owing to him, my ties with this particular monastery had become very close.) In 1980 he was the general manager, or "keeper of the keys."

(4) Geshé Jampal Gyatso was one of five resident teachers at my own guru's establishment, the Nepalese Mahayana Gompa in Kopan, just on the outer rim of Kathmandu Valley. In 1980 he was forty-nine years old. He had been a monk at Sera Monastery in Tibet and had earned his geshé degree during the examinations held in Dharamsala, India, after becoming a refugee in 1959. He had taken a degree from the Sanskrit University and from the Tantric College as well.

(5) Losang Gedun, the reigning abbot of the Gelukpa Monastery at Bodhanath. The khenpo (*mkhan po*, abbot) hailed from Tsang Panam (Gtsang Pa snam) and, after becoming a monk at age seven, had entered the great Drepung ('Bras spungs) Monastic College at age twenty-five. In 1959 he, along with countless other monks, escaped to India. He lived at the Tibetan refugee camp at Buxaduar for "about twelve years" until he was relocated to the Tibetan settlement in Mundgod, South India. Abbots for the Gelukpa Monastery were sent in rotating shifts from Mundgod. Losang Gedun-la had served as abbot there for six years when I interviewed him in August 1980. Though his tenure was

up, he had said that rather than return to Mundgod, it was his wish to remain at that monastery. Everyone connected with the monastery spoke extremely highly of his great compassion. In April 1981 he passed away—at the monastery in Bodhanāth.

All six of the Tibetans I interviewed had at least three things in common—namely, (1) they were all practicing Buddhists, (2) they were all affiliated with the Gelukpa tradition of Tibetan Buddhism (Pasang and his family counted the Geluk monastery at Bodhanath their main monastic affiliation), and (3) owing to the Chinese occupation of Tibet, they had all become refugees in Nepal and were now carrying forth their lives in a new and difficult environment.

III.

The fact that five of my "informants" were trained in and stood squarely within the Geluk tradition encouraged me to suspect that they might also be conversant with the classical tradition of Geluk namthar, though at no point did I ever raise this as an issue with any of them. On the other hand, I felt confident that my own work with these older written materials might inform my work with the contemporary accounts. Indeed, I had assumed that there might well be similarities and continuities in the contemporary narrations and certain standardized/stereotypical conventions of the written genre. Especially with regard to the account narrated by Döndrup, this assumption was proven to be correct. However, what soon become apparent to me during our early sessions together was how unprepared I was (as a Westerner? as an "objective" scholar?) for the numerous uncanny, fantastic, and even mythic correspondences that actually *did* emerge between the two biographical modes.

The written genre of namthar contain a number of standard elements—many quite similar to Western hagiographies. For example, it is often the case that (1) the "life" begins in an earlier, even "mythic" time frame; (2) there are miraculous events accompanying the birth of the "saintly" one; and (3) the child is precocious and seems, from the beginning, destined for his or her future religious role. There then follows a fairly detailed description of the saint's (4) religious training and education; (5) meditative retreats; 6) personal "mystical" experiences that "seal" his or her attainment; followed by (7) the description of his or her "good works" for humankind; and lastly (8) the events surrounding the saint's death.

Needless to say, none of my informants' narratives reached the final stage demarcated above. Moreover, modesty and Buddhist selflessness (*shunyata*; here, *atmanairatyma*) precluded their describing items 6 and 7 (though these were on occasion supplied by others in the community).

THE LIFE OF DÖNDRUP, THE KYONGRU TULKU

It should be noted that during our very first session, Döndrup spent most of the time talking about his capture and subsequent treatment by the Chinese. This subject, in fact, occupied a large part of our discussions. A review of the eight sessions I recorded from Döndrup (totaling some nineteen hours of narration) shows that close to five hours were devoted to the Chinese alone. I will speak of Döndrup's experiences with the Chinese later, and begin here with what occupied our second, third, and sixth sessions together.

During our second meeting, after explaining to Döndrup that I wished to record as much of his "life" as he'd care to tell, I suggested that he might begin by telling me about his childhood, and that his memories of his father, for example, might be a good place to start. Seeming thoroughly at ease with the Uher tape recorder in front of him, he began his narration. What follows is, in part, what he narrated at that second session:

> I see you would like the story of myself from childhood, right? At the beginning I should tell you about my family lineage (*kyekhung*). Well, as for that, my father's lineage is that of *Derma, Ling Derma*. At the beginning there was a father with four sons in our region. These five were known to be very helpful to all who were kind to them. They especially loved the poor and powerless (*nyenchung*) and were able to

protect and fight for them against anyone who sought to harm them. So they seemed to have been. They were officially named by the central Tibetan government and became known as *ngawo* and *ngawo tsang*, that is, "mighty ones."

But no one (of that region) could tell who those five people were or from where they had come. At that time there was a very venerable lama called Penpa Tulku Rinpoché. Finally some representatives of the region approached this lama and asked him to do divination, saying, "there have arrived here five such people," and asking where they came from, etc. So, in the lama's divination, it was said, "Don't have any (hostile) dealings with these five. Don't bother them in any way; just let them do whatever they want to do." So the villagers did as the lama said, and without becoming enemies with them, they just let them do whatever they wished. Finally, what happened was, from Lhasa the central government had sent a district governor who had mistreated the people a lot, so what the father and his four sons did was become helpers of the people. They brought a case against him. They charged him, saying: "You are very bad, mistreating one's own subjects is very bad, though you are the government. Without subjects how are you going to be an *pönpo* (leader, etc.)?"

When this case was brought against the district governor, the father was arrested and plans were made to punish him. So the four sons killed the district governor.... When the governor was killed the central government arrested all five of them to be punished. They took the case to Chamdo, and there they were told: "You five are real criminals, killing the district governor of your own place; there is probably no one else like you who would do such a thing!" So they were told. They answered: "The district governor had to be killed because if one's place has enemies, anyone should oppose that."

Asked the government's response to this, Döndrup continued his narration by saying:

So the central government said: "If indeed he mistreated the
subjects like you say, then you cannot be blamed. To make
up for that we will respect the wishes of the people in this
regard. But subjects killing the district governor is a very serious crime." So as a punishment for this crime, the father was
appointed as a military leader in my area.

Later, what happened was that there was a war between
China and Tibet. The Chinese at this period were called
"Ho Ho." During this war, one of the five (sons?) became
a great leader . . . and when there was the war, the Chinese
were driven back from Lhasa as far east as Dergé, up to Dergé
Drichu.

When was that?

It was during the time of the Fifth Dalai Lama.

After a tea break, Döndrup continued:

Now, since the Tibetans won this war, the central Tibetan
government called the five to come up to Lhasa and said,
"Although I punished you, you were of great help to me.
Even though I am the king, my subjects have done something of great help for me. The fact that you have been able to
drive out the outside enemies was of great significance. You
five have done a great, powerful job.'"

As a reward for their valorous conduct, Döndrup reported that the
government awarded the five with "a great deal of land." They became
landowners, and one of them was appointed Chizong (Spyi rdzong) of
Chambo, that is, "governor general" of the area.

Here, I skip ahead a bit to the beginning of our third session. Döndrup began by "completing" some of his statements of the previous
session:

Now this father of the four sons, every year during special religious or auspicious days, would get lost (disappear) for a day or two. When he returned he would have feathers all over his clothes and from the shoulders.

I questioned: "Feathers growing from him, or because he stayed at places where there were birds or feathered creatures?" Döndrup continued:

Feathers sort of grown on him naturally . . . because it was like this: on auspicious days when there was no war or sickness in the country and when he was happy he would become a vulture or eagle, and in this way wander all over the country. . . . What we Khampas call this is *pawo* and *pamo* (i.e., the masculine and feminine forms of the noun). The *pamo* is roughly like the Nyingma's Khandroma. Anyway, that one's [the father's] flesh and bone lineage is said to be that of Derma of Ling (Gling). Of many brave ones of Ling, Derma and Gukyé Pön ('Gu skye pon) were the chief ministers of King Gesar.[213]

Astonished, I sat motionless as Pasang added, or presumably translated:

That father's former reincarnation was minister to King Gesar. Whenever he was ordered to search out any place he could go to it, in a second.

Trained anthropologists often remark that they have found themselves, in spite of prior preparation, ill-prepared once actually in the field. I am sure I cannot adequately convey how ill-prepared I felt for these two early "encounters" with Döndrup. Having asked about his father, I had not only been transported back to the seventeenth century (i.e., the time of the Fifth Dalai Lama), but also found that I was now in the company of a man who, sitting just across from me, was telling me of a forefather who served in the army of King Gesar. Here we had actually reached *mythic* time!

I have thought much about these two sessions since. What does one do when confronted with accounts seemingly so fantastic? I had often come across such descriptions in the written namthar. But this man sat right across from me! Of course, I continued to return, tape recorder in hand, for more sessions; for it seemed certain that at the very least, this narration *had to be* continued.

At the beginning of our next meeting, I asked Döndrup—almost in desperation and in fear (of my own loss of "reality"?)—to try to focus more on this very reincarnation, on this life, and his parents of this present birth. I asked him to relate how he, himself, had come to be "recognized" as the Kyongru Tulku. What he related was as follows:

> "How I myself was tested by my parents at the beginning was like this: First when I was just barely able to speak a little, listen a bit, and eat things on my own, one day for some reason of misbehavior, my father slapped me on the cheek. When that happened I got angry, and while reaching out for a tea cup (a blue and white one brought from China) to drink tea, I closed the rims on the cup like a (cotton) bag when I held it in my hand. This was the first significant sign."
>
> "How old were you then ?" I asked.
>
> "Probably around seven, so I remember. At that time I had probably been taught the alphabet, nothing at all about religion and such; but because the previous reincarnations had practiced the Dharma, that was the reason I showed a unique and wondrous sign. That was the reason."
>
> "Do you remember that event?" I asked.
>
> "Yes, some. For example, I remember holding the cup like this."
>
> "Weren't you surprised?"
>
> "I didn't myself think it surprising; I don't remember being surprised. But in our Buddha Dharma, as to how profound and deep it is and how lamas and geshés become well

known takes place through the observations (and show) of such feats. . . . Then, there were many other signs too. Later they came to search for my reincarnation. My parents knew it was me but they hid me away. They knew because of the cup instance; and also I had hung a pair of boots on the rays of the sun—and such wondrous signs. But I was not given away right away."

We spent a few minutes in attempts to make sure that Döndrup did in fact mean "sun rays." He did. At the conclusion of this session, I was not only uneasy, but unnerved.

During our sixth session, Döndrup explained the meaning of his tulku name as follows:

> This name, which is *Kyongru,* is registered (since the seventeenth century) in the hand of the Tibetan government. *Ru* is one's own "bone lineage."[214] *Ru* (bone) is important. My bone (lineage) was considered very exceptional (i.e., as exceptionally "high"). Tulku is the term for reincarnate lama. As to *Kyong,* it has a lot of meanings. If one explained all the meanings, there would be a lot to explain. (But) for example, *Kyong* means someone who looks after the poor and who does not take bullying from other powerful families."

His ordination name was Khyenrab Dorjé (Mkhyen rab rdo rje). As to his given name, he said:

> "Döndrup Tsering" is my lay name, given to me by my parents. The reason I was given this name was because my father's family had become rather poor owing to many law cases and an inability to look after (our) land and property, combined with the big responsibilities the government had given us. Because of all this the family was having a tough time. But even when I was yet to be born and was merely in my mother's womb, from the time I was conceived my family had a lot

of good luck and everything worked out well. Before I was conceived, my family had really hard times. So "Döndrup" means the attainment of all goals no matter what, and this was the case for my family after I was conceived. "Tsering" of course means "long life." So I was named "Döndrup Tsering."

One is reminded here of the first two (of six) elements suggested by Otto Rank's typology of the structure of hero-myths,[215] that is, (1) the hero is the child of distinguished parents, and (2) his origin is preceded by difficulties, such as the continence, prolonged barrenness, or secret intercourse of the parents.

Much in keeping with the general pattern of hagiographies, Döndrup continued his narration with the following:

> On the day when I was born, my mother saw a completely white cock[216] on the family hearth. This was very unusual because we had never kept chickens and no one had seen any in this household before. And when the neighbors in the surrounding areas looked at my house, they saw rainbows rising on the roof of our house from all four directions. So others had seen and everyone wondered why. Then there was an old man in the village who told all the young people that a child was born in that house that day and that the child must have been a reincarnation of a lama. That man was not of my family, but he explained the situation to others like this, saying that there had been a lineage lama born in my family. Also there was behind our family house a big meadow. Before I was born, the meadow was dry and all water became scarce in the valley. But after I was born, everything became green again and colorful flowers grew everywhere, even during the winter.

And:

> It seems from the time I was old enough to think, I had told my mother that I was the reincarnation of a previous lama.

When I said this, my mother scolded me, saying, "This kid, even though he still can't talk properly, is talking about being a rebirth of a previous lama. What a loud-mouth he is! And, as I remember, by the time I was old enough to play, other children were always attracted to me. . . . Whatever snacks my parents gave me I would take out and share them with the others. Such was my nature. . . . And whenever I could steal *tsampa* from home, I would take that out, make *torma* (offering cakes), and arrange them on flat stones. Then, with imitations of drum beating and the like, I would pretend, always imitating being a lama.

As mentioned earlier, it was not that I had not read of such amazing feats or "signs" in the ancient written namthar. In fact, I had spent the months just prior to my interviewing Döndrup translating accounts that were replete with them. Nevertheless, the actual fact—the reality—of talking personally to someone who claimed such feats, however modestly, as *his own*, made me personally uneasy; and there were to be other uneasy moments, though space does not allow me to describe these in detail here. The issue I raise here might best be described as the problem of the *disjuncture of cultures*. I had expected to see similarities and carryovers between the sacred biographies as written and as narrated; between the textual data and living data. But when these similarities *did* dramatically appear, I was surprised, ill-prepared, and even frightened to recognize or give full credence to them.

"In the field," all my Western biases were immediately called into play. If I were going to continue to work with Döndrup, I had to "make sense" of what he was doing when we met for a taping session. In Nepal, I told myself that these fantastic stories had been told to Döndrup by his parents and teachers as part of the lore surrounding and justifying the fact of his tulku-ship. I formulated such rationalizations in spite of the fact that Döndrup himself said that *he remembered* the "crushed cup," "boots over sun rays," and other above-mentioned events. Even now, many months later, as I review the transcripts of our talks in their entirety, I have the strong inclination to say that Döndrup was a master storyteller. Indeed, at many points in our sessions, with the glee of childish delight and excitement, he told me stories—of the origins of certain Buddhist deities, and other humorous stories regarding Tsong-khapa and his early disciples.

Now, Tibetans generally greatly cherish the art of storytelling; and they highly prize what we might call the "gift of gab." The many difficul-ties of the language—namely, its cumbersome orthography, hierarchi-cal divisions, and numerous dialectical variants—make its mastery a feat applauded by all. (It is said of the present Dalai Lama, for example, that his is the most erudite speech among all Tibetans. "High" monks have told me that often even they are incapable of understanding perhaps as much as 80 percent of it; but this is said with much admiration. Robert Ekvall's novel *The Lama Knows*[217] goes a long way toward capturing the Tibetans' admiration of eloquence and their love for storytelling.)

Now, I should clear up here the possible misconception that I am saying that Döndrup was not telling me the truth. I had occasions to confront him on discrepancies regarding dates, spellings of names, and other matters about which I had some knowledge, but we always man-aged to settle these agreeably. But regarding the episodes related above I can only admit the uneasiness for me of being confronted with the possibility that they might very well be true!

In his recent book *Tuhami, Portrait of a Moroccan*, the anthropolo-gist Vincent Crapanzano presents on the first few pages an episode nar-rated to him by his friend and interviewee, Tuhami, wherein Tuhami describes his early life working as a sort of guard and lookout for a wealthy man's sexual forays with numerous women. We then learn that Tuhami himself "was married to a capricious, vindictive she-demon, a camel-footed *jinniyya*, a spirit, named A'isha Qandisha, who kept a firm control on his amorous life." Crapanzano then writes the following:

Tuhami was an illiterate Moroccan Arab tilemaker, and I am beginning my portrait of him with this fragment from his personal history because it raises the question of his, of any, personal history. I have been unable to integrate it into the narrative text of his life. I am unable to omit it. It resists integration because it probably never took place. It sounds more like a fragment from some *Arabian Nights* than the recollection of a contemporary Moroccan worker. It precludes omission because it speaks a truth that can only be called autobiographical.

It was Tuhami who first taught me to distinguish between the reality of personal history and the truth of autobiography. The former rests on the presumption of a correspondence between a text, or structure of words, and a body of human actions; the latter resides within the text itself without regard to any external criteria save, perhaps, the I of the narrator (Frye 1976). Their equivalence is, I believe, a Western presumption.[218]

This comes as close as I know to it.

DÖNDRUP AND THE CHINESE

As previously noted, not all of Döndrup's narration consisted of what might be termed "fantastic occurrences" of "signs." In fact, a good deal of time was focused on his direct experiences with the Chinese. Our very first taping session was devoted almost entirely to this subject, and in place of our fifth session, Döndrup requested to "speak alone into the recorder." This narration, which lasted well over three hours, dealt solely with his views regarding the wrongful takeover of Tibet by the Chinese, of their subsequent misdeeds, and their ideological inconsistencies. As an important facet of Döndrup's "life," the impact of the Chinese cannot be omitted from its telling.

Considering the possibility of doing a book that included his "life," Döndrup said, "I hope you will do it properly, without omissions," and immediately added, "On the one hand, if one practices religion, that is (good) on behalf of all sentient beings; on the other, if one talks honestly, from a political point of view, that is also religion."

Döndrup had been captured by the Chinese just one day prior to his completion of a three year meditative retreat on the deity Jikjé '(Jigs byed). He had been imprisoned and tortured. He reported having been hung up by his thumbs with his feet barely touching the floor. When his shoulders dislocated, they were popped back into their sockets and he was again hung up. (He showed me the scars encircling his thumbs.)

He had been kept in a group with some 250 other tulkus and former Tibetan officials at a prison at Drapché Thang in Lhasa. (This group had later been sent to Nyenchen Thang Lha [Gnyan chen thang lha][219] to work at mining and other hard labor for well over two years.) He was subjected to "fight struggles" and other abuses. He witnessed his group of fellow prisoners dwindle from 250 to 18 at the end.

Throughout Döndrup's accounts of his imprisonment, there are episodes where he defended a fellow prisoner or spoke up in one's behalf in spite of the danger to himself. He said he did so because he was usually the youngest in his various groups, because he was strong, and because there seemed to be little hope of their survival anyway.

But Döndrup did manage to escape in 1964 due to the aid of one of the Chinese. The account of the escape is interesting because of the blending it evidences of several elements: the dramatic, the political, and the religious:

> Later, out of 250 people, only 18 of us were left. The others were all killed. As for the 18 of us, we were all lamas (*dge bshes* and *sngags pa*,[220] etc.). Then around 9 or 10 o'clock one night, one Chinese leader came and saved us. He killed the guard and took us out with him. We wondered why, and said to ourselves, "We are probably going to be killed this night." Some said we were going to be thrown into the river; some said other things.
>
> I said, "Whatever the case, just pray to Könchok Sum (*Dkon mchog gsum*)[221] for the long life of the Dalai Lama, and for the attainment of happiness for the people of Tibet." I thought, "this man probably is trying to save us, judging from the good dreams I had last night." Dpal ldan lha mo[222] came in person and told me, "I shall save your lives," and gave me a white skull full of blood. "This is the blood of only the

Chinese. You drink it without any hesitation." I did as I was told. So while we were being taken away, I told the others this story.

Finally we were taken to an isolated place and asked what we were thinking. We said, "We have nothing else to say, except that out of the 250 of us, most of us have been killed, so we feel we too are to be killed. That is all we think. But before we die give us the chance to say three words of prayers." This I said. For, among all of us, I was the youngest, the most reckless, and the "fastest mouthed" (i.e., articulate).

He (the Chinese leader) said, "Well, I do not intend to do anything bad. You probably realize this. So tonight do not shout or anything like that, and don't go anywhere, just stay put here." Then he left, and after two hours came back with six guns complete with enough bullets. He asked how many could shoot guns, and two monks from Gaden could. So that is how he saved our lives and brought us to Mon Tawang (northeast India).

Conclusion

Though I have only been able to sketch it in part here, the "life" of Döndrup Tsering, the eighth Kyongru Tulku, is most remarkable. It is a narration of a contemporary life, but one in which the past figures as prominently as the present, and in which the standardized conventions of the ancient namthar seem to inform and impact on the present form at every point. Still, there is a sense in which the "life" is much more.

In many respects the "cultural models" approach of anthropology seems applicable to Döndrup's narration. A continuous thread does seem to unite the whole of the life, namely, the motif of the "heroic and religious warrior." If there is a "primal myth" to be unearthed here, it is this one. However this model also has limitations. While it provides a vehicle for drawing together the various elements of a "life" as complex and multivalenced as this one, it also necessitates deletions that may well have important consequence.

Döndrup's "life" is one centered squarely within the sacred biographical mode—with all its myth, wonder, and power. At the same time it
moves beyond these into the present age when Tibetans and Tibetan
religieux have been forced to come face to face with political and social
upheaval. Might not these recent historical events cause a change in
the content and form of the traditional biographical mode? Ernst Kris's
observations seem apropos here.

In 1957, David Snellgrove concluded the Preface to his *Buddhist
Himālaya* with the following assessment:

> My own general estimate of the nature of this religion is in
> the last resort derived not so much from the careful study
> of texts and balanced weighing of evidence, as from direct
> perception into the personalities of a few Tibetans, whom I
> have known closely. In this respect orientalists may well have
> a considerable advantage over the students of the Western
> classics, for it is still possible for us to meet with genuine rep-
> resentatives of the ancient traditions. Perhaps one should say
> just possible, for before this century is finished, there may be
> none left at all.[223]

Especially now, when some Tibetans are narrating their life stories,
historians of religion and students of Tibet and its people are indeed
favored with the rare opportunity of learning firsthand about the
nature of Tibetan culture and religion, about what it is and what it may
become. In this most worthy of endeavors, I wish them, and myself,
success.

II

On the Nature of Namthar:
Early Gelukpa Siddha Biographies

᳅ ᳅

In this paper I attempt to do two things. First, I seek to give a general definition of *namthar* and to indicate how, as a genre of a religious literature, it both compares and contrasts with Western hagiography. Second, I offer an example, taken from the biography of the Geluk Drupchen Chökyi Dorjé (Dge lugs Grub chen Chos kyi rdo rje), of how some namthar go beyond Western hagiography to present actual descriptions of practice and instructions. As can be seen, both these points are related and address basic hermeneutical concerns.

I.

In the Tibetan Buddhist tradition written accounts of the lives of accomplished practitioners form a separate genre of literature. The genre is referred to as *namthar*, an abbreviation for *nampar tharpa*, which literally means "complete liberation." Such liberative life stories[224] are meticulously recorded, narrated, and studied not simply as biographical accounts chronicling the details of the lives of highly regarded persons but as accounts serving to make manifest that liberation by describing its process. Thus namthar serve both as inspirational and as instructional models for practitioners of the path. Because they are revered as having actually accomplished enlightenment using tantric means, "in one lifetime, in one body, even in these degenerate times," as the traditional tantric phrase goes, the subjects of such biographies are called *siddhas*—that is, "accomplished" or "perfected ones," "those who have succeeded" (from the Skt. root *sidh*, "to succeed," "to be successful"). Namthar, as the lives of Buddhist siddhas, may appropriately, if with some qualification, be characterized as sacred biography.

As Buddhism developed and reached into Tibet, the siddhas (*grub thob* or *grub chen*) provided the concrete links between Indian and Tibetan Buddhism since they were living examples of the veracity of the Vajrayāna. Thus in Tibet the genre of *namthar* became an invaluable means of establishing a demonstrable lineage of successful ones for each new school established, and this resulted in the rapid proliferation of such sacred biographies there.[225]

While it has been suggested above that the term *namthar* may be characterized as sacred biography—and it is to be noted that many Western translators use this term or the term "hagiography" itself when working with the Tibetan genre[226]—it must be pointed out that namthar present a rather unique kind of sacred life history, one not altogether parallel with other examples of sacred biography that may be familiar in the West. There are similarities and dissimilarities, and these need to be taken into account when we work with namthar material.

What is in the West generally termed "sacred biography," or "hagiography," refers primarily to that genre of literature developed by the early Christian tradition that focuses on the lives of the saints. As the early Church grew, and especially as it later expanded into pagan Europe, it developed a large corpus of hagiographical material chronicling the lives of its hero-saints.[227] Following the end of the intermittent and violent persecutions of Christians in the early centuries, the Church extended and further refined its definitions of the terms "saint" and "martyr" so that hagiography came to encompass many differing types of saints. In time the early Western Church actually developed a threefold definition of the term "martyr." For example, Clinton Albertson notes that "the seventh-century *Cambrai Homily* lists three kinds of martyrdom—white, green, and red. The first two refer to ascetical

mortification, the third to shedding of blood."[228] Later the Church
developed the new category of "confessor" and applied this term to all
those whose "pious living and persevering lives bore witness to Christ as
effectively as did the early martyrs' deaths."[229] Through special courts of
canonization, hundreds of new confessor-saints were added to Church
calendars. Confessors became the living lineage of followers who exemplified the fruits of lives devoted to Christ in much the same way as
the siddhas evidenced for Buddhists the effectiveness of the Vajrayana.
Moreover, in terms of narrative content, much of the hagiographical
material dealing with the later confessors is quite similar to Tibetan
namthar, and, one might argue, owing to similar reasons.

The early hagiographies of the confessors portray rugged and heroic
individuals whose utter commitment to their faith was meant to uplift
and inspire others. They are men and women who, having felt the "call
to Christ," enter His service. Usually after having publicly advanced
the faith by founding monasteries or stewarding large numbers of disciples, they bravely and willingly choose the hard, solitary life of the
contemplative; and to a few devoted followers they reveal their holiness
through the performance of miracles.

The Western scholarly tradition has generally taken a dim view of
hagiography. Indeed in the West hagiography has come to be defined
as "any idealizing or worshipful biography,"[230] the implication being
that such texts are naively exaggerated accounts written to edify a
devoted, though gullible, popular audience, and as a consequence
are of little historical worth. The two most common accusations
leveled against hagiography are that (1) there are numerous duplications of descriptions of holiness in them, and (2) there is a preponderance of miracles. Similar negative assessments are often lodged
against Buddhist namthar by Buddhist scholars who claim that they
too are "of no direct historical worth."[231] While most of the miracles
recorded in Western hagiography are of the nature of curing ill-
nesses, there are examples of other types that bear close resemblance
to the so-called worldly or mundane (*laukika*) siddhis ("powers")
possessed by siddhas—namely, reading others' thoughts, traveling in
unconventional ways, etc.[232] Moreover a confessor's birth is usually

accompanied by wondrous signs, just as is the siddha's. There are also other similarities.

There are also, however, important differences, and we as Buddhist scholars have to keep these in mind as we work with this material. Aside from the fact that Buddhism has no canonization courts to determine sainthood or, here, siddhahood, it would seem that Buddhist namthar differ from Western hagiography in at least one important way: unlike most hagiographies, namthar do more than just inspire and edify; they *instruct* as well, setting forth, albeit in veiled language, detailed descriptions of practice and instructions for future practitioners of the path.

II.

In Nepal in early 1980 I began translation work on a group of six namthar portraying the lives of some of the earliest Gelukpa Chakya Chenpo (*Dge lugs pa phyag rgya chen po*; Skt. *mahamudra*) practitioners.[233] These six practitioners, along with thirty other such lineage-holders, are found enumerated in the short Geluk liturgical text called *Dga' ldan bha' srol phyag rgya chen po'i 'khrid kyi bla brgyud gsol 'debs lkha skong bcas bzhugs/*—that is, "The Prayer (with Supplement) to the Lineage-Lamas of the Ganden Mahāmudrā Tradition."[234] The prayer's colophon declares that it was originally composed by the eighteenth-century Yongzin Yeshé Gyaltsen (Yongs 'dzin Ye shes rgyal mtshan, 1713–1792), and that the later, supplementary additions were made by the first Phabongkha Rinpoché, Dechen Nyingpo (Bde chen snying po, 1878–1941).

With regard to the lineage-holders enumerated, the vanguard is a three-membered group consisting of (1) the great Lord Vajradhara, patron Buddha of all Mahamudra adepts; (2) Arya Manjushri ('Phags pa 'Jam dpal [dbyaṅs]); and (3) Losang Drakpa (Blo bzang grags pa), the great Jé Rinpoché Tsongkhapa. Immediately following in succession from Tsongkhapa come the six Geluk siddhas (Tib. *grub thob* or *grub chen*) on whom my current studies primarily focus.[235] These are:

4. Tokden Jampal Gyatso (Rtogs ldan 'Jam dpal rgya mtsho, 1356–1428);

5. Baso Chökyi Gyaltsen (Ba so Chos kyi rgyal mtshan, 1402–1473);

6. Drupchok Chökyi Dorjé (Grub mchog Chos kyi rdo rje; Dharmavajra, dates?);

7. Gyalwa Ensapa (Rgyal ba Dben sa pa)—i.e., Losang Dönyö Drupa (Blo bzang don yod grub pa, 1505–1566);

8. Khedrup Sangyé Yeshé (Mkhas grub Sangs rgyas ye shes, 1525–1591); and

9. Jetsun Losang Chögyan (Rje btsun Blo bzang chos rgyan)— i.e., Losang Chökyi Gyaltsen (Blo bzang Chos kyi rgyal mtshan), the First Panchen (1570–1662).

Following these six siddhas, twenty-seven other lineage-holders are named, coming down to Phabongkha Rinpoché, H. H. Trijang Rinpoché, H. H. Ling Rinpoché, and ending with the mention of one's own kind root-guru (Tib. *drinchen tsawai lama*). The third siddha of the group, Drupchok Chökyi Dorjé, will be considered in some detail below, to exemplify the nature of these namthar in general.

As sources for the complete written accounts of the lives of the six siddhas I had recourse to two versions of the great compendium of Kadam/Gelukpa biographies compiled in the late eighteenth century (circa 1787) by Yeshé Gyaltsen and known under the title *Byang chub lam gyi rim pa'i bla ma brgyud pa'i rnam par thar pa rgyal bstan mdzes pa'i rgyan mchog phul byung nor bu'i phreng ba*. One version is a block-printed copy kept in the library of the Nepalese Mahayana Gompa of my own guru, Lama Thubten Yeshe, at Kopan, Nepal, and the second is an edited and abbreviated version found in vol. 5 of Khetsun Sangpo's *Biographical Dictionary of Tibet*.[236]

As can be seen from their dates, their six contiguous lives span some three hundred years of Tibetan religious history covering the most crucial period of the rise to power of the Yellow Hat school.[237] Through them one learns who knew whom, what places were frequented, where certain monasteries were founded, and why. Moreover, especially through this particular set of lives, one can observe fairly directly the intricate interweaving of politics and religion in Tibet during this period.[238] Lastly, these accounts help to clarify the distinctive ways in which the Geluk conceived of and actually practiced the Mahamudra meditative tradition.

A namthar, by presenting the significant experiences of a tantric adept in his or her quest for enlightenment, is first and foremost a piece of tantric literature. That is, in terms of content, sacred biographies of *siddhas* are comparable to and complement the tantras and their commentaries.[239] As such, one of the main functions of namthar is the imparting of actual descriptions of tantric practices. Viewed in this way, namthar are not simply vehicles for providing inspirational models, but vehicles for providing detailed practical instructions to persons seeking to put the particular teachings of a given *siddha* into practice.

All Tibetan namthar contain elements of what are actually three distinct levels of life story—namely, (1) *chi namthar*, the so-called outer biography that most resembles our Western notions of biography, presenting details of birth, schooling, education, specific teachers, and texts consulted; (2) *nangi namthar*, or inner biography, which chronicles the specific meditative cycles, initiations, etc., imparted to the future siddha; and (3) the *sangwai namthar*, or secret biography.[240] This last level or element of the narrative is said to describe the meditative or mystical visions and other experiences of the accomplished one. The first two levels of namthar are not problematic. It is from the third, the so-called secret biography, that most scholars have shied away, dubbing it "magical," or "fantastic," "folkloric," or "obscure."[241] My suggestion is to view this third level of namthar as actually providing detailed descriptions of practice and instructions.

As an example of this I cite here one episode from the namthar of Drupchok Chökyi Dorjé. Chökyi Dorjé is known in the Geluk tradition as a *vidyadhara*—that is, as one who not only attained enlightenment but who successfully won the siddhi of immortality as well. There are therefore no dates associated with him.[242] His parents were wandering ascetic (*ja dral, bya bral*). After the boy was born, near Tanak (Rta nag) Monastery in Tsang (Gtsang), the parents carried him along with them as they continued their sacred pilgrimages. When the three arrived at Ganden, the abbot Baso Chökyi Gyaltsen gave the parents money and other goods in exchange for the boy. He was given over willingly and with devotion, and going close to Baso, the young boy forgot everything of this life. Baso Jé gave him the complete teachings, especially those of the special oral tradition stemming from Tsonkhapa, the *snan rgyud* which shows the way to enlightenment in one life, together with initiations into the three chief Gelukpa deities, Guhyasamaja, Chakrasamvara-Heruka, and Vajrabhairava. His time with his Mahamudra teacher lasted five years, and then, with a vow to secrecy, Chökyi Dorjé took leave of Baso, went to study philosophy at Drepung, and became known as a greatly learned one, and as a great "holder of the vinaya." The account goes on to present a long song composed by Chökyi Dorjé out of devotion to his teacher; it shows him as continually meditating and doing extended retreats in numerous isolated places. There follows the description of his actual attainment of the ultimate siddhi of mahamudra followed by his choosing to remain in a "physical body" (Tib. *za ma tog*) until he is able to impart the complete instructions to the future *siddha* Gyalwa Ensapa. Until Gyalwa Ensapa reaches the age of seventeen Chökyi Dorjé gives instructions to countless *dakas* and *dakinis*, as well as to human disciples. After meeting Gyalwa Ensapa and imparting the teachings to him, Chökyi Dorjé dissolves his own physical body into the clear light and enters into what is called the "diamond rainbow body," whence, until this very day, according to the Gelukpa tradition, he continues to manifest whenever there is a sincere request for aid from any being living a pure and virtuous life.

Now let us look more closely at the description of the consummation of Chökyi Dorjé's practice. The text reads:

> In accordance with the words of advice of [Baso] Chökyi Gyaltsen, he [that is, Chökyi Gyaltsen] wandered to many solitary places—to lonely forests and ravines, as well as to snow [-covered mountains]. Then at one time during this period [as he meditated] near the sacred water of Pema Chan (Padma can), all the surrounding areas were suddenly

transformed, becoming in an instant like the actual twenty-four places [in India], while the earth surrounding the water itself turned into *sindhura* [a bright scarlet powdery substance consisting of red lead, or vermillion. In tantric practices involving the female yidam Vajrayogini, it is used to mark the "three doors" of body, speech, and mind of the disciple]. Thereupon at that famous spot he performed the contemplations on guru-yoga related to the Completion Stage, and he beheld the countenance of the King of Dharma, the great Tsongkhapa. It was then that Jé Rinpoché himself gave to this holy one the complete instructions of the ordinary and extraordinary oral tradition.[243]

Several features of this passage are intriguing. To begin with, the name of the supposed place[244] where this event occurred is of interest because the term *padma can*, or, literally, "having a lotus," is often an esoteric way of referring to a woman. ("Lotus" in such a context may mean the vagina.) The term *padma can*, in particular, is used to refer to a female sexual partner in certain tantric practices, particularly those of the *mahanuttarayoga* tantric category. While I am not prepared here to suggest that the Padma can of the Chökyi Dorjé account is a flesh-and-blood being (i.e., a *karmamudra*), I do think that, reading this passage as a tantric text, there is the strong implication that the seeming place name of Pema Chan is indicative of the completion-stage practice of using sexual union (whether actual or imaginary) as a means to higher insight.[245]

Next, the "twenty-four places": here I think there can be little doubt that the twenty-four places refer at once to the so-called outer pilgrimage places (cited in not a few tantras, where they are usually called *pithas* or *upapithas*, and are said to be the dwelling places for various groups of yoginis or dakinis—that is, female beings who give assistance to a tantric practitioner)—and also to the inner places yogically generated and located throughout an adept's body. The body-mandala of the long "Heruka (Chakrasamvara) sadhana" mentions these twenty-four places, and the theory of the twenty-four places is also found in the *Hevajra Tantra*.

Shin'ichi Tsuda has given a detailed analysis based on the *Hevajra Tantra* of the various correspondences among these external and internal pithas in his *A Critical Tantrism*.²⁴⁶ As with tantric literature and practices in general, the whole of ultimate reality, external and internal, is made manifest through an intricate and delicately balanced ordering of correspondences. These correspondences are expressed symbolically. As there are external pithas, so there are internal pithas. The external pithas have corresponding points on the vajra body once this is successfully generated by a tantric adept, such that the twenty-four sacred external places are matched with corresponding places on the body— namely, head, fingernails, teeth, ear, backbone, liver, shoulders, eyes, nose, penis, thighs, thumbs, knees, etc. Successfully generating the vajra body adorned with these twenty-four spots, the tantric practitioner is said to be able to coerce the dakinis of the external pithas to approach and enter the corresponding spots on his or her body. This again is symbolic, or intentional, language. To quote from Tsuda:

> "Internal *pīṭhas*" are abodes of veins (*nāḍīsthāna*, VII.3) as "external *pīṭhas*" are abodes of *ḍākinīs*. There are twenty four parts of a body such as "the head" corresponding to the external *pīṭha* Pullīramalya (VII.4.) etc. There are twenty four veins (*nāḍī*) which rely on these internal *pīṭhas* such as "(a vein) flowing through fingernails and teeth" (*nakhadantavahā*, VII.4.) etc. These veins (*nāḍī*) are regarded as deities (*devatā*, IX.21.), that is, *ḍākinīs*. A *nāḍī* is nothing other than a *ḍākinī*. . . .
>
> A human body is composed of these twenty-four "internal *pīṭhas*" such as "the head" (VII.4.) etc., as the world, that is, the *Jambudvīpa* in this case, is composed of twenty-four "external *pīṭhas*," i.e., twenty-four countries such as Pullīramalya, etc. An "internal *pīṭha*" is existent as long as it is an abode of a vein. A vein in turn is existent as long as it conveys a humour in it or it flows in an internal organ. Therefore, if one makes [the] twenty-four veins of one's own body *active*, through [the] yogic practice of making each of the

humours flow through the corresponding veins or each of
[the] veins flow through the corresponding internal organs,
he transforms his body into an aggregate of internal *pīṭhas* or
aggregate of *ḍākinīs*, a homologous miniaturization of the
world as an aggregate of external *pīṭhas* or an aggregate of
ḍākinī (ḍākinījāla). Thus he can unite himself with the ultimate reality on the basis of the Tantric logic of symbolism.[247]

One other element in the passage from Chökyi Dorjé's namthar
deserves mention—namely, the sacred water itself (Tib. *drupchu*).
Tibetan tradition says that there is a certain type of water found in
sacred caves in Tibet that is a kind of holy nectar. Padmasambhava,
the Indian siddha revered as having first firmly established Buddhism
in Tibet, is said to have given long-life initiations to his disciples using
such holy nectar.[248] Here again there is room for further elaboration
with respect to this *drupchu*. In tantric literature water is often a symbol
for the female or, more specifically, for menstrual blood.[249] The fact that
the earth surrounding the water is here said to turn to *sindhura* would
seem to have specific reference to the supreme dakini-consort, the Goddess Vajrayogini, chief consort to Lord Chakrasamvara, for marking the
disciple's three doors (i.e., forehead, throat, and heart) with sindhura
powder is a special feature of the initiation into the higher tantric practice of this particular deity (i.e., Vajrayogini) or of the pair of deities
(i.e., Chakrasamvara and Vajrayogini) in union. In fact it would seem
that this episode, using the veiled language of the tantras, narrates the
unfolding and the acting out in Chökyi Dorjé's own body of the Yoga of
the completion-stage techniques involved, in this case with the practice
based on the cycle of Chakrasamvara.

The above is an analysis of a brief and isolated event in a single
namthar. But other events similar in nature appear in the other five
Gelukpa lives with which I have worked. Studying these texts has
strongly suggested to me that approaching this literature in the manner
I indicate above may prove helpful. Treating a given namthar as a piece
of tantric literature intended to impart instructions to practitioners, in
addition to inspiration, can help us to glean valuable information about

the Vajrayana in general, and about specific tantric practices in particular. In this way Tibetan sacred biographies become less obscure, certainly less folkloric, and capable of providing us with a valuable entrée into the *lived* world of Tibetan tantric Buddhism.

Dakini: Some Comments on Its Nature and Meaning

❧ ❧

In the literature and tantric practice contexts of Tibetan Buddhism, the term *dakini* (Tib. *mkha' 'gro ma*) is fairly ubiquitous. Indeed, it occurs so often these days in Western translations of tantric texts that one expects it will soon be appearing in *The American Heritage Dictionary* along with such other recently incorporated commonplaces as "satori," "zen," and "mandala." Still, apart from the quite literal definition of the term—that is, as a feminine noun meaning "one who goes in the sky"—there remains little consensus about its meaning and, in my opinion, little precision in the various attempts to further delineate and characterize its nature and function.

Without doubt, *dakini* represents one of the most important, potent, and dynamic images/ideas/symbols within all of Tantra. Yet precisely owing to such dynamism and power, and owing to the all-encompassing nature of this symbol, it is almost impossible to pin it down or to limit it to a single definition. To do so is not the intention of the present essay. Instead, what I want to do briefly here is: first, to survey and review some of the diverse assessments of its meaning offered by scholars previously, and second, to suggest perhaps some new ways of thinking about it in a more holistic way.

Dakinis are said to be beings that are "tricky and playful:"[250] the term is thus sometimes glossed by translations like "sky-dancer"[251] or "sky-enjoyer."[252] They are often described as "wrathful or semiwrathful deities,"[253] though it is also recognized that they may have human (or other, animate or inanimate) form as well. In some contexts they are termed "demoniacal beings" and "witches."[254] One scholar seemed to like to call them "furies;"[255] others have referred to them as "sprites" and "fairies."[256] They have been called the "genii of meditation."[257] For tantric adepts, they are viewed as "messengers" or "prophetesses," "protectresses," and "inspirers." Additionally, they are at times regarded as *rikmas*, or "mystic consorts." And most inclusive of all, within Buddhist tantric contexts, *dakini* is viewed as the supreme embodiment of the highest wisdom itself. Embracing such wisdom, one becomes Buddha.

I believe it is this latter sense of *dakini*—that is, the embodiment of the highest wisdom and the symbolic concretization of the direct, unmediated, and nonconceptual experience of voidness (Skt., *shunyata*; Tib., *stong pa nyid*)—that makes the term so difficult to discuss. For in the ultimate, absolute, and final sense, "she" stands for ineffable reality itself. In a tantric universe replete with symbols, dakini, one may say, is *the* symbol par excellence; and being preeminently, constitutively, and inherently *symbolic*, the dakini always remains a symbol within the "Tibetan symbolic world."[258] As such, "she" serves always only to represent and suggest—even for the tantric adept—other and deeper, nondiscursive experiential meanings. Inevitably, then, "she" remains elusive to academic or intellectual analyses.

All this notwithstanding, a number of scholars (Western, Indian, and Tibetan) have offered various definitions, as well as symbolic and psychological interpretations, of the term. One extremely thoughtful analysis, by Nathan Katz, appeared in *The Tibet Journal*.[259] By way of review, I now turn to some of these.

1. DEFINITIONS AND ETYMOLOGIES

In 1895, L. Austine Waddell's classic study of Tibetan Buddhism called dakinis "furies," further defined them as being synonymous with

yoginis, and stated that both terms referred to "goddesses with magical powers."²⁶⁰ In his estimation, it was because such "goddesses and
she-devils were the bestowers of natural and supernatural powers and
were especially malignant [that] they were especially worshipped."²⁶¹ S.
C. Das's great *Dictionary*, which was finished shortly after that time,
defined *mkha' 'gro ma* as "a class, mainly of female sprites, akin to our
witches, but not necessarily ugly or deformed."²⁶² He went on to further
delineate two types of such beings: "those still in the world and those
that have passed out of the world," and to include a group called the
"goddesses of wisdom" (*ye shes kyi mkha' 'gro ma*) in the latter class.²⁶³

Some six decades later David Snellgrove would write the following,
giving a much fuller description of *dakini*:

> Especially associated with Uḍḍiyāna is a class of feminine
> beings known as ḍākinī. There is frequent reference to them
> in the tantric texts, where they appear as the partners of the
> yogins, flocking around them when they visit the great places
> of pilgrimage. Their presence was essential to the perfor-
> mance of the psycho-sexual rites and their activities generally
> are so gruesome and obscene as to earn them quite properly
> the name witch. They enter Tibetan mythology in a rather
> more gentle aspect, and ceasing altogether to be beings of
> flesh and blood, they become the bestowers of mystic doc-
> trines and bringers of divine offerings. They become the
> individual symbols of divine wisdom with which the medi-
> tator must mystically unite, and although iconographically
> they retain their fierce and gruesome forms, in such a con-
> text witch seems rather a harsh name for them. The Tibetans
> translated the name as sky-goer (mkha-'gro-ma) [khan-
> droma], which Mr. Evans-Wentz regularly translates as fairy,
> but this scarcely does justice to their composite character.²⁶⁴

Snellgrove's description is certainly fuller, incorporating many of the
ideas mentioned here earlier, while indicating still others.

A more recent study by Martin Kalff informs us further about the dakini's pre-Buddhist origins, as well as "her" early iconographic representations. Kalff writes:

> The Ḍākinīs alluded to here [i.e., in the *Cakrasaṃvara Tantra*], female aspects of the enlightened Buddha, have to be differentiated from a lower type of Ḍākinī, a class of harmful female demons who feed on human meat. The relationship between the two types of Ḍākinī is suggested by the fact that the lower unenlightened type represents a remnant of a pre-Buddhist form which, with the ascendancy of Tantra, became integrated into Buddhism.[265]

Continuing his description of these "pre-Buddhist" demonic dakinis, Kalff notes:

> An example of the demonic type of Ḍākinī can be found in the *Laṅkāvatāra Sūtra*. In that text the one who eats meat is threatened with the following words: From the womb of Ḍākinī he will be born in the meat-eaters' family and then into the womb of a Rākṣasī and a cat; he belongs to the lowest class of men.
>
> Here the Ḍākinī is mentioned in the same breath with a Rākṣasī, another type of meat-eating female demon who haunts the cemeteries. The Ḍākinīs, too, are at home in the cemeteries. They are very well described in a biography of Padmasambhava which includes his visit to eight cemeteries in eight different regions.[266]

Again, detailing his description of the "gruesome" iconographic depiction of these dakini, Kalff quotes from Eva Dargyay's dissertation on the *Mataraḥ* and *Ma mo*. Kalff's English translation of Dargyay's German reads as follows:

And there is the uncountable host of Ḍākinīs. Some of them
with loose hair ride on lions, in their hands they raise up the
skull and the nine-pointed emblem of victory. Some of them
are mounted on birds and they scream. In their hands they
hold the lion's emblem of victory. Some of them have one
body and ten faces. They eat intestines and hearts.[267]

In such ways are the "pre-Buddhist" dakinis described. Within Buddhism, however, a change occurs, and the dakini's nature is softened
and transformed. One may recall here, for example, that Padmasambhava's "journey to Tibet" is narrated almost solely in terms of his "tam-
ings" and "subjugations" of various "demons" in route, the bulk of them
female.[268] Following each such "taming," that demonic spirit-being
pledges to aid and support the new religion, that is, Buddhism. Thence,
the dakini is viewed as a helper and an ally to the Buddhist cause. Now,
as descriptions of "Buddhist" dakinis, we hear definitions like the following: "Dakinis, [or] female sky travelers, [are] the Tantric Goddesses
who protect and serve the Tantric Doctrine. They are not invariably
enlightened beings; there are many so-called Worldly Ḍākinīs . . . who
are still bound in Saṃsāra."[269]

What then, one may ask, of the term's precise etymology? The Sanskrit term may have derived from a root meaning "to fly,"[270] but as the
term is normally defined in the Sanskrit (at least as evidenced by most
of the Purāṇic literature), it refers to the "female attendants of Kali,"
who are said moreover to "feed on human flesh."[271] The Tibetan etymology certainly softens this portrayal of dakini! In Tibetan, the equivalent
for the term ḍākinī is composed of three syllables: mkha', meaning "sky"
or "space" (Skt. akasha); 'gro, a verbal contraction meaning "to go"; and
ma, a feminine particle marker. Hence, the compound term in Tibetan
could justifiably be translated as "sky-goer" or "she who goes in the sky."
Still, this does not fully explain the term.

I now cite three interpretations by Western scholars who attempt to
offer further clarification of the Tibetan etymology. Herbert Guenther
offers the following gloss: "The Tibetan explanation of the word for
'sky,' 'celestial space' is a term for 'no-thing-ness' (stong pa nyid) (Skt.

shunyata) and 'to go' means 'to understand.' The Ḍākinī is therefore an understanding of no-thing-ness."[272] According to Anagarika Govinda,

> *mkha'* means "space" as well as "ether," the fifth element . . . in other words, that which makes *movement* possible . . . and makes form appear without being itself movement or appearance. . . . *Hgro'* means "to go," "to move about." According to popular conception a *Khadoma* is therefore a heavenly being of female appearance (as indicated by the suffix *ma*), who partakes of the luminous nature of space or ether, in which she moves.[273]

Again, James Robinson, in a description that is perhaps too anthropomorphic, comments: "The Tibetans render dakini as *mkha' 'gro ma*, 'the sky-walking woman.' But the idea of 'sky' was interpreted as standing for 'emptiness,' and 'walking' is equivalent to 'understanding,' so that the dakini is 'the woman who understands emptiness,' that is to say, the feminine embodiment of wisdom."[274]

SYMBOLIC AND PSYCHOLOGICAL INTERPRETATIONS

Individual terms function in contexts, and it is within such contexts that they take on life and meaning. (One is reminded of Wittgenstein's famed maxim that "the meaning of a word is its *use* in the language."[275]) Definitions and etymologies are useful only to a point. To begin to see what the term *ḍākinī* means, we need to see it in action, in context; that is to say, to see how it functions—as narrated in siddha biographies, as enacted in tantric ritual, and as depicted in tantric art.

First, it is necessary—even if only briefly—to investigate its function in actual texts—that is, what one scholar has called the role the dakini plays in the "spiritual imagery" of Tibetan tantric texts.[276] As Katz rightly noted, among the chief sources for such an investigation are the biographies (Tib. *namthar*) of the siddhas (tantric adepts who are famed for having attained enlightenment in their lifetimes by using tantric means). Such texts are replete with mentions of the dakini, and the stories they narrate are told and retold throughout the Tibetan world of practice. Undoubtedly, one of the most famous stories is that which narrates the episode of Naropa's encounter with the grand dame of all dakinis, the great Vajrayogini. As wonderfully translated by Guenther,[277] this story goes as follows:

> Once when 'Jigs-med grags-pa [Jikmé Drakpa] (Abhayakīrti [=Nāropa]), with his back to the sun, was studying the books on grammar, epistemology, spiritual precepts, and logic, a terrifying shadow fell on them. Looking around he saw behind him an old woman with thirty-seven ugly features: her eyes were red and deep-hollowed; her hair was fox-coloured and dishevelled; her forehead large and protruding; her face had many wrinkles and was shrivelled up; her ears were long and lumpy; her nose was twisted and inflamed; she had a yellow beard streaked with white; her mouth was distorted and gaping; her teeth were turned in and decayed; her tongue made chewing noises and licked her lips; she whistled when she yawned; she was weeping and tears ran down her cheeks; she was shivering and panting for breath; her complexion was darkish blue; her skin rough and thick; her body bent and askew; her neck curved; she was hump-backed; and, being lame, she supported herself on a stick. She said to Nāropa: "What are you looking into?"
>
> "I study the books on grammar, epistemology, spiritual precepts, and logic," he replied.
>
> "Do you understand them?"
>
> "Yes."
>
> "Do you understand the words or the sense?"
>
> "The words."
>
> The old woman was delighted, rocked with laughter, and began to dance, waving her stick in the air. Thinking that she might feel still happier, Nāropa added: "I also understand the sense." But then the woman began to weep and tremble and she threw her stick down.

"How is it that you were happy when I said that I understood the words, but became miserable when I added that I also understood the sense?"

"I felt happy because you, a great scholar, did not lie and frankly admitted that you only understood the words. But I felt sad when you told a lie by stating that you understood the sense, which you do not."

"Who, then, understands the sense?"

"My brother."

"Introduce me to him wherever he may be."

"Go yourself, pay your respects to him, and beg him that you may come to grasp the sense."

With these words the old woman disappeared like a rainbow in the sky.

(It has been my experience that whenever I have asked a lama to explain to me the nature and meaning of the term *ḍākinī*, he has answered, first, by narrating this particular story!)

Guenther, applying Karl Jasper's term, has called dakinis "ciphers of transcendence."[278] In the Introduction to his translation of Naropa's namthar he posits his own interpretation of the above passage:

The vision which induced Nāropa to resign from his post and to abandon worldly honours, was that of an old and ugly woman who mercilessly revealed to him his psychological state.... All that he had neglected and failed to develop was symbolically revealed to him as the vision of an old and ugly woman. She is old because all that the female symbol stands for, emotionally and passionately moving, is older than the cold rationality of the intellect which itself could not be if it were not supported by feelings and moods which it usually misconceives and misjudges. And she is ugly, because that which she stands for has not been allowed to become alive or only in an undeveloped and distorted manner. Lastly, she is a deity because all that is not incorporated in the conscious mental makeup of the individual and appears other-than and more-than himself is, traditionally, spoken of as the divine. Thus he himself is the old, ugly, and divine woman, who in the religious symbolism of the Tantras is the deity rDo-rje phag-mo [Dorjé Phakmo] (Vajravārāhī) and who in a psychological setting acts as "messenger" (pho-ña).[279]

The siddha biographies give us numerous other examples of the "play" of the dakini. Another example of the dakini as shock therapist is provided by the namthar of Abhayakaragupta. As translated by B. N. Datta, the pertinent passage reads as follows:

> Once, as he was sitting in the court of [a] temple cloister, there appeared a young maiden who dragged on a piece of beef near to him which was dripping in blood, shoved it to the ācārya and said: "I am a Candāla [out-caste] maiden, but eat what is slaughtered for you." But he answered: "I am a Bhiksu of purer order. How shall I eat meat which is extraordinarily offered to me?" But she sank back and disappeared in the court below. That was again Vajrayoginī who gave him the Siddhi, but he did not take it.[280]

Like Nāropa (in later sections of his namthar), Abhayakaragupta here missed his chance to attain special power and insight even though the dakini offered him the opportunity (read: "chance," "moment," or "space") in which to do so. The dakinis burst upon the scene (here, consciousness) at any moment, to test, to shock, to "stop the [habitual] world"[281] of the future siddha. Thus they may be said to function as "tricksters."

As "messengers" they are often also "triggers," "instigators," or "inspirers." Again, as Katz has noted, "the influence of the *mkha' 'gro ma* is virtually [a] universal [motif] in *rnam thar* to mark the 'turning-point' stage."[282] "Her" appearance catches the future siddha's attention and creates a space in which old habitual patterns are either mildly called into question or shattered completely. Indeed, it is because "she" ushers in insight that is totally new, and because the experience of insight seems to *burst* in upon the intellectually barren and stagnant mind, that the dakini is described as "playful" and "capricious." Of course, "her" very abruptness also explains why "she" is also so often described as "horrific" and "terrifying."

As "trickster," the dakini *tests* the tantric adept in numerous ways, usually revealing his or her own mental rigidness and neurosis. Commenting on this "trickster" quality of the dakini, Trungpa Rinpoché has said:

> The playful maiden is all-present. She loves you. She hates you. Without her your life would be continual boredom. But she continually plays tricks on you. When you want to get rid of her she clings. To get rid of her is to get rid of your own body—she is that close. In Tantric literature she is referred to as the dakini principle. The dakini is playful. She gambles with your life.[283]

The dakini is not always, however, a terrifying messenger. Sometimes in various namthar we see "her" as trusted companion and prophetess. In the namthar of Gyalwa Ensapa,[284] for example, the following passage is found:

> During that time [Gyalwa Ensapa] occupied himself performing penances and behaving in such a way as to have [the experience of] bliss and voidness arise [continuously] in his consciousness. Then by the Wisdom Dakini he was advised thusly: "Tomorrow you will meet a pandita who is the reincarnation of the great siddha Paldré Dorjé. To that one you should impart all the detailed practice instructions without holding back."

While the above example contains implicit reference to the dakini principle in "her" iconographic form as the great Vajrayogini, other namthar refer to this principle in other forms, whether deific, human, or formless. For example, from the namthar of Sangyé Yeshé (Sangs rgyas ye shes) we learn that he determined not to remain in Lhasa (but to return to his Mahamudra guru—that is, Gyalwa Ensapa—in Tsang) on account of (1) a mysterious illness, and (2) a dream in which a "young girl" admonished him to do so. The pertinent passage reads:

> When Sangyé Yeshé had developed the illness in his legs while in Lhasa, he had strongly determined at that time to return to Tsang as soon as his illness left him. Moreover, it had also happened that one night in a dream, a young girl had said to him, "Now you have accomplished your aims (here). Let's go back go Tsang!"

Just prior to this passage and, interestingly, offered as an "explanation" of it, one finds another passage in the namthar that alludes to the dakini by way of showing its influential presence and workings in the spiritual life of Gyalwa Ensapa himself. This passage states:

> Now, in the meantime, it had occurred that an inner voice spoke to . . . Gyalwa Ensapa, saying, "It is good that my Rab 'byams pa [Sangyé Yeshé] has not wandered too far away. I must ask [the great goddess] Palden Lhamo (Dpal ldan lha mo) to bring my brilliant one back to me, since his remaining [in Lhasa] could be harmful [to him]."

The *coda* that connects and encapsulates these two passages is intriguing, both for its picturing of the inner dynamics of spiritual clairvoyance and telekinesis, and for the tender and loving concern it illustrates in connection with the guru-disciple relationship. The text says, "This explains why . . . [Sangyé Yeshé decided to return to Tsang]" and, finally, "Those events occurred owing to Gyalwa Ensapa's feelings of concern [for his heart-disciple]." Moreover, it may be noted that in these two passages, Sangyé Yeshé's illness, Gyalwa Ensapa's "inner voice," the grand protective deity Palden Lhamo, and the "young girl" in the dream are *all* manifestations of the dakini.

In the above examples, a certain pattern can be clearly discerned. Namely, the appearance of the dakini in each case marks a particular and unique *communicative moment* for the tantric adept. In terms of specific functions, during such moments, or "spaces," "she" prophesies to, advises, or carries out the wishes of the advanced adept. For the siddha-to-be, she provides protection. Manifesting in multifarious forms, "she" serves as the spur, inspiration, and helpful companion for successfully accomplishing the arduous path of tantric practice.

In order to perform such functions, the dakini does not always manifest as a phantom of dreams, nor as the divine apparition of a deity. Nor does "she" necessarily take human form. In one account "she" appears as a stone statue.[285] In the namthar of the siddha Kukkuripa, the dakini is his dog![286]

Still, if we judge from the evidence of the siddha biographies, we note that quite often the dakini does appear in human, female form, and that in this form, "she" is often the sexual partner or "mystic consort" (Tib. *rikma*)[287] of the siddha. Such human dakinis are integrally and intimately connected with the sexual symbolism of tantric ritual and practice and, by extension, to the notion that for certain advanced tantric practices, the aid of an actual flesh-and-blood partner is useful and/or required.[288] According to Katz's count, "fully fifty-six of the eighty-four [Indian mahasiddhas] are depicted in the company of a woman."[289] Citing examples, Katz notes:

> The attainment of mahāmudrāsiddhi by Vaidyāpāda is dependent upon his taking up residence with a Candāla [outcaste woman]. Anaṅgavajra is instructed by his guru, Padmavajra: "Put yourself in touch with the swine-keeping woman by keeping swine and then step by step you will be a Vajrasattva." ...We hear of Dhari-ka-pa, a king, becoming the servant of a harlot. Puta-lo-ki in the same verse "...won the harlot and perfection."[290]

And, of course, owing to recent English translations, we are all quite familiar now with such illustrious human dakinis as Niguma[291] ("wife" of the siddha Naropa, who developed and taught her own system of the famed "six yogas"); Yeshé Tsogyal (Ye shes mtsho rgyal,)[292] chief Tibetan consort of Padmasambhava; Dagmema (Bdag med ma),[293] Marpa's accomplished wife; and Machik Lapdrönma (Ma gcig lab sgron ma),[294] Phad-ampa Sangyé's (Pha dam pa Sangs rgya's) chief consort, and fashioner of the advanced meditative system of Chö (Gcod). These examples remind us that the tantras were, and remain, effective for producing enlightened beings regardless of sex. They should also remind us that these were no ordinary women practitioners! They were all tantric masters in their own right, who left society's constraints to follow the treacherous path of tantric practice. It should be stressed, moreover, that within the contexts of certain advanced tantric practices, the processes of sexual intercourse may be performed either between human partners or conducted solely as an internal and imagined series of yogic actions. In the case of human practitioners, the sexual act is not performed by "ordinary beings," but rather by "deities"—by beings who have put aside their ordinary mind-body complex and assumed the arcane body and the subtle awareness of a particular deity. Summarizing the major functions of the dakini in the tantric siddha biographical tradition—what one might call a summary of the dakini as a central leitmotif—Katz has enumerated the following:

> (1) inspiring and directing the siddha; (2) directly or indirectly initiating the siddha; (3) [serving as] the patron of the siddha . . . ; (4) the source of power of the siddha; (5) guardians of the *gter-ma*; and (6) biographers of the siddha.[295]

He goes on to reiterate that "the *mkha' 'gro ma* may appear in visions, dreams, meditations and as actual women. They are also revered as preceptors of particular yogic practices [i.e., Chö (Gcod); Tummo (Gtum mo)] and may be demoniacal as well as beneficent. . . . Their role in the lives of the siddha is tremendous . . . ."[296]

It remains only necessary now to mention how the dakini functions within the contexts and symbolism of tantric ritual and practice itself. According to the symbolism of tantric, or Vajrayana, Buddhism, enlightenment (*bodhi*) is represented as the perfect "sexual union" (Skt. *yuganaddha*; Tib. *zungjuk*) of ultimate wisdom and compassionate activity. In Mahayana Buddhism generally, these two are referred to as *prajna* (Tib. *sherab*) and *upaya* (Tib. *thap*), respectively. *Prajna* is represented as being female, and *upaya* as being male. (Of course, the perfection of sexual union, simultaneous orgasm, is a familiar and direct symbol for the loss of "self"—what might be called a readily understandable description of *shunyata*. During such orgasm, both partners experience the "transcendental emotion" called in the Tantras *samarasa*, or "one taste." Here, neither partner is distinct. It is impossible to distinguish where one ends and the other begins. This experience of "wholeness" and "sameness" is accompanied by intensely blissful feeling.)

In terms of tantric symbolism, these two are iconographically represented as two deities, usually semi-wrathful in form, who are embracing in sexual union. The pair of deities are said to be in the aspect of *yap yum* (Tib., lit., "Father-Mother"). Comprising this most revered pair are the great Wisdom Dakini (Tib., *Ye shes mkha' 'gro ma* [Yeshé Khandroma]) who is usually in her form as the Goddess Vajrayogini or Vajravarahi,[297] and "her" consort (whether Chakrasamvara, Guhyasamaja, Hevajra, or whatever chief "male" deity of the given ritual cycle). Their blissful union symbolizes complete enlightenment, the direct, blissful experience of ultimate voidness.

Since our discussion focuses on the dakini, it is fitting here to describe "her" *deific* form. To do so, I refer to one of "her" chief iconographic forms, that is, as the great yidam, the Goddess Vajrayogini:

> Her body is a vibrant blood-red color. Apart from the bone ornaments that are draped around her waist and a necklace of skulls around her neck, she is completely naked. She holds aloft in her raised left hand a *kapala* [Skt., a skull cup, here filled with *amṛta* (Tib. *bdud rtsi*, nectar)], and her right hand wields a hooked knife [Skt. *kartari*]. Resting on her left shoulder is the trident staff, or *khatvanga* [that represents her consort, the Heruka, Chakrasamvara]. The top of the staff is decorated with three skulls. Standing with bent left leg and outstretched right leg on two corpses, her entire figure is encircled in flames.[298]

In such a manner is "she" envisioned and contemplated by the practicing adept.

2. Overview and Concluding Remarks

In the above materials, in addition to briefly reviewing how some scholars have defined and interpreted the phenomenon of dakini, I have tried to indicate a sampling of the multiplicity of forms and guises in which the symbol, or principle, of dakini manifests. To be sure, such a multiplicity of forms, together with the fact of "her" special ambiguity—that is, that "she" is at once the witch, the trickster, and wisdom incarnate—combine to make "her" a most *elusive* phenomenon. Yet, in spite of such divergent images, "her" nature, it seems to me, is *allusive* as well. Viewing the dakini in a number of different textual and ritual practice contexts allows us to perhaps develop some appreciation of its multivalent character. Here, then, I wish to offer some general comments regarding "her" nature and meaning.

To begin, it allows us to note that, while her nature is feminine, "she" is *not* necessarily female. Though the dakini assuredly most often appears in female form (whether as a female deity or a female human being), this is but one of the myriad of ways absolute insight chooses to make manifest its facticity. Modern-day women practitioners who pride themselves on being "already halfway there" owing solely to their sex need only be reminded of two pristine teachings on voidness:

> In the *Diamond Cutter (of Doubts) Sutra*,[299] the Buddha said:

> Those who by my form did see me,
> and those who followed me by my voice,
> wrong the efforts they engaged in,
> me those people will not see.

> From the Dharma (alone) should one see the buddhas,
> from the Dharmakāya comes their guidance.
> Yet Dharma's true nature cannot be discerned,
> and no one can be conscious of it as an object.[300]

And in the *Vimalakirtinirdesha Sutra*, the goddess who lives in Vimalakirti's house (herself a dakini!) has this dialogue with Shariputra (who represents the conservatism of early Buddhism wherein distinctions based on sex still held sway):

> *Shariputra*: Goddess, what prevents you from transforming yourself out of your female state?
>
> *Goddess*: Although I have sought my "female state" for these twelve years, I have not yet found it. Reverend Shariputra, if a magician were to incarnate a woman by magic, would you ask her, "What prevents you from transforming yourself out of your female state?"
>
> *Shariputra*: No! Such a woman would not really exist, so what would there be to transform?
>
> *Goddess*: Just so, Reverend Shariputra, all things do not really exist.[301]

(Of course, modern-day men practitioners who think this lets them off the hook from respecting their female counterparts might reflect on the last of the "Fourteen Root Vows of Vajrayana," which makes it clear that it is a serious downfall "to disparage women, who are of the nature of wisdom"!)[302]

The dakini is, however, a *feminine* principle. The term used to refer to the phenomenon is a feminine noun; and within the tantric symbolism employed to represent supreme enlightenment, the dakini most assuredly takes feminine form. Of course, one of the most interesting questions in this regard is, "Why is *that* the case?"[303] An attempted answer would require at least a book; but I would like to suggest that apart from such ancient characterizations, constructs, and divisions based on sex and/or gender differences—as, for example, male=intellect, female=intuition; male=activity, female=passivity and receptivity; and the like—the main idea being articulated here is that the dakini is the *necessary complement*[304] to render us (whether male or female) whole beings. To put it another way, "she" is what is lacking, the lacking of which prevents our complete enlightenment.

Given that we unenlightened beings normally exist in rather narrowly limited "spaces," it is not surprising that the appearance in our lives of the dakini's vastness ("she" is *all* that we lack!) might be, at least initially, overwhelming, horrific, and terrifying. Some of the portrayals of the dakini as "gruesome, demonic, flesh-eating ghouls" no doubt spring from this perspective. And with the most stubborn and most self-righteous, "she" is least gentle!

Making contact with the dakini, then, is sometimes terrifying and always dangerous, but doing so offers the chance for dramatic and highly-prized fruit. The biographies of the siddhas show that these brave ones actually seek "her" out. To do so, they are usually shown making perilous journeys and visiting cemeteries and charnel grounds. The logic of such imagery operates on several levels at once. The outer journey, of course, is more accurately an inner or spiritual one, and because in order to fully make contact with "her," the adept's own ordinary psychophysical being must "die," the cemetery is a most appropriate symbolic place for such an encounter. Even in nontantric Buddhism, the utter destruction of the false idea of a "self" must be accomplished prior to (or concomitant with) the attainment of the insight that cognizes voidness (*shunyata*) directly. Having finally won access to the dakini, the tantric adept is thereafter graced by "her" to receive new powers and insight and, ultimately, full enlightenment itself.

From the absolute point of view, then, the dakini is highest wisdom itself. That is, "she" is the direct, unmediated, nonconceptual understanding of voidness (*shunyata*). "She" is, as her chief iconographic representation suggests, the "naked" experience of voidness in itself—limitless, uncontained, effusive, and entirely blissful. How could such an experience be adequately described in words?

In the tantric world of ritual and meditative practice, the older Buddhist trilogy of Buddha, Dharma, and Sangha is replaced by the triad of lama (*bla ma*), yidam (*yi dam*), and khandroma (*mkha' 'gro ma*)— that is, dakini. But in practice, each of the three includes both of the other members of the triad, so that one regards one's guru as the yidam and as the dakini (since both are *embodiments* of the highest wisdom). Likewise, the dakini is both lama and yidam. In highest tantra practice contexts, one is continually reminded that one should not be confused about this. The dakini is all the "Three Roots" in one.

Within tantric contexts (and Mahayana contexts, generally), we speak of the *trikaya*, or so-called Three Bodies of the Buddha. Since "she" embodies the highest wisdom, the dakini is all three of these bodies. "She" is the formless "Body of Truth," the Dharmakaya. In "her" communicative role, bringing inspiration and insight to advanced practitioners, "she" is the magnificent and eloquent "Enjoyment Body," the yidam, or Sambhogakaya. And in "her" infinite manifestations that serve to communicate with us ordinary beings and to trigger havoc in our habitual samsaric patterns of thought, "she" sports in countless configurations of the "Emanation Body," the Nirmanakaya. The dakini is thus, in her vastness, the embodiment of the entirety of trikaya.

Also within the world of tantric *practice*, another triad is commonly posited—namely, that which delineates the "outer, inner, and secret" (Tib., *phyi*, *nang*, and *gsang ba*) levels of experience. (These three may be seen as reflecting the trikaya, in reverse order.) According to this manner of speaking, we may say that the *outer* dakini is those varied forms in which the dakini appears, whether human or deific, benign or wrathful, beneficent or malevolent; the *inner dakini* manifests when the advanced meditator successfully transforms him- or herself into the great dakini (usually Vajrayogini, herself); and the *secret dakini* is the formless power, energy, and pure bliss of voidness.[305]

In this last aspect, the dakini is synonymous with another extremely important concept in the Tantras—namely, Mahamudra, the "Great Gesture" or "Great Symbol"—for "she" appears when the highest intellectual grasp of "voidness" is transcended. There since beginningless time, "she" is the ultimate, unchanging basis and reality of being. At the end of the arduous path of practice of highest yoga tantra, "she" reveals "herself," naked before us. And regardless of whether we are "male" or "female" beings, if we wish to become enlightened beings, we must embrace, and be embraced by, "her."

13

Namthar as Literature and Liturgy

❧ ❧

GENERAL DEFINITION

In the Tibetan Buddhist tradition, written accounts of the lives of accomplished practitioners form a distinct genre of literature. That genre is referred to as *namthar*, an abbreviation of *nampar tharpa*, which literally means "complete liberation." Such liberation life stories are meticulously recorded, narrated, and studied, not simply as the biographies of highly regarded persons, but as accounts serving to make manifest that liberation by describing its process. Thus, namthar serve as both inspirational and instructional models for practitioners of the Buddhist path. Because they center on beings who are revered as having accomplished enlightenment by using tantric means—"in one lifetime, in one body, even in these degenerate times," as the traditional phrase goes—the subjects of these biographies are called *siddhas*, "accomplished" or "perfected ones." Namthar, then, as the lives of Buddhist siddhas, present the lives of enlightened beings, and thus they may be characterized as sacred biography.

The very definition of namthar highlights an important distinction between Western and Buddhist notions concerning the biographies of holy persons. In the West, the term "sacred biography" is generally reserved only for the life of the founder of a particular religion, while the term "hagiography" is used in reference to the biographies of all the succeeding saints in that tradition.[306] In Buddhism, however, and especially in its Mahayana and Vajrayana forms, the belief is that anyone can become a buddha. In fact, these forms of Buddhism assert that it is not only possible but incumbent on the adept to attain buddhahood. There are thus countless enlightened beings, and for Tibetan Buddhists the written lives of all of them are considered to be sacred biography.

It is important to note that Buddhism traveled from India into Tibet primarily in its tantric or Vajrayana form.[307] Thus, while figures like Shantiraksita[308] and Kamalashila[309] were instrumental in propagating the rules of monastic discipline and the nontantric philosophy and practice of both the Theravada and Mahayana branches of Buddhism, it was tantric Buddhism that successfully captured the minds of Tibetans, and thus it was the tantric adepts, the siddhas, who succeeded in effectively advancing the new religious tradition of Buddhism in Tibet.

The pre-Buddhist world of Tibetan folk religion was populated by multifarious spirit beings, many of them malevolent. Even after the various strains of the broader-based shamanism of the area and the more localized folk traditions were finally brought together and systematized as the religion of Bön, this basic psychospiritual worldview continued to hold sway.[310] For Buddhism to gain acceptance in such an environment it would have to prove itself on that environment's own terms. Thus almost all accounts agree that Padmasambhava, the figure usually credited with establishing Buddhism in Tibet,[311] was able to do this precisely because he was a siddha possessed of a siddha's wonder-working powers. By subjugating Tibet's malevolent spirits, Padmasambhava effectively demonstrated the power and efficacy of the Buddhist religion, and it was owing to this superior display of power that, together with Shantiraksita, he was able to found the first Tibetan lineage of Buddhism, called the Nyingmapa (Rnying ma pa).

Over the next seven centuries, several other schools were founded in Tibet as the Buddhist Dharma made continued inroads there. And as each new order came into its own, more and more namthar were produced glorifying the persons most influential to a given school's creation and development.

Generally speaking, though the style and content of siddha biographies may differ from one historical period and setting to another (as

between Indian and Tibetan examples of the genre),[312] and from one
Tibetan order to another,[313] all share some of the same ingredients. It is
to these shared ingredients, and to a method of interpreting them, that
I now turn.

First, all siddhas are said to have attained *siddhis*, or magical powers
of various sorts. Indeed, the terms *siddha* and *siddhi* go hand in hand,
each term being part of the definition of the other. In written accounts,
siddhas are said to speak at birth, to fly through the air, to read other's
thoughts, and to pass through walls unhindered. Additionally, miracles
are said to have accompanied their births, and they are said to have had
exceptional childhoods. (It is interesting to note that many of the early
Christian "confessor" hagiographies include similar descriptions.)[314]

It is largely in reaction to the prominent place of siddhis in siddhas'
life stories that some Western Buddhist scholars have judged namthar
to be the products of popular spirituality and therefore of little scholarly or historical value.[315] Using this "peculiar hermeneutical device,"[316]
such scholars belittle the genre and close themselves off to the wealth of
information and inspiration that it contains.

The six Gelukpa namthar presented here reveal quite another picture of this literature's value and richness, for they provide us not only
with a wealth of valid historical information but with an entrée into
the world of tantric practice itself by setting forth, even if only in veiled
language,[317] descriptions and instructions regarding tantric meditations.
It is particularly with respect to this latter feature that, I believe, Tibetan
namthar go beyond Western hagiography in creating a religious literature of richness and depth.

We can begin to appreciate this by considering two important points.
First, a namthar, by presenting the significant experiences of a tantric
adept in his or her quest for enlightenment, is first and foremost a piece
of tantric literature. To put it another way, siddha biographies, in terms
of their content and function, are comparable to and complement the
tantras and their commentaries.[318] One of their main functions is thus
the imparting of esoteric and exoteric practice descriptions and instructions. Viewed in this way, namthar are indeed vehicles for providing
inspirational models; but they are, in addition, vehicles for providing

detailed instructions to persons seeking to put the teachings of a particular siddha into practice.

Second, it should be borne in mind that all Tibetan namthar contain elements of what are actually three distinct levels or kinds of life story:[319] (1) *chi namthar (phyi'i rnam thar)*, the so-called outer biography, which most resembles Western notions of biography, presenting details about birth, schooling, specific teachers, texts consulted, etc.; (2) *nangi namthar (nang gi rnam thar)*, or "inner biography," which chronicles the specific meditation cycles, initiations, etc., imparted to the future siddha; and (3) *sangwai namthar (gsang ba'i rnam thar)*, or "secret biography." This last level or kind of narrative describes the meditative accomplishments, mystic visions, and other spiritual realizations and experiences of the accomplished one.[320] The first two levels of namthar as described here do not seem to present problems for the scholars who work with this literature. It is from the third, the so-called secret biography, that most have usually shied away, calling it magical or fantastic, folkloric or obscure. My own suggestion, as I have already stated, is to view this third level as providing inspiration and encouragement, along with descriptions of esoteric practices and instructions for their accomplishment.

This traditional threefold structured model of namthar can be usefully employed to introduce Western readers of these life stories to their multifaceted richness and ambiance. I suggest that we take it to represent, respectively, what, for purposes of organization, I term: (1) the "historical," (2) the "inspirational," and (3) the "instructional" levels of the stories. Furthermore, I suggest that levels 1 and 3 may be fruitfully discussed under the broader rubric of "literature" (where the first level speaks to us directly, though the third level requires further elaboration),[321] and that level 2 naturally lends itself to consideration under the heading of "liturgy" and, in fact, often functions that way within the tradition. Moreover, as might be expected, the "inspirational" and the "instructional" levels of namthar overlap in many respects.

Applying this three-tiered model to the six biographies presented here, one could say that the outer or "historical" level of these accounts introduces us in a direct way to the lived world of mid-fourteenth- to mid-seventeenth-century Gelukpa practitioners. Figures previously known only because their names appear in lineage enumerations or religious chronicles become living, breathing human beings. We witness their childhoods and education, their practice hardships and triumphs. In addition to learning more about them as individuals, we see the world, with all its historical and political vicissitudes, in which they moved: the cultural, social, and political contexts in which they practiced the Dharma. Moreover, we learn about the world experienced by these siddhas' disciples and by the general populace of Tibet during this time.

Next, by "inspirational" I refer to the data within these stories that serve to inspire Buddhist practitioners themselves, the *nangpa*, or "insiders,"[322] those who already profess the faith and wish to emulate its exemplary figures. Here we witness the utter devotion and commitment to practice demonstrated by these siddhas, how each pleased his guru, the dynamics of the guru-disciple relationship, and how, for each of these "realized ones," study and compassionate teaching—both verbal and through written compositions—were continued unbroken. All of this combines to uplift, encourage, inspire, and empower those seeking to practice.

Lastly, by "instructional" I mean those elements in the stories that serve advanced practitioners seeking to learn more about how and when to put into practice the diverse skillful methods of the Vajrayana. Even today, the most erudite Tibetan teachers continually refer to ancient namthar. Within namthar themselves, a future siddha is often shown searching out a particular namthar or requesting permission to study it. Moreover, the authors and the readers of such biographies have often been the most venerated teachers, the elite of the tantric tradition, precisely because namthar *are* instructional. Thus, in addition to shedding much light on what the world of the traditional Tibetan tantric practitioner was like, the particular accounts translated here tell us how these Gelukpas practiced Mahamudra and inform us about the specific contours of the Ganden oral tradition. They are not just fantastic tales. Nor are they "merely inspirational," if by that one means products of, and for, popular spirituality. Rather, they are spiritual biographies brimming with information on many levels.

In what follows I briefly attempt to indicate how the threefold model
I have suggested and the two rubrics of literature and liturgy can help
reveal the depth and richness of this genre. Because each translation is
accompanied by abundant annotation, I will address only a few points
by way of example here.

CHI, THE HISTORICAL

In his monumental work *Tibetan Painted Scrolls*, published in 1949, the
great Tibetologist Giuseppe Tucci compared namthar with Christian
hagiography and suggested that history was never the intended purview
of the genre. He wrote:

> *rNam t'ar* much resemble the lives of saints widely circu-
> lated during our Middle Ages; they must be considered
> neither histories nor chronicles. The events they relate
> with a particular satisfaction are spiritual conquests,
> visions and ecstasies; they follow the long apprentice-
> ship through which man becomes divine, they give lists
> of the texts upon which saints trained and disciplined
> their minds, for each lama they record the masters who
> opened up his spirit to serene visions, or caused the
> ambrosia of supreme revelations to rain down upon him.
> Human events have nothing to do with these works, and
> how could they, being a vain flow of appearances in the
> motionless gleam of that void, never to be grasped, into
> which the experience of truth dissolves and annuls us? . . .
> All the rest is shadows.[323]

For all its poetry, it must be admitted that Tucci's description of
namthar does not do much to inform us about the actual nature or
function of the genre. To be sure, the siddha's spiritual biography (the
inner and secret levels) takes precedence over the outer biography in
such literature. Still, for the six Gelukpa examples translated here, Tucci's assessment would be quite inappropriate. For in these six, human

events do figure in. Names, places, and verifiable dates are mentioned, and human beings are historical as well as religious actors in the central drama that unfolds the path to enlightenment.

To begin, the six siddhas and their respective dates should be considered. They are:

1. Tokden Jampal Gyatso (1356–1428)
2. Baso Chökyi Gyaltsen (1402–1473)
3. Drupchen Chökyi Dorjé (?)
4. Gyalwa Ensapa (1505–1566)
5. Khedrup Sangyé Yeshé (1525–1591)
6. Jetsün Losang Chökyi Gyaltsen (1570–1662)

As can be seen from their dates, these six lives span some three hundred years of Tibetan religious history, particularly that period covering the rise to power of the Yellow Hat,[324] or Gelukpa, order. Because the lives are contiguous, through them we are able not only to witness a continuous lineage of Gelukpa Mahamudra practitioners but to view continuously unfolding historical developments, both as they impacted on and were influenced by these six. Through them, one learns who knew whom, what places were frequented, and where certain monasteries were founded and why. Moreover, through this particular set of lives, we can observe directly the intricate interweaving of politics and religion in Tibet during this period.

It is of interest, for example, to learn that four of these six siddhas, who succeeded Tsongkhapa (1357–1419) in the Geluk Mahamudra lineage, were personally connected with the first five Dalai Lamas. Baso Chökyi Gyaltsen became abbot of Ganden (Dga' ldan) Monastery on the order of the First Dalai Lama, Gendundrub (Gde 'dun grub, 1391–1475). One of Baso's Mahāmudrā disciples, Palden Dorjé (Dpal ldan rdo rje), studied with and taught the Second Dalai Lama, Gendun Gyatso (Gde 'dun rgya mtsho, 1476–1542). Later, Gyalwa Ensapa was ordained by the Second Dalai Lama and studied under him. Following the death of Gyalwa Ensapa, Sangyé Yeshé accompanied and served the Third Dalai Lama, Sönam Gyatso (Bsod nams rgya mtsho, 1543–1588), until the latter went to Mongolia. Lastly, the First Panchen Lama, Losang Chökyi Gyaltsen, was the chief tutor of both the Fourth Dalai Lama, Yönten Gyatso (Yon tan rgya mtsho, 1589–1616), and the Great Fifth Dalai Lama, Ngawang Losang Gyatso (Ngag dbang blo bzang rgya mtsho, 1617–1682).

Tsongkhapa had not been seeking to found a new order of Buddhism in Tibet. Yet, owing to his vast intelligence, the great assiduity he evidenced toward his studies, the purity of his moral and monastic discipline, and his tireless energy for teaching, that new order gradually came into being. Two other factors, however, contributed to its development: an ever-growing number of devoted disciples and a conducive political climate in and around the environs of Lhasa. Speaking to this latter point, Snellgrove has observed:

> In and around Lhasa Tsong-kha-pa found ready support from the local nobility and people. This was a sort of border zone between the old religious rivals, 'Bri-khung and Sa-skya, and had more recently come under the influence of the Phag-mo-gru and gDan-sa-mthil who gave a friendly welcome to the teachings of Tsong-kha-pa and his disciples. The example of a religious school which was as yet taking no part in the political rivalries of the day and insisted on the observance of strict monastic discipline, may well have appealed to many who were critical of the apparent worldliness of the older established orders.[325]

While it would be impossible in the space of an introduction such as this to go into any detail regarding the numerous vicissitudes of Tibetan history, one general comment can be posited: one would be hard-pressed to distinguish Tibet's religious history from its political history. Owing to the pervasive power exerted by religion throughout Tibet, whatever rival factions existed—whether indigenous royal houses or foreign hegemonies—all found it necessary to ally themselves with sectors of the religious community. Similarly, a religious order often waxed or waned depending on the stabilities of its secular alliances.[326]

If the political climate during Tsongkhapa's own lifetime greatly served his new order, the situation immediately following his death took a turn for the worse. Prior to his death, not only had Tsongkhapa founded—with the aid of his disciples Jé Darma Rinchen (Rje Dar ma rin chen) and Jé Dulwa Dzin (Rje 'Dul ba 'dzin)—his own monastery, called Ganden (erected in 1409), but two others of his disciples, Jamyang Chöjé Tashi Palden ('Jam dbangs Chos rje Bkra shis dpal ldan) and Jamchen Chöjé Shakya Yeshé (Byams chen Chos rje Shakya ye shes),³²⁷ had founded the great monastic establishments of Drepung ('Bras spungs) in 1416 and Sera (Se ra) in 1419, respectively. These monasteries are famed as the Three Great Seats of the Gelukpa.³²⁸ All were constructed very near to Lhasa during Tsongkhapa's lifetime.

Now the namthar of Baso Chökyi Gyaltsen translated here provides us with a brief but interesting comment on the Gelukpa tradition's development just after Tsongkhapa had passed away. One of Tsongkhapa's youngest and most energetic disciples was Gendundrub (Dge 'dun grub).³²⁹ He was twenty-five years old when, in 1415, he joined Tsongkhapa in Lhasa and became one of his most devoted followers. Tsongkhapa was already advanced in age. Later, in 1445, Gendundrub founded what became the fourth most important Gelukpa monastic establishment, the famed Tashi Lhunpo (Bkra shis lhun po).³³⁰ Even more important, he built this monastery not in Lhasa but far to the west of it, near the town of Shigatse (Gzhis ka rtse) in Tsang (Gtsang).³³¹ This action was of great importance and is usually interpreted as the chief activity that signaled the active expansion of the new order and its ever-growing prestige. However, this expansion was not, by Gendundrub's time, viewed with the acceptance and warmth that Tsongkhapa had experienced some thirty-five years before.

As previously noted, Baso Chökyi Gyaltsen became abbot of Ganden on the order of Gendundrub. From Baso Jé's namthar we get an insider's view of the reasons behind this decision, for here we find the dramatic words of Gendundrub himself. The relevant passage reads:

> At that time, the All-knowing Gendundrub Pelsangpo was
> residing at Tashi Lhunpo, carrying out numerous virtuous
> activities. . . . Then the precious throneholder of Ganden
> and many other illustrious lamas of that institution prayed
> to the Venerable Gendundrub, urging him to become the
> next Regent of the Second Buddha [Tsongkhapa]. But
> Gendundrub replied: "I myself must hold the Dharma reins
> of Jé Rinpoché right here [at Tashi Lhunpo] since it is neces-
> sary to build a fortified mansion [here] in the midst of an
> enemy camp."³³²

After offering appropriate praise to Baso Jé, Gendundrub then advised
the monks of Ganden to name Baso Jé to the position, which they did.

Within the few years between Tsongkhapa's passing and the founding of Tashi Lhunpo, many changes had occurred, and these would
continue as the growing prestige and power of the new order began to
arouse the hostility of the older orders and their lay patrons. Without
going into this quite complicated history here, suffice it to say that the
above remarks by Gendundrub are of *historical* importance and that
they appear within a namthar.

A survey of the next five namthar in this set shows that while all of
these siddhas continued to journey to and study at one or another of the
Gelukpa monasteries in Lhasa, for the most part the main seats of their
religious activity remained in the province of Tsang. Monasteries like
Gangchen Chöpel (Gangs can chos 'phel), Rong Jamchen (Rong byams
chen), Nenying (Gnas rnying), and especially Ensa, and hermitages like
Riwo Dechen (Ri bo bde chen) and Garmo Chö Dzong (Mgar mo chos
rdzong)—all located in Tsang—were the primary centers for this group.
And for all of them, the great Tashi Lhunpo shone like a dazzling bea-
con, signaling the Gelukpa's expanding influence throughout the region.
Thus, through the lives of these six, we witness the Wheel of Dharma of
the Gelukpa advancing into and establishing itself in new territory.

This particular set of six namthar concludes with a figure of great
importance to Tibet's religious and political history: the First Panchen,
Losang Chökyi Gyaltsen.³³³ In his namthar we can observe the various

ebbs and flows of seventeenth-century Tibet, when not only the various orders and royal families vied for authority, but foreign powers as well. The First Panchen is renowned not only because he served as chief tutor to two Dalai Lamas (one, the greatly powerful Fifth Dalai Lama) but also because on numerous occasions he himself sued for peace among various rival factions.[334] The First Panchen was extremely important to the Gelukpa Mahamudra lineage and to other practice lineages for his compositions explicating them. Like those of the great Gyalwa Ensapa, the First Panchen's writings extended and clarified Gelukpa meditative practice, ritual, and liturgy.[335] His namthar reveals him to be a humble though greatly influential figure, incredibly learned, and an accomplished yogi, astute diplomat, prolific writer, and thoroughly compassionate teacher of the Buddha's doctrine.

An important issue relating both to Tibetan religious and political history is the concept of "reincarnation." In Tibet, the older Buddhist notions of "transmigration" and "rebirth" were transformed and refined in such a way as to become a tool for ensuring the stability of religious authority, prestige, and wealth. Thus the concept of the *tulku* (*sprul sku*), or incarnate lama, evolved.[336] Prior to the general acceptance of this new concept, "the previous pattern in Tibetan society had been one of a religious aristocracy passing both religious and secular power from father to son or from paternal uncle to nephew."[337] The Sakya order, for example, made use of the latter "inheritance" channel. However, in time, the incarnate lama lineages took priority over familial claims in the transmission and safeguarding of religious authority.

While the Gelukpa did not invent this practice in Tibet, reincarnation did become a most important means of ensuring the stability of the new order's ever-growing authority, given the fact that it enjoined strict celibacy on its monks. Within the six namthar presented here, we see accounts of early instances of the use of reincarnation within the Gelukpa tradition.

For example, the First Panchen was recognized as being the reincarnation of Gyalwa Ensapa. The fact that Gyalwa Ensapa had chosen to reincarnate is recorded both in the namthar of Sangyé Yeshé and in the namthar of the First Panchen. In the latter's namthar, we are told that Gyalwa Ensapa had informed his chief spiritual son, Sangyé Yeshé, regarding the details of his next incarnation, and we learn how Sangye Yeshé went about having his teacher's rebirth verified.

The concept of "reincarnation" is mentioned as well with regard to other teachers referred to in the six stories. For example, Gyalwa Ensapa is instructed by the dakini Vajrayogini to entrust his teachings to one Kunkhyen Lekpa Döndrup (Kun mkhyen Legs pa don grub), who is further described as being "the reincarnation of the great siddha Pal-dré Dorjé (Dpal 'bras rdo rje)." Likewise, Langmikpa (Glang mig pa), one of the chief tutors of Sangyé Yeshé, and the lama who confirmed the First Panchen as being Gyalwa Ensapa's reincarnation, is himself described as "the reincarnation of Jamyang Lekpai Lodrö ('Jam dbyangs legs pa'i blo gros)."

In other passages, the subjects of these stories are given additional prestige by being born in places where other revered masters had been born, taught, or served as abbots. Thus, Gyalwa Ensapa's birth is said to have occurred "in a place that had itself been blessed by the presence of many holy ones of the past, all of princely lineage, like Sönam Choklang (Bsod nams phyogs glang) and others. . . ." Now, this Sönam Choklang is none other than the lama who retroactively became recognized as the second in the lineage of Panchens, in which Gyalwa Ensapa himself was later recognized as the third.[338]

Not all of the "outer" information in these namthar concerns religious or political issues. For example, we are told twice about a widespread epidemic of smallpox. Gyalwa Ensapa first meets his Mahamudra guru, Chökyi Dorjé, when he [Ensapa] is continuing his meditations in spite of having contracted the disease. The relevant passage reads:

> When the great Gyalwa Ensapa was seventeen years old, there was a widespread epidemic of smallpox, and he also contracted the disease. One day, while reciting verses regarding dependent origination near his door, he heard a voice. The moment he heard the sound of this voice, the hairs of his skin stood on end, and [immediately] he went outside. There he saw a monk with a white mustache and goatee, wearing

religious robes of the finest cloth, whose bearing and purity
were striking. Instantly realizing that this person must certainly be a great siddha, Gyalwa Ensapa invited him inside
and there paid him the appropriate respect.

Because the passage mentions Gyalwa Ensapa's age at the time of his
meeting his chief guru, we know that Tibetans, at least in the regions of
Tsang, experienced an epidemic sometime in 1521. Another epidemic
is mentioned in the namthar of the First Panchen. Reference is also
made to it in Sangyé Yeshé's story. We are told that this second epidemic
occurred when the First Panchen was nineteen years old, making the
year 1588. Since the time of each epidemic is remembered and recorded,
it can be assumed that the disease had a widespread and perhaps even
devastating impact on Tibetan society. One other bit of information is
of interest in this connection. It is the fact that, of these six Geluk siddhas, the two who are remembered as having contracted the disease are
the same two who are said to be bound directly to each other through
the process of reincarnation. Gyalwa Ensapa contracted the disease,
and, some sixty-seven years later during another epidemic, his reincarnation, the First Panchen, also contracted it.

But these stories inform us about more than just the various external factors affecting these six practitioners; they also provide an inside
look at the dynamics of Gelukpa monastic life, describing in detail such
things as monastic organization, college curricula and examinations,
and ordination ceremonies. Most of the subjects of these six stories
were at some time affiliated with one or more of the Three Great Seats
of Gelukpa learning near Lhasa, though Sangyé Yeshé and the First
Panchen were more closely tied to Tashi Lhunpo in Tsang. We hear of
all these institutions and of their respective colleges. We also hear of
important colleges or institutions that by the seventeenth century were
no longer thriving, like Sangpu (Gsang phu),[339] the famed college of
logic where Jampal Gyatso had studied.

From these accounts, we get a clear sense of what Tibetan monastic
education involved. The Gelukpa order has emphasized that training in
logic be coupled with proper meditation on the Buddha's teaching, and

we see that approach come to life in these stories. Siddhas are usually viewed as wild yogis who shun book learning in preference for yogic meditation. These stories, though, show the Gelukpa's style of joining the two. Jampal Gyatso's namthar gives a good example of this through its descriptions of his early encounters and subsequent meditation retreats with Tsongkhapa.

Further, all of these siddhas, being followers of the Gelukpa, became at some point in their lives fully ordained monks and, therefore, holders of the three sets of vows. Here, we are allowed to view the ordination ceremonies for each, and all relevant data regarding their ordinations are described in detail.

None of these six enlightened beings founded great monastic institutions. One could say that that is to be expected of siddhas. While each was affiliated with one or more of the famed Geluk monasteries (the First Panchen at one time served as abbot of five such institutions simultaneously!), each spent considerable time meditating in isolated retreat. Some, like Chökyi Dorjé, became primarily associated with specific retreat sites[340] rather than with any monastery. Gyalwa Ensapa's small monastery[341] is probably the most venerated of those places today. Still, Baso Jé, Sangyé Yeshé, and the First Panchen are remembered for the generous financial and other donations each made to the monasteries with which they were connected. Each was a true patron of the arts and did much to enrich the Dharma through art.

Another fact becomes apparent as one reads these six accounts: each siddha studied not only the major treatises that formed the standard curricula for Gelukpa institutions but also a wide variety of other texts and meditative systems, including many that are usually associated only with the other Tibetan orders. Thus, these siddhas are shown studying the manuals of Lamdré (Lam 'bras) and Taknyi (Brtag gnis),[342] two systems associated mainly with the Sakya tradition. The First Panchen not only observed for a time the Kagyü practice of wearing only a cotton covering but also, on another occasion, made the practice of "taking only essences"[343] his main meditative endeavor. All six siddhas received instructions on the oral tradition of Chöd (Gcod), and, because they were Mahamudra siddhas, they of course received full instruction in

Naropa's six yogas.[344] Thus, like the great Tsongkhapa, these six men are examples of the unbiased and true nonsectarian character and spirit with which the lamas of old approached the Buddha's teachings.

Lastly, each of these six contributed to the Gelukpa lineage in direct and lasting ways. Jampal Gyatso upheld the purity of the Ganden oral tradition of Mahamudra through his strenuous efforts in meditating just as his guru had instructed him. He thus maintained the practice lineage for future disciples. Baso Jé successfully trained three disciples in the oral tradition. Chökyi Dorjé won the siddhi of immortality, becoming a vidyadhara,[345] and passed on the living practice tradition to the great Gyalwa Ensapa. Gyalwa Ensapa not only successfully completed the tantric path but also composed numerous treatises on its practice, as well as texts that clarified, refined, and advanced Gelukpa ritual and liturgy in general. Sangyé Yeshé upheld the teachings of Gyalwa Ensapa even as he generously provided for the spiritual and material well-being of his followers. And the First Panchen—owing as much to his peacemaking activities as to his tireless efforts in study, meditation, and teaching—placed the Gelukpa order on sound footing to continue its spiritual work.

Many other observations regarding Tibet's religious, political, and social history could be cited, drawn solely from the information provided by the "outer" level of the six namthar translated here. It is my hope that the notes accompanying each translation will help the reader to draw out more of these, and I move on now to what I have called the "inspirational" level of these accounts.

NANG, THE INSPIRATIONAL

It is easy to see how such exemplary figures as these six siddhas would inspire those coming after them. The accounts of their selfless deeds, often performed under the most difficult circumstances, have remained as trusted guides for later practitioners.

The names of these six are found enumerated—along with those of thirty other Geluk Mahamudra lineage-holders—in the short liturgical text called the *Prayer, with Supplement, to the Lineage Lamas of the*

Ganden Oral Tradition of Mahamudra.[346] This prayer, written in verse, is chanted daily in convocations of monks and nuns engaged in tantric practice and by individuals practicing in isolated retreats. It is usually intoned very slowly and with great sincerity, solemnity, and devotion.

After offering homage to the Mahamudra meditative system, the prayer proceeds in thirty-six verses, each composed of two eight-syllable lines that briefly describe the life and merits of each lineage-holder, with a third line bearing that one's name. These are then followed by refrains of four eight-syllable lines. For example, after naming Vajradhara, the first member of the lineage, the refrain is recited as follows:

> By generating a mind of compassion and loving kindness,
>   and by completely severing the continuum that clings to holding
>   a "self,"
>   may I be blessed to quickly attain the highest state
>   of Mahamudra, [through] the path of total integration.[347]

As this prayer is solemnly intoned, attention is focused on the verse summations of each lineage holder's liberation life story: his struggles, efforts, and accomplishments. Supplication is made to each lineage-holder in turn, and the practitioner prays to be blessed by each of them so as to attain the ultimate realization of Mahamudra[348] in his or her own lifetime.

At the prayer's conclusion, a fervent wish is posited, a wish characteristic of tantric practice in general and of this system of guru yoga in particular: that one be enabled to receive the direct transmission of insight from one's own root guru, which alone can usher in consummate realization. The prayer's concluding verses state:

> Having developed strong revulsion for dwelling in samsara
>   and taking full responsibility for liberating all sentient beings
>   [without exception],
>   and seeing my Blessed Guru as Lord Buddha himself,
>   may I be blessed to quickly attain the state of Mahamudra,
>   that most exquisite state of total integration.

Your body, Father, and my own body;
your speech, Father, and my own speech;
your mind, Father, and my own mind:
may I be blessed to realize quickly
their true inseparability![349]

Chanting this prayer helps to bring to mind the continuous *living* lineage of those who have, in following the Buddhist path, successfully reached its goal. Moreover, because it causes one to contemplate the good qualities of each siddha of the lineage, it trains the mind to appreciate goodness and virtue and to dwell on such qualities as a direct and practical means of generating them in oneself. The solemn request for inspiring strength from those who are identical with the Buddha himself is continuously made. Whenever there is a break in the daily routine of practice, the fuller namthar themselves are read and contemplated if they are available.[350] Throughout all these activities, there is an air of heartfelt devotion; the accomplishments of the siddhas are inspiring. And they are *empowering*.

"What concrete benefits do people derive from reading namthar?" "How do namthar function within the lived world of Tibetan Buddhist thought and practice?" I asked these questions of many lamas. A remarkably concise and candid response was given to me by the Gelukpa Geshé Jampal Thardö, who said:

Well, some people use them in their teaching or to write books! Lamas, too, use them to teach and write books. But they are much more useful and interesting when associated with one's practice. For example, if one is practicing the *Guhyasamaja Tantra*, first one reads the prayer to the lineage lamas. Second, for understanding in detail the qualities of each lama in the lineage—in order to obtain that lama's *power*—one reads the namthar of that lama.[351]

In point of fact, lamas often use namthar in their teaching activities. No lama would, for example, introduce a new teaching or begin a series of initiations without first narrating one or more namthar of the teachers in the lineage who practiced that teaching or meditation successfully. This makes for very practical instruction. The recitation of namthar sets the stage for practice by giving authority and credence to the lineage of teachings, by prefiguring the conditions conducive to practice, and by subtly sowing the seeds for similar liberation.[352]

Such preparations are all the more necessary when the imminent undertaking is tantric practice. Deciding to commit oneself fully to the tantric path—with its strict discipline, rigorous yogic practices, and numerous pitfalls—is by no means a small matter. Thus it is only natural that it is inspirational, even joyously uplifting, to contemplate real persons who have traveled that path successfully. Namthar provide examples of human beings not very different from ourselves, who, owing to the guidance of a kind teacher and through their own efforts in practice, were able to transform themselves for the better. Were namthar solely tales of miraculous births and fantastic feats, their capacity to inspire would be lacking, as they would seem to place success out of the reach of ordinary human beings. In truth, only those examples that are capable of being replicated are capable of inspiring.

Central to all of this—to the success of the siddhas of the past and to our own future success—is the guru. One could say, in fact, that devotion to the guru is the central thread running through all namthar. In the Tibetan tradition, the lama (*bla ma*), or "superior teacher," is the *sine qua non* of all practice. The title of "lama" is not applied, as is sometimes wrongly assumed, to just any Tibetan monk, but rather is strictly reserved for a teacher who is capable of leading disciples to a direct and genuine experience of the Buddha's teachings. Anyone may teach the words of a particular doctrine, but only a lama is able to give those words life, to reveal to a disciple their ultimate meaning and true spirit. Thus, a lama is one who can confer both instruction and power, the living spirit of the teachings. We see this central theme of guru devotion echoed in the concluding verses of the Geluk Mahamudra Lineage Prayer and throughout these six accounts. It is what lies behind the statement in Sangyé Yeshé's namthar that "Gyalwa Ensapa gave him instructions for *tasting* [the teachings]."

Indeed, the lama is so essential for preserving and ensuring the continued vitality and purity of the teachings that he or she is placed first in the traditional Tibetan Buddhist refuge formula.[353] Tibetans hold that "without the lama, there is no Buddha," and it is said that Sangyé Yeshé always advised his followers that "before there is the guru, there is not even the name of the Buddha!" Gyalwa Ensapa's main practice was always "to train the mind to see the guru as the Buddha," and he is quoted as having said: "The size of one's realizations is completely dependent on the size of one's guru devotion."

It is the lama who introduces us to the teachings, and it is he or she who assists us all along the way. It is from the lama that we derive the benefit of the Buddha's actual presence as a teacher. The Buddha Shakyamuni passed away more than 2,500 years ago. We cannot see or communicate directly with that historical being, but we can do these things with our guru of this life. Since the guru embodies all good qualities, he or she is identical in essence with the absolute nature of the Buddha.

Commenting on the importance of guru devotion, His Holiness the Fourteenth Dalai Lama has said:

> In order to safely traverse the paths and stages that untie the knots of emotional and karmic bondage, one must correctly apply an effective method. The most certain way to ensure this correct application is to rely upon a fully qualified spiritual friend, someone who has personally realized the fruits of spiritual training and who has gained the ability to communicate his or her experiences to trainees.... In general, the more powerful the method being applied, the more qualified must the teacher be. For instance, one must rely upon a guru who is a fully enlightened Buddha in order to engage successfully in the final yogas of Highest Tantra....[354]

Another account says: "Without the guru, there would be no teachings and no path. Therefore devotion makes possible the transmission of sacred outlook, enlightened mind, from guru to disciple. Devotion to one's guru is thus the ground, path, and fruition of vajrayāna."[355]

This is especially true with regard to tantric practices such as the Mahamudra. In fact, it is held that the ultimate realization of the supreme siddhi, Mahamudra itself, is attainable *only* through the guru's blessing.[356] This realization is not something that can be learned from books. In order to experience it, one must learn directly from a teacher who has such realization. Then one must follow that teacher's instructions. The practices of guru devotion and guru yoga are therefore the ones that immediately precede Mahamudra practice itself.[357]

After carefully choosing a guru—and there are numerous texts on how one ought to go about investigating before doing so[358]—the disciple should observe three general types of behavior toward him or her. These behaviors are known as the "three ways to delight a guru" or the "three joys":[359] to make material offerings to the guru, always to show respectful behavior toward the guru, and always to follow the guru's instructions. In this context, the special bonds between lama and disciple are unique, and owing to their closeness, the two are often referred to as "father and son" (or "father and daughter").

In these six namthar we see the dynamics of these guru-disciple relationships played out, and we witness in them the continuous transmission of the living lineage of Buddhist realization. The Buddha's teachings have come down to us without interruption through a continuous stream of realized ones, all of whom, it may be said, now stand before us in the form of the guru.[360] This is the central meaning of "lineage" in Tibetan Buddhism.

Jampal Gyatso's utter commitment to practice, for example, not only pleased his root guru, Tsongkhapa, but also greatly inspired the other members of the famed Wölka ('Ol kha) retreat. When Chökyi Dorjé first approached his Mahamudra guru, Baso Jé, his namthar tells us that he did so "as if he were approaching his own father; and arriving at his feet, with much reverence and single-pointed devotion, he no longer thought of anything of this world, not even of his actual mother and father of this life." The great Gyalwa Ensapa had two gurus whom he counted as his root gurus, and through his strenuous efforts he delighted them both. Sangyé Yeshé was incredibly intelligent, but it was only after surrendering himself to Gyalwa Ensapa that he became "truly learned, both from the side of thought and of practice." The first meeting of a future siddha with the lama destined to become his guide to the ultimate siddhi is a momentous event. Often the disciple has had many illustrious teachers prior to this all-important meeting and has trained with zeal in numerous studies as well as in practice. Gyalwa Ensapa's story is an excellent example of this; Chökyi Dorjé has a dramatic impact on him! Jampal Gyatso is completely turned around when he finally comes face to face with Tsongkhapa. Each disciple knows when the real lama comes along. And for each future siddha, once the bond is made, there is the complete giving over of full commitment to the lama. Knowing that the lama's instruction is the vital link to highest attainment, nothing is held back.

These six life stories show us that not only were these six practitioners inspired by their own gurus and by siddhas previous to them, but they themselves were inspiring to their own contemporaries. Thus, there are numerous layerings of inspiration woven throughout these stories that continually become manifest to the reader.

For example, having won the ultimate fruit of practice, these siddhas go on to exhort and to inspire those around them. Thus Gyalwa Ensapa, famed for having completely abandoned the eight mundane concerns,[361] and who was therefore, it is said, "completely without guile," exhorted practitioners of the Dharma with these simple words of advice:

> If the Dharma is listened to, pondered, and practiced merely for the sake of attaining honor and reputation in this life— even if one really desires to learn the path to enlighten-ment—these actions, being connected with samsara, become tainted, like turning *amṛta* into poison, and serve only to render this precious human rebirth completely empty.[362] Instead, when hearing, pondering, and practicing the Dharma, one's aim should be first of all to subdue one's own mind. Then one should carefully investigate the path, continuously using stainless reasoning as the antidote for the defiling emotions. Moreover, anyone who claims to study the Dharma without out thoroughly investigating all the traditions of the Maha-

yana, and who likes to bicker over the slightest points of language—saying "You say this, but I say this"—completely misses the point!

Even though Jampal Gyatso desired only to meditate in isolated retreat, news of his unique intimacy with Lord Manjushri brought people of every sort to him seeking counsel. As already mentioned, the First Panchen was admired so much that at one time he was requested to assume the abbacy of five Gelukpa monasteries simultaneously. In Baso Jé's namthar he is praised by the distinguished Shapdrung (Zhabs drung) of Nenying, Kunga Delek (Kun dga' bde legs), with the following words:

> I do not take pride in having been born into an ancient lineage, but I do take pride in being a student of Baso Chöjé.

One of the students of the First Panchen, known as Shungkhang Rabjampa (Gzhun khang rab 'byams pa), was himself a famous teacher from the Gomang (Sgo mang) college at Drepung. Still, referring to the First Panchen, he said:

> Even though I have received many Dharma teachings from many lamas in Central Tibet and Tsang, including even Ganden's throneholder himself, and even though I am myself extremely hardheaded, all of your teachings have so helped my mind that a supreme reverence for you has been born in me that formerly was not possible for any others.

Finally, through these accounts we witness the reverence with which each of these six regarded the great siddhas who lived and practiced before them, like the tantric master Naropa. The First Panchen wished to imitate the great siddhas Milarepa and Shabaripa. His namthar mentions Chökyi Dorjé and Saraha in the same sentence. Like others of the six, he also went on pilgrimage to visit the places where the famed Wölka retreat had taken place, and where Jampal Gyatso had later practiced and his relics were enshrined. Naturally, they all revered Tsong-khapa, that living example of the "model of virtue" and of accomplished practice; we see each of them reflecting continuously on the life of Tsongkhapa as inspiration for their own practice.

The Tibetan tradition holds that in addition to a lama's ability to confer instruction and initiation, he or she should also possess three other "perfect virtues." These are the abilities to explain the doctrine; to debate, skillfully refuting an antagonist's position; and to compose, committing one's own system of explanation to writing.[363] As their respective namthar attest, these six Gelukpa siddhas were masters in all these areas, and their tradition greatly reveres them for this.

SANG, THE INSTRUCTIONAL

I have already suggested that one of the major ways in which namthar surpass Western hagiography is in their role as vehicles for specific instruction. This is because, being the biographies of tantric practitioners, they operate in ways similar to other tantric literature. One of the things we know about tantric literature in general is that, in it, things are not always as they seem. Intricate systems of symbolic correspondences are used, and ordinary language is called on to function in an extraordinary way to suggest the richness and taste of a reality that is ultimately ineffable.

The "secret biography" of a siddha is said to describe that siddha's meditative accomplishments, mystical visions, and other spiritual experiences. For many who work with this material, this amounts to saying that a secret biography simply presents descriptions of siddhis. In the judgment of some Western scholars, it is the inclusion of this kind of material that makes namthar "popular" compositions of dubious value. I would only suggest again that these assessments betray a narrow and elitist perspective that prevents such scholars from seeing that these texts can be, at the same time, both popular *and* profound.

Now it seems to me only natural that the biographies of siddhas should include some mention of siddhis, or magical powers, since the latter go hand-in-hand with the very definition of the former. Moreover, the inclusion of descriptions of siddhis not only testifies to the truth of the title "siddha" but enhances the siddha's capacity to inspire as well. The importance attached to Padmasambhava's ability to display such powers has already been noted. These six Geluk siddhas also, owing to their success in practice, are said to have had these attainments.

Jampal Gyatso's namthar tells us that he came to possess "fierce siddhis" to cure illness, subjugate evil spirits, make predictions, and even prolong life. He is even credited with extending Tsongkhapa's life through his prayers to Manjushri.[364] Chökyi Dorjé is famed for having won the siddhi of immortality. The great Gyalwa Ensapa, as a result of his training with Chökyi Dorjé, was able to pass through walls unhindered, count the individual particles of a mountain, and speak foreign languages without prior study.

Gyalwa Ensapa's life was also tremendously rich in visionary experiences. At a very early age, as he was practicing meditation in a cave, he was visited by the Buddha and Tsongkhapa, both of whom blessed him. At the age of eight, he envisioned that he flew upward one night and seated himself upon the moon, holding in his hands a *dorjé* (rdo rje) and bell with which he proclaimed the spread of the Buddhist Dharma. Numerous miraculous displays are said to have accompanied Gyalwa Ensapa's birth. It is said that upon being born he uttered the six-syllable mantra of Avalokiteshvara,[365] and that the gods, in response, rained down flowers throughout the region.

Having successfully mastered the propitiation of the wrathful Lord of Wisdom, Vajrabhairava, Sangyé Yeshé overpowered frightening apparitions with the force of his samadhi. The First Panchen Chökyi Gyaltsen also enjoyed a rich visionary life. He was visited and blessed by goddesses and yoginis, and by Tsongkhapa himself. Using his "subtle body" in the dream state, he is said to have memorized by heart all the root commentaries of the Mahayana. These are but a few examples.

Because they do figure so prominently within namthar, the question of siddhis must be tackled head-on. Magic plays no part in a siddha's meditative discipline, nor is it viewed as a means to his or her ultimate realization. Indeed, the term "magic" is itself so negatively charged in the West as to be almost completely inappropriate in such contexts.

Still, so-called magical or miraculous displays do have a prominent place in almost all namthar. Because of this, siddhas are often referred to in Western translations as "magicians" and even as "sorcerers"! All such characterizations, however, miss the mark of accurately describing a siddha, who, viewed properly, is an accomplished one, possessed of *power*. Now, the Buddhist tantric practitioner's main goal is not to gain such powers but rather to win ultimate realization in this very life. This is the highest, the superior, siddhi, or success. All other siddhis are subordinate; however, the lesser siddhis are said to come by the way as one advances along the path. Buddhist texts are very careful to distinguish between "mundane" or "worldly powers," attainable by yogis of any ascetic tradition, and the highest, supramundane siddhi, enlightenment, which alone is to be sought by the true Buddhist adept. In the six namthar translated here, this highest siddhi is called the "siddhi of Mahamudra" because it was by using this particular tantric method that these six practitioners attained enlightenment.

The crux of the problem regarding siddhis seems to have to do not so much with "magic" as with "power." Siddhas are said to possess powers, mainly powers to control natural phenomena. Still, and in spite of the fact that quantum mechanics has discredited much of Newtonian physics, as one modern scholar puts it: "Contemporary science continues, despite its relativistic tendencies, to expect a certain stability and uniformity in nature, and to be suspicious still of alleged events which seem to disturb its expected order."[366] Within the Buddhist tradition, though, siddhis are viewed as quite natural phenomena: the results that accrue to those who, through rigorous meditation, have gained an increased awareness regarding the true nature of reality. Owing to such increased awareness, reality itself becomes malleable in a siddha's hands. It is then said that such a one has gained extraordinary powers: the ability to control or to alter certain natural and psychic forces.

It should be noted that while much is made of the possession and displays of siddhis in tantric literature, this same sense of power appears under the term *ṛddhi* in some of the earliest strata of Buddhist literature. For example, perhaps the best known enumeration of the mundane siddhis is that found in the Dīgha Nikāya, I. 78. There, when the Buddha enumerates for King Ajatasattu the fruits of the life of a monk, he mentions the attainment of various ṛddhi and describes them as follows:

> Being one, he becomes many, or having become many, he
> becomes one again; he becomes visible or invisible; without
> obstruction he passes through walls, through fences, through
> mountains, as if they were but air; he penetrates up and down
> through solid earth, as if it were but water; he walks on water
> without parting it, as if it were solid ground; cross-legged he
> travels through the air, as a bird on the wing; he touches and
> handles the moon and the sun, though they be so potent and
> mighty; even in this body of his, he scales the heights of the
> world up to the heaven of Brahma; just as a clever potter
> could succeed in making out of clay any shape of vessel he
> wanted to have.[367]

In the context of this sutra, the Buddha describes thirteen progressively higher fruits of asceticism and the monastic life. His description of the attainment of such magical powers immediately precedes the final fruit for the Theravadin monk: "realization of the Four Noble Truths, the destruction of the defiling emotions, and the full attainment of arhatship." Even while such ṛddhi are subordinate to complete liberation, they are ranked high in terms of the aspirant's progressive meditational development and accomplishment.

Indeed, accounts of the Buddha's own life—especially the later, more embellished ones—record numerous instances when he himself demonstrated such powers. The Sanskrit *Lalitavistara*[368] as well as the earlier *Mahavastu*[369] offer good examples of this. And it is well known, even in the early Theravadin literature, that the Buddha had two greatly renowned disciples: Shariputra, famed for his wisdom and insight, and Maha-Maudgalyayana, renowned for his mastery of rddhi.

As mentioned above, all siddhis, except the supreme siddhi of complete enlightenment, are regarded as only mundane and worldly powers—even if they appear extraordinary to us! Nonetheless, such siddhis are a feature of namthar. Their presence highlights the esteem accorded to a given siddha; they are signs of his or her holiness and success along the path. Moreover, such powers are said to be employed by tantric adepts as a means to aid, teach, and inspire others. For a true Buddhist practitioner who has abandoned the false idea of "self" and who, with developed compassion for all beings, treads the path toward complete enlightenment, siddhis are never sought after or used as ends in themselves. A Buddhist tantric adept must already have had some genuine realization of the bodhisattva's vow of compassion before even embarking on the tantric path. Thus the tradition holds that all powers are manifested and employed only to "help a bodhisattva in the attainment of all his aims for his own good and for the good of others."[370]

Having noted all of this, I wish here to make an additional observation that bears directly on the special nature—and what I suggest is the *dual sense*—of the term "secret" in the context of namthar. Within the genre of Buddhist sacred biography as a whole there are various kinds of narrative, which bear different titles. For example, there are the namthar, or "complete liberation" life stories; there are other narratives termed *dzepa* (*mdzad pa*) that focus primarily on the specific deeds and spiritual activities of the accomplished one; and there are still others that bear the name *tokjo* (*rtogs brjod*). This latter group is of particular interest here, since this title literally means an "utterance" or "declaration" (*jopa*) of the siddha's own spiritual realization (*tok*).

Above, I have given a general definition of the "secret" level of siddha biographies. Here, I present what an eminent Tibetan lama had to say on the subject. Geshe Losang Jampa[371] described for me what "secret" means in the context of a secret biography:

A true yogi does not wish to become famous in the world. That would be to mix up Dharma practice with worldly concerns. The great yogis, therefore, would keep their innermost realizations and meditative accomplishments secret. They might sometimes, however, have told their very closest disciples about such experiences in order to spur the disciples' faith, and sometimes these disciples later wrote down these experiences.

While such an explication of "secret" may be surprising to those intrigued solely by the esoteric features of tantric Buddhism, Geshe Jampa's remarks are surely reliable and are borne out by many examples. One need only recall, for example, a text that forms an essential part of every Gelukpa monk's recitations: the *Secret Biography of Tsongkhapa*,[372] written by Jamyang Chöje Tashi Palden (1379–1449), one of Tsong-khapa's direct disciples. After some initial verses of praise, the text consists almost entirely of an enumeration of Tsongkhapa's meditative and mystic experiences and realizations:[373]

> At the age of seven you directly perceived
> Dīpaṃkara Atīśa, the great Path Clearer,
> and Vajrapāṇi, Lord of the Secret.
> The exhortations of both the sūtras
> and tantras dawned upon you.
>
> O illustrious lama, at your feet I pay homage . . .
> You directly perceived Mañjuśrī . . .
> Seated in a radiant aura as blue
> as the color of perfect sapphire . . .
> From this time onward, O High One,
> whenever you desired you could invoke
> Mañjuśrī . . . and listen to the teachings . . .
> When practicing the seven-limbed ritual
> of the Thirty-five Purification Buddhas,
> continually and clearly you beheld them
> and all their forms, *mudrās* and symbols . . .
> All the mahāsiddhas of India and Tibet . . .
> appeared to, then constantly cared for, you . . .
> Having touched your heart
> to the wisdom sword of Mañjuśrī,
> a stream of undefiled ambrosia
> flowed into the depths of your being
> spontaneously arousing the propitious
> absorption of highest joy . . .

Your mind absorbed in the mystic circle of Heruka ...
Myriads of ḍākinīs of the outer, inner, and secret places
made you offerings of vajra songs,
transporting you in ecstasy;
O illustrious lama, at your feet I pay homage.

Clearly, the meditative realizations and achievements being described above are Tsongkhapa's own; they are visions and mystical events that could have been experienced and known only by him. They were later told to Tashi Palden, who recorded them. According to tradition, such personal disclosures qualify as secret biography.

Countless other examples of this level of biography can be found throughout the vast corpus of Tibetan sacred literature. When we read, for example, in the namthar of Jampal Gyatso that he "experienced a continuous, steady, and clear appearance of the body and speech of Jetsun Manjushri," we are reading secret biography. We are also reading secret biography when, in a passage describing the performance of the completion-stage practice of Guhyasamaja, Jampal Gyatso says, "During that time, I held to the practice [of not allowing the bodhicitta—here, semen—to slip away] for twenty-six full days." But is a secret biography merely an enumeration of the siddha's magical or mystical accomplishments? Is it only a listing of siddhis? I think not. The enumeration of such realizations and powers is what defines and validates a siddha, and in a sense there would *be* no siddha biography without the incorporation of at least some of these descriptions and accounts. Yet, while such a listing may certainly be viewed as a basis for faith, inspiration itself is not the sole aim of the secret level of these stories. This is why I suggest that they also often contain the siddha's own personal advice and pith instructions on practice for future practitioners, and this is why I believe that this instructional character is the second meaning of "secret" in these contexts. On the one hand, "secret" refers to those innermost meditative achievements experienced by the siddha. On the other, it refers to the tantric text's use of veiled or hidden analogical and symbolic language to prevent the uninitiated reader's ready access to practice instructions that might be too advanced. The meanings of these passages are thus hidden or secret until one is prepared and able to interpret the symbolic language with the proper understanding. Thus, what is "instructional" to advanced practitioners is "secret" to unskilled, ordinary beings.

The following passage from the namthar of the Gelukpa siddha Chökyi Dorjé (there are no dates given for him since he is said to have gained the siddhi of immortality), best demonstrates the convergence of these two meanings of the term "secret":

> In accordance with the words of advice of Chökyi Gyalt-sen, he wandered to many solitary places—to lonely forests and ravines as well as to snow-covered mountains. Then, at one time during this period, as he meditated near the sacred water of Pema Chan (Padma can), all the surrounding areas were suddenly transformed, becoming in an instant like the actual twenty-four places [in India], while the earth surrounding the water itself turned into *sindhura*. Thereupon at that famous spot, he performed the contemplations on guru yoga related to the completion stage, and he beheld the countenance of the King of Dharma, the great Tsongkhapa. It was then that Jé Rinpoché himself gave to this holy one the complete instructions of the ordinary and extraordinary oral tradition. In particular, Jé Rinpoché taught him the extraordinary practice of the three-tiered mental exercise of guru yoga wherein he visualized his own outward form as that of an Indian pandit and his inner aggregates and sense organs as a host of deities. In his heart, the Buddha Shakyatubpa was clearly manifest, and in that one's heart resided Vajradhara.[374]

It is clear that this passage describes events that could have been experienced directly and known only by Chökyi Dorjé himself. We are given a description of his meditative visions: his surroundings are "transformed," and Tsongkhapa appears and instructs him. We, too, are "told" these instructions. Even so, there is yet another level to this particular account, and several of its features are intriguing. To begin

with, the name of the supposed "place"[375] where this event occurred is
of interest because Pema Chan (Tib. Padma can)—literally, "having a
lotus"—is often a veiled reference to a woman. ("Lotus" in this context
may mean the vagina.)[376] Moreover, Pema Chan sometimes refers to a
female sexual partner in certain advanced tantric practices, particularly
those of the *mahanuttara yoga* category. The Pema Chan of the Chökyi
Dorjé account may or may not be a tantric consort, but I do think that
there is at least the suggestion that the place name Pema Chan may
indicate the completion-stage practice of using sexual union, whether
actual or imaginary, as a means to higher insight.

Now with regard to the "twenty-four places" mentioned in the passage, there can be little doubt that these refer simultaneously to the
so-called outer pilgrimage places, called *pithas*, said to be the dwelling
places for various groups of yoginis or dakinis, and also to the inner
places, yogically generated and located throughout an adept's body. The
body-mandala of the long Heruka Sadhana mentions these twenty-four
places,[377] and the theory of the twenty-four places is also found in the
Hevajra Tantra.

Shin'ichi Tsuda has given a detailed analysis based on the *Hevajra
Tantra* of the various correspondences among these external and internal pithas in his *A Critical Tantrism*.[378] As with tantric literature and
practices in general, the whole of ultimate reality, external and internal,
is made manifest through an intricate and delicately balanced ordering
of correspondences. These correspondences are expressed symbolically.
As there are external pithas, so there are internal pithas. The external
pithas have corresponding points on the "vajra body" once this is successfully generated by a tantric adept, such that the twenty-four sacred
external places are matched with corresponding places on the body:
head, fingernails, teeth, ears, backbone, liver, shoulders, eyes, nose,
penis, thighs, thumbs, knees, etc. Successfully generating the vajra body
adorned with these twenty-four spots, the tantric practitioner is said
to be able to compel the dakinis of the external pithas to approach and
enter the corresponding spots on his or her body. This again is symbolic,
or intentional, language. To quote from Tsuda:

"Internal *pīṭhas*" are abodes of veins (*nāḍisthāna*) as "external *pīṭhas*" are abodes of *ḍākinīs*. There are twenty-four parts of a body, such as the head corresponding to the external *pīṭha Pullīramalya*, etc. There are twenty-four veins (*nāḍī*) which rely on these internal pīṭhas such as (a vein) flowing through fingernails and teeth (*nakhadantavahā*), etc. These veins (*nāḍī*) are regarded as deities (*devatā*), that is, *ḍākinīs*. A *nāḍī* is nothing other than a *ḍākinī* . . . A human body is composed of these twenty-four "internal *pīṭhas*" such as the head, etc., as the world, that is, the *Jambudvīpa* in this case, is composed of twenty-four "external *pīṭhas*," i.e., twenty-four countries such as *Pullīramalya*, etc. An "internal *pīṭha*" is existent as long as it is an abode for a vein. A vein in turn is existent as long as it conveys a humour in it or it flows in an internal organ. Therefore, if one makes (the) twenty-four veins of one's own body *active*, through (the) yogic practice of making each of the humours flow through the corresponding veins or each of (the) veins flow through the corresponding internal organs, he transforms his body into an aggregate of internal *pīṭhas* or an aggregate of *ḍākinīs*, a homologous miniaturization of the world as an aggregate of external *pīṭhas* or an aggregate of *ḍākinīs* (*ḍākinījāla*). Thus he can unite himself with the ultimate reality on the basis of the Tantric logic of symbolism.[379]

One other element of this passage from Chökyi Dorjé's namthar deserves mention here—namely, the "sacred water" itself. Tibetan tradition says that there is a certain type of water found in sacred caves in Tibet that is a kind of holy nectar. Padmasambhava is said to have given long-life initiations to his disciples using this holy nectar.[380] However, there is room for further elaboration with respect to this. In tantric literature, water is often a symbol for the female or, more specifically, for menstrual blood.[381] The fact that the earth surrounding the water mentioned here is said to have turned into sindhura would seem to have specific reference to the supreme dakini-consort, the Goddess Vajrayogini, chief consort to Lord Chakrasamvara, since marking the disciple's "three doors"[382] with a sindhura powder is a special feature of the initiation into the higher tantric practice focusing on this particular deity. In fact, it would seem that this episode narrates—using the veiled language of the tantras—the unfolding and acting out in Chökyi Dorjé's own body of the yoga of the completion-stage techniques involved, in this case, with the practice based on the cycle of Chakrasamvara. If this is so, then this passage, in addition to providing us with a list of siddhis, or mystical visions, also employs the symbolic language of the tantras to describe and to impart information about the advanced practice associated with Chakrasamvara.

The above is an analysis of a brief and isolated event in a single namthar, but similar events appear in other life stories as well. Studying these texts has strongly suggested to me that an approach to this literature like the one I have indicated above may indeed prove helpful. Treating a given namthar as a piece of tantric literature that is intended to provide instructions and inspiration to practitioners can help us to glean valuable information about the Vajrayana in general and about specific practices in particular. In this way, Tibetan sacred biographies become less obscure, and certainly less folkloric, and are shown to be capable of providing us with valuable insights into the lived world of Tibetan tantric Buddhism.

Before concluding this introduction, one specific and unique feature of these six namthar should be mentioned: the so-called *Miraculous Volume* of the Gelukpa. It is said that the text is of "mystical origin" and that it is "accessible only to the most holy of the lineage gurus."[383] As will be seen, the *Miraculous Volume* figures prominently in these namthar, where it is said to be entrusted to each succeeding disciple once that one has accomplished the highest goal of practice. It thus functions in these stories as a type of seal of accomplishment. It should be noted that many Gelukpa lamas claim that, from the time of the First Panchen, the *Volume* has been entrusted to the deity Kalarupa for safekeeping. One can find more information about the *Miraculous Volume* in the notes to the various translations here.

Regardless of our individual approaches, I believe that there is much in these namthar to inspire us. These six figures contributed greatly to ensuring the purity and vitality of the Gelukpa tradition in particular and of Buddhism in Tibet in general. For their selfless efforts in mastering and spreading the Dharma, they have fully earned the title "siddha" and "enlightened being." Such exemplary figures have continued to inspire those within the Tibetan tradition to this very day. May that inspiration, like ambrosia, spill across cultural boundaries to inspire us as well.

Part IV
Buddhist-Christian
Comparative Reflections

❧ ❧

14

The Goddess and the Flowers

◦⧸⧸ ⧹⧹◦

India, Second Century

During the time of the Buddha, a great congregation of bodhisattvas, celestial beings, and monks were all gathered at Layman Vimalakirti's house, debating the teachings together. A goddess was there too, and one day she was so full of joy that she scattered celestial flowers over the whole congregation. The flowers that landed on the bodhisattvas fell to the floor, but those that landed on the monks stuck to them. The monks tried to shake the flowers from their robes, to no avail.

The goddess then asked the monk Shariputra, "Reverend Shariputra, why are you trying to brush away these flowers?"

Shariputra replied, "Because flowers are not proper for religious people."

Then the goddess spoke: "Why shouldn't flowers be proper for religious people? Flowers do not conceptualize or discriminate; you monks are conceptualizing and discriminating. Even though you have renounced your homes for the sake of the Dharma, if you make discriminations, you are not religious. If you make no discriminations, then you are truly religious. Evil spirits have power over the fearful but cannot disturb the fearless. So those afraid of forms, sounds, smells, tastes, and textures are under the power of the passions that arise from these things. The flowers stick to those who are afraid of them; they fall from the bodies of those who are free from the discriminations that lead to fear."

JAN WILLIS'S REFLECTION

This is a wonderful story on so many levels. It is basically a story about the error of focusing on religious "purity" and the observance of religious "rules" rather than on the core of religion and spirituality, which is the good heart. The story is also about fear, and it tells us that often it is fear that holds us back from acting freely and rightly in the world. Thus, if we want to act in accordance with the heart-core of practice, we need to loosen such discriminations and fears. Because Shariputra and the other monks have not done this, the flowers stick to them but not to the bodhisattvas, those who see the ultimate truth without discrimination and whose trademark is, therefore, the truly altruistic heart.

When the goddess asks Shariputra why he is brushing away the flowers she offered, he responds, "Because flowers are not proper for religious people." Here we see clearly that, for Shariputra at least, some things are "proper" and some things are not. There are rules! Moreover, he believes that following the rules ought to be paramount for "religious people." The goddess's response—that flowers do not discriminate and neither would the monks if they were truly religious—is a marvelous pronouncement. She points to the heart of the matter: namely, that "religious" folk need to put into practice the heart-teachings of their religious tradition and not just follow, by rote, its prescriptions.

Now, because I see myself as a Baptist Buddhist, I also see a strong Christian parallel with this story in the parable of the Good Samaritan. You'll remember that in the parable, a man is robbed and beaten and left to die by the wayside on the road to Jericho. First a priest comes along and sees him. But the priest chooses not to help the man and instead crosses to the other side of the road. Next comes along a Levite, and he, too, passes over to other side. But then a Samaritan happens by, and seeing the man's poor condition—and without judging and discriminating about it—the Samaritan approaches the man, binds his wounds, places him on his own donkey, takes him to an inn, and gives the innkeeper money to continue the care of the man until his return. At the end of his narration of the parable, Jesus asks, "Now which of the three was truly the man's neighbor?" Or, put another way, which of the three was truly a "religious" man?

Perhaps the first two "religious" men, the priest and the Levite, were afraid that they would themselves be harmed if they stopped to help the wounded man. The robbers might still be around. Or perhaps they thought that stopping to help the wounded man might somehow be defiling to them because he might not be of their tribe or clan. Either way, it was the priest's and the Levite's fears that prevented them from acting religiously.

Interestingly, in Jesus's time, Jews regarded Samaritans with scorn. They considered them to be polluting and didn't want any physical contact with them. What a good thing that this particular Samaritan did not see the world this way! Rather than ask, "If I help this man, what might happen to *me*?" the good Samaritan asked, "If I don't help this man, what will happen to *him*?" In Martin Luther King's words, "the good Samaritan engaged in a dangerous altruism."

I was once soundly berated by a young African American man, a newly "reborn" Christian, who told me that, by seeing goodness and virtue in the Buddha's teachings, I was not accepting Jesus Christ as my sole salvation and was therefore destined for eternal damnation. I told him that I didn't believe that Jesus himself would see it that way!

Discriminations and judgments usually serve only to alienate us, one from another, rather than bring us closer. According to Mahayana scriptures (where bodhisattvas figure so prominently), a tenth-stage bodhisattva—that is, a buddha—is referred to as a "cloud of Dharma" because, like rain, he shares the teachings with all, equally and without discrimination. Whether we speak of Dharma rain or of the flowers of this story, the lesson is, "Give up fear and don't discriminate, and then you'll truly be practicing!" It seems very good advice.

15

Community of "Neighbors": A Baptist-Buddhist Reflects on the Common Ground of Love

❧ ❧

Today we are all aware that the concept of "race" is a mere construction. There is only one "race": the human race; to think otherwise is like still believing that the earth is flat. But "racism" is a different matter. It exists as a system of beliefs and prejudices that people differ along biological and genetic lines and that one's own group is superior to another group. When these beliefs and prejudices are coupled with power—especially the power to negatively affect the lives of those perceived to be inferior—we have a serious problem. And no one should downplay or underestimate the harm that such an ideology inflicts on everyone who participates in it. According to one African American professor of social work, "America's history is inextricably bound to this racist ideology. From the codifying of slavery, to the belief in 'Manifest Destiny,' to the treatment of 'illegal immigrants,' many of America's actions continue to conflict with its creed that 'All men are created equal.'"[384]

Over the past decade or so, I have written a number of pieces that focus on racism in America and racism in so-called American Buddhism.[385] Being African American myself, my reasons for this focus may perhaps be clear though not necessarily inevitable. I have written on a number of other topics: Buddhist philosophical discourses and life

stories of Buddhist "saints," for example. In my writings on racism, I
have tried to communicate something of the emotional and psychic toll
it takes to live in this country as a person of color. In a number of these
writings, I have called myself a "Baptist Buddhist," and thus this is also
one of my "dual belongings," one of my "multiple identities."

When I speak of racism, I am not concerned with garnering pity, or
playing the "race card" of guilt, or telling you, from some assumed position of superiority on the matter, that there is simply no way for you to
understand this toll. I certainly cannot speak for all African Americans,
or even for most of them. Early on in the process of writing this paper,
I emailed the organizers of this conference, Jung and Paul, to say that I
found the title of the panel both much too broad and much too narrow.
Too broad because one person cannot possibly channel and/or verbal-
ize the countless instances of suffering endured by African Americans
(and more broadly, by persons of color) throughout space and over
centuries in this country owing to slavery and its aftermath. And too
narrow because, ultimately, we want to do more than just rehash our
many sufferings. We don't want to wallow in victimhood. We want to
move on—from the recognition of that immense suffering, seen and
unseen—and to go out into the world and act to bring about racial,
social, economic, and ecological justice. That's what we are called on to
do: to form a new community wherein there is compassion and caring
for one another, where there is love and peace, nonviolence, reconciliation, and justice.

So even though I am quite frankly tired—as are so many people of
color—of being the token African American who can add visible diversity to a group in order to show that it is now more inclusive than before,
nevertheless, in this so-called postracial society where we have a black
president and the demographic of "persons of color" now comprises an
actual majority of the United States' population, I must still rise to say
that, sadly, racism is not dead in this country! Its painful vestiges exist,
and those vestiges are far from being either innocent or unharmful.

I truly believe that—for African Americans, in particular—it is the
trauma and the legacy of slavery that haunts us in the deepest recesses
of our souls. It is hard to imagine what having been bartered and sold as

though mere property does to a human being, what being dehumanized, infanticized, and divested of all rights and liberties does to one's sense of self-worth and well-being. As I once wrote, the trauma of slavery "is the chief issue for us. It needs to be dealt with, head-on—not denied, not forgotten, not suppressed. Indeed, its suppression and denial only hurts us more deeply, causing us to accept a limited, disparaging, and even repugnant view of ourselves. We cannot move forward until we have grappled in a serious way with all the negative effects of this trauma."[386]

Some of the wounds of slavery are buried very deep within. I grew up in the Jim Crow South where traces of the system of human chattel were everywhere apparent, where Black Codes and the rules of segregation defined and dictated for us our "places," where the water fountains were designated "white" and "colored" and our parents warned us against ever drinking from the wrong one! And yet I was fortunate enough to be a fifteen-year-old teenager when the Rev. Dr. Martin Luther King Jr. decided to bring the civil rights movement to Birmingham and to let us children lead the marches there. So I got that invaluable opportunity to march with King, and I wouldn't trade that for anything.

Some say those days of overt racism and segregation are over.[387] But they are not. Racism in America still shows its face each and every day— for those of us who experience it directly—in ways great and small. We may have heard about James Byrd Jr., the black man in Texas whose body was chained to a truck and dragged for several miles before being finally decapitated.[388] We probably know the sad history of Emmett Till, the fourteen-year-old boy visiting from Chicago who was savagely beaten and then shot outside his relative's home in Money, Mississippi.[389] We may lament the countless lynchings of blacks that occurred throughout the southern states in the 1920s and 1930s. We may suspect that if today there are more young African American males imprisoned in this country than are in its institutions of higher education, then something is wrong. But, even apart from these bigger examples, people of color continue to suffer countless small indignities each day in this country as well. In my memoir, *Dreaming Me: Black, Baptist, and Buddhist*, I titled a chapter "Little Things" to point to these experiences—to the unseen and perhaps unconscious behaviors of others that inflict real wounds. Let me quote here just a couple of passages from that chapter by way of example:

A woman in Jasper, Texas—a baby-boomer, modern, "with-it" liberal—said on *Racism in America*, a TV documentary in the 1990s, that she hadn't known how badly divided her community had become or that the division between whites and blacks had widened rather than narrowed. She hadn't known that day in and day out, blacks in her own community still suffered so from racism's soul-crushing hatefulness. She told the documentary's interviewer, "It's the little things, like not putting their change actually back into their hands, just laying it on the counter." She recounted, as if in amazement, the simple question raised by a local black man, "Why can't you put the change back in my hands? Am I so low, so disgusting to you, that you can't touch me?" The liberal-minded baby-boomer hadn't known it was so bad, went so deep, and was reflected in such little things.

Not long after I arrived in Middletown, Connecticut, and assumed my new position as a tenured professor of religion at Wesleyan in the late 1970s, I ventured down the three blocks from campus to Main Street. It was almost Christmas. I had a smoking friend, and I had decided to get her a nice cigarette lighter. Off I went, happily. There were already several lines of shoppers in the first jewelry store I entered. It was Christmas, I thought to myself. I waited patiently, with all the rest of the shoppers. When finally my turn came at the counter, I said to the slim, gray-haired, bespectacled saleswoman facing me, "Hello, I'd like to see some lighters, please."

"We only have *expensive* lighters here!" she said, dismissing me abruptly. For a moment, I was completely stunned. I wasn't sure I had heard her right. I stood there in silence.

Before her remark could register and draw forth an outburst from my innermost core, a young white man in the line next to me said aloud, "Ah, lady! Show the woman the lighters!" He had recognized the woman's dart as being intended to wound me. He had seen what I had just suffered, and it embarrassed and angered him. But I was too angry and too hurt to speak. My inability to respond to her made me even angrier. I turned away from the counter and thanked the man as I exited the store.[390]

These are the "little things," the small indignities that aren't easily seen.

Now, to be fair, whites, too, experience the effects and legacies of slavery. For the most part, however, these are little noticed. Why would one notice? They are, after all, what we consider "normative." They are what are now being termed by some "white privilege." When whites look in the mirror each morning, it may well be to notice new wrinkles or unaligned teeth, but rarely, I suspect, does the image reflected there engender a worry about what small indignities might have to be suffered this day. If we like, we might read the famed 1961 account by the journalist John Howard Griffin, *Black Like Me*,[391] to get some idea of what it may have felt like to be black in the southern states in the late 1950s. But the real story today is what is not felt by whites, owing to their possession of white privilege. This fairly new focus of research suggests that rather than focus exclusively on the human cost of racism, we might explore instead the ways in which some people or groups actually benefit, deliberately or inadvertently, from racial bias. There are some good resources available.[392]

In the end, I don't like the term "racism." I feel that it sensationalizes things. The term immediately makes everything more loaded and heavy. I'd rather readers of my work first read what I'm trying to say than be turned off before attempting to understand me. "Racism" is a big, heavy thing. Its mention has the power to shut down conversations before they can even begin. I don't like the term "racism" because it is ugly; it is about violence—whether to body, soul, or spirit. It is about hate. I much prefer to think about and to meditate on love.

LOVE

As most of us know, love is a cardinal principle of all of the world's religious traditions. It stands at the center of what we, as religious and spiritual beings, are called on to practice. But its practice is not easy!

As Christians, we are taught that the "good news" (the Gospel, from the Old English *godspell*) is that God loves us. He is no longer solely a vengeful God—as so much of the Old Testament tells us— but he now shows us a new, softer face and gives us a new chance for salvation (through the loving sacrifice of His Son, Jesus Christ, as a ransom for our sins). Over and over again, we are reminded that the hallmark of true Christian behavior is love. For example, there is the oft-quoted New Testament passage found in 1 Corinthians, "Though I speak with the tongues of men and of angels, and have not love, I am become but as a sounding brass or tinkling cymbal. . . . And though I have the gift of prophecy, and understand all mysteries, and all knowledge; and though I have faith, so that I could remove moun- tains, but have not love, I am nothing. . . . And now abideth faith, hope, and love, but the greatest of these is love" (1 Corinthians 13, vv. 1–2 and 13).

In his First Epistle General, the apostle John (who tells us the mean- ing of Jesus's life and resurrection) tells us: "Beloved, let us love one another: for love is of God; and every one that loveth is born of God, and knoweth God. He that loveth not, knoweth not God; for God is love" (1 John 4:7–8). Having defined "God" as "love," the apostle John then goes on to tell us how God has used, has employed the life, death, and resurrection of Jesus, as a means for our individual salvation: "In this was manifested the love of God toward us, because God sent his only begotten Son into the world, that we might live through him. Herein is love, not that we loved God, but that he loved us, and sent his Son to be propitiation for our sins" (1 John 4:9–10).

The apostle John then announces how we, in recognition of the fact that Jesus has died for us, should or ought to behave. Interestingly, and importantly, it is not how we should behave toward God or toward Jesus, but toward each other—toward our fellow human beings. John writes: "Beloved, if God so loved us, we ought also to love one another" (1 John 4:11).

As I mentioned earlier, I call myself a "Baptist Buddhist." This is not a theological stance for me, but rather an empirical description of who I feel I am. I was once on a plane that came very close to crashing. And in those tense moments, I found that I called on both my Baptist and Buddhist spiritual backgrounds. These are very deep responses. As Kierkegaard once wrote, "One doesn't truly know what one believes until one is forced to act."[393] Moreover, because I grew up in Alabama just outside of Birmingham, and as a teenager marched with King during the Birmingham campaign, I learned about nonviolent social activism at that time. Many of the ideas that I later encountered in Buddhist teachings I had already heard from King and other civil rights activists. So finding once again the themes of nonviolence, interdependence, and love in Buddhism was, for me, like coming home.

In Buddhism also, love is a cardinal principle, a central tenet. For example, in the famed early Buddhist classic the *Dhammapada*,[394] at verse 5 one finds this concise description of Buddhist belief and practice: "Hatred is never appeased by hatred. Hatred is only appeased by love. This is an eternal law." The term translated here as "eternal law" is *Dhamma* (in the Pali), or *Dharma* (in Sanskrit). In short, this message is at the very heart of all Buddhist teachings: We must practice love. (The Dalai Lama often says, "My religion is kindness.") If this is so, how are we to practice it? Another *Dhammapada* verse, number 183, encapsulates the entirety of the Buddhist path as follows: "Do no harm. Practice virtue. Purify the mind. This is the teaching [i.e., the Dhamma] of all the buddhas."

Again, the Dalai Lama—paraphrasing the great eighth-century Buddhist poet Shantideva—often says, "We all desire to be happy and to avoid suffering. In this respect, we are all exactly alike. Therefore, as much as possible, let us seek to do good to one another; and if we cannot do good, let us at least try not to harm!"

The Buddha founded a community, a sangha, to foster and encourage these principles. It consisted of four parts: monks, nuns, laymen, and laywomen, in that order, in deference to his time and cultural milieu. One should note that the Buddha's sangha was diverse; it consisted of young and old members, of men and women, and, importantly, of beings drawn from all the four *varnas* or castes of India at that time.[395] The Buddha said, "The members of a sangha look after one another," and again, "When you look after each other, you are looking after the Tathāgata (or, me)." (There seem to be some echoes here of later New Testament passages.)

Now, I would like for a moment to focus on a well-known Christian story known as the parable of the Good Samaritan. This story is found in two separate places in the Gospels, in the accounts of Matthew and in those of Luke. At Matthew 22, we find the following, when a lawyer among Jesus's listeners asks him:

> "Master, which is the greatest commandment in the law?"
> And Jesus said unto him, "Thou shalt love the Lord thy God with all thy heart, and with all thy soul, and with all thy mind. This is the first and great commandment. And the second is like unto it: Thou shalt love thy neighbor as thyself."

I believe that this is as compact a declaration of Christian doctrine and practice as one will find. For here, one finds both the letter and the spirit of the law. What does a Christian accept fully in mind? And how ought a Christian to behave, ethically? That is, what kind of heart should she seek to develop? (In Buddhist thought, it should be noted, these two—mind and heart—are so integrally connected that the same term, *citta*, is often used to denote them.)

Now, at Luke 10:25–27, we get the fuller context as well as the afore-mentioned complete parable. Here we find the following:

> And, behold, a certain lawyer stood up, and tempted him, saying, "Master, what shall I do to inherit eternal life?"
> Jesus said unto him, "What is written in the law? How readest thou?"
> And he, answering, said, "Thou shalt love the Lord thy God with all thy heart, and with all thy soul, and with all thy strength, and with all thy mind; and thy neighbor as thyself."

And Jesus said unto him, "Thou hast answered right: this do, and thou shalt live."

But he, willing to justify himself, said unto Jesus, "And who is my neighbor?"

And Jesus, answering, said, "A certain man went down from Jerusalem to Jericho, and fell among thieves, who stripped him of his raiment, and wounded him, and departed, leaving him half dead. And by chance a certain priest came down that way; and when he saw the wounded man, he passed by on the other side. And likewise a Levite, when he was at the place, came and looked on him, and passed by on the other side. But a certain Samaritan, as he journeyed, came where the wounded man lay: and when he saw him, he had compassion on him, and went to him, and bound up his wounds, pouring in oil and wine, and set him on his own beast, and brought him to an inn, and took care of him. And on the morrow when he departed, he took out two pence, and gave them to the host, and said unto him, 'Take care of him; and whatsoever more thou spendest, when I come again, I will repay thee.' Now which of these three, thinkest thou, was neighbor unto him that fell among the thieves?"

And he said, "He that showed mercy on him."

Then said Jesus unto him, "Go, and do thou likewise."

This is certainly a quite rich narrative, with many intricate and subtle twists. But the heart of the story is this: We are human beings, we are children of God, and, as such, we must love one another. For it is only in the acting out of this love that we truly perform our sacred duty and act in accordance with God's laws and God's wishes. How do we show that we love God? We show it by loving our neighbors! This is our job; this is how we show, how we demonstrate, who we truly are.

When Jesus asks, "Now which of the three was [truly] neighbor unto the man?" he is really asking which of the three was truly the religious man. Perhaps the first two "religious" men, the priest and the Levite, were afraid that they might themselves be harmed if they stopped to help the wounded man; the robbers might still be around. Or perhaps they thought that by stopping to help the wounded man, they might somehow be defiled or polluted by him since he was not of their tribe or clan. But—either way—it was the priest's and the Levite's fears that prevented them from acting religiously. In Jesus's time, Jews regarded all Samaritans with scorn. Samaritans were considered to be polluting, and so no Jew wanted any physical contact with them. What a good thing that this particular Samaritan did not see the world this way! Rather than ask, "If I help this man, what might happen to me?" the Good Samaritan asked, "If I don't help this man, what will happen to him? In King's words, "the Good Samaritan engaged in a dangerous altruism."[396] He was willing to practice putting another's well-being above his own. (In Buddhism, this is called being a compassionate bodhisattva.)

In his book *No Future without Forgiveness*, Desmond Tutu beautifully explains this care and compassion for one another as the idea of *ubuntu*.[397] Tutu notes that we are human beings by virtue of acting humanely in a community of beings who all belong, and who therefore care for one another.

But practicing in this way is not always easy. In fact, it is most times very difficult. We are all accustomed to putting our own selves first. So it does not come naturally to us to love our neighbors, much less so to love those we consider our "enemies." Yet love must become for us a sustained habit, an attitude, not simply a one-time knee-jerk response; and to generate this transformed view requires serious practice. Buddhism offers many meditative tools to help bring about this transformed view. The methods employed are both calming and analytical in nature. A key notion is that of our interconnectedness. It is a positive take on the universal Buddhist idea of *shunyata* (Skt.; Pali *sunna*). Usually the term is misleadingly translated as "emptiness" or "voidness," but the concept more appropriately connotes the idea that we are "empty" or "void" of independence and so are dependent beings, unable to truly live or to be ultimately satisfied on our own, completely without others. We are interconnected by our very nature.

Dr. King knew about this interconnectedness also. Indeed, he spoke about it often and often tied it into social justice issues. For example, he wrote:

> In a real sense, all life is interrelated. All men are caught in an inescapable network of mutuality, tied in a single garment of destiny. Whatever affects one directly affects all indirectly. I can never be what I ought to be until you are what you ought to be, and you can never be what you ought to be until I am what I ought to be. This is the interrelated structure of reality.[398]

We do not exist independently. We need only breathe to know this. This is the real—not virtual—Internet. We are inextricably bound together. And therefore, unless we find a way to live together, we shall—all of us—perish together. And since this is the case, since this is our reality, we must have compassion for one another. Another way of saying this is, "If you suffer, I suffer, and if you are happy, I am happy." And this is just exactly what the bodhisattva—and the true Christian—knows and feels.

In King's sermon "On Being a Good Neighbor," he notes that "the ultimate measure of a man is not where he stands in moments of comfort and convenience, but where he stands at times of challenge and controversy. The true neighbor will risk his position, his prestige, and even his life for the welfare of others."[399] King concluded with the following: "No longer can we afford the luxury of passing by on the other side. Such folly was once called moral failure; today it will lead to universal suicide. We cannot long survive spiritually in a world that is geographically together. In the final analysis, I must not ignore the wounded man on life's Jericho Road, because he is a part of me and I am a part of him. His agony diminishes me, and his salvation enlarges me."[400]

The great Buddhist poet Shantideva wrote:

> All the joy the world contains
> has come from wishing happiness for others,
> while all the misery the world contains
> has come from wishing happiness for myself alone.[401]

Though it is not an easy practice, this practice of love, it is the practice that gives our lives true meaning. In this interconnected world, there is no one who is not, and no thing that is not, our neighbor. With this deep recognition of our very being, we need to go forth and act in the world.

KING'S "BELOVED COMMUNITY"

Dr. King had a vision of a "Beloved Community."[402] That vision calls for us to join together in a society wherein, recognizing our interdependence, we belong and share compassionately with one another. Recognizing that "God is Love" (a New Testament Christian notion), that "we exist in dependence on one another" (a Buddhist notion), and that nonviolence and nonharm (*ahimsa*) and love (*agape*) must be our sole methods of dealing with one another, King envisioned a society in which we could be our best selves by seeking the benefit of others, knowing that when we seek to lift others up, we ourselves are raised up.

This is how the King Center in Atlanta website describes King's vision:

> For Dr. King, The Beloved Community was not a lofty utopian goal to be confused with the rapturous image of the Peaceable Kingdom, in which lions and lambs coexist in idyllic harmony. Rather, The Beloved Community was for him a realistic, achievable goal that could be attained by a critical mass of people committed to and trained in the philosophy and methods of nonviolence.
>
> Dr. King's Beloved Community is a global vision, in which all people can share in the wealth of the earth. In the Beloved Community, poverty, hunger and homelessness will not be tolerated because international standards of human decency will not allow it. Racism and all forms of discrimination, bigotry and prejudice will be replaced by an all-inclusive spirit of sisterhood and brotherhood. In the Beloved Community, international disputes will be resolved by peaceful conflict-

resolution and reconciliation of adversaries, instead of military power. Love and trust will triumph over fear and hatred. Peace with justice will prevail over war and military conflict.[403]

The concept of "the Beloved Community" may seem to us today to be too grandiose, too idealistic and, in the end, impossible. I disagree. It is certainly not a new proposition. If we look at the grand sweep of history, we see that no nation or people seem to have yet actually achieved it. Why? Because, where there are wars with "winners" and "losers," bitterness lingers. Because, as King said over and over, hatred only gives rise to more hatred, and therefore only love can bring an end to hate. Only reconciliation, rather than selfish one-sided victory, can bring lasting peace and justice.

Again, the King Center records:

> In his 1963 sermon, *Loving Your Enemies,* published in his book, *Strength to Love,* Dr. King addressed the role of unconditional love in struggling for the beloved Community. "With every ounce of our energy we must continue to rid this nation of the incubus of segregation. But we shall not in the process relinquish our privilege and our obligation to love. While abhorring segregation, we shall love the segregationist. This is the only way to create the beloved community."

One expression of agape love in King's Beloved Community is justice, not for any one oppressed group, but for all people. As Dr. King said, "Injustice anywhere is a threat to justice everywhere."[404] He felt that justice could not be parceled out to individuals or groups, but was the birthright of every human being in the Beloved Community. "I have fought too long and hard against segregated public accommodations to end up segregating my moral concerns," he said. "Justice is indivisible."[405]

The Buddha exhorted his first sixty ordained sangha members—while they were still practicing their own meditations—saying, "Go forth, O Bhikkhus, for the welfare of the many, for the happiness of the many, for the good, well-being, and happiness of gods and men. Preach the sublime Dhamma, excellent in the beginning, excellent in the middle, excellent in the end. Proclaim the Holy Life, altogether perfect and pure."[406]

So, how do we demonstrate that we have understood the Buddha's— or Christ's—teachings? By being compassionate, by loving our neighbors, by loving our enemies, indeed by working for the weal of humankind, for the welfare of the many, for the happiness of the many, for the good, well-being, and happiness of gods and men.

As 1 Corinthians reminds us, "Love does not delight in evil but rejoices with the truth. It always protects, always trusts, always hopes, always perseveres. Love never fails." The important thing is our doing. Compassion is our wisdom in action. Therefore, with courage, and together, may we begin to act.

16

A Professor's Dilemma

⊶ ⊷

I have taught undergraduate-level courses in Buddhism for almost thirty-five years, but I still wonder whether I've succeeded in imparting to students what I see as the compelling qualities of this compassionate religion. In short, I find myself asking, is there anything "Buddhist" about a college course in Buddhism?

I wonder what particular skills and qualities we scholar-practitioners of Buddhism within the academy are trying to foster in our students when we offer our various classes on Buddhist subjects. Are we attempting simply to get students to facility with a Buddhist vocabulary, to help them comprehend a few major tenets of the Dharma, or to somehow encounter Buddhism's essence (pardon the misnomer)?

The Buddha famously announced to his followers, *Ehi passika!*—that is, "Come and see (for yourself)!" He went on to lay out a hermeneutical code to be followed when engaging in gaining knowledge of his Dharma, namely, "Do not be led by reports or tradition or hearsay. Be not led by the authority of religious texts, nor by mere logic or inference, nor by considering appearances, nor by delight in speculative opinions, nor by seeming possibilities, nor by the idea, 'This is our teacher.'"

Though clearly challenging, these principles are decidedly *not* the ones that guide most university courses! Rather, an "established body of knowledge" is the professor's—and the students'—presumed stock in trade.

I am not trying to suggest that intellectual pursuits are not good things; they are. In Buddhism also, critical reasoning is highly regarded. Wherever we look in Buddhist discourses, we read over and over again about the importance of developing critical reasoning and insight. Still, ultimately, there are limits to discursive reasoning, and nirvana is beyond concepts. Thinking alone will not get to it, and no matter how fine-tuned our reasoning ability, it will not save us from the facts of birth and death.

Buddhist studies professors are not lamas or geshes (the true scholar-practitioners), capable of imparting *lung* and *dbang*—that is, direct spiritual guidance and empowerment. But it seems that our aim as professors is not even to offer the students *experience*, though this is what true knowledge and insight into Buddhist thought and practice requires. We cannot sit on the cushions for our students. And yet, if they don't sit on the cushions, what are they, or we, really doing?

On occasion, I offer students the chance to sit with me and meditate. However, this is always offered apart from and outside of class, without obligation and without penalty for those who choose not to participate. Our universities have long ceased to be theological institutions, and, in this secular and scientific age, talk of spiritual experience is viewed with a good dose of skepticism.

Still, rather than simply teaching our students to discuss and debate the concept of "buddha nature," I wish that we could somehow teach them to recognize their own. If it were up to me, I might require that my students (and I) attend a ten-day vipassana retreat along with each of my classes, to try, as Phillip Moffitt recently said in *Shambhala Sun*, "to teach through the body itself." There is enough discursive mind-flexing already.

It is no accident that the Buddha's earliest discourse on meditation was the *Satipatthana Sutra* (Foundations of Mindfulness). I have often thought that such vipassana, or mindfulness practice (and its corollary metta, or loving-kindness meditation) is ideal for Westerners, being the least encumbered by cultural baggage. Such practices are stripped down, direct, and immediate—Buddhism embodied at its heart.

In the end, though we can attempt to articulate it, we cannot simply hand over that all-important Buddhist view, the view that not only distinguishes Buddhism from all other traditions but also grants ultimate freedom and liberation. If the Buddha himself could have enlightened others, we would all already be enlightened. (Of course we *are*, but as yet we don't fully know or realize this.) But even he could not. He told us at his leaving that each of us would have to work out our own salvation, with diligence. In the absence of meditation practice in the classroom, we academics can only advise students to seek out a practice center.

"Be diligent!" I say to students as the semester ends. "Be diligent, and be kind."

17

Teaching Buddhism in the Western Academy

❧ ❧

INTRODUCTION

I have been teaching university courses in Buddhism for over forty years. While my main area of expertise is Tibetan Buddhism, I teach the entry-level course in Buddhism as well as a number of more specialized seminars. After taking my large lecture course, "Introduction to Buddhism," students are allowed entrance into the seminars "Tibetan Buddhism," "Women in Buddhist Literature," "Buddhism in America," and "Socially Engaged Buddhism." Typically, students who have completed the Intro course have gained a fairly good grasp of major Buddhist ideas and historical developments and are thus equipped to take up these more focused investigations. I can offer such a variety of courses in Buddhism at the undergraduate level because, for the most part, I have taught primarily at highly selective liberal arts institutions that have always wanted their students to know about other world cultures, and because I first began teaching in the mid-1970s when Asia was being viewed by the Western academy with renewed interest.

Teaching Tibetan Buddhism at the undergraduate level, however, does offer unique challenges. Many of these have to do with the difficulty of the terms in Asian languages, as names and places are difficult for untrained students to read, pronounce, and remember. Finding accurate and engaging teaching materials that are neither too watered-down nor overly laced with Tibetan names and terms is difficult. A far larger issue, however, has to do with the distinctive features of Tibetan Buddhist tantrism, with its incorporation of esoteric yogic and meditative practices and with its focus on the mythic versus literal forms of presentation and interpretation. Determining how best to present this to typically young undergraduate students is a challenge.

Moreover, as a corollary of Tibetan Buddhism's esoteric character, one must typically study the tantric tradition—as I did—with, and from, Tibetan practitioners within a cultural matrix and milieu where a close teacher–disciple relationship is a necessary requirement. This model of study, however, where one is in many respects dependent on a living teacher (rather than, say, a text or group of texts), is viewed in Western academia with suspicion and as preventing the objective "distance" deemed a requirement of academic studies in institutions in the West. I have personally witnessed the intra-departmental tensions surrounding the phenomenon of the "scholar-practitioner" and of the idea of introducing "practice"[407] into the classroom. My challenge has been to teach this subject in an honest, engaging, and balanced way. In this chapter, I will take up these broader topics—teaching Buddhism, teaching Tibetan Buddhism, and the "scholar-practitioner" issue—each in turn.

TEACHING BUDDHISM IN THE WESTERN ACADEMY

A "liberal arts education" ought to be, it seems to me, "liberative" and liberating. After all, that is the essential meaning of the phrase.[408] Students (and their parents) choose a liberal arts college or university—over a vocational or technical or professional school—precisely because the liberal education is intended to steer students away from the narrow foci on specific practical training and to open them up to broader perspectives. A liberal arts education ought to render to the student a freedom from narrowness, other ways of viewing and living in the world, and the ability to imagine alternative solutions to problems. At its best, a liberal education should produce a thinking citizen of the world with high ethical values and compassionate concern for others. It is, arguably, within such an educational environment—and, certainly, with this as my goal—that I teach a series of courses on Buddhism at one of the elite colleges in the Northeast.[409]

Let me begin with a brief description or outline of my "Introduction to Buddhism" course. There is a rather standard progression: I begin with a focus on the Indian background prior to the advent of "Buddhism," discussing the subcontinent's geography, history, peoples, and pre-Buddhist religious traditions. Having established this as context, I then turn to the "life" of the Buddha and his impact on "Aryan society" (mentioning, but not discussing at length, the contentious modern debates surrounding the issues of dating and myth-making as I do so[410]). Next, I take up the Buddha's teachings, or Dharma, laying out and honing in, over the course of the next three weeks, on key ideas: the Four Noble Truths, the middle way, the eightfold path, *karma, nirvana, shunyata,* and Theravada versus Mahayana views. This takes us through the first half of the Introduction course.

During the second half of the course, my focus becomes topical. Usually I address, in turn, three specific areas from a possible number of headings: "Women and Buddhism," "Tibetan Buddhism," "Chan and Zen Buddhism," "Socially Engaged Buddhism," or "Buddhism in the West"—devoting two weeks each to the three rubrics chosen. If I focus two weeks on Tibetan Buddhism in this course, I use Lama Yeshe's *Introduction to Tantra* along with a selection on "The Distinctive Features of Tantra" from the Dalai Lama's *The World of Tibetan Buddhism.* I also "pair" the readings of two *namthar* (sacred biographies), one of the famed yogi Milarepa and the other of the Indian *siddha* Naropa.[411] These two legendary life stories in particular highlight the importance of the notion of "guru devotion" in Tibetan Buddhism as well as provide exciting tales of liberation, each in their own right. In the beginning of the Introduction course, I typically have students read the entirety of Walpola Rahula's *What the Buddha Taught;*[412] at the course's end, I have them read Stephen Batchelor's *Buddhism without Beliefs.* This pair makes for a lively comparison and is helpful in showing students how their own "modernity" issues cause them, mostly unconsciously, to re-envision "what the Buddha taught" according to their own needs, desires, and contemporary cultural and social milieus.

I think that, broadly speaking, my Introduction to Buddhism course in its earliest years could be seen as privileging texts over contexts and philosophical discourse over narrative, but I have tried each subsequent year to balance this out by offering more and more narratives[413]—after all, so much of the Buddhist canon, whether sutra or vinaya, is actually framed within narrative—and by showing students that Buddhism is a living tradition that is practiced by actual living Buddhists.[414] In order to drive home this point, my courses now emphasize narratives as well as philosophical discourses. I love to tell stories and I do so, liberally. I also show Buddhists practicing, whether through the use of Power-Point presentations or contemporary DVDs. A recent film like *Zen Buddhism: In Search of Self*,[415] for example, provides a visual context in which to anchor discussions not only about Zen practice but also about the life of ordained communities and about Buddhist women practitioners in particular. For a visual sense of "engaged Buddhism," I show the film *Dhamma Brothers*,[416] which also introduces students to vipassana practice as well as serves as an exemplar of one of the most established practices of engaged Buddhism, namely, "prison Dharma."

Students come to this introductory Buddhism course anxious to learn primarily about two things: "emptiness" and meditation. They have done retreats themselves or know someone—perhaps a parent—who has done one. They have read Hermann Hesse's *Siddhartha* or Kerouac's *Dharma Bums*. They have seen images of His Holiness the Dalai Lama on the jumbotron in Times Square. They have seen Buddhist monks on TV commercials. They have watched Bertolucci's *Little Buddha* or Scorsese's *Kundun*. They have traveled to India, or Nepal, or Japan. They are the epitome—and more—of what Thomas Tweed has dubbed "night-stand Buddhists."[417]

Within this gathering of highly intelligent, well-read, well-traveled, multitasking, and theory-driven students, I want to make space for the unhurried contemplation of Buddhist ideas;[418] I want these ideas to touch them where they live, in their minds and also in their bodies. Often this involves—as in the case with the Buddhist notion of "selflessness" (*anatman* or *shunyata*; variously translated as "nonself," "emptiness," "voidness," or "interbeing")—subtle and not-so-subtle simple repetition of the idea from different angles. Stories are also helpful here. At other times, introducing students to actual methods of meditation is helpful.[419] In the end, as much as I might sometimes like to, I know that I cannot make the whole class about meditation, nor can I simply turn over to them the all-important view (owing to which one is said to be a true follower of the Buddhist path).[420] That is not what I do in the university venue. Although meditation is intriguing to students, it is not the main focus of my class.

The main focus is on the teachings, or Dharma, of the Buddha; on what sets it apart from other traditions and what constitutes its principal ideas. I present these as best I can with the aid of Rahula, *What the Buddha Taught*; and Harvey, *An Introduction to Buddhism*; Nhat Hanh, *Being Peace* and *Old Path, White Clouds*;[421] and others, and through careful unpacking of key Buddhist Sanskrit and Pali terminology. We are together exploring what the Buddha taught and how what he taught was interpreted and expanded over time and in different cultural regions. In doing this, I see myself as a philosopher, philologist, and historian. I ask students to take the time to ponder meanings and to try to discern what might be fundamental and enduring about Buddhist thought.

Students in this course are asked to read as well as to ponder, and also to write. Written assignments include essays on key doctrines and on contextual history: for example, I might ask students to give a careful explication of the Four Noble Truths, or to describe in some detail how specific details of the Buddha's life explain the origin of key notions articulated in his First Sermon. And because I enjoy narrative so much and view it as such an excellent way of engaging students, I also always assign at least one essay in which students are asked to imagine themselves as an actual person in the Buddha's time and to create a narrative based on that. An example of this type of assignment follows:

> *Imagine yourself* as a sixth century BCE Indian woman (whether young or old, daughter, wife, widow, etc.). One day,

a Buddhist nun appears in your village or town teaching the Buddha's doctrine and inviting you to join the order. *What would be your response? Why?* This question is designed to invite your *creativity*, as well as to help you to *bring together* much of the material we've covered thus far. It is designed, therefore, to have you do *three* distinct things:

1. portray and comment upon a given woman's social situation;
2. deftly summarize the Buddha's main teaching; and
3. react to the teaching's attractiveness—or unattractiveness—given the circumstances *you* have *initially posited.*

Make sure your essay addresses *all three* of the above.

After getting their creative juices engaged—giving their chief character a name, an age, a familial relationship, and so on—students usually delight in this exercise; and they have produced some remarkably fine narratives.

Throughout the course, I ask students to seek to formulate ever-more precise expressions of the heart of Buddhist Dharma. "Compassion," some say; "wisdom," say others. I sometimes lead them in a short recitation of the *Dhammapada*'s verse 183: "To do no harm. To practice virtue. To discipline the mind. This is the teaching of all the Buddhas."

TEACHING TIBETAN BUDDHISM

The course description I last used when I taught my Tibetan Buddhism seminar read as follows:

> For centuries Tibet and Tibetan Buddhism have held an allure and mystique for Westerners that is akin to the magical kingdom of Shangri-la. This course will explore the realities as well as the myths of Tibet and Tibetan Buddhism. We shall survey the geographical, cultural, and religious

landscape of Tibet prior to the advent of Buddhism and, thereafter, focus on the introduction of Buddhism and its subsequent development there. We shall attempt to plumb the complex interface of religion, culture, and politics as practiced within the Tibetan context as well as to glean an appreciation of the distinctly Tibetan flavor of Buddhist tantric theory and practice. In order to do the latter, we shall draw both on a number of Tibetan biographies as well as specific Tibetan Buddhist rituals. Lastly, we shall look at the situation of Tibetans today.

The description sets forth a pretty tall order and promises a great deal for a group of students who can neither spell nor pronounce most Tibetan terms. Still, they know about the allure. While they probably have not read—or seen—*Lost Horizon*,[422] many have gone to concerts by the Beastie Boys[423] and watched the Dalai Lama on YouTube.

In former years I'd had to piece together a number of disparate readings to cover the broad sweep of Tibetan religious and political history, but, more recently, thanks to the work of John Powers, I could assign a single textbook for the course—his *Introduction to Tibetan Buddhism*[424]—along with more specialized readings. These readings are primarily life stories and narratives. We read, for example, the biography of the Dalai Lama and other Tibetan figures in John Avedon's *In Exile from the Land of Snows* (1984). I pair an ancient namthar (of Yeshé Tsogyal)[425] with the life of a contemporary nun, Ani Pachen's *Sorrow Mountain* (2000). To discuss the issues of "othering" and "exoticization" of Tibet and Tibetans, I have students read James Hilton's *Lost Horizon* and Donald Lopez Jr.'s *Prisoners of Shangri-La* (1999). I make sure that we read a large number of essays written by Tibetans[426] themselves in order to counter the purely Western gaze. We read and discuss *The Tibetan Book of the Dead*[427] and then watch a film about its practice in modern-day Ladakh.[428] We read about mandalas of various sorts, then all take turns constructing and offering an actual mandala.[429] This seminar is both more theoretical and more hands-on than the larger "Introduction to Buddhism" course. It is where the mythic must come to life in order to be understood: in tantric-speak, where the "secret" and "inner" worlds must touch the "outer."[430] My task is to explain to students and to show them how this threefold structuring and ordering of the tantric materials operates.

I find this last remark almost confessional in nature, and it is here where I sometimes hesitate. I know something that the students do not, and my task is to share that knowledge with them, at least in a general and nonspecific way. However, sometimes this means share it with them even though they have not—as dictated by the tradition's tantric requirements—received the proper initiations to render them ready to receive it. What am I to do then? Of course, the sharing of knowledge is exactly what all good teachers do, and, generally speaking, we all also know that knowledge is best when it is drawn out of the student themselves and is thus "discovered" rather than simply handed over. However, the idea of sharing "with the *uninitiated*" is the source of my conundrum here, and it is a sensitive, and intimate, issue for me. It is here that the theory and controversy surrounding the "insider/ outsider" model in contemporary religious studies[431] actually has some teeth for me, since it is clearly by virtue of my quasi-"insider"[432] status that I have gained, and am capable of sharing, this particular information and knowledge. But scholarly detachment is the rule within the academy. Yet scholarly detachment here would almost certainly ensure that my knowledge of the subject matter is incomplete or inaccurate. Should I not teach this because of the manner in which I learned it— namely, at the feet of a lama?

I am a teacher within a university setting. I am neither a lama nor a guru to my students. In the Tibetan traditions, a lama is one who can show her heart-disciples the "three kindnesses" of (1) teaching the sutras and their commentaries, (2) offering sound oral instructions on the tantras, and (3) giving empowerments.[433] While I may be able to offer instructions and commentary, I certainly cannot impart *spiritual empowerments (dbang)* to my students in the way that experienced lamas can. Nor is that "kindness" the same kindness that occurs in academe. And yet, I take heart in remembering that when I won Wesleyan's Binswanger Prize for excellence in teaching in 2003, the plaque that I was given announced that it was due to my "ability to make learning a *shared* process" and that I "open [the] eyes [of my students] to a culture far different from our own." It continued, movingly, by remarking that "having lived the transformative message of Tibetan Buddhism, you *teach from the heart.*" Did they really mean it, I wondered? Is there, can there be, true appreciation—within the academy—for this?

THE "SCHOLAR-PRACTITIONER"

Not long ago, when two of my colleagues and I were interviewing a prospective job candidate via Skype, a savvy young job seeker who had done her homework for the interview, the candidate asked me, "How do you manage teaching Tibetan Buddhism when you also practice? Do you ever find that to be *problematic?*" I responded, "Well, what I teach is a form of Buddhism known for its esoteric character. It would be impossible for me to teach it—or to know anything about it, really— without knowing something about its internal workings and practices." The candidate seemed satisfied. What was especially of note, however, was the surprise and seemingly new insight on the part of my two colleagues. Immediately after we had disconnected from the interview, one said, "Jan, that was an *amazing* response! *How did you come up with that?*" It was as if she had seen and understood what it was that I did at the university for the very first time. "I simply told her the truth," I replied. "It wasn't as if I had to make something up!" Again, the usually unspoken suspicion—that I might not really belong on a university faculty—had surfaced.

A few years before, while conducting a departmental self-evaluation, the department's chair was attempting to categorize what each of us faculty members contributed to the department. Some offered theoretical expertise, others a more "thematic" approach. When it came to me, and my courses on Buddhism, I was deemed a contributor of the "experiential" approach! It seemed clear to me at the time that this odd categorization was intended to mean that what I did was something other—and, probably, something less—than "academic" and "scholarly." Sadly, over the course of my nearly four decades of teaching, most members of my department and of my university's administration have maintained the narrow-minded and misguided misperception that scholarly engagement within a religious studies department—if possible at all—necessitates complete objectivity from the subject matter, even downright (though often denied) hostility toward it. Any affinity for one's area of expertise is therefore viewed with suspicion. Furthermore, as a teacher of a religious tradition that espouses the importance of one's own experience, my subject matter, Buddhism, is doubly anathema to them.

In the fall of 1969, I had the great good fortune of traveling to Nepal and meeting Lama Thubten Yeshe there. I went, as part of that countercultural movement of the late 1960s and early 1970s, seeking spiritual awakening and healing for the traumatic effects wrought by the legacy of slavery and an early childhood spent in the Jim Crow South. I carried an abundance of low self-esteem, feelings of hurt, anger, and unworthiness, and I sought relief. I loved Lama Yeshe from the instant I met him, but my pride would not let me admit it. He sent me for a time to study with his guru in India, a task befitting me, I thought, since I had studied physics and philosophy at Cornell (pride is often the other side of insecurity). But Lama Yeshe nourished and encouraged me, showering me with compassion and extolling my intelligence. Over the course of the next fifteen years, while I studied Tibetan and Sanskrit and translated a work that served as the basis of my PhD dissertation, Lama Yeshe helped me to build confidence in myself, to accept who I was, and to see my basic goodness (my buddha nature). No academic degree can equal that![434] And so, my career as a Buddhist scholar was launched.

Charles Prebish claims to have been the earliest American scholar to coin the phrase "scholar-practitioner" to refer to "professors, who, in addition to having sophisticated academic credentials in Buddhist studies, also happen to be practicing Buddhists."[435] Prebish discussed his own "coming out" as a Buddhist to his department head, who thereafter, Prebish noted, "no longer took my academic scholarship seriously" (67). José Cabezón, a former Tibetan Buddhist monk and holder of a PhD in Buddhist studies from the University of Wisconsin, is quoted by Prebish as describing why scholar-practitioners are viewed negatively. Cabezón remarked: "One of the prevailing views in the study of religion is that 'critical distance'from the object of intellectual analysis is necessary. Buddhists, by virtue of their religious commitment, lack such critical distance from Buddhism. Hence, Buddhists are *never* good Buddhologists."⁴³⁶ Of course, as Prebish rightly noted, this is a stereotype, as well as a faulty argument. Even so, it exists; and it produces consequences.

Religious studies professors are, ironically, often the very individuals who are most hostile to any form of religion. Perhaps defensive about their profession, it seems to me they often confuse "critical, scholarly distance" with "arrogance" and "condescension." (I often wonder what led them into the field!) As a consequence of their perspective, they never really get to know their subject matter. So intent on deconstructing, they can never quite construct, see anything as being constructive, or even allow the possibility that anything might be spiritually meaningful. It is bad enough that this is their opinion and perspective, it is much worse, however, when this is what they teach their students.

As I have noted above, I try to make a distinction between what is appropriate for the classroom and what is appropriate for the Dharma hall or meditation room.⁴³⁷ None of my Buddhism courses is designed to convert students to Buddhism or to guide them in a specific spiritual lineage as if I were their guru or Dharma teacher. I recognize that I teach, primarily, within a university—not a Dharma center—setting. But I don't hate, or belittle, or disparage Buddhism. And this fact comes through to my students.

I had answered the young job candidate honestly. Had I not studied with and learned from a true Tibetan guru about the internal (outer, inner, and secret) meanings of tantric texts and practices, I would have an inaccurate and faulty sense of what they are about. I might think, for example, that *chöd* practices are violent and sadistic sacrificial rites—as some Western authors have actually described them. I might think that mangy dogs are capable of offering insight, rather than seeing that the dogs are markers of moments of insights, as dakini, or wisdom-beings breaking suddenly into consciousness.⁴³⁸ I might think that Tibetan mandalas are only pretty art forms. In fact, I know a number of scholars of Tibetan Buddhism who do not know much about the internal logic or workings of Tibetan tantric practice and would never dream of asking for, or practicing, any form of Tibetan tantric meditation. These scholars are knowledgeable about other aspects of Tibetan culture; they are adept at the languages and even at describing certain rituals in exacting detail. Yet they have often entirely misread and consequently misunderstood the meaning of a given text or ritual precisely because they tend to approach, and to read, literally what is intended to be read—and what is actually operating—symbolically.

The history of the clash of cultures and misconceptions resulting from Tibetan Buddhism's various encounters with its Western interpreters is full of examples of this phenomenon.[439] Reading literally is a characteristic of the Western mind and its penchant for left-brain functioning; but many, if not most, non-Western cultures—and certainly non-Western religious traditions—"read" differently. And while bridging this divide may be challenging, it is not impossible. Some people can actually see and allow for the possibility of more than one level of experience operating at one time!

Several different causes and conditions came together in the late 1990s that ultimately resulted in my writing a memoir. I would never have thought to do this on my own; I did not feel old enough or wise enough. And yet, after several persistent requests to do so by an editor at Doubleday publishers and the urging of friends, I took up the challenge. It was an intense, emotion-filled, and difficult three-year project that in the end was far more rewarding than I could ever have imagined when I began. I spent the time remembering, going back over key events in my life, and weighing and reflecting on them. In discovering and retracing early memories from my life, I found my true self. And I began to let go of old wounds.

In the book, I recognized and spoke openly about the crippling effects of racism; and I saw and spoke openly about the redemptive benefits of spiritual practice, whether Baptist or Buddhist. Titled *Dreaming Me: Black, Baptist, and Buddhist: One Woman's Spiritual Journey*,[440] the book was originally published in 2001 and received starred reviews from both the *Library Journal* and *Publishers Weekly*. One review remarked that I "could be the first African-American Buddhist feminist guru to be embraced by reading groups across America." A good bit of hyperbole there!

Writing the memoir was good for me on several levels. First, in order to write it, I had to convince myself that writing a book about myself was a worthwhile project to undertake, especially within an academic environment. Second, after writing it, the book's success made my religious studies colleagues—at least outwardly—show a bit more respect for what I did (whether they actually felt this or not). Third, I guess one could say that, in *Dreaming Me*, I "came out" as being a practitioner, someone who cares about religion and religious studies, someone who doesn't mind the appellation "scholar-practitioner." I had written a number of other more scholarly works before the memoir, but it was the memoir that seemed to bring real recognition. Still, my day-to-day life within academia did not change very much; I continued to teach my courses as I had before and to give outside lectures, albeit in more and more impressive and distinguished venues. I attributed this to my age rather than to any particular recognition within the guild of religious studies, or within the Dharma world for that matter.

Then in midsummer of 2011, I found myself among two hundred other Buddhist teachers[441] at a conference held at the Garrison Institute in New York. For the four days of the conference I happily joined with friends and colleagues for meals and discussion groups and evening chats. But it was only near the conference's end that I could put into words the feeling I had been trying to capture throughout those days: only I and a very few others were academics. Indeed, I counted only one other university professor, and she, unlike myself, was now retired. What I finally experienced was a sense of grateful recognition for being included among Buddhist, not Buddhist studies, teachers. I had been included and invited to that particular conference because I was considered to be a practitioner and a Dharma teacher. (Perhaps presciently, I had titled one of the chapters in *Dreaming Me* "Teaching as My Practice.") I was, indeed, a *scholar-practitioner*. And that felt pretty good.

18

A Baptist-Buddhist

It was the kind of slow-motion thing that you see in movies. My car was skidding, swerving out of control on the slush and ice of a highway recently plowed—but not recently enough. I was returning from Boston, trying to get back home to Middletown before the big snow-and-ice storm forecasted for later that afternoon arrived. Now I knew that I should have taken my hosts' advice and stayed in Boston.

The storm had been the delight of weather forecasters for days, and I did not want to be caught in those treacherous driving conditions that had been their gleeful theme all week. As I left Boston on the Mass Pike around 7:00 am, things had seemed all right. I put on some music and applauded myself for making the right decision. But after driving for about an hour, the flurries began. It was a beautiful thing, snow; and I'd soon be home. By the time I turned off onto I-84, the roads were getting pretty bad. Attempting to calm myself, I determined that if I slowed down, keeping ample space between my car and the ones in front of me, I'd still make it okay.

Just after passing Hartford, the snow got really heavy. I cut off the music and gripped the steering wheel a bit tighter. At least now there were only three lanes to worry about, not the five that had led into the Hartford area. Traffic slowed but was moving. I told myself, "Only twenty minutes. Then home." I tried to keep focused on the cars ahead and the tracks they were making. "Follow in the tracks," I told myself. "Keep inside the tracks. You'll make it." I was scared.

Suddenly I began to see things from the perspective of an observer. The car was spinning out. It turned almost sideways, then somehow righted itself. Finally, it began to slide toward the center guardrails. I silently mused, "So, this is how it is. Just like that, one's last moments." Images of my father and sister flashed by. No time to say anything to them. I saw the guardrails rushing toward me. The car would hit them in the next second and that would be that.

A booming *OM MANI PADME HUM!* woke me up. I was screaming the mantra at the top of my lungs. I saw myself leaning forward, clutching the steering wheel so tightly that my knuckles stood out. My car had moved back into the tracks of the middle lane. I don't know how it got there. In less than a split-second, it had simply jumped back into the tracks of the lane, as if some giant invisible hand had snapped it up and placed it down again.

I looked to my rearview mirror. Behind me, cars were braking and swerving. They had been attempting to stop as they saw me careening into the guardrails. I said another few *OM MANIs* for them while I squeezed my steering wheel.

As I continued on, now moving very slowly, I thought more about that near brush with death—how quickly our treasured selves can be extinguished; how fragile life really is. And I thought about how surprisingly that booming *OM MANI* had come out of me, in what I thought was my last moment of this life. It is the mantra of Avalokiteshvara, the Buddha of Compassion. I regularly intoned it whenever I passed a dead animal on the highway, to wish it peace and blessings.

Perhaps in those compressed seconds I saw myself as a dead animal. The best I can figure, however, is that it was the shortest prayer I knew. What went along with it, I think, was the wish not to be separated from Lama Yeshe in whatever future rebirth. Perhaps I was a Buddhist after all.

Once, when I was teaching at UCSC, the car I was driving had suddenly stalled out less than a foot from a railroad crossing. The next instant a speeding train roared by, its warning horns blaring, while my car trembled and shook as though it would fly away. Then, I had not called out the mantra. At least I didn't think I had.

And returning one night to Hartford's Bradley Airport, after two Christmas holiday weeks spent with my family in Alabama, another thoroughly frightening event took place. As usual, I was flying on Delta Airlines. The company's biggest hub is Atlanta; they fly hundreds of flights into Birmingham and their pilots have a first-rate flying record. Hence, for most of the flight into Hartford, I was feeling pretty relaxed. However, temperatures all up and down the East Coast were pretty frigid, and this caused a good deal of turbulence. As we bumped along, dipping and rolling in the rough air, there were more than a few clenched fists in evidence. Buckled in at my window seat, for most of the hour-and-fifty-minute trip I tried to maintain a relaxed attitude, trusting in our pilots to steer us safely in. Still, as Bradley's airfield came into view, I found myself being more than a little relieved.

From the window, I could see the lights of the air strip. Like most others on this particular flight, I let out a sigh of relief. Seated beside me were an older woman who had seemed frightened for most of the trip and a young girl who was, presumably, her grandchild. I smiled encouragingly before I spoke to her, "Okay! See, there's the runway! It won't be long now."

We were no more than a few feet above the tarmac. The plane's landing gear was down, its headlights illuminating the field. Then things abruptly changed. In an instant, the plane veered steeply upward. It went into a climb that was almost perpendicular. We were like astronauts, our heads pressed back against our seats, our bodies feeling the G-forces of lift-off. My own knuckles went white. Papers from somewhere started blowing through the compartment. Overhead doors snapped open. Oxygen masks dropped. Some people started to scream. I started to pray, at first aloud and then silently, but speeded up, with urgency. I called on both my guru, Lama Yeshe, and on Jesus. "Lama Yeshe!" I screamed, "May I never be separated from you in this or future lives!" Gripping my armrests, I continued in silence, "May you and all the buddhas help and bless us now!" Without pausing, I then fervently intoned, "Christ Jesus, please help us. Please, I pray, bless me and all these people!"

That plane climbed straight up for almost four minutes. My prayers became continuous mantras. Finally, the engines' roar lessened and the plane began to level off. The pilot's voice came over the speakers. He sounded nervous himself but tried to speak reassuringly, "Ah-h, ladies and gentlemen, I'm sorry it's taken so long to get back to you. It seems that just as we were landing we hit one of those stiff wind shears and we had to get out of it. We're going to try this landing again, this time from the east." A collective sigh went up from all of us.

❧ ☙

I call myself a "Baptist-Buddhist" not to be cute or witty. I call myself a "Baptist-Buddhist" because it is an honest description of who I feel I am. When I was on that plane, racing straight upward through the frigid night air, I did not feel as though I were simply hedging my bets. I felt sheer and utter terror, and I called on both traditions for help. Long ago, Kierkegaard had argued that one doesn't know what one really believes until one is forced to act. That climbing plane showed me what I believed.

Most times, actually, I think of myself as being more an African American Buddhist. When I seek to make sense of things or to analyze a particular situation, I am more likely to draw on Buddhist principles than Baptist ones. But when it seems as though the plane I'm on might actually go down, I call on both traditions. It is a deep response.

About this dual description, my folks seem generally accepting. Though one day while telling me that she thought my years with Lama Yeshe hadn't caused me any harm, my mother did let me know, in subtle and not so subtle ways, that she worried for my soul and its salvation. Many others, who've had occasion—or taken the license—to comment on it, have stridently voiced disdain and disapproval: "Either you believe in Christ, our Lord, as your sole and only savior, or you're lost!" A young, well-educated, and articulate black man who was visit-

ing Wesleyan once told me exactly this. To this vociferous attack by
a newly reborn Christian, and to others like it, I can only say, "Well,
I trust that Jesus Himself is more understanding and compassionate."
The Jesus I knew from the Gospel stories was the Jesus who had min-
istered to women, to the poor and the downtrodden; and He was the
Jesus I knew personally, because He had ridden with me on that bus ride
to Cornell. Moreover, it seems to me that those who see a disjuncture in
my being a Baptist-Buddhist haven't spent any amount of time reflecting on what, or who, a Buddha really is—or a Christ, for that matter. As
always, in matters of faith and of the heart, a little concrete experience
and practice usually takes one higher, and at the same time sets one on
firmer ground.

   If I have learned anything about myself thus far it is that in my deepest core I am a human being, graced by the eternal truths espoused both
by Baptists and by Buddhists. And more than that, I am aware that it is
not any particular appellation that matters. For ultimately, what I have
come to know is that life—precious life—is not a destination. Life is
the journey.

Notes

꧁꧂

Chapter 1: Nuns and Benefactresses

1   See, for example, Nancy Falk, "An Image of Woman in Old Buddhist Literature: The Daughters of Mara," in *Women and Religion*, ed. Judith Plaskow and Joan Arnold (Chico, CA: AAR/Scholars Press, 1974), 105–12; Diana Paul, *Women in Buddhism: Images of the Feminine in Mahāyāna Tradition* (Berkeley, CA: Asian Humanities Press, 1979); Nancy Schuster, "Changing the Female Body: Wise Women and the Bodhisattva Career in Some *Mahāratnakūṭasūtras*," *Journal of the International Association of Buddhist Studies* 4, no. 1 (1981): 24–69; Andre Bareau, "Un personnage bien mysterieux: L'espouse du Buddha," in *Indological and Buddhist Studies: Volume in Honour of Professor J. W. de Jong* (Canberra: Faculty of Asian Studies, 1982), 31–59; and Yuichi Kajiyama, "Women in Buddhism," *Eastern Buddhist* (new series) 15, no. 2 (1982): 53–70.

2   Speaking to this problem in relationship to early Christianity and current New Testament scholarship, Wayne Meeks, in his *The First Urban Christians: The Social World of the Apostle Paul* (New Haven: Yale University Press, 1983), 1–2, states:

> [An] air of unreality ... pervades much of the recent scholarly literature about the New Testament and early Christianity. A clear symptom of the malaise is the isolation of New Testament study from other kinds of historical scholarship—not only from secular study of the Roman Empire, but even from church history. Some New Testament students have begun to retreat from critical history into theological positivism. Others no longer claim to do history at all, but favor a purely literary or literary-philosophical reading of the canonical texts.... If we ask, "What was it like to become

and be an ordinary Christian in the first century?" we receive only vague and stammering replies.

To be sure, ordinary Christians did not write our texts and rarely appear in them explicitly. Yet the texts were written in some sense for them, and were used in some ways by them. If we do not ever see their world, we cannot claim to understand early Christianity.

3   Even the *Therigatha*, a collection of hymns recording the "triumphant songs" (or *annas*) said to have been composed by women *arhats* upon their attainment of deliverance, was compiled, written, edited, and extensively commented on by a monk named Dhammapala. All the texts comprising the orthodox Buddhist canon (of whatever country) were authored exclusively by men.

4   "Theravada" and "Mahayana" are terms denoting the two main divisions of Buddhist thought and practice: (1) the early and more conservative or "individualist" phase called here the Theravada, and (2) the later, more progressive and "universalist" phase known as the Mahayana.

5   For references to the lapse of "five years" between the Buddha's establishing his male order and his decision to found a female order, see I. B. Horner, *Women under Primitive Buddhism: Laywomen and Almswomen* (New Delhi: Motilal Banarsidass, 1975 [1930]), 98, 103, and 295.

6   Horner, *Women under Primitive Buddhism*, devotes an entire section to Ananda and Gautama Buddha's relationship to women (see 295–312). Horner writes on 295: "Of all Gotama's disciples, Ānanda was the most popular among the almswomen . . . they would have felt that in him they had a friend—one who had a definitely feministic bias." What is so interesting about the overall character of Ananda as described in the scriptures (and what reveals their humor, as well as posits the reason for Ananda's strong connection to feminine causes) is that, prior to his conversion, Ananda's chief (samsaric) bondage was his addiction to women. A number of humorous passages in the scriptures show the lengths to which the Buddha had to go in order to wean Ananda from this addiction so that in the end he joined the sangha. In I. B. Horner, trans., *The Book of the Discipline (Vinaya-Piṭaka)*, vol. 20 of the Sacred Books of the Buddhists (London: Pali Text Society, 1975), 353, she notes that at "*Vin.* ii 289 . . . Ānanda was charged at the Council of Rajagaha with having persuaded Gotama to admit women to the Order, thus causing its decay."

7   According to Mahayana accounts, Buddhas are "always said to be born parthenogenetically, that is, without the sexual intercourse of the parents." Additionally, all mothers of Buddhas are destined "to die seven days after giving birth in order to preclude any sexual intercourse after such a miraculous event" (Paul, *Women in Buddhism*, 63). In this world age, Queen Mahamaya, Gautama Buddha's mother, died seven days after his birth. From that time on he was raised by

his aunt, Mahaprajapati. Both Horner, *Women under Primitive Buddhism*, 102, and Paul, *Women in Buddhism*, 81, suggest that the myth-making process may have intruded into the orthodox account of the founding of the women's order, for its history parallels in many ways that of the Jains. In Jaina accounts also, it is Mahavira's aunt, Canda, who instigates the establishment of a nuns' order.

8   See Horner, *Cullavagga* X (i.e., "Lesser Division," chap. 10), in part 5 of *The Book of the Discipline (Vinaya-Piṭaka)*, 352.

9   Again *Cullavagga* X; here my own translation. This passage is also cited, with slight differences in translation, by Horner, *Cullavagga* X; Henry Clarke Warren, *Buddhism in Translations* (Cambridge: Harvard University Press, 1896; reprint, New York: Atheneum, 1968), 443; and Ananda K. Coomaraswamy, *Buddha and the Gospel of Buddhism* (New York: Harper Torchbooks, 1964), 161.

10   In fact, the Buddha says that his doctrine's presence in India would be cut in half. The explicit words of the Buddha's predictions are given in the text of this essay.

11   This is Warren's translation for the Pali, *garudhammā*. See his *Buddhism in Translations*, 444–47. Otherwise, the eight are referred to generally as the "eight chief rules."

12   In Paul, *Women in Buddhism*, 85–86. Other translations of this passage differ, giving stronger wording especially with regard to the chief rule listed here as eighth. For example, Warren, *Buddhism in Translations*, 444, writes: "A priestess of even a hundred years' standing shall salute, rise to meet, entreat humbly, and perform all respectful offices for a priest, *even if he be but that day ordained*." Similar wording is found in Horner, *Women under Primitive Buddhism*, 119; and in Horner's translation in Edward Conze, *Buddhist Texts through the Ages* (New York: Harper Torchbooks, 1964), 24. Clearly such a rule was intended to solidify for all time the subordinate place of women within the Buddhist order. Moreover, in addition to an extra two-year probationary period for nuns, there were more rules set down for them than for monks. Further, it often happened that monks incurred a lesser penalty than did nuns for a similar kind of offense.

13   See Horner, *Cullavagga* X, 355; Warren, *Buddhism in Translations*, 446; and Conze, *Buddhist Texts*, 25.

14   See Paul, *Women in Buddhism*, 86–87; Caroline A. F. Rhys Davids, trans., *Psalms of the Sisters (the Therīgāthā)* (London: Pāli Text Society, 1948 [1909]), 7; and *Poems of Early Buddhist Nuns* (revised edition of the *Therīgāthā*) (Oxford: The Pali Text Society, 1989).

15   A similar phenomenon had happened earlier, when women were allowed to become Jaina nuns. Referring to Mrs. Sinclair Stevenson's *Heart of Jainism* (Oxford: Oxford University Press, 1915), Horner, *Women under Primitive*

Buddhism, 102, states that "more than twice as many women as men, thirty-six thousand women to fourteen thousand men, left the world and became nuns under the Śvetāmbara sect of the Jain Order." That Jaina nuns have continued until the present to outnumber Jaina monks is attested to by Padmanabh Jaini's study, *The Jaina Path of Purification* (Berkeley: University of California Press, 1979), 246–47. Horner, *Women under Primitive Buddhism*, reiterates that "women . . . flocked in large numbers to ask for admission" (115).

16   For a history of the development of permanent monastic structures, see Sukumar Dutt, *Buddhist Monks and Monasteries of India* (London: George Allen and Unwin, 1962).

17   Horner, *Cullavagga* X, 356.

18   According to such texts as the *Apadana* and *Therigatha*, several nuns became famous as preachers of the Dharma: Paṭacara, Sukka, Mahaprajapati, Dhammadinna, Thullananda, Bhadda Kapilani, and Khema. The *Apadana* cites seven illustrious women, calling them the "Seven Sisters." They were Khema, Uppalavanna, Patacara, Bhadda, Kisagotami, Dhammadinna, and Visakha (the last mentioned being a famed laywoman disciple). On numerous occasions throughout the *Therīgāthā* women are said to have joined the Buddhist order after listening to a discourse propounded by a "brilliant-talker" *(citta-kathī)* nun. For more on the specific epithets used of these teachers, see Horner, *Women under Primitive Buddhism*, 254–58.

19   See Caroline A. F. Rhys Davids, *Psalms of the Sisters* (the *Therīgāthā*).

20   See Horner, *Cullavagga* X, 357ff. It should also be noted that the *Bhikkuni-vibhaṅga*, "The Nun's Analysis," or "rules for the nuns," found in I. B. Horner, *The Book of the Discipline (Vinaya-Piṭaka)*, vol. 20 of the Sacred Books of the Buddhists (London: Pali Text Society, 1975), 80–122, is composed of rules laid down by the Buddha in response to individual occasions of specific problems associated with the nuns' order.

21   See Coomaraswamy, *Buddha and the Gospel of Buddhism*, 160.

22   The point is forcefully made by Falk, "An Image of Woman in Old Buddhist Literature," 110.

23   See Paul, *Women in Buddhism*, 51.

24   Ibid.

25   Ibid.

26   Ibid., 52.

27   Ibid.

28   This is the assessment of the Jātakas in Coomaraswamy, *Buddha and the Gospel of Buddhism*, 159.

29   Ibid., 160.

30   See Paul, *Women in Buddhism*, 51.

31   Coomaraswamy, *Buddha and the Gospel of Buddhism*, 160.

32   The *Maharatnakuta* is an early Mahayana anthology of texts, comprising forty-nine individual tales. The text was translated into Chinese by Bodhiruci between 706 and 713 AD. The tales of the anthology are quite diverse and seem clearly not to have been composed either by a single author or in a single location.

33   See Paul, *Women in Buddhism*, 31–41.

34   See Richard Robinson, *The Buddhist Religion: A Historical Introduction* (Belmont, CA: Dickenson Publishing, 1970). When describing the early precursor to the Mahayana, i.e., the Mahasanghika, 37, Robinson notes: "The Mahāsaṅghikas admitted upāsakas and non-arhant monks to their meetings, and were sensitive to popular religious values and aspirations."

35   Regarding this interesting phenomenon in early Mahayana accounts, see Schuster, "Changing the Female Body," and Paul, *Women in Buddhism*. Paul devotes an entire chapter (166–216) to what she terms "The Bodhisattvas with Sexual Transformation."

36   The *Lotus Sūtra* (Skt. *Saddharmapuṇḍarīkasūtra*) is one of the earliest and most influential of the Mahayana scriptures. It was composed sometime between 100 BC and 100 AD. Two popular English translations of the *Lotus* are Hendrick Kern (from the Sanskrit), *The Saddharma-Puṇḍarīka, or the Lotus of the True Law* (Oxford: Clarendon Press, 1909 [1884]); and Leon Hurvitz (from the Chinese of Kumārajīva), *Scripture of the Lotus Blossom of the Fine Dharma (The Lotus Sutra)* (New York: Columbia University Press, 1976).

37   Hurvitz, *Scripture*, chap. 23, 300.

38   This translation is by Paul, *Women in Buddhism*, 189.

39   In some of the early Mahayana literature, the claim is put forward that a woman's physical characteristics bar her from becoming either a buddha or a *cakravartin* (i.e., world monarch), this by virtue of the fact that both of these conform to a specific physical type, called the *Mahapuruṣa*, or "Great Man," having thirty-two major marks (Skt. *lakṣaṇa*) and eighty minor marks. Listed tenth among the thirty-two marks is "having the male sex organ concealed within a sheath." A pre-Mahayana Pāli scripture, the *Lakkhana-suttanta* discusses these thirty-two major marks in detail. See Dīgha Nikāya, 3, translated by T. W. Rhys Davids as *Dialogues of the Buddha*, in Sacred Books of the Buddhists, vol. 4 (Oxford: Oxford University Press, 1921; reprint, London: Pāli Text Society, 1977), 132–67.

40   My own translation, from the Sanskrit version of the *Bodhisattvabhūmi: Being the XVth Section of Asangapāda's Yogācarabhūmiḥ*, ed. Nalinaksha Dutt (Patna: K. P. Jayaswal Research Institute, 1978), chap. 7, 66. See also Har Dayal's summary of some of this literature in his *The Bodhisattva Doctrine in Buddhist Sanskrit Literature* (New Delhi: Motilal Banarsidass, 1975 [1932]), 224.

41   The Perfection of Wisdom literature was composed primarily in southern India and over a few centuries, beginning circa 100 BC and continuing well beyond the fifth century AD. For a detailed review of this literature, see Edward Conze, *The Prajñāpāramitā Literature* (The Hague: Mouton and Co., 1960), and the Introduction to his *Selected Sayings from the Perfection of Wisdom* (Boulder, CO: Prajna Press, 1978).

In *The Prajnaparamita Literature*, 10, Conze offers a very interesting suggestion regarding the southern Indian origins of the female deity known as "Prajñāpāramitā," the "Mother of all Buddhas." He notes that the "Perfection of Wisdom" goddess first appeared in an area of southern India where "both Dravidian and Greek influences made themselves felt . . . . In view of the close analogies which exist between the Prajnaparamita and the Mediterranean literature on Sophia, this seems to me significant. Also the Andhras were a non-Aryan people . . . and the matriarchal traditions of the Dravidians may well have something to do with the introduction of the worship of the 'Mother of the Buddhas' into Buddhism."

42   The *Diamond Sutra* (Skt. *Vajracchedikasutra*), composed circa fourth century AD.

43   See E. Conze's translation of the *Diamond Sutra* in his *Buddhist Wisdom Books* (New York: Harper Torchbooks, 1972), 63.

44   The *Vimalakirtinirdesha Sutra* was composed circa first century AD. It is one of the oldest and most popular works of the Mahayana. Two English translations are popular: Charles Luk's translation from the Chinese, *The Vimalakīrti Nirdeśa Sūtra* (Boulder, CO: Shambhala Publications, 1972); and Robert A. F. Thurman's translation of the sutra from the Tibetan, *The Holy Teachings of Vimalakīrti: A Mahāyāna Scripture* (University Park: The Pennsylvania State University Press, 1976).

45   The *Shrimala Sutra* is thought to have been originally composed in the Andhra district of South India sometime during the third century AD. Alex and Hideko Wayman have translated the sutra. See their *The Lion's Roar of Queen Śrīmālā* (New York: Columbia University Press, 1974).

46   Thurman, *Holy Teachings of Vimalakīrti*, 61.

47   Paul, *Women in Buddhism*, 287–88.

48   One could go on to mention later examples of women who excelled in Buddhist practice, especially in connection with the development of the Buddhist tantric systems—such as Niguma, the "sister" of Nāropa, who developed her own system known as the "Six Yogas of Niguma"; Dagmema (Bdag med ma), Marpa's accomplished wife; and Machik Lapdrönma (Ma gcig lab sgron ma), who founded the celebrated system of Chö (Gcod) practice—but there is no space to go into these here.

49   For more on the important connections between the development of *stūpas* and the rise of the Mahayana, see Akira Hirakawa, "The Rise of Mahāyāna Buddhism and Its Relationship to the Worship of Stūpas," in *Memoirs of the Research Department of the Toyo Bunko* 22 (Tokyo: Toyo Bunko, 1963).

50   The scriptures show that the Buddha consorted with important kings of his day—such as King Bimbisara of Magadha (who donated the famed Bamboo Grove located six miles outside of Rajagṛha); his son and successor, Ajatasatthu; and Prasenajit of Koshala—as well as with powerful merchants. His first lay converts are reported to have been the wealthy merchant couple who were the father and mother of Yasa, the "noble youth" who became the Buddha's sixth monk-disciple. The powerful merchant Anathapiṇḍaka donated the land for the famous Jetavana Monastery at Shravasti. Thus, as Robinson notes in *The Buddhist Religion*, 34, "even during the Buddha's lifetime his saṅgha became a wealthy landowner."

51   Romila Thapar, *A History of India*, 2 vols. (London: Penguin Books, 1990 [1966]), 1:109.

52   Robinson, *The Buddhist Religion*, 32.

53   For whatever reasons, the order of nuns did not remain a strong component of Buddhism's development. Though exceptional personalities were counted among the nuns described in such texts as the *Therigatha*, as Paul notes, *Women in Buddhism*, 82:

> The nun's life is not well marked in the Mahāyāna sūtra tradition or in the philosophical writing of that tradition. Participation in an intellectual life by the Mahāyāna Buddhist nun is not recorded. The nun seems not to have been a significant part of the student body of the great Buddhist universities which were the central gem in the crown of the monk's order, an order which was extensive, prosperous, and productive of extraordinary thought and art.

Women benefactresses, on the other hand, played, as shall be seen, a powerful role in developing and sustaining the tradition.

54   I am well aware of the problems associated with the use of such terms as "patron" and "patronize" in these contexts. Though the *American Heritage Dictionary* defines "patron" as "anyone who supports, protects, or champions; a benefactor," the term clearly derives from the Latin *pater* and, even earlier, the Sanskrit *pati*, both denoting a male and meaning "father" or "protector." The closest feminine counterpart, i.e., "matron," is clearly inadequate here.

55   The life of Visakha, also known as the "mother of Migara," is recounted in the *Dhammapada* commentary, and references to her are found in the Udana and in the Anguttara Nikāya. Warren gives a translation of her life in his *Buddhism in Translations*, 451–81. Horner, *Women under Primitive Buddhism*, 345–61;

and Coomaraswamy, *Buddha and the Gospel of Buddhism*, 163–64, also mention her. Coomaraswamy quotes H. Oldenberg, *Buddha, His Life, His Doctrine, His Order*, trans. from the German by W. Hoey (London, 1882), as saying:

> Pictures like this of Visākhā, benefactresses of the Church, with their inexhaustible religious zeal, and their not less inexhaustible resources of money, are certainly, if anything ever was, drawn from the life of India in those days: they cannot be left out of sight, if we desire to get an idea of the actors who made the oldest Buddhist community what it was.

56 Warren, *Buddhism in Translations*, 471. Visakha is said to have "lived to be a hundred and twenty years old, but there was not a single gray hair on her head—always she appeared as if about sixteen."

57 Shravasti was an important city during the Buddha's day and a main seat for his order. It figures as the setting of numerous sutras.

58 Warren, *Buddhism in Translations*, 477–78.

59 That is, they were usually Hindus and worshipped either Viṣṇu or Shiva.

60 Ambapali is also known as "Amrapali." Her name means "daughter of the mango-guardian" according to the *Therīgāthā* LXVI. Her life is found recorded in that text because she later became a Buddhist nun. She is said to have had a son (named Vimala-Kondanna) who became a monk under the Buddha's care. That son, it is said, taught Ambapali the meaning of the Buddhist doctrine of impermanence by illustrating it in relationship to her own aging body. She was thus "converted."

61 Horner, *Women under Primitive Buddhism*, 89.

62 See Rhys Davids, *Psalms of the Sisters* (*Therīgāthā* LXVI), 120–25.

63 Coomaraswamy, *Buddha and the Gospel of Buddhism*, 74–75. A contingent of "Licchavi princes" are said to have become upset when the Buddha refused their invitation to dine with them in order to honor his former acceptance to do so with Ambapali.

64 See Horner, *Women under Primitive Buddhism*, 89; and Rhys Davids, *Psalms of the Sisters* (*Therīgāthā* XXVI), 30. Padumavati, too, it is said in the *Therigatha*, was converted to the Buddha's teaching after hearing her son preach the Dharma.

65 King Bimbisāra apparently had three wives: (1) Khema (Skt. Kṣema), called his "queen-consort"; (2) a princess from Videha, sometimes called Koshshaladeva, who was the sister of King (?) Prasenajit (and the mother of Ajatasatthu); and (3) Chellana. Queen Kṣema was said to have purposely tried to avoid meeting the Buddha since, addicted to her own beauty, she was afraid of his censure. When through a trick carried out by King Bimbisara she and the Buddha did meet, having listened to the Buddha's discourse, she attained arhatship (one

of the only persons said to have done so while not enrobed). For more on this woman who became a famous nun-teacher, see *Therīgāthā* LII; and Horner, *Women under Primitive Buddhism*, 36, 167–69, 180, 183, 191, etc.

66 Nilakanta Sastri, *A History of South India* (Madras, 1963), 96.

67 Alex and Hideko Wayman, *The Lion's Roar of Queen Śrīmālā*, 2.

68 The T'ang empress Wu Tse-t'ien apparently invited Bodhiruci, the famous Indian translator, to China, and for some twenty years she and her two sons and successors provided support for him. Schuster, "Changing the Female Body," 26, claims that "in return, Bodhiruci lent his prestige to the Empress's claim to be legitimate ruler of China in her own right . . . . The Empress's Buddhist supporters, with at least the tacit approval of Bodhiruci, agreed further that the Empress's reign had been predicted by the Buddha himself in certain Mahāyāna sūtras (the *Ratnamegha*, *Pao-yü ching*, and the *Mahāmegha*, *Ta-yün ching*). One of the sūtras Bodhiruci retranslated for the Empress was the Śrīmālā-sūtra."

69 The Kushana empire (or Kushana dynasty) in northwest India (with its famed king, Kaniska, accession date 78 AD [?]) lasted from the first century AD until the middle of the third century AD. From that time onward, the northwest region came under Iranian influence following the victorious invasion by the Sasanian dynasty of Persia.

70 Nalinaksha Dutt, *Mahāyāna Buddhism* (New Delhi: Motilal Banarsidass, 1977), 56–58, 61–62.

CHAPTER 2: THE *CHOMOS* OF LADAKH

71 Anna Grimshaw, *Servants of the Buddha: Winter in a Himalayan Convent* (Cleveland, OH: Pilgrim Press, 1994).

CHAPTER 3: TIBETAN ANIS

72 This English translation by Tarthang Tulku is found in *Mother of Knowledge: The Enlightenment of Yeshe Tsogyal*, by Nam-mkha'i snying-po (Berkeley: Dharma Publishing, 1985), 105.

73 That Padmasambhava was not alone in this important endeavor has been amply shown by recent scholarship. See for example Eva Dargyay's study, *The Rise of Esoteric Buddhism in Tibet* (Delhi: Motilal Banarsidass, 1977), which goes a long way toward filling out the actual historical circumstances and figures involved in the early establishment of Buddhism in Tibet. Dr. Dargyay shows that such figures as Vimalamitra and Vairocana were of equal (or even

more) importance to the founding of the earliest—that is, Nyingma—tradition there.

74   Two recent translations of Yeshé Tsogyal's namthar have been published: (1) Tarthang Tulku's *Mother of Knowledge*; and (2) Keith Dowman's *Sky Dancer: The Secret Life and Songs of the Lady Yeshe Tsogyel* (London: Routledge & Kegan Paul, 1984).

75   English translation given in *Mother of Knowledge*, 102.

76   As examples, see Nancy Falk and Rita Gross, eds., *Unspoken Worlds: Women's Religious Lives in Non-Western Cultures* (San Francisco: Harper & Row, 1979); and Judith Plaskow and Joan Arnold, eds., *Women and Religion* (Chico, CA: AAR/Scholars Press, 1974).

77   See, for example, Nancy Falk, "An Image of Woman in Old Buddhist Literature: The Daughters of Māra," in Plaskow and Arnold, *Women and Religion*, 102–12; Paul, *Women in Buddhism*; Schuster, "Changing the Female Body," 24–69; Bareau, "Un personnage bien mysterieux," 31–59; and Kajiyama, "Women in Buddhism," 53–70.

78   I have argued this point somewhat differently and more fully in an article entitled "Nuns and Benefactresses: The Role of Women in the Development of Buddhism," in *Women, Religion and Social Change*, ed. Y. Haddad and E. Findly (Albany: State University of New York Press, 1985), 59–85.

79   To date, only the life of Yeshé Tsogyal has received full treatment in English translation. Abbreviated biographies of the four female luminaries of the famed Indian "eighty-four siddha(s)" appear in James Robinson's *Buddha's Lions: The Lives of the Eighty-Four Siddhas* (Berkeley, CA: Dharma Press, 1979); and in Keith Dowman's *Masters of Mahāmudrā* (Albany: State University of New York Press, 1985); and brief accounts of some of the eminent female followers of Phadampa Sangyé (Pha dam pa Sangs rgya), called "nuns" (Tib. *ma jo*) or "ladies" (*jo mo*), are given in *The Blue Annals*, trans. George N. Roerich (Calcutta: Royal Asiatic Society of Bengal, 1949; reprint, Delhi: Motilal Banarsidass, 1979), 915–20. However, full treatment of such female tantric adepts as Niguma, Machik Lapdrönma (Ma gcig lab sgron ma), and Dagmema (Bdag med ma) remain to be done. Several women scholars are presently working on translations of the lives of these women. See, for example, Sarah Harding, *Machik's Complete Explanation Clarifying the Meaning of Chod* (Ithaca, NY: Snow Lion Publications, 2003), and her *Niguma, Lady of Illusion* (Ithaca, NY: Snow Lion Publications, 2010). An account of the history of the Samding incarnates is given in Hildegard Diemberger, *When a Woman Becomes a Religious Dynasty: The Samding Dorje Phagmo of Tibet* (New York: Columbia University Press, 2007).

80   I use the term here in its technical, rather than general sense. Generally, in

Tibetan, *chos pa* refers to any follower of the Buddha's Dharma (Tib. *chos*). Here, however, it is used specifically in reference to a practitioner who has some training in particular disciplines or rituals.

81   For more information on *lhakhas* and *pawo*, see Barbara Aziz, *Tibetan Frontier Families* (New Delhi: Vikas Publishing House, 1978), esp. 253; and Per-Arne Berglie, "On the Question of Tibetan Shamanism," in *Tibetan Studies* (Zurich: Völkerkundermuseum Universität Zürich, 1978), 39–51.

82   For recent accounts of the nuns' tradition in India and Sri Lanka, see Nancy Falk, "The Case of the Vanishing Nuns: The Fruits of Ambivalence in Ancient Indian Buddhism," in Falk and Gross, *Unspoken Worlds*, 207–24; and Ellen Goldberg, "Buddhist Nuns Make Comeback in Sri Lanka—To Monks' Dislike," *The Christian Science Monitor*, April 2, 1984, 14 and 44.

83   Tsepon W. D. Shakabpa, *Tibet: A Political History* (New Haven, CT: Yale University Press, 1967). Shakabpa's population figures are given on 6.

84   I suspect that both these figures are considerably higher than the actual number of monks and nuns in pre-1959 Tibet.

85   Shakabpa, *Tibet*, 6–7.

86   The distortions introduced by translating the term *gönpa* in English as "monastery" have not gone unnoticed by David Snellgrove. See for example his discussion in *Buddhist Himālaya: Travels and Studies in Quest of the Origins and Nature of Tibetan Religion* (Oxford: Bruno Cassirer, 1957), 200–201.

The proper translation and application of the Tibetan term also may be seen to explain how it is that each of the four major Tibetan Buddhist traditions, now in exile, commonly estimates the number of gönpa belonging to each of their respective sects as 2,000–3,000 establishments. For example, Tarthang Tulku, a teacher of the Nyingma tradition, in *Crystal Mirror Volume V* (Berkeley, CA: Dharma Publishing, 1977), estimates that there were in Tibet 3,000 Nyingma gönpa. He provides a listing of such establishments together with the enrollments at each. A few were relatively large complexes with upward of 1,000 members. Most had populations of under 100, and some are listed which had only one member.

87   Of course, this nonspecificity with regard to the sex of a member of a given religious community is also echoed in the original meaning of the English term "convent." The term derives from the Latin *conventus*, i.e., "a coming together, an assembly." Only later did the term come to be popularly applied specifically to a place where nuns convened.

88   David Snellgrove and Hugh Richardson, *A Cultural History of Tibet* (London: Weidenfeld & Nicolson, 1968; reprint, Boulder, CO: Prajna Press, 1980), 247–48.

89   Aziz, *Tibetan Frontier Families*, 228.

90   The chief cause of hardships for Buddhist nuns, of whatever country or histori-
     cal period, was economic. Tibet was no exception here. But, as I and some oth-
     ers (Diana Paul and Nancy Falk, for example) have argued, the nuns' troubles
     were also created by an ambivalent image, fostered by some Buddhist litera-
     ture, of women's ability to successfully practice the renunciant's life. One other
     feature peculiar to Tibetan monastic life should be mentioned here, namely,
     the so-called monk/nun tax, or levy. C. W. Cassinelli and Robert Ekvall, in *A
     Tibetan Principality: The Political System of Sa-skya* (Ithaca, NY: Cornell Uni-
     versity Press, 1969), explore the workings of this system of conscripting monks
     and nuns in Sakya. For monks, their study shows, this system often proved to
     be of benefit, offering upward mobility. The same was not so for the nuns. In
     two dramatically different descriptions, Cassinelli and Ekvall report on monks
     (296):

> Levy monks had certain advantages over volunteer monks,
> especially the opportunity for attaining personal wealth. This
> opportunity—and the general advantages of monkhood, such
> as education, high prestige, material comfort, proximity to the
> sources of power and authority, and the chance to become a sKu
> Drag official—apparently made the levy of monks a quite bearable
> institution. Moreover, the family that produced a boy upon call
> had its revenue lowered in compensation. It must also be remem-
> bered that the average Tibetan family felt a kind of duty to provide
> at least one son to the monkhood.

And on nuns (297):

> There was also a levy of nuns to staff the two nunneries near the capi-
> tal, Sa bZang and Rin Chen sGang, with a total of about 110 nuns,
> of whom not more than 10 percent were volunteers. The nun levy
> was also based on the schedule of revenue in kind, and a family that
> gave up a little girl also had its revenue lowered. The levy of nuns,
> like the levy of monks, no doubt helped tie the polity together, but
> in a much less significant way. The life of a nun had few attractions.
> Monks always served as abbots of the nunneries, and hence only
> lesser positions were open to the nuns. No nuns were sent out of Sa
> sKya proper, and the most a nun could aspire to was becoming a per-
> sonal servant of the royal family, usually of its unmarried daughters.
> Ordinary nuns, moreover, usually had to spend about half their time
> in physical labor outside their nunneries. The levy of nuns was prob-
> ably the only way to keep enough nuns in the capital nunneries in
> order to maintain the religious prestige of the sect.

91   Except for a fairly early Indian anthology of nuns' "triumphant songs" (or

annas) known as the Therigatha, which is also our main source for claiming an
early tradition of women *arhats* (those who have attained nirvāṇa) and famed
women teachers, nuns do not appear in the later literature. In India, Gautama
Buddha (563–483 BC) had been reluctant to establish an order of nuns, and
though he had finally agreed to do so, his enjoining of the so-called eight
weighty regulations (Pāli: *garudhammā*) on the female order had fixed forever
its inferior status vis-à-vis the monkhood.

In *Women in Buddhism*, 82, Diana Paul notes:

> the nun's life is not well marked in the Mahāyāna sutra tradition
> or in the philosophical writing of that tradition. Participation in
> an intellectual life by the Mahāyāna Buddhist nun is not recorded.
> The nun seems not to have been a significant part of the student
> body of the great Buddhist universities which were the central gem
> in the crown of the monk's order, an order which was extensive,
> prosperous, and productive of extraordinary thought and art.

And Nancy Falk writes in "The Case of the Vanishing Nuns," 208:

> At the root, the major problem of the women's order probably
> rested in the Buddhist tradition's inability to affirm completely the
> idea of women pursuing the renunciant's role. This led to an insti-
> tutional structure that offered women admirable opportunities for
> spiritual and intellectual growth, but not for the institutional and
> scholarly leadership that such growth should have fitted them to
> assume. The nuns' troubles were compounded by an ambivalent
> image created in a tradition of Buddhist stories that sometimes
> praised their achievements but just as often undercut and attacked
> them.

92 L. Austine Waddell, *The Buddhism of Tibet, or Lamaism; with Its Mystic Cults, Symbolism and Mythology, and in Its Relation to Indian Buddhism* (London: W. H. Allen, 1895; reprint, New York: Dover Publications, 1972), 275.

93 Ibid.

94 Giuseppe Tucci, *To Lhasa and Beyond: Diary of the Expedition to Tibet in the Year MCMXLVIII* (Rome: Instituto Poligrafico dell Stato, 1956), 64.

95 See Turrell Wylie's translation, *The Geography of Tibet according to the 'Dzam-gling-rgyas-bshad* (Rome: Istituto Italiano per il Medio ed Estremo Orient, 1962), 73–74, 144, and 271.

96 Rinchen Dölma Taring, *Daughter of Tibet: The Autobiography of Rinchen Dölma Taring* (New Delhi: Allied Press, 1970), 167.

97 Waddell, *The Buddhism of Tibet*, 276.

98 Taring, *Daughter of Tibet*, 167.

99 Ibid.

100 The current incarnation, age fifty at the time of this writing, occupies a government office in the Chinese-controlled Tibetan Autonomous Region. A sweeping history of the Samding lineage was published in 2007. See Diemberger, *When a Woman Becomes a Dynasty*.

101 Machik Lapdrönma, famed in Tibetan religious annals as the fashioner of the Chö system of tantric practice, is said, in turn, to have been the reincarnation of Yeshé Tsogyal.

102 Taring, *Daughter of Tibet*, 165.

103 Ibid., page facing 225.

104 Lobsang Lhalungpa, the son of a powerful ex-state oracle of Tibet, has written many important works dealing with Tibetan Buddhism, not least of which is his fine English translation of *The Life of Milarepa* (New York: E. P. Dutton, 1977).

105 See *Parabola* 3, no. 4 (1978): 49.

106 I join with many others in mourning the recent passing of both these revered teachers of the Geluk tradition: the senior tutor to His Holiness the Fourteenth Dalai Lama, the sixth Kyabjé Yongdzin Ling Rinpoché, Thupten Lungtok Namgyal Thinley (1903–83); and His Holiness's junior tutor, the third Kyabjé Trijang Rinpoché, Lobsang Yeshe Tenzin Gyatso (1901–81).

107 Lobsang P. Lhalungpa, *Tibet, the Sacred Realm: Photographs 1880–1950* (New York: Aperture, 1983), 33. Lhalungpa continues his description of Ani Lochen with the following:

> Endorsing my eclectic attitude, she said to me: "I always looked upon every Buddhist order as being a different vehicle capable of transporting fortunate seekers across the great ocean of Saṃsāra [the cycle of birth and death]." The essence of her message can be summed up as follows: What matters most in this troubled world is compassion and wisdom. The form and institution of the practice matters less. A seeker who perceives the illusory nature of all things is on the threshold of wisdom.

108 Taring, *Daughter of Tibet*, 269.

109 Aziz, *Tibetan Frontier Families*, 244. Aziz first published materials regarding this *ani* in an article entitled "Ani Chodron: Portrait of a Buddhist Nun," in *Loka 2, Journal from Nāropa Institute*, ed. Rick Fields (New York: Doubleday/Anchor, 1976).

110 Aziz, *Tibetan Frontier Families*, 244.

111 Ibid., 245.

112 Ibid., 245–46.

113 For more on this particular monastery in Kyirong (Skyid grong), see Wylie, *The Geography of Tibet*, 65 and 129. Wylie notes, 129, that "this monastery

is reported as having been erected at the place where Ras-pa zhiba-'od [Repa Shiwa Öd], a disciple of Milarepa, had meditated. Later on, it was changed into a Gelukpa monastery by Kong-po Chab-nagpa Sangs-rgyas-dpal-'byor [Kongpo Chapnagpa Sangyé Paljor], a lama of the Shel-dkar Chos-sde [Shelkar Chode] monastery. He established a new school there and gave it this name."

114 It is to be noted here that Ani Drölkar did not at first equate "freedom" with the lack of material hardship; rather she spoke of it in political terms. Still, as her subsequent comments reveal, the realities of economic and material hardship and nonfreedom once again enter into her description.

115 These nuns apparently had all been formerly associated with the Samten Ling Gönpa.

116 Aziz, "Ani Chodron," 245.

117 Ibid., 243.

Chapter 4: Tibetan Buddhist Women Practitioners, Past and Present

118 See Kalu Rinpoché, *The Dharma That Illuminates All Beings Impartially Like the Light of the Sun and the Moon* (Albany: State University of New York Press, 1986), 91–92.

119 Surya Das, *The Snow Lion's Turquoise Mane: Wisdom Tales from Tibet* (New York: HarperCollins, 1992), 250.

120 Resources on Tibetan Buddhism include Keith Dowman, *The Power-Places of Central Tibet: The Pilgrim's Guide* (London: Routledge & Kegan Paul, 1988); Lhalungpa, *The Life of Milarepa*; Nalanda Translation Committee, *The Life of Marpa the Translator* (Boulder, CO: Prajna Press, 1982); Kalu Rinpoché, *Dharma That Illuminates*; Sogyal Rinpoché, *The Tibetan Book of Living and Dying* (San Francisco: HarperCollins, 1992); Lama Zopa Rinpoche, Lama Thubten, and George Churinoff, trans., *The Seventh Dalai Lama, Nyung Na: The Means of Achievement of the Eleven-Headed Great Compassionate One, Avalokitesvara* (Boston: Wisdom Publications, 1995); and Roerich, *The Blue Annals*.

121 See Anna Grimshaw, *Servants of the Buddha: Winter in a Himalayan Convent* (Cleveland, OH: Pilgrim Press, 1994).

122 See Grimshaw's review of *The World of Buddhism*, entitled "Spiritual Corporations," *Times Literary Review*, February 15, 1985, 181.

123 Several authors have briefly alluded to Gelongma Palmo, who is perhaps better known by her Indian name, Bhiksuni Laksmi. See, for example, Miranda Shaw, *Passionate Enlightenment: Women in Tantric Buddhism* (Princeton, NJ:

Princeton University Press, 1994), 126–30; and Lama Zopa Rinopche, Lama Tubten, and Churinoff, *The Seventh Dalai Lama, Nyung Na,* 193–96.

124 The suggestion that the current Drigung Khandro is a reincarnation of Āchi Chökyi Drölma is made in Das, *The Snow Lion's Turquoise Mane,* 111.

125 For more on Ayu Khandro, see Rita Gross, *Buddhism after Patriarchy: A Feminist History, Analysis, and Reconstruction of Buddhism* (Albany: State University of New York Press, 1993), 87–88; and Tsultrim Allione, *Women of Wisdom* (London: Routledge & Kegan Paul, 1984), 236–57.

126 A video about this great *chod* practitioner has recently been produced, called *We Will Meet Again in the Land of the Dakini,* distributed by Mystic Fire Video.

127 Sogyal Rinpoché narrates a number of stories about his two aunts in *The Tibetan Book of Living and Dying,* 225–27, 241, and 366.

128 A recent interview with Khandro Chenmo Rinpoché appears in *Cho Yang: The Voice of Tibetan Religion and Culture* 5 (1992): 61–64.

129 Rinchen Dölma Taring's life is narrated in her autobiography *Daughter of Tibet: The Autobiography of Rinchen Dolma Taring* (London: Wisdom Publications, 1986 [1970]).

130 Ama Adhe is one of two Tibetans whose life and imprisonment in Tibet is chronicled in David Patt, *A Strange Liberation: Tibetan Lives in Chinese Hands* (Ithaca, NY: Snow Lion Publications, 1992).

131 A video chronicling a day in the life of this amazing Tibetan woman doctor has been produced by Sheldon Rochlin and Mikki Maher: *Tibetan Medicine: A Buddhist Approach to Healing,* distributed by Mystic Fire Video.

132 Much of this account is taken from Kalu Rinpoché, *Dharma That Illuminates,* 96–97.

133 See Tarthang Tulku, *Mother of Knowledge: The Enlightenment of Yeshe Tsogyal* (Berkeley, CA: Dharma Publishing, 1985).

134 Keith Dowman, *Sky Dancer: The Secret Life and Songs of the Lady Yeshe Tsogyel* (London: Routledge & Kegan Paul, 1984).

135 See Rita Gross, "Yeshe Tsogyel: Enlightened Consort, Great Teacher, Female Role Model," in *Feminine Ground: Essays on Women and Tibet,* ed. Janice D. Willis (Ithaca, NY: Snow Lion Publications, 1995), 11–32.

136 See Kenneth Douglas and Gwendolyn Bays, trans., *The Life and Liberation of Padmasambhava,* 2 vols. (Emeryville, CA: Dharma Publishing, 1978).

137 Three English translations of *The Tibetan Book of the Dead* are now available. In order of publication, these are: W. E. Evans-Wentz's *The Tibetan Book of the Dead* (Oxford: Oxford University Press, 1957); Francesca Fremantle and Chögyam Trungpa's *The Tibetan Book of the Dead: The Great Liberation through Hearing in the Bardo* (Boulder, CO: Shambhala Publications, 1975); and Robert A. F. Thurman's *The Tibetan Book of the Dead: Liberation through Understanding in the Between* (New York: Bantam Books, 1994).

138 See Roerich, *The Blue Annals*.

139 Tsultrim Allione, *Women of Wisdom*, 141–204.

140 Jérôme Edou, trans., *Machig Labdrön and the Foundations of Chöd* (Ithaca, NY: Snow Lion Publications, 1996).

141 Dowman, *The Power-Places of Central Tibet*, 248.

142 Chögyam Trungpa and Nalanda Translation Committee, *The Life of Marpa the Translator*.

143 For an account of Catharine Burroughs' life, see Vicki Mackenzie, *Reborn in the West* (New York: Marlowe & Company, 1996).

144 Also the copyeditor of my book *Enlightened Beings: Life Stories from the Ganden Oral Tradition* (Boston: Wisdom Publications, 1995).

145 So far these materials have not yet appeared in published form.

146 Jan Willis, "Tibetan Ani-s: The Nun's Life in Tibet," in Willis, *Feminine Ground*, 105–9; reprinted in chapter 3 of this volume.

147 See Taring, *Daughter of Tibet*, 165–67.

148 See *Parabola* 3, no. 4 (1978): 49.

149 See Lhalungpa, *Tibet, the Sacred Realm*, 33.

150 Publication data not available.

151 See *Chö Yang: The Voice of Tibetan Religion and Culture*, "Year of Tibet Edition" (Dharamsala, India: Council for Religious and Cultural Affairs, 1991), 130–43.

152 Ibid., 142–43.

153 Ibid., 130.

154 Delog Dawa Drölma, *Delog: Journey to Realms Beyond Death* (Junction City, CA: Padma Publishing, 1995).

155 Taring, *Daughter of Tibet*.

156 After some publication delays, Canyon Sam's book was published in 2015 with the title *Sky Train: Tibetan Women on the Edge of History* (Seattle: The University of Washington Press, 2015).

CHAPTER 5: FEMALE PATRONAGE IN INDIAN BUDDHISM

157 In *Women, Religion, and Social Change*, ed. Y. Haddad and E. Findly (Albany: State University of New York Press, 1985), 59–85. Reprinted as chapter 1 of the present volume.

158 For more on the important connections between the development of stupas and the rise of the Mahayana, see Akira Hirakawa, "The Rise of Mahāyāna Buddhism and Its Relationship to the Worship of Stūpas."

159 See W. G. Weeraratne's entry on "Avadāna" in *Encyclopaedia of Buddhism*, vol. 2, fasc. 3 (Ceylon: Government of Ceylon Press, 1967), 397.

160 For a translation of this text, see Caroline A. F. Rhys Davids, *Psalms of the Sisters* (the *Therīgāthā*).

161 The life of Visakha, also known as the "mother of Migara," is recounted in the Dhammapada commentary, and references to her are found both in the Udana and in the Anguttara Nikaya. H. Warren gives a translation of her life in his *Buddhism in Translations*, 451–81. I. B. Horner, in *Women under Primitive Buddhism*, 345–61, also discusses Visakha; and A. Coomaraswamy, in *Buddha and the Gospel of Buddhism*, 163–4, also mentions her. Coomaraswamy quotes Oldenberg's *Buddha, His Life, His Doctrine, His Order* (1882) as saying: "Pictures like this of Visakha, benefactresses of the Church, with their inexhaustible religious zeal, and their not less inexhaustible resources of money, are certainly, if anything ever was, drawn from the life of India in those days: they cannot be left out of sight, if we desire to get an idea of the actors who made the oldest Buddhist community what it was."

162 Warren, *Buddhism in Translations*, 471. Visakha is said to have "lived to be a hundred and twenty years old, but there was not a single gray hair on her head—always she appeared as if about sixteen."

163 Shravasti was an important city during the Buddha's day and a main seat for his order. It figures as the setting of numerous sutras.

164 Warren, *Buddhism in Translations*, 477–78.

165 Coomaraswamy, *Buddha and the Gospel of Buddhism*, 74–75. A contingent of "Licchavi princes" are said to have become upset when Buddha refused their invitation to dine with them in order to honor his former acceptance to do so with Ambapali.

166 See Nancy Falk's "The Case of the Vanishing Nuns," 209–10.

167 For example, see such works as: J. Burgess, *Buddhist Stūpas of Amarāvatī and Jaggayapeṭa* (Archaeological Survey of South India, 1870); A. Coomaraswamy, *History of Indian and Indonesian Art* (New York, 1927), and *La sculpture de Bharhut* (Paris, 1956); and A. Cunningham, *The Bhilsa Topes* (London, 1854), and *The Stupa of Bharhut, A Buddhist Monument Ornamented with Numerous Sculptures Illustrative of Buddhist Legend and History in the Third Century BC* (London, 1879; reprint, India, 1962).

168 Shastri, *A History of South India*, 96. Cf. Wayman, *The Lion's Roar of Queen Śrīmālā*, 2.

169 Wayman, *The Lion's Roar of Queen Śrīmālā*, 2.

170 Nalinaksha Dutt, *Mahāyāna Buddhism*, 56–58.

171 Ibid., 61–62.

CHAPTER 6: BUDDHISM AND RACE

172 Rodger Kamenetz, *The Jew in the Lotus* (New York: HarperCollins, 1995).

173 Larry L. Saxon, "Nattier Storm Alert," Letters, *Tricycle: The Buddhist Review* 5, no. 2 (1995): 8.

174 Quoted in Tensho David Schneider, "Accidents and Calculations: The Emergence of Three AIDS Hospices," *Tricycle: The Buddhist Review* 1, no. 3 (1992): 81.

175 Faith Adiele, "Standing Alone with Myself," in *Life Notes: Personal Writings by Contemporary Black Women*, ed. Patricia Bell-Scott (New York: W. W. Norton, 1994), 364–88.

176 Sandy Boucher, *Turning the Wheel: American Women Creating the New Buddhism* (San Francisco: Harper & Row, 1988), 306.

177 Ibid., 311.

178 Quoted in Clark Strand, "Buddha in the Market: An Interview with Korean Zen Master Samu Sunim," *Tricycle: The Buddhist Review* 5, no. 2 (1995): 91–92.

179 Lama Yeshe, *Introduction to Tantra: The Transformation of Desire* (Boston: Wisdom Publications, 2001 [1987]), 41.

180 Ibid., 42.

181 Ibid., 46.

182 Amiri Baraka [Leroi Jones], *Blues People: Negro Music in White America* (New York: Morrow Quill, 1963), 136.

CHAPTER 7: DIVERSITY AND RACE

183 See my "Buddhism and Race: An African American Baptist-Buddhist Perspective," in *Buddhist Women on the Edge: Contemporary Perspectives from the Western Frontier*, ed. Marianne Dresser (Berkeley, CA: North Atlantic Books, 1996), 81–91.

184 Lori Pierce makes this observation in her essay "Outside In: Buddhism in America," in Dresser, *Buddhist Women on the Edge*, 98. She writes: "Most of the published material by, for, and about Buddhism in America is about Buddhism as a spiritual path and practice. Though this is certainly interesting and important (and necessary, if Buddhism is to be a tool in understanding and destroying discriminatory practices), this emphasis can distract us from questions concerning racism and sexism. Feminist scholars and female Sangha members have vociferously critiqued Buddhism at the institutional level and examined how through hierarchical structures or adherence to unsuitable cultural forms, it has exacerbated problems between male and female teachers and students and other Sangha members."

Jan Nattier, in an essay entitled "Visible and Invisible: The Politics of Representation in Buddhist America," *Tricycle: The Buddhist Review* 5, no. 1 (1995): 42–49, had earlier described those she termed "elite Buddhists" as having "redefined Buddhism as [being] synonymous with the practice of meditation."

185 One need only glance at the several publications devoted to the subject of Buddhism in America in the past decade to see that these works focus almost exclusively on the spiritual path and practice of the various traditions of Buddhism here. Besides Rick Fields' journalistic social history, *How the Swans Came to the Lake: The American Encounter with Buddhism* (Boston: Shambhala Publications, 1992), most other publications treat one or more Buddhist traditions but always emphasize meditation. In the 568-page 1998 book *Buddhism in America: Proceedings of the First Buddhism in America Conference*, edited by Brian Hotchkiss, conference organizer Al Rapaport left no doubt about it. In his introduction (xiii) he states, "I envisioned the Buddhism in America Conference as a forum at which modern-day meditation teachers could present, and attendees could experience, the essence of the Buddhist teachings on life, death, compassion, and enlightenment."

186 *Shambhala Sun* 7, no. 2 (1998): ii.

187 See Ralph Steele, *Tending the Fire: Through War and the Path of Meditation* (n.p.: Sacred Life Publishers, 2014).

188 "Buddhism and Race: An African American Baptist-Buddhist Perspective," in Dresser, *Buddhist Women on the* Edge, 81. Reprinted in chapter 6 of this volume.

189 Ibid., 87.

190 That is, Maurine Stuart Roshi, the head of the Cambridge Buddhist Association from the early 1980s until her death in 1991. Information about Stuart Roshi's life can be found in Helen Tworkov's *Zen in America: Profiles of Five Teachers* (San Francisco: North Point Press, 1989), 153–97. Following her death, a series of lectures by Stuart Roshi were collected in *Subtle Sound: The Zen Teachings of Maurine Stuart*, ed. Roko Sherry Chayat (Boston: Shambhala Publications, 1996).

191 That was none other than Rosa Zubizarreta, the member of the Buddhism and Racism Working Group who was quoted in the November 1998 advertisement I had read in *Shambhala Sun*.

CHAPTER 8: DHARMA HAS NO COLOR

192 The full text of the parable of the raft can be found in the Majjhima Nikaya of the Pali canon. The translation from which I have excerpted the story is by

Walpola Rahula, *What the Buddha Taught, Revised and Expanded Edition with Texts from Suttas and Dhammapada* (New York: Grove Press, 1974 [1959]), 11–12.

193 Clearly, I am not the only person who holds this opinion. I am reminded, for example, of Sylvia Boorstein's book, *That's Funny, You Don't Look Buddhist: On Being a Faithful Jew and a Passionate Buddhist* (San Francisco: HarperSanFrancisco, 1998). And His Holiness the Dalai Lama often begins his talks today, in various parts of the world, by saying that one need not leave the religious tradition of one's upbringing in order to take advantage of the Buddha's teachings.

194 The *Diamond Cutter Sutra* (Skt. *Vajracchedikasutra*) was composed circa fourth century AD. This particular translation was done by Edward Conze and appears in his *Buddhist Wisdom Books*, 63.

195 The Buddhist theory of the "two truths" is perhaps most thoroughly presented and analyzed by the great Mahayana philosopher and founder of the Madhyamaka school, Nagarjuna (ca. 150–250 AD). The theory explains that words and language constitute and create a conventional, relative world wherein communication and action takes place among ordinary beings. Yet the experience and view of an enlightened being ultimately transcends all conventional structures, being unmediated, ultimate, and ineffable.

196 The speech, entitled "Criteria of Negro Art," was delivered by Du Bois in Chicago in 1923. This section of the speech is quoted by John Malkin as part of an interview conducted with Charles Johnson and recorded in *Shambhala Sun*, January 2004, 84.

197 The Dalai Lama begins many of his lectures with this gentle, but realistic, declaration.

CHAPTER 9: YES, WE'RE BUDDHISTS, TOO!

198 See Pew Forum, "U.S. Religious Landscape Survey" (Washington, DC: Pew Research Center, 2008), https://www.pewforum.org/religious-landscape-study/; and R. Wuthnow and W. Cadge, "Buddhists and Buddhism in the United States: The Scope of Influence," *Journal for the Scientific Study of Religion* 43, no. 3 (2004), 365.

199 See Gurinder Singh Mann, Paul Numrich, and Raymond Williams, *Buddhists, Hindus, and Sikhs in America: A Short History* (Oxford: Oxford University Press, 2008), 15.

CHAPTER 10: THE LIFE OF KYONGRU TULKU

200 Tib. Don grub lags; *lags* (pronounced "la" or "lah") is an honorific particle.

201 Tulku (*sprul sku*) is the Tibetan equivalent for the Sanskrit term *nirmanakaya*, literally, "magical emanation body." It is used in reference to an "incarnate being," usually a lama, and indicates that such a being personally "incarnates" either a certain deity or a former high lama.

202 Clifford Geertz, *Islam Observed: Religious Development in Morocco and Indonesia* (New Haven, CT: Yale University Press, 1968), 25–35. Cited in *The Biographical Process: Studies in the History and Psychology of Religion*, ed. Frank Reynolds and Donald Capps (The Hague: Mouton, 1976), 10.

203 W. E. H. Stanner works with Australian aborigines. See his essay "The Dreaming," in *Reader in Comparative Religion: An Anthropological Approach*, ed. William A. Lessa and Evon Z. Vogt (New York: Harper & Row, 1979), 158–67; and "Religion, Totemism, and Symbolism," in *Aboriginal Man in Australia: Essays in Honour of Emeritus Prof. A. P. Elkin*, ed. R. M. and C. H. Berndt (Sydney: Angus and Robertson, 1965).

204 This discussion by Bateson is reported by Ernst Kris, in *Psychoanalytic Explorations in Art* (New York: International Universities Press, 1952), 83, note 27.

205 See, for example, the works of Gregory Bateson and Kenelm Burridge.

206 For example, Otto Rank's classic 1922 study, *The Myth of the Birth of the Hero: A Psychological Exploration of Myth*, trans. Gregory Richter and E. James Lieberman (Baltimore, MD: Johns Hopkins University Press, 2004); and Joseph Campbell's *The Hero with a Thousand Faces* (Novato, CA: The Joseph Campbell Foundation and New World Library, 2008).

207 In his review of Leo Simmons' *Sun Chief*, Claude Levi-Strauss suggested that there is basis for the view that through biography the alien character of other cultures is immediately transcended. He wrote, in *Social Research* 1, no. 10 (1943): 515–17: "The function of primitive biographies is to provide a psychological expression of cultural phenomena. This psychological expression— because it is psychological—is immediately accessible to any human being, even to one who belongs to a quite different cultural surrounding."

208 For an overview of the "life history" approach as it has developed in anthropology, see Clyde Kluckhohn, *The Use of Personal Documents in Anthropology*, Bulletin 55 (New York: Social Science Research Council, 1945); and Lewis Langness, *The Life History in Anthropological Science* (New York: Holt, Rinehart and Winston, 1965).

209 See Langness, *The Life History in Anthropological Science*, 3–21, for a survey. Of course, Freudians are the chief referents here.

210 A primary example is Ernst Kretschmer, *The Psychology of Men of Genius*, trans.

R. B. Cattell (London: Kegan Paul, Trench, Trubner and Co., 1931). Also, Erik Erikson, *Young Man Luther: A Study in Psychoanalysis and History* (W. W. Norton, 1958); *Gandhi's Truth: On the Origins of Militant Nonviolence* (W. W. Norton, 1969); and his studies of Hitler and Gorky, "The Legend of Hitler's Childhood" and "The Legend of Maxim Gorky's Youth," in *Childhood and Society* (New York: W. W. Norton, 1950), 326–28 and 359–402, could be included here.

211 In his *Psychoanalytic Explorations in Art* (New York: International Universities Press, 2000), Ernst Kris devotes a chapter to "The Image of the Artist: A Psychological Study of the Role of Tradition in Ancient Biographies," 64–84.

212 This summary of one of Kris's main points is stated in Reynolds and Capps, *The Biographical Process*, 18.

213 Gesar (pronounced "Kesar") is the name of the legendary king of the mythic kingdom called Gling. He is the chief hero of Tibet's oldest epic.

214 The Tibetan term *ru* (bone) is closely linked to *rva* or *rus* (both meaning "horn"), and all three terms are used to connote male potency and patrilineal descent.

215 The other four elements of the hero-pattern as outlined by Rank in *The Myth of the Birth of the Hero* are: (3) during or before the pregnancy, there is a prophecy cautioning against his birth and usually threatening danger to the father or fathersurrogate; (4) he is surrendered to the water, then saved by animals or lowly people and suckled by a female animal or a humble woman; (5) after he grows up, he finds his parents, takes his revenge and is acknowledged as heir; and (6) he finally achieves rank and honors.

216 The present Dalai Lama, Tenzin Gyatso, reported that after his birth "a pair of crows came to roost on the roof" of his house. "They would arrive each morning, stay for a while, and then leave." He continued, "This is of particular interest, as similar incidents occurred at the birth of the First, Seventh, Eighth, and Twelfth Dalai Lamas. After the births, a pair of crows came and remained." See John Avedon, *An Interview with the Dalai Lama* (New York: Littlebird Publications, 1980), 17.

The black crows in the accounts of the Dalai Lamas are viewed as emanations of the wrathful deity Mahakala, said to be the special protector (i.e., *kyong*) of each Dalai Lama.

Döndrup's mention of the appearance of a white cock in connection with his birth is of particular interest here because of its link with a much older tradition: that is, two of King Gesar's protective deities, born (or appearing) simultaneously with him, were a white eagle and a white crow.

217 See Robert Ekvall's *The Lama Knows: A Tibetan Legend Is Born*, originally published in India in 1979 and reprinted in 1980 by Chandler and Sharp Publishers.

218 Vincent Crapanzano, *Tuhami: Portrait of a Moroccan* (Chicago: The University of Chicago Press, 1980), 4–5.

219 Nyenchen Thang Lha is located far to the north of Lhasa. The mountain, which is situated on the southern border of Namtso (Gnan mtsho) Lake, enjoys special veneration owing to its connection with a popular pre-Buddhist deity of the same name. It is thus one of the most sacred mountains in Tibet, and it would be considered great sacrilege to "violate" it by digging or mining there.

220 *Dge bshes* is an abbreviation for *dge ba'i bshes gnen* (Skt. *kalyanamitra*). The term means "virtuous friend" and connotes one's spiritual guide and benefactor. Additionally, the contracted form, i.e., *dge bshes*, is used (especially by adherents of the Gelukpa school) to refer to its revered teachers, who have earned the highest monastic degrees. *Sngags pa* in this context refers to advanced tantric practitioners and to renowned graduates of one of the Tantric Colleges.

221 Tibetan for the "Three Jewels" of the Buddhist refuge formula, i.e., the Buddha, the Dharma, and the Sangha; or again, the Buddha, his teaching, and his monastic order.

222 Dpal ldan Lha mo (pronounced "Pelden lhamo") is the name of a goddess (Indian, "Shri Devi") in wrathful form, viewed as a protectoress and guardian of the Buddhist faith.

223 Snellgrove, *Buddhist Himālaya*, xii.

CHAPTER 11: ON THE NATURE OF NAMTHAR

224 This useful translation is borrowed from Robert A. F. Thurman's discussion of how Vimalakirti's namthar may be viewed as being *upaya* (usually translated as "skillful means" but here by Thurman as "liberative technique.") See his *The Holy Teaching of Vimalakirti*, 6–9 and 161–62.

225 Tucci has given an excellent summary of the development of Tibetan historical literature in his *Tibetan Painted Scrolls*, vol. 1 (Rome: Libreria dello Stato, 1949), 139–50. In brief, Tucci argues that at an early date Tibetans, following the Chinese rather than the Indian tradition, showed "a particular interest, if not precisely a great accuracy, in recording facts . . . ." Accordingly, the first historical writings produced by Tibetans were *yik tshang* (*yig tshang*), or chronicles—that is, books in which events affecting national life were recorded along with their dates. In its second phase Tibetan historical writing took on a different character and broadened to include Tibet's growing national and religious consciousness, and the first expansive histories, known as *chöjung* (*chos 'byung*), were produced. *Chöjung* literally means "growth and expansion of the Dharma," and thus it is within *chöjung* that we find the first real attempts

at biographical writing. Tucci writes (140): "With this [i.e., *chöjung*] a new historiography appears: the bare facts are not listed year by year according to the simple system of the chronicles; they assume decorous literary draperies in which reminiscences of Buddhist hagiography recur."

226 For example, see Eva Dargyay's *The Rise of Esoteric Buddhism in Tibet*; Tucci's *Tibetan Painted Scrolls*; and James Robinson's *Buddha's Lions*.

227 This rendering is used by Clinton Albertson in his *Anglo-Saxon Saints and Heroes* (New York: Fordham University Press, 1967). Throughout the accounts of confessor lives, one finds epithets like "Christ's soldier," "warriors of the spirit," and "God's hero." One is reminded that a common Tibetan rendering for the Sanskrit bodhisattva is *pawo jangchup sempa* (*dpa' bo byang chub sems dpa'*)—that is, brave or courageous bodhisattva.

228 Ibid., 75.

229 See Donald Attwater, *A Dictionary of Saints* (London: Penguin, 1979), 4.

230 This is the entry given under "hagiography" in *The American Heritage Dictionary of the English Language* (1978), 592. Albertson, *Anglo-Saxon Saints and Heroes*, 25–26, duly notes and responds to the negative assessments usually made with regard to hagiographic materials.

231 This specific assessment was voiced by David Snellgrove in his *Buddhist Himālaya*, 85, with particular reference to the eighty-four siddhas of the Saivite and Buddhist traditions. However, Snellgrove finds namthar of value for depicting the general religious climate of the times. The relevant passage reads: "Both Buddhist and Shaivite tradition preserve the memory of eighty-four great yogins or perfected ones (*siddha*). Their biographies are to be found in the Tibetan canon, and although the tales related of them are of no direct historical worth, they portray well enough the general religious setting, in which the actual tantric texts originated."

232 Perhaps the best-known enumeration of the *laukika siddhis* is that found at Dīgha Nikāya, I. 78. There, when the Buddha enumerates for King Ajatasattu the fruits of the life of a monk (in the *Samannaphala Sutta*), he describes them as follows: "Being one he becomes many, or having become many, he becomes one again; he becomes visible or invisible; without obstruction he passes through walls, through fences, through mountains, as if they were but air; he penetrates up and down through solid earth, as if it were but water; he walks on water without parting it, as if it were solid ground; cross-legged he travels through the air, as a bird on the wing; he touches and handles the moon and the sun, though they be so potent and mighty; even in this body of his, he scales the heights of the world up to the heaven of Brahma; just as a clever potter could succeed in making out of clay any shape of vessel he wanted to have." Translated by H. G. A. van Zeyst in his "Abhiññā" article in the *Encyclopaedia*

of Buddhism, vol. 1, ed. G. P. Malalasekera (Colombo: The Government Press, 1961), 99. (I have substituted "obstruction" for van Zeyst's "let.") For more on the worldly siddhis, see 97–102; and Dayal, *The Bodhisattva Doctrine in Buddhist Sanskrit Literature*, 104–16. The superior (*lokottara*) siddhi is the realization of Mahamudra.

233 The tantric meditative system of practice known as *chakya chenpo* (Skt. *mahamudra*) is sometimes thought to be associated only with the Kagyüpa school of Tibetan Buddhism. This is especially true in Western accounts of the system. However, as the prayer and related namthar presently under discussion attest, this practice lineage was incorporated into the Gelukpa tradition as well.

234 The text is written in verse form. After offering salutations to the Mahamudra, or Great Seal, meditative system, it proceeds by presenting thirty-six verses, each comprised of two eightsyllable descriptive lines, with a third line bearing the name of the respective lineage-holder. This is followed in each case by a refrain of four eight-syllable lines: *rgyud bdag 'dzin 'khri ba chod pa dang/ byams sning rje byang sems 'byongs ba dang/ lam zung 'jug phyag rgya chen po yi/ mchog myur du thob par byin gyis rlobs/* (By generating a mind of compassion and loving kindness,/ and by completely severing the continuity which clings to holding a self,/ may I be blessed to attain quickly the Highest (state)/ of Mahāmudrā, (by means of) the path of total integration.)

235 My book *Enlightened Beings: Life Stories from the Ganden Oral Tradition* (Boston: Wisdom Publications, 1995) treats the shared lineage of Kagyü/Geluk Mahamudra and presents complete translations of the biographies of these six Geluk siddhas.

236 See Khetsun Sangpo, ed., *Biographical Dictionary of Tibet and Tibetan Buddhism*, vol. 5 (Dharamsala: Library of Tibetan Works & Archives, 1973). In each case, for the Geluk lives, Khetsun Sangpo's version omits the verse that in the standard *Byang chub lam gyi rim pa'i bla ma brgyud pa'i rnam thar* immediately precedes the narration of the life. These verses, together with the refrain given above (note 11), constitute the Geluk liturgical prayer. The Khetsun Sangpo version also abbreviates by summarizing certain sections of the lengthier standard namthar.

237 The school founded by Tsongkhapa was known by various names—namely, Riwo Gendenpa, Kadam Sarmapa, and Gelukpa. The Gelukpa became known as the "Yellow Hats" presumably because of Tsongkhapa's innovation, in Tibet, of having the monks of his school wear yellow or saffron apparel, as did the original Buddhist monks in India. This innovation signaled the great reform he instituted in Tibet, which is set forth doctrinally in his mammoth work, *The Great Stages of the Path to Enlightenment* (abbreviated in Tibetan as the Lamrim Chenmo [*Lam rim chen mo*]). Snellgrove tells us, in *A Cultural History of*

Tibet, 181, that "Westerners have borrowed from the Chinese the term 'Yellow Hat' for the dGe-lugs-pa . . . ." Whatever the actual origin of the term, it has come to be an unambiguous and readily identifiable feature of the school. The six lives cover the three hundred years from the mid-fourteenth to the mid-seventeenth centuries, during which the Gelukpa successfully appropriated more and more power and firmly established itself in Tibet.

238 For example, of the six Gelukpa *siddhas* immediately succeeding Tsongkhapa, four were personally connected with the first five Dalai Lamas. Baso Jé became abbot of Ganden Monastery on the order of the First Dalai Lama, Gendun Drup (Dge 'dun grub). One of Baso's Mahamudra disciples, Palden Dorjé (Dpal ldan rdo rje), studied with and taught the Second Dalai Lama, Gedun Gyatson (Dge 'dun rgya mtsho). Following the death of Gyalwa Ensapa, Sangyé Yeshé accompanied and served the Third Dalai Lama, Sönam Gyatso (Bsod nams rgya mtsho), until the latter went to Mongolia. Finally, the Panchen Lama Losang Chökyi Gyaltsen (Blo bzang chos kyi rgyal mtshan) was the direct tutor of both the Fourth Dalai Lama, Yönten Gyatso (Yon tan rgya mtsho) and the Great Fifth Dalai Lama, Ngawang Losang Gyatso (Ngag dbang blo bzang rgya mtsho).

239 This point was forcefully made by Reginald Ray in a paper delivered to the American Academy of Religion in San Francisco (December 1977) entitled "The Vajrayāna Mahāsiddhas: Some Principles of Interpretation" (unpublished).

240 This is well known to those within the tradition. Most namthar contain all three levels, though one or the other is most emphasized. Some few namthar treat specifically only one level. For example, there are separate secret biographies (i.e., *sangwai namthar*) of such great masters as Padmasambhava, Tsongkhapa, and Sakya Pandita. Tucci, *Tibetan Painted Scrolls*, 1:161, for example, cites Tsongkhapa's secret biography, entitled *Rje rin po che'i gsang ba'i rnam thar rgya mtsho lta bu las cha shas nyung ngu zhig yongs su brjod pa'i gtam rin po che'i snye ma* (*Complete Works*, Potala ed., vol. *ka*, 1–16), and says it "contains a narrative of his visions, of his mystical realizations, of the revelations he received from divine masters in dreams or ecstasy. . . . The author of this work is Dge legs dpal bzan po" (i.e., Khedrup Jé). Khedrup Jé also authored another namthar of Tsongkhapa that treats primarily the first and second levels. Luciano Petech, in his introduction to Alfonsa Ferrari's *Mk'yen brtse's Guide to the Holy Places of Central Tibet*, ed. Luciano Petech with the collaboration of Hugh Richardson (Rome: Istituto Italiano per il Medio ed Estremo Oriente, 1958), xix, takes note of this traditional threefold pattern of Tibetan namthar, setting out the specific shifts from one to the other in the life of Khyentsé Kunga Tenpa'i Gyaltsen (Mkhyen brtse Kun dga' bstan pa'i rgyal mtshan), the author of the

Guide. David Ruegg, in *The Life of Bu ston Rinpoché, with the Tibetan Text of the Bu ston rNam thar*, Serie Orientale Roma 34 (Rome: Istituto Italiano per il Medio ed Estremo Oriente, 1966), 44–45, also notes the threefold structure of namthar.

241 Many scholars working with this material have tended to confine it to the province of popular literature, viewing siddha biographies as the products of popular spirituality and as folkloric. For example, Mircea Eliade notes in his *Yoga, Immortality and Freedom* (Princeton, NJ: Princeton University Press, 2009), 305: "a number of the Nāthas and Siddhas put more emphasis than their predecessors had done upon the value of magic and Yoga as inestimable means for the conquest of freedom and immortality. It was especially this aspect of their message that struck the popular imagination; we still find it echoed today in folklore and vernacular literatures." For Eliade this feature of namthar was valuable, and he followed the above remark with this statement: "It is for this reason that the latter seem to us of great value for our inquiry." David Snellgrove, too, agrees with this assessment of namthar. In *Buddhist Himālaya*, 86, he calls namthar "popular accounts (in which) the goal of perfection seems to be immortality." Giuseppe Tucci, *Tibetan Painted Scrolls*, 1:151, admits that "an historian cannot ignore the *rnam t'ar*," and indeed Tucci makes good use of them. However his own general definition of *namthar* appears to me to be more obscuring of their true nature than clarifying. He writes (150–51): "*rnam t'ar* much resemble the lives of saints widely circulated during our Middle Ages; they must be considered neither histories nor chronicles. The events they relate with a particular satisfaction are spiritual conquests, visions and ecstasies; they follow the long apprenticeship through which man becomes divine, they give lists of the texts upon which saints trained and disciplined their minds, for each lama they record the masters who opened up his spirit to serene visions, or caused the ambrosia of supreme revelations to rain down upon him. Human events have nothing to do with these works, and how could they, being a vain flow of appearances in the motionless gleam of that void, never to be grasped, into which the experience of truth dissolves and annuls us?... All the rest is shadows." Albert Grünwedel, in *Die Geschichten der vierundachtzig Zauberer: Mahāsiddhas* (Berlin: Reimer, 1916), refers to namthar as both "fantastic" and "obscure."

242 The *Byang chub lam gyi rim pa'i bla ma brgyud pa'i rnam thar*... (block-printed edition), 930, wherein Chökyi Dorjé's biography is recorded, gives no dates for this great siddha. Indeed, there his life is preceded by the following verse: *Rgyal ba kun gyis gsungs pa'i chos rnams kyil bcud rnams bsdus nas nams su blangs pa'i mthus/ tshe gcig nid la rdo rje'i sku brnes pal 'chi med rnal 'byor mchog la gsol ba 'debs/ zhes bsngags pal grub chen chos-kyi-rdo-rje ni/* (To you, O best of immortal yogis I bow,/ who, after abridging into one the essences of all the Dharmas

expounded by all the Buddhas,/ put those into practice,/ and attained the Diamond-body in this very life). However, in the *Catalogue of the Toyo Bunko Collection of Tibetan Works on History* (Tokyo: The Toyo Bunko, 1970), vol. 1, 129, the editor, Zuiho Yamaguchi, assigns to him the dates "1457–1541?" Chökyi Dorjé's own namthar attests to the fact that he lived far beyond one hundred years of age even before he met his most eminent disciple Gyalwa Ensapa and carried him through his training.

243   The Tibetan reads as follows: *De nas pan chen chos kyi rgyal mtshan gyi bka' bzhin/ gangs/ ri sul/ nags khrod sogs du ma 'grims/ de'i tshe padma can gyi sgrub chu'i ne 'khor gyi sa rnams skad cig de la sin dhu rar 'gyur ba zhig yod pas yul ner bzhi dngos dang mtshungs pa zhig yod ces grags pa der rdzogs rim dang 'brel ba'i bla ma lha'i rnal 'byor bsgoms par mdzad pas chos gyi rgyal po tsong kha pa chen pos zhal gzigs/ de'i tshe rje rin po ches dam pa 'di la thun mong dang thun mong ma yin pa'i snan brgyud kyi gdams ngag yongs su rdzogs par gnang//*

244   Sarat Chandra Das, in his *Contributions on the Religion and History of Tibet* (New Delhi: Mañjuśrī Publishing House, 1970 [1881]), 109–10, summarizes the life of "Gyal-wa Ton-Dub [Gyalwa Döndrup]." Toward the end of his summary he writes, "At the age of seventeen he became a pupil of the sage Chhokyi Dorje [Chökyi Dorjé] and fully mastered the volume of precepts called Gahdan-Nen-gyud. Afterwards returning to Tsan he resided at the temple of Pamachen near the Panam-Chomolha-ri. Here his teacher the sage showed him the volumes of illusive mysticism." Of course, what is of interest here is Das's treatment of Pema Chan (which he writes as "Pamachen") as a geographical location. In fact, in a note directly connected with his mention of "Pamachen," he attempts to give even more precise details of the whereabouts of this "temple," though, in reality, the note only speaks of the Chomolhari mountain range.

245   It should be noted, however, that Pema Chan occurs also as the proper name of the twelfth stage (*bhumi*) of the path approaching enlightenment in some Vajrayana works. See, for example, 'Jam mgon Kong sprul Blo gros mtha' yas, *Śes-bya kunkhyab mdzod* (Paro: Lama Ngodup, 1976), vol. 4, 337.

246   See Shin'ichi Tsuda, *A Critical Tantrism*, Memoirs of the Research Department of the Toyo Bunko 36 (Tokyo: The Toyo Bunko, 1978). Tsuda devotes a section of chapter 5 (215–21) to "The Theory of Pilgrimage Places."

247   Ibid., 221.

248   This was told to me by Lama Zopa Rinpoche.

249   See Alex Wayman's discussion of this idea in his *Yoga of the Guhyasamājatantra: The Arcane Lore of Forty Verses: A Buddhist Tantra Commentary* (Delhi: Motilal Banarsidass, 1999 [1977]), 234–35. Using Tsongkhapa's Pancakrama commentary, Wayman (383) illustrates that "rivers as external water agree with menses and blood as personal [or internal] water."

CHAPTER 12: DAKINI

250 This characterization of dakini is found in the glossaries appended to both *The Life of Marpa the Translator* (Boulder, CO: Prajna Press, 1982), 219, and *The Rain of Wisdom* (Boulder, CO: Shambhala Publications, 1980), 345. Both works were translated by the Nalanda Translation Committee under the direction of Chögyam Trungpa Rinpoché.

251 For example, this gloss is used by Keith Dowman in the title of his translation of the life of the dakini Yeshe Tsogyel. See his *Sky Dancer: The Secret Life and Songs of the Lady Yeshe Tsogyel.*

252 See Geshe Kelsang Gyatso's *Clear Light of Bliss: Mahamudra in Vajrayana Buddhism* (London: Wisdom Publications, 1982).

253 Both glossaries mentioned in note 250 define *dakini* as "a wrathful or semi-wrathful female yidam."

254 Austine Waddell often referred to dakinis as being "demoniacal." Waddell, *The Buddhism of Tibet*; Evans-Wentz, *The Tibetan Book of the Dead*; and Das, *A Tibetan-English Dictionary* (Delhi: Motilal Banarsidass, 1970), all used the term "witch" in their characterizations.

255 See Waddell, *The Buddhism of Tibet*, 366.

256 Sarat Chandra Das used both "sprites" and "fairies" in his definition of the term *mkha' gro ma*. See his *A Tibetan-English Dictionary*, 180. Interestingly, "fairies" is also the term used by Robert Paul in his *The Tibetan Symbolic World: Psychoanalytic Explorations* (Chicago: The University of Chicago Press, 1982); on 132, for example, he calls dakinis "sky-going fairies."

257 This is one of the descriptions used by Anagarika Govinda. See his *Foundations of Tibetan Mysticism* (New York: Samuel Weiser, 1975), 192.

258 Here I am playing on the title of Robert Paul's valuable work of the same name.

259 See Nathan Katz's "Anima and Mkha'-'gro-ma: A Critical Comparative Study of Jung and Tibetan Buddhism," *The Tibet Journal* 2, no. 3 (1977): 13–43.

260 Waddell, *The Buddhism of Tibet*, 180.

261 Ibid., 129–30.

262 Das, *A Tibetan-English Dictionary*, 180.

263 Ibid.

264 See Snellgrove, *Buddhist Himālaya*, 175.

265 Martin Kalff, "Dakinis in the Cakrasaṃvara Tradition," in *Tibetan Studies*, ed. M. Brauen and P. Kvaerne (Zurich: Volkerkundemuseum der Universitat Zurich, 1978), 149–150.

266 Ibid., 150.

267 Ibid.

268 For two interesting translations of Padmasambhava's "journey" to Tibet, see

Keith Dowman's *The Legend of the Great Stupa and the Life of the Lotus Born Guru* (Berkeley, CA: Dharma Publishing, 1973), 82–85; and Tarthang Tulku, *Crystal Mirror, Volume IV* (Berkeley, CA: Dharma Publishing, 1975), 18–25.

269 See Garma C. C. Chang, *Teachings of Tibetan Yoga* (Secaucus, NJ: Citadel Press, 1977), 122. (An interesting note on the inadequacy of this definition is provided by John Wilson in his "Introduction," 8–9.)

270 This suggestion was posited by James Robinson in his translation, *Buddha's Lions*, 394.

271 The definition of *dakini* as "a female imp attending Kālī (feeding on human flesh)" is found in Sir Monier Monier-Williams, *A Sanskrit-English Dictionary* (Oxford: Clarendon Press, 1964 [1899]), 430. J. N. Banerjea, in *Paurāṇic and Tantric Religion* (Calcutta: University of Calcutta, 1966), 128, states that "the later lexicons explain the name Ḍākinī as a special kind of the attendants of Kālī (*Ḍākinī Kālīgaṇaviśeshaḥ*)," and suggests that an earlier or parallel phenomenon may have been the *ghoshini*, who occur in the *Atharvaveda* as the "female attendants of the terrific god Rudra."

272 See Herbert V. Guenther, *Treasures on the Tibetan Middle Way* (Berkeley, CA: Shambhala Publications, 1971), 103, n. l. , and Katz, "Anima and Mkha'-'gro-ma," 24.

273 Govinda, *Foundations of Tibetan Mysticism*, 196.

274 Robinson, *Buddha's Lions*, 394.

275 Wittgenstein, *Philosophical Investigations*, trans. G. E. M. Anscombe (New York: The Macmillan Company, 1953), 43. The fuller statement by Wittgenstein is: "For a *large* class of cases—though not for all—in which we employ the word 'meaning' it can be explained thus: the meaning of a word is its *use* in the language." Wittgenstein was aware of two other points of importance to this study—namely, he realized that language has *multiple* functions, and that words and expressions function *relationally*, getting their meanings in social [and/or cultural] contexts.

276 This language is that used by Lobsang Lhalungpa in the Introduction to his translation of *The Life of Milarepa*, xxiii.

277 See Guenther's translation, *The Life and Teaching of Nāropa* (Oxford: Oxford University Press, 1974), 24–25.

278 Guenther, *Treasures on the Tibetan Middle Way*, 103, n. 1. Also cited in Katz, "Anima and Mkha'-'gro-ma," 13.

279 Guenther, *The Life and Teaching of Naropa*. Guenther clearly recognizes the parallels between the dakini and Jung's *anima*. In a note to this passage, he writes: "This aspect has a great similarity to what the Swiss psychologist C. G. Jung calls the 'anima.'" Katz's article, "Anima and Mkha'-'gro-ma," investigates and elaborates on these similarities and on some dissimilarities.

280 Bhupendranath Datta, trans., *Mystic Tales of Lāma Tarānātha* (Calcutta: Ramakrishna Vedanta Math, 1957), 65. This story, with some minor changes in translation, is also cited in Katz, "Anima and Mkha'-'gro-ma," 23. It is paraphrased in Tsultrim Allione's *Women of Wisdom*, 37.

281 This type of language was used, one may recall, in several of Carlos Castaneda's novels for describing part of the method, and experience, of training in the Yaqui Indian tradition. See especially Castaneda's *Journey to Ixtlan: The Lessons of Don Juan* (New York: Simon and Schuster, 1972).

282 Katz, "Anima and Mkha'-'gro-ma," 22. (I have slightly rearranged the structure of Katz's original sentence here.)

283 These remarks by Chögyam Trungpa Rinpoché are to be found in the journal *Maitreya* 4 (1973): 25. They are also quoted in Allione, *Women of Wisdom*, 38.

284 This namthar and that of Sangyé Yeshé (which follows) were translated by me. The complete translations of these namthar, together with four others, has been published as *Enlightened Beings: Life Stories from the Ganden Oral Tradition* (Boston: Wisdom Publications, 1995).

285 See Katz, "Anima and Mkha'-'gro-ma," 27.

286 For the story of Kukkuripa, see Robinson, *Buddha's Lions*, 128–30; and Dowman, *Masters of Mahāmudrā*, 199–203.

287 Often the term *karmamudra* is used in such contexts as an alternative for *rikma*. However, in my opinion, there is already so much confusion regarding the many, and varied, meanings of *karmamudra* that I prefer not to use it.

288 An interesting analysis of the benefits of having an actual flesh-and-blood partner, and of "living with an insightful consort," is presented in Allione, *Women of Wisdom*, 39–40.

289 Katz, "Anima and Mkha'-'gro-ma," 24.

290 Ibid.

291 There is as yet no full-scale biography of Niguma published in English. One can, however, learn something of her life from Guenther's translation of *The Life and Teaching of Nāropa*. Additional information can be gleaned from Roerich, *The Blue Annals*; and from Glenn Mullin's *Selected Works of the Dalai Lama II* (Ithaca, NY: Snow Lion Publications, 1985). (In 2010 Sarah Harding's *Niguma, Lady of Illusion* was published by Snow Lion.)

292 There are two English translations of the life of Yeshé Tsogyal: Tarthang Tulku's translation, *Mother of Knowledge*; and Keith Dowman's *Sky Dancer*.

293 Again, there is no single work which narrates the life of Dagmema, but information regarding her may be gleaned from Roerich, *The Blue Annals*; and from Nalanda Translation Committee, *The Life of Marpa the Translator*.

294 Apart from the accounts of it in *The Blue Annals*, the life of Machik Lapdrönma appears in Allione's *Women of Wisdom*, 141–87. Also see Jérôme Edou's *Machig*

Labdron and the Foundations of Chod (Ithaca, NY: Snow Lion Publications, 1995); and Sarah Harding's *Machik's Complete Explanation Clarifying the Meaning of Chod*, wherein Machik's life is narrated on 57–102. Additionally, four of the "eighty-four siddhas" of Indian fame were women. Their life stories can be found in Robinson's *Buddha's Lions* and in Keith Dowman's *Masters of Mahāmudrā*.

295 Katz, "Anima and Mkha'-'gro-ma," 28. In the quote, I have substituted "siddha" for Katz's phonetic rendering of its Tibetan equivalent, grub thob.

296 Ibid.

297 In essence these "two" goddesses are actually one. Vajrayogini is the female deity who is the chief consort of Lord Chakrasamvara. It is explained that the name "Vajravarahi" (that is, "Diamond Sow") is used of her to emphasize her *function* (which is to destroy the ignorance of holding the view of an inherently existent "I"—symbolized by the pig's head), while the name "Vajrayogini" is used to indicate her *essence* (namely, the adamantine insight that cognizes the inseparability of bliss and voidness).

298 Here, I describe Vajrayogini's iconographic form based on the descriptions of it found in a number of her meditative sadhanas. For a description and discussion of the iconographic form of Vajravarahi and her "ornaments," see Allione, *Women of Wisdom*, 31–36. For more detail on Vajrayogini's form in general, see Jonathan Landaw and Andy Weber's *Images of Enlightenment: Tibetan Art in Practice* (Ithaca, NY: Snow Lion Publications, 1993), 139–43.

299 That is, the *Vajracchedika Sutra*, one of the group of smaller sutras comprising the Prajnaparamita, or Transcendent Wisdom, literature.

300 From Edward Conze's translation of the *Vajracchedika*. See his *Buddhist Wisdom Books*, 63. For Conze's "Dharmabodies" I have substituted "Dharmakaya."

301 This translation is quoted from Thurman, *The Holy Teaching of Vimalakīrti*, 61.

302 For a full enumeration and discussion of these, see my *The Diamond Light of the Eastern Dawn: A Collection of Tibetan Buddhist Meditations* (New York: Simon and Schuster, 1972), 100–106.

303 It is, I believe, too simplistic to assert that the Tantras are written from a male point of view because most tantric practitioners were or are men. I would agree that the texts do seem to take this point of view. However, there seem in addition actually to be qualities that are "feminine" in nature, and that hence require feminine characterization. A thorough discussion of such a premise would, of course, require at least a book.

304 I find this way of speaking more appropriate, and much more helpful, than language like: the dakini represents one's "other" or one's "opposite." It seems to me to be also less combative; and certainly, if we're seeking enlightenment, we had better try to be less combative.

305 For explanations and descriptions of the dakini based on this threefold schema
     of outer, inner, and secret, I am grateful to Geshé Jampal Thardö.

CHAPTER 13: NAMTHAR AS LITERATURE AND LITURGY

306 For example, see the "Introduction" to Reynolds and Capps, *The Biographical
     Process*, especially 3–5, where this distinction is discussed in some detail.
307 Basically, there are only two major divisions or "vehicles" (Skt. *yana*) of Bud-
     dhist doctrine and practice: (1) the Hinayana, or "Lesser Vehicle," which aims
     at individual liberation, and (2) the Mahayana, or "Great Vehicle," which aims
     at universal liberation. The Vajrayana, variously referred to as the "Diamond
     Vehicle" and the "speedy path," is in actuality a subdivision of the Mahayana,
     being based firmly on those ideals. Because it makes use of the yogic techniques
     offered in the Tantras, the Vajrayana is also referred to as the Tantrayana. Medi-
     tation has always remained the heart of Buddhist practice. Still, as Buddhism
     developed over time, such practice came to be overshadowed by concerns with
     scholarly disputations and expositions of the doctrine. Two major movements
     within Buddhism sought to moderate the emphasis on such scholasticism. The
     first was the emergence of the Mahayana, which stressed the bodhisattva ideal
     and the practice of compassion, and which also placed these goals within the
     reach of the lay community. However, the Mahayana movement also produced
     its own resurgence of philosophical interests, owing most notably to its "two
     crown jewels," Nagarjuna and Asanga. These two great sages, who were also
     master meditation practitioners, splendidly articulated Buddhism's quintessen-
     tial doctrine, that of *shunyata*, the voidness of inherent existence in all things as
     well as in the so-called self. Thereafter, basing itself firmly on the fruits of the
     Mahayana's explication of voidness, a second movement emerged, which, while
     not repudiating the value of such crystalline exposition, sought to reemphasize
     the practice side of Buddhism as a balance to theoretical preoccupations. This
     supplementary movement within the Mahayana is known as the Vajrayana, the
     "Diamond Vehicle," which posits the goal of complete liberation in one's own
     lifetime through rigorous practice aimed at bringing about direct realization
     of the teachings. Practitioners who enter upon this "speedy path" and who are
     successful in winning its fruits are called *siddhas*. It was primarily this latter
     form of Buddhism that was successful in winning over Tibetan converts.
308 Shantaraksita, a learned Indian Buddhist monk from the great Nalanda Uni-
     versity, was invited to Tibet during the reign of King Trisong Detsen (Khri
     srong lde brtsan, 755–797[?]). He was initially unsuccessful in his attempts to
     establish Buddhism there and advised that the tantric adept Padmasambhava

be sent for. Later, these two worked together to introduce Buddhism. History records that it was actually Shantaraksita who presided over the architectural design and construction of the first Buddhist monastery in Tibet, called Samyé (Bsam yas), and that it was he who served as its first abbot and who ordained the first seven indigenous Tibetan monks. For more on the life of Shantaraksita, see chapter 25 of Alaka Chattopadhyaya, trans., *Atísa and Tibet: Life and Works of Dīpaṃkara Śrījñāna in Relation to the History and Religion of Tibet* (Delhi: Motilal Banarsidass, 1967); and my own summary of his life in the entry "Śāntaraksita," in *The Encyclopedia of Religion*, ed. Mircea Eliade (New York: Macmillan, 1987), 13:68–69.

309 Kamalasila, on the counsel of the aged Shantaraksita, was later summoned from India. He is remembered in the annals of Tibetan religious history especially owing to the part he played in the famed Council of Lhasa debates convened to settle the issue of which form of Buddhism—the Indian or the Chinese— would predominate in Tibet. Kamalasila, representing the Indian side, defeated the Chinese representative, one Hua-shang Mahayana, and the Tibetans opted for Indian Buddhism. The debates, which took place at Samyé circa 792–94, were not without serious results, however, and it appears that Kamalasīia was later murdered. For more on this famed debate and its aftermath, see Paul Demiéville, *Le concile de Lhasa: Une controverse sur le quietisme entre bouddhistes de l'Inde et de la Chine au XIIe siècle de l'ère chrétienne*, Bibliothèque de l'Institut des Hautes Études Chinoises 7 (Paris: Collège de France, Institut des Hautes Études Chinoises, 2006); and on the life of Kamalasila, see my summary in the entry "Kamalaśīla," in *The Encyclopedia of Religion*, 8:242–43.

310 Much still remains to be learned regarding Tibet's indigenous folk traditions. Major studies have been done by Stein, Marcelle Lalou, Tucci, Hoffman, Eliade, Walther Heissig, Snellgrove, and other historians of religion. Recently, studies by young anthropologists and musicologists such as Geoffrey Samuel, Martin Brauen, Samten Karmay, Robert Paul, Ricardo Canzio, and others promise to help expand our understanding of these traditions even further.

311 Eva Dargyay's study, *The Rise of Esoteric Buddhism in Tibet*, goes a long way toward filling out the actual historical circumstances surrounding the early establishment of Buddhism in Tibet. In particular, she argues convincingly that Padmasambhava was not the only early siddha responsible for advancing the cause of Buddhism there. Rather, such figures as the Vairotsana and Vimalamitra played roles of equal importance in the founding of the earliest order there.

312 This topic is much too large to adequately address here, and I am working on a separate monograph that fully discusses the history of Buddhist sacred biography in India and Tibet. Here, however, a few brief and general comments

may be posited. Our main source for Buddhist siddha biographies in India is Abhayadatta's late eleventh- or early twelfth-century work on the eighty-four siddhas (see English translations by James Robinson, *Buddha's Lions*; and Keith Dowman, *Masters of Mahamudra*). Regarding these biographies, we may note that they are all much briefer than their later Tibetan counterparts; that they invariably recount the lives of lay (as opposed to monastic) practitioners; and that they fall into two distinct types: (1) the majority of them (four-fifths of the eighty-four) focus in stylized ways on the importance of the Mahamudra guru himself rather than on the training of the siddha-to-be or on the latter's subsequent enlightened activity, (2) while a fifth of them are longer and more individuated in style and focus on the accomplished siddha, usually publicly accompanied by a tantric consort who performs often bizarre examples of wonder-working enlightened activity and power.

Generally speaking, all Tibetan namthar rely on Abhayadatta's work and include compositions of both types: those that emphasize the future siddha's training and those that emphasize the accomplished siddha's powers. However, in Tibet, over time we see the interesting reunification of yogic practice and monasticism, and as a consequence we witness shifts of emphasis in the Tibetan examples.

313 Again generally speaking, because Tantric Buddhism had to prove its veracity and effectiveness over Tibet's older indigenous beliefs, the namthar produced in connection with the founding of the earliest orders (the Nyingmapa and the Kagyüpa) are those that most greatly emphasize the siddha's wonder-working powers, giving scant attention to that siddha's background, education, training, or gurus. Again, one notes that such namthar focus on the lay tantric practitioner in the company of his or her tantric consort. One has only to consider the famed namthar of Padmasambhava as an example of this type of composition. The later Tibetan namthar, on the other hand, such as those produced in connection with the Sakyapa and Gelukpa orders, demonstrate that tantric practice and monastic life have been reunited, and the whole career of the siddha, from early training through post-enlightenment activity, is recounted while the displays of wonder-working power are downplayed.

314 The early hagiographies of the Christian "confessor saints" portray rugged and heroic individuals whose utter commitment to their faith was meant to uplift and inspire others. They chronicle the lives of men and women who, having felt the "call to Christ," entered his service. Usually after having publicly advanced the faith by founding monasteries or stewarding large numbers of disciples, they bravely and willingly chose the hard, solitary life of the contemplative, and to a few devoted followers they revealed their holiness through the performance of miracles.

The Western scholarly tradition has generally taken a dim view of hagiography. Indeed, in the West "hagiography" has come to be defined as any idealizing or worshipful biography, the implication being that such texts are naively exaggerated accounts written to edify a devoted, though gullible, popular audience and, as a consequence, are of little historical worth. One need only peruse the writings of Père Hippolyte Delehaye on this subject to see with what condescension such texts are regarded. The two most common accusations leveled against hagiography are that there are in them numerous duplications of descriptions of holiness and that they describe a preponderance of miracles.

315 Many scholars working with this material have tended to confine it to the province of popular literature, viewing siddha lives as the products of, and for, popular spirituality, and as being folkloric. For example, Mircea Eliade writes, in his *Yoga, Immortality and Freedom*, 305: "A number of the Nāthas and Siddhas put more emphasis than their predecessors had done upon the value of magic and Yoga as inestimable means for the conquest of freedom and immortality. It was especially this aspect of their message that struck the popular imagination; we still find it echoed today in folklore and the vernacular literatures." It must be noted that Eliade found this feature of namthar valuable, however, and he followed the above remark with the statement: "It is for this reason that the latter seem to us of great value for our inquiry."

David Snellgrove, too, agrees with this assessment of namthar. In *Buddhist Himalāya*, 86, he calls namthar "popular accounts (in which) the goal of perfection seems to be immortality." Snellgrove voiced this assessment with specific reference to the lives of the eighty-four siddhas of the Śaivitic and Buddhist traditions. He considers that such namthar have value for depicting the general religious climate of the times. The full relevant passage here reads: "Both Buddhist and Shaivitic tradition preserve the memory of eighty-four great yogins or perfected ones (siddhas). Their biographies are to be found in the Tibetan canon, and although the tales related of them are of no direct historical worth, they portray well enough the general religious setting, in which the actual tantric texts originated" (85). Giuseppe Tucci, in *Tibetan Painted Scrolls*, 1:151, admits that "an historian cannot ignore the *rnam-t'ar*," and indeed Tucci himself makes good use of them. However, his own general definition of namthar (see text of "Introduction") appears to me to be more obscuring of their true nature than clarifying. Albert Grünwedel, in *Die Geschichten der vier und achtzig Zauberers:Mahāsiddhas*, published in 1916, refers to namthar as both "fantastic" and "obscure." It seems to me that a negative and elitist bias shines through all of the above assessments, for all of them overlook the fact that these texts may be simultaneously both popular and profound.

316 This terminology was aptly applied by Reginald Ray in an unpublished paper,

"The Vajrayāna Mahāsiddhas; Some Principles of Interpretation," read at the
American Academy of Religion meeting in San Francisco in December 1977.

317 Tantric literature is often described as "esoteric" or "hidden." The meanings of tantric texts are said to be "veiled" from the ordinary, or uninitiated,
reader owing to their being written in symbolic or so-called twilight language
[sandhyabhaṣa]. This is especially the case when practice instructions are to
be communicated, since these are not intended to be readily grasped or to be
practiced by persons not properly prepared to undertake such practice. Thus,
the meanings of these texts are "hidden" or "veiled" until, being properly prepared, one can read their symbolic language with understanding. Again, what
is instructional to advanced practitioners is "hidden" to unskilled ordinary
beings. An interesting discussion of the language of the tantras can be found
in Agehananda Bharati's The Tantric Tradition (New York: Doubleday, 1970),
164–84. Bharati argues throughout that such language should properly be
understood as "intentional language" [sandhyabhaṣa].

318 his point was duly noted in Reginald Ray's conference paper "The Vajrayāna
Mahāsiddhas": "When one compares the contents of the Siddha biographies
with those of the classical Tantras and their commentaries, one finds that they
are basically the same, if presented in very different styles" (4).

319 This fact is well noted by those within the Tibetan tradition. Other Western
scholars working with namthar have also recognized this tripartite pattern. Tucci's work, Tibetan Painted Scrolls, for example, is cognizant of it. David Ruegg,
in his translation of The Life of Bu-ston Rinpoché, 44–45, notes the threefold
structure of namthar. And Luciano Petech's "Introduction" to Alfonsa Ferrari's
translation of Mk'yen brtse's Guide to the Holy Places of Central Tibet, xix, takes
note of this traditional threefold pattern.

320 Most namthar contain all three levels of life story, though one or the other is
most emphasized. Tucci, Tibetan Painted Scrolls, 1:159–61, notes that Khedrup
Jé (Mkhas grub rje) authored a "secret biography" of his guru, Tsongkhapa, in
addition to one treating primarily the first two levels only. Another disciple of
Tsongkhapa, Jamyang Chöjé Tashi Palden (1379–1449), who helped to found
Drepung Monastery, is also remembered as the author of a famous "secret biography" of his teacher, called Je Rin po che gsang ba'i rnam thar, and translated
in several English versions as Song of the Mystic Experiences of Lama Jé Rinpoché.

321 By this suggestion I do not mean to become embroiled here in the hairsplitting
philosophical debates that have continued throughout the history of Buddhist
literature over the issue of nitartha ("direct" or "definitive meaning") versus
neyartha ("indirect" or "interpretable meaning") teaching and scripture. There
are already a number of excellent discussions of this important question. For
example, see the fine essay by Robert Thurman, "Buddhist Hermeneutics,"

Journal of the American Academy of Religion 46, no. 1 (1978): 19–39; and his translation of Tsongkhapa's analysis of this issue in *The Central Philosophy of Tibet: A Study and Translation of Jey Tsong Khapa's Essence of True Eloquence* (Princeton, NJ: Princeton University Press, 1984), originally published under the title *Tsong Khapa's Speech of Gold in the "Essence of True Eloquence."* I mean only to assert quite simply that the authors of tantric literature used skillful means and that they employed language in such a way that its "literal" meaning is not always its "final" meaning.

322 "Insider" is a literal translation of the Tibetan term *nangpa*. In Buddhist contexts it is used to refer to "those who stand inside" the Buddha's Dharma, as opposed to *chipa* (*phyid pa*), or "those standing outside" of it. Further, among the nangpa two divisions are recognized: (1) lay followers of the Dharma, and (2) ordained monastic practitioners.

323 See Tucci, *Tibetan Painted Scrolls*, 1:150–51.

324 The new order founded by Tsongkhapa was known by various names: Riwo Gandenpa, Kadam Sarmapa, Gendenpa, and Gelukpa. Presumably, the order also came to be referred to as the "Yellow Hats" because of Tsongkhapa's innovation of having the monks of his order wear yellow or saffron apparel, as did the original Buddhist monks of India. This signaled the great reform that he instituted in Tibet and that is set forth doctrinally in his mammoth work *The Great Stages of the Path to Enlightenment* (titled in Tibetan the Lamrim Chenmo [*Lam rim chen mo*]). Snellgrove suggests, in *A Cultural History of Tibet*, 181, that "Westerners have borrowed from the Chinese the term 'Yellow Hat' for the Gelukpa." Whatever the actual origin of the epithet, it has come to be an unambiguous and readily identifiable feature of the order. The six life stories translated here cover the three-hundred-year period during which the Gelukpas successfully appropriated more and more power and firmly established themselves in Tibet.

325 Snellgrove, *A Cultural History of Tibet*, 181.

326 For studies devoted primarily to the relationships between religion and politics in Tibet, see the works of Shakabpa, *Tibet: A Political History* (New Haven, CT: Yale University Press, 1967); Melvyn Goldstein, "The Circulation of Estates in Tibet: Reincarnation, Land, and Politics," *The Journal of Asian Studies* 32, no. 3 (1973), 445–55; Bina Roy Burman, *Religion and Politics in Tibet* (New Delhi: Vikas Publishing House, 1976); Luciano Petech, "The Dalai-Lamas and Regents of Tibet: A Chronological Study," *T'oung Pao* 47 (1959): 368–94; W. Rockhill, "The Dalai Lamas of Lhasa and Their Relations with the Manchu Emperors of China 1644–1908," *T'oung Pao* 11 (1910): 1–104; Pedro Carrasco, *Land and Polity in Tibet* (Seattle: University of Washington Press, 1959); and Franz Michael, *Rule by Incarnation: Tibetan Buddhism and Its Role in Society and State* (Boulder, CO: Westview Press, 1982).

327 This is the same Jamchen Chöjé Shakya Yeshé whom Tsongkhapa had sent in
his stead to the Ming court during the reign of the Chinese Emperor Yung-lo
(reigned 1403–1424). Tsongkhapa received two invitations from the emperor
to visit China. He declined the first, but after receiving the second, he sent
Shakya Yeshé as his representative. Following his return from China, Jamchen
Chöjé founded Sera Monastery in 1419. For further information, see Shakabpa, *Tibet: A Political History*, 84–85.

328 Descriptive information on these famed Gelukpa institutions can be found in
Waddell's *The Buddhism of Tibet*; Tucci's *To Lhasa and Beyond*; Wylie's *The
Geography of Tibet*; and Ferrari's *mK'yen brtse's Guide to the Holy Places of Cen-
tral Tibet*.

329 Some 125 years after his death, Gendundrub (1391–1475) was retroactively
recognized as being the first Dalai Lama. An excellent English version of the
life of Gendundrub can be found in Glenn Mullin, *Selected Works of the Dalai
Lama I: Bridging the Sūtras and Tantras* (Ithaca, NY: Snow Lion Publications,
1985), 203–50. A very brief summary of Gendundrub's life is also provided by
Sarat Chandra Das in his *Contributions on the Religion and History of Tibet*,
110–11. Snellgrove, in *A Cultural History of Tibet*, 182, rightly notes that it was
Gendundrub's "energy and ability which was mainly responsible for building
up Tsong-kha-pa's school into an active expansive order ready and anxious to
compete with the others on an equal footing."

330 According to Gendundrub's namthar, he was instructed by a vision of the
Goddess Palden lamo to construct Tashi Lhunpo. Shakabpa, *Tibet: A Political
History*, 91, says that Gendundrub was able to build the monastery because of
the generous financial help he received from one "Dargyas Pon Palzang." The
monastic facilities housed about three thousand monks.

331 The site chosen by Gendundrub for Tashi Lhunpo is important because, as
Snellgrove, *Buddhist Himālaya* or *A Cultural History of Tibet*, 182, points out,
this location was "on the very edge of the territory dominated by the powerful
princes of Rin-spungs who had the militant support of the Karmapa Red Hat
hierarchy." Over the course of its history, Tashi Lhunpo Monastery in particular came under violent attack from the rival Karma Kagyü order, and as Gendundrub's own remarks show, he was aware of this potential threat from the very
outset.

332 The Tibetan reads as follows: *De'i tshe bkra shis lhun por thams cad mkhyen pa
Dge'dun grub dpal bzang po 'phrin las dbyar mtsho ltar rgyas par bzhugs pas khri rin
po ches gtsos Dga' ldan pa'i bla chen phal mo ches rje Dge'dun grub la rgyal ba gnyis
pa'i rgyal tshab tu 'byon dgos par gsol ba btap pas rje Dge'dun grub kyis kho bo dgra
yul du dgra mkhar brtsig dgos pa yod pas 'di kha rang du rje'i bstan pa 'dzin pa yin/*.

333 The title "Panchen," or "greatly learned one" (a contracted form of the Sanskrit

noun *paṇḍita* plus the Tibetan term *chen*) was not a new one and had been used prior to the time of Losang Chökyi Gyaltsen. However, the great prestige of the title "First Panchen" in connection with him results from the fact that it was conferred on him by his famed disciple, the Great Fifth Dalai Lama, who at the same time officially recognized him as also being the incarnation of Amitabha Buddha. (The Great Fifth claimed for himself the honor of being the incarnation of Avalokiteshvara.) The line of Panchens thus created by the Fifth Dalai Lama thereafter became primarily associated with Tashi Lhunpo Monastery. For more on the enumerations of the Panchens, see Tucci's *Tibetan Painted Scrolls,* 2:413–14; Gunther Schulemann's *Die Geschichte der Dalai-Lamas* (Leipzig: Otto Harrassowitz, 1958 [1911]); and S. Das's "The Lives of the Panchen Rinpochés or Tashi Lamas," *Journal of the Royal Asiatic Society of Bengal* (1882), and *Contributions on the Religion and History of Tibet,* 81–144.

334 The accounts of the First Panchen's activities presented both by Das, in *Contributions on the Religion and History of Tibet,* 111–17; and by Fa tsun, in *Encyclopaedia of Buddhism* 3, Fasc. 1, 163–69, stress this aspect of his life.

335 According to Longdöl Lama's (Klong rdol bla ma) famed catalog, the *Tsento* (*Mtshan tho*), the First Panchen was the author of some 108 separate works. The Tibetan listing of these compositions can be found in Lokesh Chandra's *Materials for a Study of Tibetan Literature,* vol. 3 (New Delhi: International Academy of Indian Culture, 1963), 645–47. Among the First Panchen's works are to be found his own autobiography of 450 folia, completed in 1720 by his successor, the Second Panchen, Losang Yeshé; several namthar (of Sangyé Yeshé, Gyalwa Ensapa, six of the First Panchen's predecessors from the extended enumeration beginning with Subhuti, and others); numerous sadhanas, especially devoted to Vajrabhairava, Guhyasamaja, Chakrasamvara, and Kalacakra; numerous texts on guru yoga, and some on Chöd. But perhaps most noteworthy, and certainly of vital importance to the present study, were his *Lama chöpa* (*Bla ma mchod pa*) [*Guru puja* or *Offering to the Spiritual Master*]; *Dge ldan bka' brgyud rin po che'i phyag chen rtsa ba rgal ba'i gzhung lam* [*Root Text for the Ganden Oral Tradition of Mahamudra, called the Main Path of the Conquerors*], and *Yang gsal sgron me* [an autocommentary on the latter text, called *The Lamp of Reillumination.*] These latter two texts succinctly elucidate the Ganden oral tradition regarding Mahamudra. The first has come to set the standard for performance of all subsequent Gelukpa monastic liturgy and public ritual.

336 Tucci's *The Religions of Tibet* (Berkeley: University of California Press, 1980), 134–35, gives a succinct description of the development of this religio-political phenomenon in Tibet. Also see the discussion on reincarnation in Franz Michaels's *Rule By Incarnation,* 38–41.

337 See Gene Smith's "Foreword" to L. Chandra's Indian edition of the *Tibetan*

Chronicle of Padma-dkar-po (New Delhi: International Academy of Indian Culture, 1968), 1.

338 The Fifth Dalai Lama conferred upon his guru, Losang Chökyi Gyaltsen, the title "First Panchen"; but soon, to increase the prestige of the position, retroactive validity was conferred upon the theory of his being an incarnation of Amitābha Buddha by extending those incarnations in a backwards series, said to begin with Tsongkhapa's famed disciple, Khedrup Jé. Thus, in the enumerations given by Tucci and Schulemann, we find the early list of Panchens to include Khedrup Jé, Sönam Chöklang, Gyalwa Ensapa, and Panchen Losang Chökyi Gyaltsen. Over time, the list of such incarnations was extended back even to India, with the first member of the series being declared to be Subhuti, the famed contemporary disciple of Shakyamuni Buddha himself. The most extensive enumeration of the Panchen incarnations of Tashi Lhunpo therefore lists four Indian incarnations (Subhuti, Manjushrikirti, Lekden Jé [Legs ldan 'byed], and Abhayakaragupta) and six Tibetan incarnations—Gö Lotsawa Khukpa Lhetsé ('Gos lo tsā ba Khug pa Lhas btsas), Sakya Pandita Kunga Gyaltsen (Sa skya Paṇḍita Kun dga' rgyal mtshan), Yungtön Dorjé Pal (Yung ston Rdo rje dpal), Khedrup Jé, Sönam Chöklang, and Gyalwa Ensapa prior to Losang Chökyi Gyaltsen. Thus, though Losang Chökyi Gyaltsen is actually the eleventh member of the extensive enumeration, he was the first incarnation in the series to be named with an ordinal number.

339 It would appear that at least by the beginning of the nineteenth century, this monastery was no longer a teaching college. We note, for example, Wylie's translation of the well-known 1820 Tibetan geographical work, the *'Dzam gling rgyas bshad* [the geography of the world], 76–77, where Sangpu is described as follows: "In former times (Gsang-phu) had students of Dbu-ma and Tshad-ma and a large assemblage of monks; however, since the increase of such (monasteries) as Se-ra and 'Bras-spungs, this one has gradually declined, and now there is nothing there but a few married monks who have chosen to follow the Sa-skya-pa...."

340 Chökyi Dorjé's main retreat site was Garmo Chö Dzong. This hermitage is listed in the *'Dzam gling rgyas bshad* (see Wylie's translation, 71). It is described as being "not far to the south" of Ensa Monastery. Again, while all of these six siddhas became affiliated at some point in their lives with one of the three chief Gelukpa monasteries in Central Tibet, for the most part their chief spiritual activities were concentrated in the area of Tsang.

341 Ensa Monastery was located northeast of Tashi Lhunpo, on the eastern bank of the Sangchu River. Until the Chinese takeover of Tibet in 1959, Ensa Monastery was regarded as one of the purest and most strict, in terms of monastic discipline, of all Gelukpa establishments. In 1980, Lama Thubten Zopa Rinpoche related to me the following anecdote regarding the monastery: "At devotionals,

after each round of tea was finished, the monks of Ensa Gönpa would immediately turn their cups face-down. This was done to constantly remind each of them of the uncertainty of the time of death. Nothing was ever done casually, or without alertness, at Ensa."

342 *Lamdré* literally means "path and fruit." *Taknyi* literally means the "two examinations." Both terms have reference to the tantric oral traditions transmitted from the Indian siddha tradition to early members of the Sakya order. Moreover, both these terms have particular reference to the *Hevajra Tantra* (*Hevajramulatantraraja*). For example, the great siddha Virupa's treatise, *The Path and Its Fruits*, is said to have been written on the basis of all of the sutras and tantras in general and on the *Hevajra Tantra* in particular. Likewise, *Taknyi* refers to an important commentary on the *Hevajra Tantra*, the latter itself being divided into two sections.

343 In Dargyay's *The Rise of Esoteric Buddhism in Tibet*, 222, the practice of *chulen* (*bcud len*) is described as follows: "'Taking only essences' (*bcud-len*) is a dietetic method; while practicing it the Yogi is not allowed to take any other food except the allowed essence of flowers or stones for example . . . ." In recent years "pill retreats," as they are called, have been performed by increasing numbers of Western practitioners, and a number of instruction manuals on the subject have been published. Such manuals usually describe the proper retreat conditions and prospective retreatants, as well as the pill ingredients, something of their method of production, and their proper use. In 1983, Wisdom Publications published a most informative pamphlet on this subject, written and guided by the Venerable Lama Thubten Yeshe. It is called, simply, *Taking the Essence* (https://www.lamayeshe.com/article/taking-essence).

344 Information on Naropa's six yogas can be found in a number of English-language sources. For example, see Garma C. C. Chang, *Teachings of Tibetan Yoga* (New Hyde Park, NY: University Books, 1963); Lobsang Lhalungpa, *The Life of Milarepa*; Tucci, *The Religions of Tibet* (esp. 98–109); C. A. Muses and C. C. Chang, *Esoteric Teachings of the Tibetan Tantra* (York Beach, ME: Samuel Weiser, 1982), 123–282; and Geshe Gyatso, *Clear Light of Bliss: Mahamudra in Vajrayana Buddhism* (London: Wisdom Publications, 1982).

345 The Sanskrit term *vidyadhara* literally means "possessor of knowledge." When used in relation to siddhas, however, that knowledge is always of the "magical" sort. Thus, vidyadharas are thought to be able to take birth at will, to transform themselves into any desired form or manifestation, to travel unimpededly to any destination, to assume the "rainbow body," etc.

346 The full title of the prayer is *Dga' ldan bka' srol phyag rg ya chen po'i 'khrid kyi bla brgyud gsol 'debs/ kha skong bcas bzhugs//*. The prayer's colophon declares that it was composed by the eighteenth-century Yongzin Yeshé Gyaltsen

(1713–1793) and that additions were made by the first Phabongkha Rinpoché, Dechen Nyingpo (1878–1941).

347   The Tibetan rendered here as "total integration" is *zungjuk* (*zung 'jug*). The term is of central importance in advanced tantric contexts generally and in discussions of Mahamudra practice in particular, for it is used to suggest the ultimate culmination of practice, the experience of the final and complete union, convergence, fusion, and inseparability of any number of technically defined "pairs," which results in their becoming "no longer two." Sometimes *zungjuk* is rendered simply as "enlightenment" or as "buddhahood" itself. The "pairs" are described variously (for example, as subject and object, wisdom and method, shunyata and bodhicitta, or perception and experience), but in tantric contexts they usually refer to bliss and voidness, or again to the illusory body and the clear light. For more on this important term, see Tucci's *The Religions of Tibet*, 53, 57–58, 61, and 65. The specific English rendering of "total integration" for this term was suggested by Lama Thubten Yeshe.

348   That is, enlightenment itself.

349   This verse describes in concise form the entire process of the training in and the completion of the path of guru yoga. In each case, the "three doors" of body, speech, and mind (which comprise the psychophysical totality of ordinary beings and which are subject to defilement and impurities) are juxtaposed with the three of the guru's purified form. The wish is then posited to realize the inseparability of the Buddha's holy body, speech, and mind and one's own. When such union or total integration is experienced, one becomes a buddha, an enlightened being, in actuality.

350   There are also specific times during the monastic calendar when the reading of certain namthar is enjoined on the community. For example, it is customary for Gelukpa clerics to read aloud the *Secret Biography of Tsongkhapa* on the day commemorating his death and to read the namthar of other figures important to the order's development on dates commemorating their deaths.

351   From a conversation with Geshé Thardö in Charlottesville, Virginia, in early 1985.

352   The Venerable Chögyam Trungpa Rinpoché was once asked about the importance of "lineage" for one who was practicing. Though his remarks refer to the Kagyü tradition, the answer he gave (which is found in Judith Hanson's translation of Jamgon Kongtrul's *The Torch of Certainty*, 17) is appropriate in our context as well:

> "The lineage is very important for the practitioner. Each teacher in the lineage had his particular skillful way of teaching. Each has contributed a great deal to the wealth of the Kagyü tradition. Each one's life is a perfect example for us to study. Each one has left behind and passed on his experiences to us.

The lineage shows us that 'it can be done'—even by us! It makes us aware that the teachings represent not one but many lifetimes of work. Each teacher sacrificed a lot, went through a great deal of personal hardship and finally attained enlightenment. Belonging to this lineage makes us very rich and full of enlightenment-wealth. Being part of this family gives us immense encouragement and also a sense of validity [regarding that which we are trying to practice]. We realize that the teachings we now receive have come down from all of them."

353 For example, one common refuge formula goes:

The Guru is Buddha, the Guru is Dharma, The Guru is Sangha also.

The Guru is the source of all [three]. To all the Gurus, I go for refuge.

Another version says:

To the feet of the Venerable Lama, embodiment of the Three

Jewels, profoundly I turn for refuge;

[please] bestow upon me your transforming powers.

354 See *Selected Works of the Dalai Lama III: Essence of Refined Gold*, trans. Glenn Mullin (Ithaca, NY: Snow Lion Publications, 1985), 59.

355 See Nalanda Translation Committee, *The Life of Marpa the Translator* (Boulder, CO: Prajna Press, 1982), xxxvi.

356 Gö Lotsawa, the author of the famed *Blue Annals,* explained in his discussion of the Mahamudra that the knowledge of Mahamudra, which is equivalent to knowledge of shunyata, cannot be realized in truth as long as it remains on the level of discursive reasoning. Yet one cannot use reasoning to get beyond a reason-grasped knowledge of it. Rather, in order to get beyond this reasoning state, one must use a means that is direct, nondiscursive, and intuitive, and only a guru's blessing provides such a means. Gö Lotsawa wrote (Roerich, *Blue Annals*, 839): "Thus the antidote (of this inference, i.e., understanding of Relativity [here, śūnyatā]) which is not a mere theory, represents the knowledge of Mahāmudrā. This (knowledge) can be gained only through the blessing of a holy teacher (i.e., through initiation, and not through reasoning)."

357 Indeed, for all tantric study and practice, guru devotion is deemed indispensable. Tantric practice is complicated and difficult. If performed properly, it can usher in enlightenment in this very life, but if done improperly, it can produce dangerous consequences. The direct, personal guidance of a guru is therefore essential. From the student's side, proper understanding and performance of guru devotion is essential. A key textual reference outlining the latter is Ashvaghosa's *Fifty Stanzas of Guru Devotion.* This text is often taught before the giving of tantric empowerments. See translation of the text by Alexander Berzin and Jonathan Landaw, in *The Mahāmudrā Eliminating the Darkness of Ignorance* (Dharamsala: Library of Tibetan Works & Archives, 1975).

358 In my opinion, one of the best discussions of this issue appears in Mullin, *Selected Works of the Dalai Lama III*, where, on 59–80, His Holiness the Fourteenth Dalai Lama speaks about some of the dangers inherent in the notion of "seeing every action of the Guru as Perfect." His Holiness's remarks are eloquent, judicious, and especially appropriate in these times.

359 The Tibetan is *nyepa sum*.

360 It is an often-repeated counsel, especially in Mahamudra practice contexts, that "it was Buddha Vajradhara himself who said that one's guru is to be seen as the Buddha." One of the textual loci for this assertion is the Mukhagama of Manjushri composed by the Indian Buddhist Buddhajnanapada. In this text, Buddha Vajradhara says:

> It is I who dwell in the guru's body,
> I who receive offerings from aspirants.

Therefore, to please one's guru is to please all the buddhas and to please Vajradhara, who embodies them all. The guru thus provides us with a precious opportunity. As Geshé Ngawang Dargyey states in his supplement to Ashvaghosa's *Fifty Stanzas of Guru Devotion* in *The Mahāmudrā Eliminating the Darkness of Ignorance*, trans. Alexander Berzin, 161: "Through devotion to your Guru, showing him respect, serving him and making offerings, you build up the merit that will allow you to become liberated from all your suffering. Such service is done not to benefit your Guru, but for your own sake. When you plant seeds in a field, it is not to benefit the earth. It is you yourself who will harvest the crops. Therefore with the proper devotional attitude towards your Guru—seeing him as a Buddha—the more positive energy you exert in his direction, the closer you come towards Buddhahood yourself."

361 The Tibetan for what I translate here as the "eight mundane concerns" is *'jig rten gyi chos brgyad*. This compound is often rendered "eight worldly dharmas," but I seek to avoid this translation because it leaves one of the terms (dharma) untranslated. The eight "concerns" are: gain, loss, reputation, disgrace, praise, blame, pleasure, and pain. According to Buddhist doctrine, as long as one's activities are bound up with such worldly and mundane concerns, one is not practicing the Dharma purely.

362 In this first paragraph, Gyalwa Ensapa alludes first to the three approaches to gaining insight about and mastery of the Dharma: insight gained from hearing the doctrine, that gained by pondering and reflecting on it, and that gained by cultivating meditation on it. He then tells us directly that any attempt to engage in these three approaches that mixes them with any of the eight mundane concerns will result only in the continuance of samsara. Rather than curing ourselves, we further poison ourselves. In short, Gyalwa Ensapa says: "Don't mix Dharmic activity with worldly activity! If it is mixed with worldly

activity, it is not true Dharmic activity!" (Lama Zopa Rinpoche and others are famous today for their similar admonitions.) The entire passage by Gyalwa Ensapa is recorded in Willis, *Enlightened Beings*, 62.

363 These three "perfect virtues" of a lama are mentioned by Tucci in *Tibetan Painted Scrolls*, 1:94–96; and by Lokesh Chandra in *Materials for a Study of Tibetan Literature*, 1:11. For additional "services" expected from a lama, see Franz Michael, *Rule by Incarnation*, 132–36.

364 See, for example, *A Short Biography of Je Tzong-k'a-pa*, ed. India Stevens [based on lectures by Geshe Ngawang Dhargyey] (Dharamsala: Library of Tibetan Works & Archives, 1975), 23. A slightly revised version of this same *Biography* appears in *The Life and Teachings of Tsong Khapa*, ed. Robert Thurman (Dharamsala: Library of Tibetan Works & Archives, 1982), see 21.

365 Avalokiteshvara is the Buddhist deity of "Infinite Compassion."

366 This comment is actually a summation, by C. F. Moule, of a paper by Mary Hesse entitled "Miracles and the Law of Nature." See *Miracles: Cambridge Studies in Their Philosophy and History*, ed. Moule (London: A. R. Mawbray & Co., 1965). Moule himself notes (238ff.) that the Greek word most commonly used throughout the New Testament was not *thaumasion* (marvel) but *dunamis* (power).

367 This is one of the most well-known enumerations of the various types of rddhi. For alternate translations of this particular passage, see Ria Kloppenborg, *The Paccekabuddha: A Buddhist Ascetic* (Leiden: E. J. Brill, 1974), 52–53; and Robinson, *Buddha's Lions*, 8. For a fuller discussion of rddhis, see H. G. A. van Zeyst, "Abhinna," in *Encyclopaedia of Buddhism*, vol. 1, 97–102; and T. W. Rhys Davids, trans., *Dialogues of the Buddha* (Digha Nikaya), in *Sacred Books of the Buddhists*, vol. 2 (Oxford: Oxford University Press, 1921; reprint, London: Pali Text Society, 1977), 277.

368 A recent English version of this sutra was published in two volumes; see Gwendolyn Bays, *The Voice of the Buddha: The Beauty of Compassion* (Berkeley: Dharma Publishing, 1983).

369 The *Mahāvastu*, in three volumes, was translated into English by J. J. Jones and published in the Sacred Books of the Buddhists series (London: The Pāli Text Society), in 1973, 1976, and 1978 (vols. 16, 18, and 19, respectively).

370 Dayal, *The Bodhisattva Doctrine in Buddhist Sanskrit Literature*, 106.

371 Lobsang Jampa, a geshé of the Gelukpa tradition, was the resident lama at the Kurukulla Center in Boston, Massachusetts. In April and July 1989, I met with Geshe Jampa to discuss Tibetan sacred biography. The quoted materials were recorded at the Milarepa Center in Barnet, Vermont, on July 3, 1989. I wish here to gratefully acknowledge his kind assistance. He passed away in May 1991 of cancer.

372 The full English text of this life, translated by Glenn Mullin, can be found in Robert Thurman, *Life and Teachings of Tsong Khapa* (Dharamsala: Tibetan Works & Archives, 1982), 47–55. Tucci, *Tibetan Painted Scrolls*, 1:161, mentions another "secret biography" of Tsongkhapa, written by Khedrup Jé.

373 These excerpts are taken from Glenn Mullin's translation of Tashi Palden's text in Thurman, *Life and Teachings of Tsong Khapa*, 48–53. Mullin, in a smaller collection called "Four Songs to Je Rinpoche" (Dharamsala: Library of Tibetan Works & Archives, 1978) translates this text's title as *Song of the Mystic Experiences of Lama Jé Rinpoché*. Describing the text there on 10 Mullin writes: "The word *Mystic* (*gSang ba*) in the title indicates that the song is essentially tantric in nature and imagery. *gSang-ba* also means *secret*, but in this case it is the oral explanations of the underlying meanings of the text that are secret, rather than the text itself. *Song of the Mystic Experiences* is memorized by almost all monks of the Geluk Tradition and is chanted in assemblies on all occasions especially related to Lama Tzong Khapa."

374 The Tibetan reads as follows: *De nas paṇ chen chos kyi rgyal mtshan gyi bka' bzhin/ gaṅs/ ri sul/ nags khrod sogs du ma 'grims/ de'i tshe padma can gyi sgrub chu'i ne 'khor gyi sa rnams skad cig de la sin dhu rar 'gyur ba zhig yod pas yul ner bzhi dngos dang mtshuṅs pa zhig yod ces grags pa der rdzogs rim daṅ 'brel ba'i bla ma lha'i rnal 'byor bsgoms par mdzad pas chos kyi rgyal po tsong kha pa chen pos zhal gzigs/ de'i tshe rje rin po ches dam pa 'di la thun mong dang thun mong ma yin pa'i snan brgyud kyi gdams ngag yongs su rdzogs par gnang/ lhag par rje rin po che'i phyi paṇḍi ta'i cha lugs nang gi phung khams skye mched rnams 'dus pa'i lha tshogs su gsal ba'i thugs kar rgyal ba shakya thub pa de'i thugs kar rdo rje 'chang bzhugs pa'i bla ma'i rnal 'byor thun mong ma yin pa sems dpa gsum rtseg can de gnang ngo//.* The passage immediately following this one tells us: "Thereafter, for a time the great siddha Chökyi Dorjé chose not to completely abandon his coarse karmic body, but rather to remain in a sort of mystic support body that was nevertheless of the nature of a fully accomplished total integration buddha body."

375 Sarat Chandra Das, in his *Contributions on the Religion and History of Tibet*, devotes a page (109–10 in the 1970 edition) to summarizing the life of "Gyalwa Ton-Dub [Gyalwa Döndrup]." Toward the end of his summary he writes, "At the age of seventeen he became a pupil of the sage Chhokyi Dorje [Chökyi Dorjé] and fully mastered the volume of precepts called Gahdan-Nen-gyud. Afterwards returning to Tsan he resided at the temple of Pamachen near the Panam-Chomolha-ri. Here his teacher the sage showed him the volumes of illusive mysticism." Of course, what is of interest here is Das's treatment of Pema Chan (which he writes as "Pamachen"). He locates it geographically. In fact, in a note directly connected with his mention of "Pamachen," Das attempts to

give even more precise details of the location of this "temple," though his note
speaks only of the Chomolhari mountain range. Das's reading may be derived
from his assumption that this location is associated with one of the "hidden
countries" of Tibetan lore.

376 A. Bharati, *The Tantric Tradition*, 175, for example cites M. Shahidullah's *Les
chants mystiques de Kāṇha et de Sarāhā* as the locus for a list of "intentional"
or "*sandhā*-words" in which *padma* as "lotus" is symbolically equivalent to the
Sanskrit *bhaga*, or "vulva." Dasgupta's *An Introduction to Tantric Buddhism*
(Berkeley, CA: Shambala, 1974), 105, notes that according to the *Hevajra Tantra*, "Prajñā [i.e., highest insight] is called the female organ [*bhaga*] because it is
the abode of all pleasure which is great bliss (*mahāsukha*)."

377 On the "twenty-four places" according to the body mandala of Heruka
Chakrasamvara, see Geshe Kelsang Gyatso, *Clear Light of Bliss*, 23.

378 Tsuda devotes a section of his chapter 5 (215–21) to "The Theory of Pilgrimage
Places."

379 Ibid., 221.

380 This was told to me by Lama Thubten Zopa Rinpoche.

381 For example, see Alex Wayman's discussion of this idea in his *Yoga of the
Guhyasamājatantra*, 234–35. Using Tsongkhapa's *Pañcakrama* commentary,
Wayman suggests (238) that "rivers as external water agree with menses and
blood as personal [or internal] water."

382 That is, by marking the disciple's forehead, throat, and heart, thereby symbolically blessing the "doors" of that one's body, speech, and mind, respectively.

383 This characterization of the *Miraculous Volume* is given by Sermey Geshé
Lobsang Tharchin in his translation of Phabongkha Rinpoché's *Liberation in
Our Hands: A Series of Oral Discourses, Part 1: The Preliminaries by Pabongka
Rinpoche* (Howell, NJ: Mahayana Sutra & Tantra, 1990), 172. Geshe Tharchin translates the Tibetan, *Dga' ldan sprul pa'i glegs bam*, as *Ganden Emanation Scripture*. In Michael Richards' translation of Phabongkha Rinpoché's
teachings, called *Liberation in the Palm of Your Hand: A Concise Discourse on
the Path to Enlightenment* (Boston: Wisdom Publications, 1991, 2006), the
Tibetan is rendered *The Miraculous Book of the Gelugpas*. It should be noted
that in Richards' translation, it appears as though Phabongkha Rinpoché is
directly quoting from the *Volume*. The pertinent passage (244) reads: "The following verses are taken from *The Miraculous Book of the Gelugpas*, so they are
especially blessed . . . ."

Chapter 15: Community of "Neighbors"

384 See Joy DeGruy's *Post Traumatic Slave Syndrome: America's Legacy of Enduring Injury and Healing* (Portland, OR: Uptone Press, 2005), 23.

385 See, for example, these articles and essays: "Buddhism and Race: An African American Baptist-Buddhist Perspective"; "Diversity and Race: New Koans for American Buddhism," in *Women's Buddhism, Buddhism's Women: Tradition, Revision, Renewal*, ed. Elli Findly (Boston: Wisdom Publications, 2000); "A New Spirit at Spirit Rock," *Tricycle: The Buddhist Review* (Winter 2002); "You're Already a Buddha, So Be a Buddha," *Turning Wheel* (Summer 2003); "The Dharma Has No Color," in *Dharma, Color, and Culture: New Voices in Western Buddhism*, ed. Hilda Baldoquin (Berkeley, CA: Parallax Press, 2004); and "Yes, We're Buddhists, Too!" *Buddhadharma* (Winter 2011). My most sustained essay on racism in America is my memoir, *Dreaming Me: Black, Baptist, and Buddhist: One Woman's Spiritual Journey* (Boston: Wisdom Publications, 2008).

386 Willis, "Buddhism and Race," 88.

387 A recent United States Supreme Court decision called for Congress to drop section V from the Voting Rights Bill, asserting that the kinds of racial discriminations experienced in the 1960s no longer exist. On June 25, 2013 *The New York Times* reported the following: "The Supreme Court on Tuesday effectively struck down the heart of the Voting Rights Act of 1965 by a 5-to-4 vote, freeing nine states, mostly in the South, to change their election laws without advance federal approval." The article continued, "At the core of the disagreement was whether racial minorities continued to face barriers to voting in states with a history of discrimination. 'Our country has changed,' Chief Justice John G. Roberts Jr. wrote for the majority. 'While any racial discrimination in voting is too much, Congress must ensure that the legislation it passes to remedy that problem speaks to current conditions.'"

388 James Byrd Jr. was an African American man who was murdered by three men, of whom at least two were white supremacists, in Jasper, Texas, on June 7, 1998.

389 Emmett Till's story is often credited with having spurred the American civil rights movement. He reportedly flirted with a white cashier at a grocery store in Money, Mississippi. Four days later, two white men kidnapped Till, beat him, and shot him in the head. The men were tried for murder, but an all-white male jury acquitted them.

390 See *Dreaming Me*, 257–58.

391 John Howard Griffin's *Black Like Me* was published in 1961 and became a best-seller. In 2011, a fiftieth-anniversary edition was published.

392 On the subject of white privilege, Paula Rothenberg's anthology, *White Privilege: Essential Readings on the Other Side of Racism*, 5th ed. (New York: Worth

Publishers, 2016), offers an excellent place to begin reading. Tim Wise, who is included in that volume, has also written a number of books on this subject.

393 The existentialist Christian philosopher Søren Kierkegaard argued this point in his classic treatise on faith, *Fear and Trembling.*

394 There are a number of English translations of the *Dhammapada.* I'd suggest those of Gil Fronsdal, Thomas Cleary, and John Ross Carter and Mahinda Palihawadana. The translations here are my own.

395 This diverse community was quite radical for its time. I have written about the Buddha's choice to include women in an essay titled "Nuns and Benefactresses," in Haddad and Findly, *Women, Religion, and Social Change,* 59–85. It is the first chapter of this volume. The fact that the Buddha admitted into the sangha diverse castes was equally as radical and revolutionary, given India's strict laws against mingling of the *varnas.*

396 See King's 1963 sermon "On Being a Good Neighbor," in *Strength to Love* (Philadelphia: Fortress Press, 1981 [1963]), 34.

397 See Desmond Tutu's *No Future without Forgiveness* (New York: Doubleday, 1999), 31.

398 See King's sermon "The Man Who Was a Fool," in *Strength to Love,* 72.

399 See King's sermon "On Being a Good Neighbor," in *Strength to Love,* 35.

400 Ibid., 38.

401 See Shantideva's *The Way of the Bodhisattva,* translated by the Padmakara Translation Group (Boston: Shambhala Publications, 2008). This is my own, slighted edited, translation of verse 129 of chapter 8.

402 The term "Beloved Community" was not originated by King, but it was he who brought the idea into prominence. The term had been coined by the philosopher-theologian Josiah Royce (1855–1916), and a year after Royce's death, it became a central ideal of the organization Fellowship of Reconciliation (FOR). King was a member of the organization, and its members helped him during the Montgomery campaign. Beginning in 1956, King began speaking about the Beloved Community in his talks and sermons.

403 See the King Center website, https://thekingcenter.org/king-philosophy/.

404 One of the best-known sources for this quote is Dr. King's famed "Letter from a Birmingham Jail" written in 1963, wherein he writes: "Injustice anywhere is a threat to justice everywhere. We are caught in an inescapable network of mutuality, tied in a single garment of destiny. Whatever affects one directly affects all indirectly. Never again can we afford to live with the narrow, provincial 'outside agitator' idea. Anyone who lives inside the United States can never be considered an outsider."

405 Ibid., and see https://thekingcenter.org/king-philosophy/.

406 *Mahavagga* I, 11, 1.

CHAPTER 17: TEACHING BUDDHISM IN THE WESTERN ACADEMY

407 Presumably, this means meditation, though there are many other forms of Buddhist practice.

408 Among many others on this topic, see remarks by Frank Reynolds, *Teaching Buddhism in the West: From the Wheel to the Web* (London: RoutledgeCurzon, 2002), 6–7.

409 Wesleyan University, Middletown, Connecticut. Named after the founder of Methodism, John Wesley, the school was initially affiliated with the Methodist Church but became nonaffiliated early in its history. I believe there may still be a sense of defensiveness about the earlier church connection. One need only read the number of times the term "*secular* institution" is repeated throughout the school's various advertisements and mission statement to get an idea of this.

410 I save the explorations of Heinz Bechert and others for more advanced seminars. For this course, the dates 563–483 BCE are functional.

411 For Milarepa's life, I have most often relied on the English translation by Lobsang Lhalungpa, *The Life of Milarepa*, though there is now available the less-Tibetan-language-laden translation by Andrew Quintman, *The Life of Milarepa* (New York: Penguin Classics, 2010). For the life of Nāropa, I use Guenther, *The Life and Teaching of Nāropa*.

412 This wonderful little text was first published in 1959.

413 I am in agreement here with Todd Lewis's assessment of the value of narrative, as articulated in his essay "Representation of Buddhism in Undergraduate Teaching: The Centrality of Ritual and Story Narratives," in *Teaching Buddhism in the West*, ed. Victor Hori and Richard P. Hayes (London: RoutledgeCurzon, 2002), 39–56.

414 Much of my work over the years has had this primary message. My translation of the early Geluk Mahamudra siddhas, *Enlightened Beings: The Ganden Oral Tradition*, attempted to make this point. Roughly two-thirds of that text is comprised of annotations that are intended to show these siddhas to be actual historical figures who practiced. I sometimes guide students to envision themselves as investigative reporters during the time of ancient figures, to put them on the ground in former times and other cultures. This method has had good results.

415 *Zen Buddhism: In Search of Self* is a 2007 film, 62 minutes long, produced by Gong Jae Sung, which chronicles a ninety-day gathering of two dozen Zen Buddhist nuns observing Winter Zen Retreat at Baek Hung Temple in South Korea.

416 See *Dhamma Brothers*, a 2007 documentary film directed by Jenny Phillips about a meditation program held at Donaldson Correctional Facility near Bessemer, Alabama.

417 Thomas Tweed, "Night-Stand Buddhists and Other Creatures: Sympathizers, Adherents, and the Study of Religion," in *American Buddhism: Methods and Findings in Recent Scholarship*, ed. Duncan Ryūken Williams and Christopher S. Queen (London: Routledge, 1999), 71–99.

418 Traditional Buddhism says that there are three types of wisdom: that which arises from hearing and study (*sruta mayi prajna*), that which arises from contemplation (*cinta mayi prajna*), and that which arises from meditation (or, *bhavana mayi prajna*). In my classes, I try to provide the space for the first two of these activities.

419 Over the years, I have tried various means to accomplish this. Early on, I offered to guide students who had completed the first half of the course in a Tibetan practice. I "prepped" all the students for the practice during class but did not make attending the ceremony or doing the practice a requirement of the course. I then invited all interested students to come together for a special abbreviated *rjes nang*, or "permission to practice" ceremony. After that ceremony, we met as a group once each week outside the classroom until the end of the semester. After the first few weeks, the number of students attending these sessions usually trailed off; students wanted to know what the practice(s) were like, but not everyone found them captivating, especially as the schedules of other extracurricular events picked up. In those early years, I lectured a bit on the theory of Buddhist meditation in class and "practiced" with a few students outside of class. More recently, I have incorporated into the actual class a week or week-and-a-half of lectures and discussions that focus solely on the varieties of Buddhist meditation, wherein we all briefly try them out during class time. Students read selections from Peter Harvey, Ayya Khema, Thich Nhat Hanh, and others, and we then devote a period of class time to practice. It turns out that this sampling technique has spurred much engagement in and, subsequently, outside the classroom.

420 An interesting account of what constitutes this Buddhist view is provided by Dzongsar Jamyang Khyentse in his *What Makes You Not a Buddhist* (Boston: Shambhala Publications, 2008).

421 I use both Thich Nhat Hanh's *Being Peace* and a hefty selection from *Old Path, White Clouds: Walking in the Footsteps of the Buddha*, which is a composite narrative of the "life" of the Buddha.

422 The novel *Lost Horizon* was written by James Hilton and published in 1933. The book was made into a film directed by Frank Capra in 1937.

423 Adam Yauch of the group is known for his song "Bodhisattva Vow," which became the anthem of concerts for the Students for a Free Tibet organization.

424 John Powers, *Introduction to Tibetan* Buddhism (Ithaca, NY: Snow Lion Publications, 2007). The smaller *Concise Introduction to Tibetan Buddhism* appeared in 2008.

425 I use the translation by Tarthang Tulku and Jane Wilhelms called *Mother of Knowledge* (1983).

426 Fortunately, in the past few years, a lot have become available. Works by Jamyang Norbu, Tsering Namgyal, Tenzin Tsundue, and Dagyab Kyabgon Rinpoché provide useful counterbalances to Western misperceptions. A useful collection of such essays can be found in *Imaginging Tibet: Perceptions, Projections, and Fantasies*, ed. Thierry Dodin and Heinz Rather (New Delhi: Sanctum Books, 2001).

427 I like Francesca Fremantle and Trungpa Tulku's translation and commentary in *The Tibetan Book of the Dead*.

428 See the 2004 DVD, *Tibetan Book of the Dead*, directed by Hiroaki Mota and Barrie McLean.

429 The short text I use for guiding us here in the construction and offering of a maṇḍala is taken from Sermey Geshé Lobsang Tharchin's *A Commentary on Guru Yoga and Offering of the Mandala* (Ithaca, NY: Snow Lion Publications, 1987).

430 According to tantric rules of interpretation, all texts and rituals are said to consist of and to operate on three levels—to wit, the outer, inner, and secret levels—and may therefore be read and interpreted on these three distinct levels. See a fuller account of these three in the Introduction to my *Enlightened Beings: the Ganden Oral Tradition*, 3–29.

431 For a collection of essays on this subject by eminent scholars, see *The Insider/ Outsider Problem in the Study of Religion: A Reader*, ed. Russell T. McCutcheon (London: Bloomsbury, 1999).

432 I harbor no delusions that my few years of study with Tibetans qualify me fully to officiate or to assume the role of a qualified guru or lama. Still, Lama Yeshe entrusted me with certain ritual and practice instructions that, he said, were "to be used in your capacity as a teacher."

433 There are various translations of the lama's capabilities or "kindnesses" (*kadrin, bka' drin*). In *The Sacred Sites of the Dalai Lamas* (Studio City, CA: Divine Arts, 2011), Glenn Mullin calls the three the "legacies of a master" and defines them as: "giving spiritual teachings that reveal the essential thought of the Buddhas, leading discussions that dispel mistaken dogma, and composing texts that fill with delight the fortunate beings that love profound realizations" (82). A teacher must be a master at teaching, inquiry and debate, and composition. Some of these skills are also enjoined by the university on its faculty. But spiritual empowerment is the province of an experienced spiritual master.

434 In this way my meeting and studying with Lama Yeshe was quite different than the encounter that Donald Lopez Jr. discusses in his provocative essay, "Foreigner at the Lama's Feet," in *Curators of the Buddha: The Study of Buddhism*

under Colonialism, ed. Donald S. Lopez Jr. (Chicago: University of Chicago Press,1995), 251–95. There he notes that most of us went to the lamas' feet seeking our PhDs. Lopez develops a number of intriguing ideas in this essay about what he calls "four moments of urgency" in our encounters with Tibetan refugees, about working with a lama as with "a native scholar who was made to serve as both informant and guru," and about how, in order to gain our degrees, we had to render the teacher's voice and words secondary to the printed words of our newly created texts.

435 See Charles S. Prebish, "The New Panditas," in *Buddhadharma: The Practitioner's Quarterly* (Spring 2006): 64. In fact, the phrase is fairly commonplace within the various Buddhist traditions. For example, as Prebish notes here, *gantha dhura*, or the "vocation of books," was one name for early Buddhist monks who upheld and valued teaching above practice. In the Tibetan tradition, especially within the Gelukpa school, *khedrup (mkhas grub)* is an often-used form of respect. The term literally means "a learned master" *(mkhas)* who is also an accomplished practitioner *(grub)*, as in the name of one of Tsongkhapa's greatest disciples, Khedrup Gelek Pelzang (Mkhas grub rje).

436 Ibid., 67. (Spoken like a true J. Z. Smithian!)

437 Three articles exploring this theme are found in the *Journal of Global Buddhism* 9 (2008). See John Makransky, "The Emergence of Buddhist Critical-Constructive Reflection in the Academy as a Resource for Buddhist Communities and for the Contemporary World," 113–53; Ian Reader, "Buddhism and the Perils of Advocacy," 83–112; and Duncaan Ryuken Williams, "At Ease in Between: The Middle Position of a Scholar-Practitioner," 155–63. All are available at http://www.globalbuddhism.org/.

438 I prefer not to single out here the particular scholars and their misinterpretations I refer to above. They know who they are.

439 We all know about the infamous L. Austine Waddell, for example, and his tirades against what he mistakenly called "lamaism." For more on the issue of the West's encounters with Tibetan Buddhism, see Donald Lopez, Jr., *Prisoners of Shangri-La: Tibetan Buddhism and the West* (Chicago: Chicago University Press, 1999).

440 The memoir was first published in 2001 by Riverhead Books, under the title *Dreaming Me: An African American Woman's Spiritual Journey*. In 2008, a slightly revised and expanded edition was published by Wisdom Publications as *Dreaming Me: Black, Baptist, and Buddhist: One Woman's Spiritual Journey*.

441 This was not a scholarly convocation of Buddhist studies scholars and academics, but rather a gathering of teacher-practitioners from Dharma centers around the world.

Bibliography

❧❧

Adiele, Faith. "Standing Alone with Myself." In *Life Notes: Personal Writings by Contemporary Black Women*, edited by Patricia Bell-Scott, 364–88. New York: W. W. Norton, 1994.

Allione, Tsultrim. *Women of Wisdom*. London: Routledge & Kegan Paul, 1984, 2000.

Avedon, John F. *In Exile from the Land of Snows: The Definitive Account of the Dalai Lama and Tibet since the Chinese Conquest*. New York: Alfred A. Knopf, 1984.

Aziz, Barbara. "Ani Chodron: Portrait of a Buddhist Nun." In *Loka 2, Journal from Nāropa Institute*, edited by Rick Fields. New York: Doubleday/Anchor, 1976.

———. *Tibetan Frontier Families*. New Delhi: Vikas Publishing House, 1978.

Banerjea, J. N. *Paurāṇic and Tantric Religion*. Calcutta: University of Calcutta, 1966.

Baraka, Amiri [Leroi Jones]. *Blues People: Negro Music in White America*. New York: Morrow Quill, 1963.

Bareau, Andre. "Un personnage bien mysterieux: L'espouse du Buddha." In *Indological and Buddhist Studies: Volume in Honour of Professor J. W. de Jong*, 31–59. Canberra: Faculty of Asian Studies, Australian National University, 1982.

Batchelor, Stephen. *Buddhism without Beliefs: A Contemporary Guide to Awakening*. New York: Riverhead Books, 1997.

Bays, Gwendolyn, trans. *The Voice of the Buddha: The Beauty of Compassion*. 2 vols. Tibetan Translation Series. Berkeley: Dharma Publishing, 1983.

Berglie, Per-Arne. "On the Question of Tibetan Shamanism." In *Tibetan Studies*. Zurich: Völkerkundermuseum Universität Zürich, 1978.

Berzin, Alexander, and Jonathan Landaw, trans. *The Mahāmudrā Eliminating the Darkness of Ignorance*. Dharamsala: Library of Tibetan Works & Archives, 1978.

Bharati, Agehananda. *The Tantric Tradition*. New York: Doubleday, 1970.

Boorstein, Sylvia. *That's Funny, You Don't Look Buddhist: On Being a Faithful Jew and a Passionate Buddhist*. San Francisco: HarperSanFrancisco, 1998.

Boucher, Sandy. *Turning the Wheel: American Women Creating the New Buddhism*. San Francisco: Harper & Row, 1988.

Burgess, J. *Buddhist Stūpas of Amarāvatī and Jaggayapeṭa*. Archaeological Survey of South India, 1870.

Burman, Bina Roy. *Religion and Politics in Tibet*. New Delhi: Vikas Publishing House, 1976.

Campbell, Joseph. *The Hero with a Thousand Faces*. 3d revised ed. Novato, CA: The Joseph Campbell Foundation and New World Library, 2008 [1949].

Caplow, Zenshin Florence, and Reigetsu Susan Mood, eds. *The Hidden Lamp: Stories from Twenty-Five Centuries of Awakened Women*. Somerville, MA: Wisdom Publications, 2013.

Carrasco, Pedro. *Land and Polity in Tibet*. Seattle: University of Washington Press, 1959.

Castaneda, Carlos. *Journey to Ixtlan: The Lessons of Don Juan*. New York: Simon and Schuster, 1972.

Chandra, Lokesh, ed. *Materials for a Study of Tibetan Literature*, vol. 3. Śata-Piṭaka Series 30. New Delhi: International Academy of Indian Culture, 1963.

——, ed. *Tibetan Chronicle of Padma-dkar-po*. Śata-Piṭaka Series 75. New Delhi: International Academy of Indian Culture, 1968.

Chang, Garma C. C. *Teachings of Tibetan Yoga*. Secaucus, NJ: Citadel Press, 1977 [1963].

Chattopadhyaya, Alaka, trans. *Atiśa and Tibet: Life and Works of Dīpaṃkara Śrījñāna in Relation to the History and Religion of Tibet*. Delhi: Motilal Banarsidass, 1967.

Chayat, Roko Sherry, ed. *Subtle Sound: The Zen Teachings of Maurine Stuart*. Boston: Shambhala Publications, 1996.

Conze, Edward. *Buddhist Texts through the Ages*. New York: Harper Torchbooks, 1964 [1954].

———. *Buddhist Wisdom Books*. New York: Harper Torchbooks, 1972 [1958].

———. *The Prajñāpāramitā Literature*. The Hague: Mouton and Co., 1960.

———. *Selected Sayings from the Perfection of Wisdom*. Boulder, CO: Prajna Press, 1978.

Coomaraswamy, Ananda K. *Buddha and the Gospel of Buddhism*. New York: Harper Torchbooks, 1964 [1916].

———. *History of Indian and Indonesian Art*. New York: E. Weyhe, 1927.

———. *La sculpture de Bharhut*. Paris: Vanoest, 1956.

Crapanzano, Vincent. *Tuhami: Portrait of a Moroccan*. Chicago: The University of Chicago Press, 1980.

Cunningham, A. *The Bhilsa Topes*. London, 1854.

———. *The Stupa of Bharhut, A Buddhist Monument Ornamented with Numerous Sculptures Illustrative of Buddhist Legend and History in the Third Century BC*. Varanasi, India: Indological Book House, 1962 [London: W. H. Allen, 1879].

Dargyay, Eva. *The Rise of Esoteric Buddhism in Tibet*. Delhi: Motilal Banarsidass, 1977.

Das, Sarat Chandra. *Contributions on the Religion and History of Tibet*. New Delhi: Mañjuśrī Publishing House, 1970 [1881].

———. "The Lives of the Panchen Rinpochés or Tashi Lamas." *Journal of the Royal Asiatic Society of Bengal* (1882): n.p.

———. *A Tibetan-English Dictionary*. Delhi: Motilal Banarsidass, 1970.

Dasgupta, S. B. *An Introduction to Tantric Buddhism*. Berkeley, CA: Shambhala Publications, 1974 [Calcutta, 1958].

Datta, Bhupendranath, trans. *Mystic Tales of Lāma Tarānātha.* Calcutta: Ramakrishna Vedanta Math, 1957 [1944].

Dayal, Har. *The Bodhisattva Doctrine in Buddhist Sanskrit Literature.* New Delhi: Motilal Banarsidass, 1975 [London, 1932].

DeGruy, Joy. *Post-Traumatic Slave Syndrome: America's Legacy of Enduring Injury and Healing.* Portland, OR: Uptone Press, 2005.

Delog Dawa Drölma. *Delog: Journey to Realms Beyond Death.* Junction City, CA: Padma Publishing, 1995.

Demiéville, Paul. *Le concile de Lhasa: Une controverse sur le quietisme entre bouddhistes de l'Inde et de la Chine au XIIe siècle de l'ère chrétienne.* Bibliothèque de l'Institut des Hautes Études Chinoises 7. Paris: Collège de France, Institut des Hautes Études Chinoises, 2006 [1952].

Diemberger, Hildegard. *When a Woman Becomes a Dynasty: The Samding Dorje Phagmo of Tibet.* New York: Columbia University Press, 2007.

Dodin, Thierry, and Heinz Rather, eds. *Imagining Tibet: Perceptions, Projections, and Fantasies.* New Delhi: Sanctum Books, 2001.

Douglas, Kenneth, and Gwendolyn Bays, trans. *The Life and Liberation of Padmasambhava.* 2 vols. Emeryville, CA: Dharma Publishing, 1978.

Dowman, Keith. *The Legend of the Great Stupa and the Life of the Lotus Born Guru.* Berkeley, CA: Dharma Publishing, 1973.

———. *Masters of Mahāmudrā.* Albany: State University of New York Press, 1985.

———. *The Power-Places of Central Tibet: The Pilgrim's Guide.* London: Routledge & Kegan Paul, 1988.

———. *Sky Dancer: The Secret Life and Songs of the Lady Yeshe Tsogyel.* London: Routledge & Kegan Paul, 1984.

Dresser, Marianne, ed. *Buddhist Women on the Edge: Contemporary Perspectives from the Western Frontier.* Berkeley, CA: North Atlantic Books, 1996.

Dutt, Nalinaksha, ed. *Bodhisattvabhūmi: Being the XVth Section of Asangapāda's Yogācarabhūmiḥ.* Patna: K. P. Jayaswal Research Institute, 1978.

——. *Mahāyāna Buddhism*. New Delhi: Motilal Banarsidass, 1977.

Dutt, Sukumar. *Buddhist Monks and Monasteries of India*. London: George Allen and Unwin, 1962.

Dzongsar Jamyang Khyentse. *What Makes You Not a Buddhist*. Boston: Shambhala Publications, 2008.

Edou, Jérôme, trans. *Machig Labdrön and the Foundations of Chöd*. Ithaca, NY: Snow Lion Publications, 1996.

Ekvall, Robert. *The Lama Knows: A Tibetan Legend Is Born*. Novato, CA: Chandler and Sharp Publishers, 1980 [India, 1979].

Eliade, Mircea. *Yoga, Immortality and Freedom*. Translated from the French by Willard R. Trask. Bollinger Series 56. Princeton, NJ: Princeton University Press, 2009 [1958].

Ericson, Erik. *Childhood and Society*. New York: W. W. Norton, 1950.

——. *Gandhi's Truth: On the Origins of Militant Nonviolence*. W. W. Norton, 1969.

——. "The Legend of Hitler's Childhood." In *Childhood and Society*, 326–28.

——. "The Legend of Maxim Gorky's Youth." In *Childhood and Society*, 359–402.

——. *Young Man Luther: A Study in Psychoanalysis and History*. W. W. Norton, 1958.

Evans-Wentz, W. E. *The Tibetan Book of the Dead*. Oxford: Oxford University Press, 1957.

Falk, Nancy. "The Case of the Vanishing Nuns: The Fruits of Ambivalence in Ancient Indian Buddhism." In Falk and Gross, *Unspoken Worlds*, 207–24.

——. "An Image of Woman in Old Buddhist Literature: The Daughters of Mara." In Plaskow and Arnold, *Women and Religion*, 105–12.

Falk, Nancy, and Rita Gross, eds. *Unspoken Worlds: Women's Religious Lives in Non-Western Cultures*. San Francisco: Harper & Row, 1979.

Ferrari, Alfonsa, trans. *mK'yen brtse's Guide to the Holy Places of Central Tibet*. Edited by Luciano Petech with the collaboration of Hugh Richardson. Serie Orientale Roma 16. Rome: Istituto Italiano per il Medio ed Estremo Oriente, 1958.

Fields, Rick. *How the Swans Came to the Lake: The American Encounter with Buddhism.* Boston: Shambhala Publications, 1992.

Findly, Ellison, ed. *Women's Buddhism, Buddhism's Women: Tradition, Revision, Renewal.* Boston: Wisdom Publications, 2000.

Fremantle, Francesca, and Chögyam Trungpa, trans. *The Tibetan Book of the Dead: The Great Liberation through Hearing in the Bardo.* Boulder, CO: Shambhala Publications, 1975.

Geertz, Clifford. *Islam Observed: Religious Development in Morocco and Indonesia.* New Haven, CT: Yale University Press, 1968.

Goldberg, Ellen. "Buddhist Nuns Make Comeback in Sri Lanka—To Monks' Dislike." *The Christian Science Monitor,* April 2, 1984, 14, 44.

Goldstein, Melvyn. "The Circulation of Estates in Tibet: Reincarnation, Land, and Politics." *Journal of Asian Studies* 32, no. 3 (1973): 445–55.

Govinda, Anagarika. *Foundations of Tibetan Mysticism.* New York: Samuel Weiser, 1975 [London, 1960].

Grimshaw, Anna. *Servants of the Buddha: Winter in a Himalayan Convent.* Cleveland, OH: Pilgrim Press, 1994.

Gross, Rita. *Buddhism after Patriarchy: A Feminist History, Analysis, and Reconstruction of Buddhism.* Albany: State University of New York Press, 1993.

———. "Yeshe Tsogyel: Enlightened Consort, Great Teacher, Female Role Model." In Willis, *Feminine Ground,* 11–32.

Grünwedel, Albert. *Die Geschichten der vierundachtzig Zauberer: Mahasiddhas.* Berlin: Reimer, 1916.

Guenther, Herbert V., trans. *The Life and Teaching of Nāropa.* Oxford: Oxford University Press, 1974 [1963].

———. *Treasures on the Tibetan Middle Way.* Berkeley, CA: Shambhala Publications, 1971.

Gyatso, Geshe Kelsang. *Clear Light of Bliss: Mahamudra in Vajrayana Buddhism.* London: Wisdom Publications, 1982.

Gyatso, Janet. *Apparitions of the Self: The Secret Autobiographies of a Tibetan Visionary.* Princeton, NJ: Princeton University Press, 1998.

Gyatso, Tenzin, the Fourteenth Dalai Lama. *The World of Tibetan*

Buddhism: An Overview of Its Philosophy and Practice. Translated, edited, and annotated by Geshe Thupten Jinpa. Somerville, MA: Wisdom Publications, 2015 [1995].

Hanson, Judith, trans. *The Torch of Certainty*. Boulder, CO: Shambhala Publications, 1977.

Harding, Sarah, trans. *Machik's Complete Explanation Clarifying the Meaning of Chod*. Ithaca, NY: Snow Lion, 2003.

———. *Niguma, Lady of Illusion*. Ithaca, NY: Snow Lion, 2010.

Harvey, Peter. *An Introduction to Buddhism: Teachings, History and Practices*. Cambridge: Cambridge University Press, 1990.

Hirakawa, Akira. "The Rise of Mahāyāna Buddhism and Its Relationship to the Worship of Stūpas." In *Memoirs of the Research Department of the Toyo Bunko* 22. Tokyo: Toyo Bunko, 1963.

Horner, I. B., trans. *Bhikkuni-vibhaṅga*. In *The Book of the Discipline (Vinaya-Piṭaka)*. Sacred Books of the Buddhists, vol. 20, 80–122. London: Pali Text Society, 1975 [1952].

———. *The Book of the Discipline (Vinaya-Piṭaka)*. In 6 Parts. Sacred Books of the Buddhists, vols. 10, 11, 13, 14, 20, 25 (1970, 1969, 1969, 1971, 1975, 1966). London: Luzac and Co., 1966.

———. *Cullavagga* X. Part 5 of *The Book of the Discipline (Vinaya-Piṭaka)*. Sacred Books of the Buddhists, vol. 20, 352–92. London: Pali Text Society, 1975.

———. *Women under Primitive Buddhism: Laywomen and Almswomen*. New Delhi: Motilal Banarsidass, 1975 [1930].

Hotchkiss, Brian, ed. *Buddhism in America: Proceedings of the First Buddhism in America Conference*. Rutland, VT: Tuttle Publishing, 1998.

Hurvitz, Leon, trans. *Scripture of the Lotus Blossom of the Fine Dharma (The Lotus Sutra)*. New York: Columbia University Press, 1976. Translated from the Chinese of Kumārajīva.

Jaini, Padmanabh. *The Jaina Path of Purification*. Berkeley: University of California Press, 1979.

Johnson, Charles. *Dr. King's Refrigerator: And Other Bedtime Stories*. New York: Scribner, 2005.

———. *Nighthawks: Stories*. New York: Scribner, 2018.

Jones, J. J., trans. *The Mahāvastu*. 3 vols. Sacred Books of the Buddhists, vols. 16, 18, 19. London: The Pāli Text Society, 1973, 1976, 1978.

Kajiyama, Yuichi. "Women in Buddhism." *Eastern Buddhist* (new series) 15, no. 2 (1982): 53–70.

Kalff, Martin. "Dakinis in the Cakrasaṃvara Tradition." In *Tibetan Studies*, edited by M. Brauen and P. Kvaerne, 149–62. Zurich: Volkerkundemuseum der Universitat Zurich, 1978.

Kalu Rinpoche. *The Dharma That Illuminates All Beings Impartially Like the Light of the Sun and the Moon*. Albany: State University of New York Press, 1986.

Kamenetz, Rodger. *The Jew in the Lotus*. New York: HarperCollins, 1995.

Katz, Nathan. "Anima and Mkha'-'gro-ma: A Critical Comparative Study of Jung and Tibetan Buddhism." *The Tibet Journal* 2, no. 3 (1977): 13–43.

Kern, Hendrick, trans. *The Saddharma-Puṇḍarīka, or the Lotus of the True Law*. Oxford: Clarendon Press, 1909 [1884]. Translated from the Sanskrit.

Khetsun Sangpo, ed. *Biographical Dictionary of Tibet and Tibetan Buddhism*. 11 vols. Dharamsala: Library of Tibetan Works & Archives, 1973–79.

King, Martin Luther, Jr. *Strength to Love*. Philadelphia: Fortress Press, 1981 [1963].

Kloppenborg, Ria. *The Paccekabuddha: A Buddhist Ascetic*. Leiden: E. J. Brill, 1974.

Kluckhohn, Clyde. *The Use of Personal Documents in Anthropology*. Bulletin 55. New York: Social Science Research Council, 1945.

Kretschmer, Ernst. *The Psychology of Men of Genius*. Translated by R. B. Cattell. London: Kegan Paul, Trench, Trubner and Co., 1931.

Kris, Ernst. *Psychoanalytic Explorations in Art*. New York: International Universities Press, 2000 [1952].

Lama Yeshe. *Introduction to Tantra: The Transformation of Desire*. Boston: Wisdom Publications, 2001 [1987].

Lama Zopa Rinpoche, Lama Thubten, and George Churinoff, trans.

The Seventh Dalai Lama, Nyung Na: The Means of Achievement of the Eleven-Headed Great Compassionate One, Avalokitesvara. Boston: Wisdom Publications, 1995.

Landaw, Jonathan, and Andy Weber, eds. *Images of Enlightenment: Tibetan Art in Practice*. Ithaca, NY: Snow Lion Publications, 1993.

Lewis, Todd. "Representation of Buddhism in Undergraduate Teaching: The Centrality of Ritual and Story Narratives." In *Teaching Buddhism in the West*, edited by Victor Hori and Richard P. Hayes, 39–56. London: RoutledgeCurzon, 2002.

Lewis, Todd, and Gary DeAngelis, eds. *Teaching Buddhism: New Insights on Understanding and Presenting the Traditions*. Oxford: Oxford University Press, 2016.

Lobsang Lhalungpa, trans. *The Life of Milarepa*. New York: E. P. Dutton, 1977.

———. *Tibet, the Sacred Realm: Photographs 1880–1950*. New York: An Aperture Book, 1983.

Lopez, Donald S., Jr. "Foreigner at the Lama's Feet." In *Curators of the Buddha: The Study of Buddhism under Colonialism*, edited by Donald S. Lopez Jr., 251–95. Chicago: University of Chicago Press, 1995.

———. *Prisoners of Shangri-La: Tibetan Buddhism and the West*. Chicago: The University of Chicago Press, 1999 [1998].

Luk, Charles, trans. *The Vimalakīrti Nirdeśa Sūtra*. Boulder, CO: Shambhala Publications, 1972. Translated from the Chinese.

Mackenzie, Vicki. *Reborn in the West*. New York: Marlowe & Company, 1996.

Makransky, John. "The Emergence of Buddhist Critical-Constructive Reflection in the Academy as a Resource for Buddhist Communities and for the Contemporary World." *Journal of Global Buddhism* 9 (2008): 113–53.

Mann, Gurinder Singh, Paul Numrich, and Raymond Williams. *Buddhists, Hindus, and Sikhs in America: A Short History*. Oxford: Oxford University Press, 2008.

McCutcheon, Russell T., ed. *The Insider/Outsider Problem in the Study of Religion: A Reader*. London: Bloomsbury, 1999.

Meeks, Wayne. *The First Urban Christians: The Social World of the Apostle Paul.* New Haven, CT: Yale University Press, 1983.

Michael, Franz. *Rule by Incarnation: Tibetan Buddhism and Its Role in Society and State.* Boulder, CO: Westview Press, 1982.

Monier-Williams, Sir Monier. *A Sanskrit-English Dictionary.* Oxford: Clarendon Press, 1964 [1899].

Moule, C. F. D., ed. *Miracles: Cambridge Studies on Their Philosophy and History.* London: A. R. Mawbray and Co., 1965.

Mullin, Glenn, trans. *Four Songs to Je Rinpoche.* Dharamsala: Library of Tibetan Works & Archives, 1978.

———. *The Sacred Sites of the Dalai Lamas.* Studio City, CA: Divine Arts, 2011.

———, "The Second Dalai Lama's 'Living on the Essence of Flowers.'" In *The Dalai Lamas on Tantra,* 318–23. Boulder, CO: Snow Lion Publications, 2006.

———, trans. *Selected Works of the Dalai Lama I: Bridging the Sūtras and Tantras.* Ithaca, NY: Snow Lion Publications, 1985.

———, trans. *Selected Works of the Dalai Lama III: Essence of Refined Gold.* Ithaca, NY: Snow Lion Publications, 1985.

———. *Song of the Mystic Experiences of Lama Jé Rinpoché.* In Thurman, *Life and Teachings of Tsong Khapa,* 47–55.

Muses, C. A., ed., and Chang, C. C. trans. *Esoteric Teachings of the Tibetan Tantra.* York Beach, ME: Samuel Weiser, 1982 [1961].

Nalanda Translation Committee. *The Life of Marpa the Translator.* Boulder, CO: Prajna Press, 1982.

———. *The Rain of Wisdom.* Boulder, CO: Shambhala Publications, 1980.

Nattier, Jan. "Visible and Invisible: The Politics of Representation in Buddhist America." *Tricycle: The Buddhist Review* 5, no. 1 (1995): 42–49.

Pachen, Ani, and Adelaide Donnelley. *Sorrow Mountain: The Journey of a Tibetan Warrior Nun.* New York: Kodansha America, Inc., 2000.

Patt, David. *A Strange Liberation: Tibetan Lives in Chinese Hands.* Ithaca, NY: Snow Lion Publications, 1992.

Paul, Diana. *Women in Buddhism: Images of the Feminine in Mahāyāna*

Tradition. Berkeley, CA: Asian Humanities Press, 1979; reprint, Berkeley: University of California Press, 1985.

Paul, Robert. *The Tibetan Symbolic World: Psychoanalytic Explorations*. Chicago: The University of Chicago Press, 1982.

Petech, Luciano. "The Dalai-Lamas and Regents of Tibet: A Chronological Study." *T'oung Pao* 47 (1959): 368–94.

Pierce, Lori. "Outside In: Buddhism in America." In Dresser, *Buddhist Women on the Edge*, 93–104.

Pintak, Lawrence. "'Something Has to Change': Blacks in American Buddhism." In *Lion's Roar*, September 1, 2001. https://www.lionsroar.com/something-has-to-change-blacks-in-american-buddhism/.

Plaskow, Judith, and Joan Arnold, eds. *Women and Religion*. Chico, CA: AAR/Scholars Press, 1974.

Powers, John. *A Concise Introduction to Tibetan Buddhism*. NY: Snow Lion Publications, 2008.

———.*Introduction to Tibetan Buddhism*. Ithaca, NY: Snow Lion Publications, 2007 [1995].

Prebish, Charles S., and Damien Keown. *Introducing Buddhism*. London: Routledge, 2006.

Prebish, Charles S., and Kenneth Tanaka, eds. *The Faces of Buddhism in America*. Berkeley: University of California Press, 1998.

Quintman, Andrew, trans. *The Life of Milarepa*. New York: Penguin Classics, 2010.

Rahula, Walpola. *What the Buddha Taught, Revised and Expanded Edition with Texts from Suttas and Dhammapada*. New York: Grove Press, 1974 [1959].

Rank, Otto. *The Myth of the Birth of the Hero: A Psychological Exploration of Myth*. Translated by Gregory Richter and E. James Lieberman. Baltimore, MD: Johns Hopkins University Press, 2004 [first German edition, 1922].

Reader, Ian. "Buddhism and the Perils of Advocacy." *Journal of Global Buddhism* 9 (2008): 83–112.

Reynolds, Frank. *Teaching Buddhism in the West: From Wheel to Web*. London: RoutledgeCurzon, 2002.

Reynolds, Frank, and Donald Capps, eds. *The Biographical Process:*

Studies in the History and Psychology of Religion. The Hague: Mouton, 1976.

Rhys Davids, Caroline A. F., trans. *Poems of Early Buddhist Nuns* (revised edition of the *Therīgāthā*). Oxford: The Pali Text Society, 1989.

———. *Psalms of the Sisters (the Therīgāthā).* London: Pāli Text Society, 1948 [1909].

Rhys Davids, T. W., trans. "Kevaddha Sutta." In *Dialogues of the Buddha (Digha Nikaya)*, Sacred Books of the Buddhists, vol. 2, part 1, 277. London: Pali Text Society, 1977 [1921].

———, trans. "Lakkhana Suttanta." In *Dialogues of the Buddha (Digha Nikaya)*, Sacred Books of the Buddhists, vol. 4, 132–67. London: Pali Text Society, 1977 [1921].

Robinson, James. *Buddha's Lions: The Lives of the Eighty-Four Siddhas.* Berkeley, CA: Dharma Press, 1979.

Robinson, Richard. *The Buddhist Religion: A Historical Introduction.* Belmont, CA: Dickenson Publishing, 1970.

Rockhill, W. "The Dalai Lamas of Lhasa and Their Relations with the Manchu Emperors of China 1644–1908." *T'oung Pao* 11 (1910): 1–104.

Roerich, George N., trans. *The Blue Annals.* Calcutta: Royal Asiatic Society of Bengal, 1949; reprint, Delhi: Motilal Banarsidass, 1979.

Rothenberg, Paula. *White Privilege: Essential Readings on the Other Side of Racism.* 5th ed. New York: Worth Publishers, 2016.

Ruegg, David. *The Life of Bu ston Rinpoché, with the Tibetan Text of the Bu ston rNam thar.* Serie Orientale Roma 34. Rome: Istituto Italiano per il Medio ed Estremo Oriente, 1966.

Sam, Canyon. *Sky Train: Tibetan Women on the Edge of History.* Seattle: The University of Washington Press, 2015.

Sastri, Nilakanta. *A History of South India.* Madras, 1963.

Schneider, Tensho David. "Accidents and Calculations: The Emergence of Three AIDS Hospices." *Tricycle: The Buddhist Review* 1, no. 3 (1992): 81.

Schulemann, Gunther. *Die Geschichte der Dalai-Lamas.* Leipzig: Otto Harrassowitz, 1958 [1911].

Schuster, Nancy. "Changing the Female Body: Wise Women and the

Bodhisattva Career in Some *Mahāratnakūṭasūtras.*" *Journal of the International Association of Buddhist Studies* 4, no. 1 (1981): 24–69.

Sermey Geshe Lobsang Tharchin. *A Commentary on Guru Yoga and Offering of the Mandala*. Ithaca, NY: Snow Lion Publications, 1987.

Sermey Geshe Lobsang Tharchin, with Artemus B. Engle, trans. *Liberation in Our Hands: A Series of Oral Discourses, Part 1: The Preliminaries by Pabongka Rinpoche*. Howell, NJ: Mahayana Sutra & Tantra Press, 1999.

Shakabpa, Tsepon W. D. *Tibet: A Political History*. New Haven, CT: Yale University Press, 1967.

Shantideva. *The Way of the Bodhisattva*. Translated by the Padmakara Translation Group. Boston: Shambhala Publications, 2008.

Shaw, Miranda. *Passionate Enlightenment: Women in Tantric Buddhism*. Princeton, NJ: Princeton University Press, 1994.

Snellgrove, David. *Buddhist Himālaya: Travels and Studies in Quest of the Origins and Nature of Tibetan Religion*. Oxford: Bruno Cassirer, 1957.

Snellgrove, David, and Hugh Richardson. *A Cultural History of Tibet*. London: Weidenfeld & Nicolson, 1968; reprint, Boulder, CO: Prajna Press, 1980.

Sogyal Rinpoche. *The Tibetan Book of Living and Dying*. San Francisco: HarperCollins, 1992.

Stanner, W. E. H. "The Dreaming." In *Reader in Comparative Religion: An Anthropological Approach*, edited by William A. Lessa and Evon Z. Vogt, 158–67. New York: Harper & Row, 1979 [1958].

———. "Religion, Totemism, and Symbolism." In *Aboriginal Man in Australia: Essays in Honour of Emeritus Prof. A. P. Elkin*, edited by R. M. and C. H. Berndt. Sydney: Angus and Robertson, 1965.

Steele, Ralph. *Tending the Fire: Through War and the Path of Meditation*. N.p.: Sacred Life Publishers, 2014.

Stein, R. A. *Tibetan Civilization*. Stanford, CA: Stanford University Press, 1972 [1962].

Stevens, India, ed. *A Short Biography of Je Tzong-k'a-pa*. Dharamsala: Library of Tibetan Works & Archives, 1975.

Stevenson, Mrs. Sinclair [Margaret]. *Heart of Jainism*. Oxford: Oxford University Press, 1915.

Strand, Clark. "Buddha in the Market: An Interview with Korean Zen Master Samu Sunim." *Tricycle: The Buddhist Review* 5, no. 2 (1995): 91–92.

Surya Das. *The Snow Lion's Turquoise Mane: Wisdom Tales from Tibet.* New York: HarperCollins, 1992.

Taring, Rinchen Dolma. *Daughter of Tibet: The Autobiography of Rinchen Dolma Taring*. New Delhi: Allied Press, 1970; reprint, London: Wisdom Publications, 1986.

Tarthang Tulku. *Crystal Mirror, Volume IV*. Berkeley, CA: Dharma Publishing, 1975.

———. *Crystal Mirror, Volume V*. Berkeley, CA: Dharma Publishing, 1977.

———, trans. *Mother of Knowledge: The Enlightenment of Yeshe Tsogyal, by Nam-mkha'i snying-po*. Berkeley, CA: Dharma Publishing, 1983.

Thapar, Romila. *A History of India*. 2 vols. Baltimore, MD: Penguin Books, 1969 [1966].

Thich Nhat Hanh. *Being Peace*. Berkeley, CA: Parallax Press, 1987.

———. *Old Path, White Clouds: Walking in the Footsteps of the Buddha*. Berkeley, CA: Parallax Press, 1991.

Thurman, Robert A. F. "Buddhist Hermeneutics." *Journal of the American Academy of Religion* 46, no. 1 (1978): 19–39.

———, trans. *The Central Philosophy of Tibet: A Study and Translation of Jey Tsong Khapa's Essence of True Eloquence*. Princeton, NJ: Princeton University Press, 1984. [Originally published under the title *Tsong Khapa's Speech of Gold in the "Essence of True Eloquence."*]

———, trans. *The Holy Teachings of Vimalakīrti: A Mahāyāna Scripture*. University Park: The Pennsylvania State University Press, 1976. Translated from the Tibetan.

———, ed. *The Life and Teachings of Tsong Khapa*. Dharamsala: Library of Tibetan Works & Archives, 1982.

———, ed. *The Life and Teachings of Tsongkhapa*. Revised edition. Somerville, MA: Wisdom Publications in collaboration with the Library of Tibetan Works & Archives, 2018.

——. *The Tibetan Book of the Dead: Liberation through Understanding in the Between*. New York: Bantam Books, 1994.

Tsuda, Shin'ichi. *A Critical Tantrism*. Memoirs of the Research Department of the Toyo Bunko 36. Tokyo: The Toyo Bunko, 1978.

Tucci, Giuseppe. *To Lhasa and Beyond: Diary of the Expedition to Tibet in the Year MCMXLVIII*. Rome: Instituto Poligrafico Dell Stato, 1956.

——. *The Religions of Tibet*. Berkeley: University of California Press, 1980 [1970].

——. *Tibetan Painted Scrolls*. 3 vols. Rome: Libreria dello Stato, 1949.

Tutu, Desmond. *No Future without Forgiveness*. New York: Doubleday, 1999.

Tweed, Thomas. "Night-Stand Buddhists and Other Creatures: Sympathizers, Adherents, and the Study of Religion." In *American Buddhism: Methods and Findings in Recent Scholarship*, edited by Duncan Ryūken Williams and Christopher S. Queen, 71–90. London: Routledge, 1999.

Tworkov, Helen. *Zen in America: Profiles of Five Teachers*. San Francisco: North Point Press, 1989.

van Zeyst, H. G. A. "Abhinna." In *Encyclopaedia of Buddhism*, edited by G. P. Malalasekera, vol. 1, 97–102. Colombo: The Government Press, 1961.

Waddell, L. Austine. *The Buddhism of Tibet, or Lamaism; with Its Mystic Cults, Symbolism and Mythology, and in Its Relation to Indian Buddhism*. New York: Dover Publications, 1972 [1895].

Warren, Henry Clarke. *Buddhism in Translations*. New York: Atheneum, 1968 [1896].

Wayman, Alex. *Yoga of the Guhyasamājatantra: The Arcane Lore of Forty Verses: A Buddhist Tantra Commentary*. Delhi: Motilal Banarsidass, 1999 [1977].

Wayman, Alex, and Hideko Wayman, trans. *The Lion's Roar of Queen Śrīmālā*. New York: Columbia University Press, 1974.

Williams, Duncan Ryuken. "At Ease in Between: The Middle Position of a Scholar-Practitioner." *Journal of Global Buddhism* 9 (2008): 155–63.

Willis, Janice D. "Buddhas, Bodhisattvas, and Arhats." In *Encyclopedia of Women and World Religion*, edited by Serenity Young, vol. 1, 107–8. New York: Macmillan, 1998.

———. "Buddhism and Race: An African American Baptist-Buddhist Perspective." In Dresser, *Buddhist Women on the Edge*, 81–91.

——— "The Dharma Has No Color." In *Dharma, Color, and Culture: New Voices in Western Buddhism*, edited by Hilda Baldoquin, 217–24. Berkeley, CA: Parallax Press, 2004.

———. *The Diamond Light of the Eastern Dawn: A Collection of Tibetan Buddhist Meditations*. New York: Simon and Schuster, 1972.

———. "Diversity and Race: New Koans for American Buddhism." In *Women's Buddhism: Buddhism's Women*, edited by Elli Findly, 303–16. Boston: Wisdom Publications, 2000.

———. *Dreaming Me: An African American Woman's Spiritual Journey*. New York: Riverhead Books, 2001.

———. *Dreaming Me: Black, Baptist, and Buddhist: One Woman's Spiritual Journey*. Boston: Wisdom Publications, 2008.

———. *Enlightened Beings: Life Stories from the Ganden Oral Tradition*. Boston: Wisdom Publications, 1995.

———, ed. *Feminine Ground: Essays on Women and Tibet*. Boulder, CO: Shambhala Publications, 1987.

———. "Kamalaśīla." In *The Encyclopedia of Religion*, edited by Mircea Eliade, vol. 8, 242–43. New York: Macmillan, 1987.

———. "A New Spirit at Spirit Rock." In *Tricycle: The Buddhist Review* (Winter 2002): 28–29.

———. "Nuns and Benefactresses: The Role of Women in the Development of Buddhism." In *Women, Religion and Social Change*, edited by Y. Haddad and E. Findly, 59–85. Albany: State University of New York Press, 1985.

———. "Śāntirakṣita." In *The Encyclopedia of Religion*, edited by Mircea Eliade, vol. 13, 68–69. New York: Macmillan, 1987.

———. "Yes, We're Buddhists, Too!" *Buddhadharma* (Winter 2011): 42–45.

Wittgenstein, Ludwig. *Philosophical Investigations*. Translated by G. E. M. Anscombe. New York: The Macmillan Company, 1953.

Wuthnow, R., and W. Cadge. "Buddhists and Buddhism in the United States: The Scope of Influence." *Journal for the Scientific Study of Religion* 43, no. 3 (2004): 363–80.

Wylie, Turrell, ed. and trans. *The Geography of Tibet according to the 'Dzam-gling-rgyas-bshad*. Rome: Istituto Italiano per il Medio ed Estremo Orient, 1962.

Yamaguchi, Zuiho, ed. *Catalogue of the Toyo Bunko Collection of Tibetan Works on History*, vol. 1. Tokyo: The Toyo Bunko, 1970.

Credits

❧❧

"Nuns and Benefactresses: The Role of Women in the Development of Buddhism" was originally published in *Women, Religion and Social Change* (Albany: State University of New York Press, 1985). Reprinted with permission of SUNY Press.

"The *Chomos* of Ladakh: From Servants to Practitioners" was originally published in *Buddhadharma: The Practitioner's Quarterly* (Summer 2004). Permission granted by Koun Franz.

"Tibetan Anis: The Nun's Life in Tibet" was originally published in *Feminine Ground: Essays on Women and Tibet*, ed. Janice D. Willis (Ithaca, NY: Snow Lion Publications, 1987). Copyright © 1987 by Janice D. Willis. Reprinted by arrangement with The Permissions Company, Inc., on behalf of Shambhala Publications.

"Tibetan Buddhist Women Practitioners, Past and Present: A Garland to Delight Those Wishing Inspiration" was originally published in *Buddhist Women Across Cultures* (Albany: State University of New York Press, 1999). Reprinted with permission of SUNY Press.

"Female Patronage in Indian Buddhism" was originally published in *The Powers of Art: Patronage in Indian Culture*, ed. Barbara Stoler Miller (Oxford: Oxford University Press, 1992). © Oxford University Press 1992. Reproduced with permission of Oxford University Press India.

1987 by Janice D. Willis. Reprinted by arrangement with The Permissions Company, Inc., on behalf of Shambhala Publications.

"Namthar as Literature and Liturgy" was originally published in *Enlightened Beings: Life Stories from the Ganden Oral Tradition* (Somerville, MA: Wisdom Publications, 1995).

"The Goddess and the Flowers" was originally published in *The Hidden Lamp: Stories from Twenty-Five Centuries of Awakened Women*, ed. Zenshin Florence Caplow and Reigetsu Susan Moon (Somerville, MA: Wisdom Publications, 2013), 325–28.

"Community of 'Neighbors': A Baptist-Buddhist Reflects on the Common Ground of Love" was originally published as "Community of Neighbors," *Buddhist-Christian Studies* 34 (2014): 97–106. Reproduced with permission.

"A Professor's Dilemma" was originally published in *Buddhadharma* (spring 2008). Permission granted by Koun Franz.

"Teaching Buddhism in the Western Academy" was originally published in Jan Willis, *Teaching Buddhism: New Insights on Understanding and Presenting the Traditions*, ed. Todd Lewis and Gary DeAngelis (Oxford: Oxford University Press, 2016), 151–65. Copyright © 2016 by Oxford University Press. Reproduced by permission of Oxford University Press.

"A Baptist-Buddhist" was originally published in Jan Willis, *Dreaming Me: An African American Woman's Spiritual Journey* (New York: Riverhead Books, 2001), reprinted as *Dreaming Me: Black, Baptist and Buddhist: One Woman's Spiritual Journey* (Somerville, MA: Wisdom Publications, 2008).

Index

❦

A

abbesses of Samding, 53–54, 70

Abhayadatta, 303–4n312

Abhayakaragupta, *namthar* of, 181

Addhakasi, 32

Adiele, Faith, 95

African American Buddhists. *See also* American Buddhism

as "anomalous," 94–95

beginners, advice to, 117–18

creating pathways for, 117–20

and disjuncture of cultures, 93, 103, 267

diversity among, 107, 134

identifying as Buddhist, 93

integrating with Christian faith, 136

personal journeys, 135

practice groups, retreats, 95, 135–36

as teachers, need for, 119

African Americans. *See also* racism

and the appeal/value of Buddhism, 98, 101, 118–19, 125–26, 130, 132

spiritual resilience, 101–2

understanding of suffering and trauma, 126–27, 135–36, 232–33

Ahkon Lhamo, Genyenma, 70, 74–75

altruism, 7, 228–29, 239–40. *See also* compassion; love

Amaravati stupa, India, 87

Ambapali, 31–32, 85, 276n60, 276n63, 286n165

American (Western) Buddhism

association with money and leisure time, 100

and Chinese and Japanese immigrants, 132–33

commodification, 99–100

convert vs. immigrant Buddhists, 133

and desire for pith above fluff, 124

diverse traditions associated with, 132–34

doctrinal rigidity, 64

female leadership, 120–21

focus on spiritual/meditation, 287–88nn184–185

lack of inclusiveness, 119–20

need for African American teachers, 136

numbers of practitioners, 96

potential contributions of African Americans to, 101–2

pretentions, 102–3

course followed by, as open to all, 82

as intrinsically male, 25

an selfless practice, 217, 229

Bön, religion of, 192

Boucher, Sandy, 96

the Buddha

ambivalence about women, 18,
187–88

buddha nature, 30–32

denouncing of the caste system, 132

emphasis on personal path and experience, 245

inclusion of women in sangha,
15–17, 84, 132, 237–38, 280–81n91, 319n395

magical powers, 216

on nonviolence, 131–32

parthenogenic birth, 270–71n7

raft parable, 127–28

rules imposed on nuns, 16–18

sangha of, 15, 19, 84, 89, 237–38,
275n50, 319n395

Satipatthana Sutra (Foundations of
Mindfulness), 246

seeing the guru as, 209, 314n360

societal position during lifetime, 29

Visakha's gifts to, 84

on voidness, 187

buddha nature, 130, 246–47, 258

Buddharaksita, 87

Buddhism. *See also* Baptist Buddhist
identity; laywomen; nuns

and the availability of Dharma to
everyone, 28–29, 83, 129

and compassion, 243–44

conventional and ultimate truth, 129

correspondences, 169, 221–22

early female patronage, 18, 84, 87,
275n50

emphasis on personal experience, 126

and forgiveness, 131–32

Four Noble Truths, 102, 126

and identifying as a Buddhist, 113–14

importance of early female patronage, 30–32, 35, 81–82, 90,
275–76nn53–54

incorporating other faith traditions
with, 127–28, 289n193

lack of dogma, 126, 322n433

meditation practices, 125

practice by women, 26–28, 67–68,
274n48, 275n53, 280–81n91

proselytizing activities, 97

secular histories, 35

and self-confidence, self-awareness, 98

and supermundane powers, 215

themes of nonviolence, interdependence, and love, 237

"Three Jewels," 292n221

types of wisdom, 321n418

vehicles of, 302n307

Buddhism and Racism Working
Group, 106

Buddhism without Beliefs (Batcheor),
251

Buddhist Himālaya (Snellgrove), 159

Buddhist Peace Fellowship, Berkeley,
California, 111

Buddhist scripture. *See also namthar*
absence of women *arhats* from,
280–81n91

diversity of views on women, 13–14

male authorship, 14

as source of historical information,
14, 35, 275n53

and Tibetan historical literature,
292–93n225

*Buddhist Women on the Edge: Contemporary Perspectives from the
Western Frontier*, 106

Kamenetz, Rodger, 93

Katz, Nathan, 174, 181–82, 184–85

Khandro, Ayu, 70

Khandro, Drigung, 70

Khandro Chenmo Rinpoché, 70

Khenpo Kunchok Molam Rinpoché, 109

Kierkegaard, Søren, 237, 266, 319n392

King, Martin Luther Jr.

"Beloved Community" vision, 242–43

Good Samaritan parable, 7

"Letter from a Birmingham Jail," 319n404

marching with, 4, 233

principles espoused by, 131–32, 237, 240–41

koans for addressing racial and gender diversity, 121

Kopan, Nepalese Mahayana Gompa, 145

Kornfield, Jack, 112

KPC. *See* Nyingmapa Buddhist Center, Poolesville, Maryland

Kris, Ernst, 143–44, 291n211

Kukkuripa, 184

the *Kunalajataka*, views of women in, 21

Kunchog, Venerable Jampa ("Yogi"), 94

Kunkhyen Lekpa Döndrup, 202

Kurukulla Center, Boston, Massachusetts, 315n371

Kushana empire, 33, 88, 277n69

Kushog, Jetsun, 70

Kyirong monastery, 61, 282–83n113

kyong (protector), 141, 152, 291n216

Kyongru Tulku, meaning of name, 152–53. *See also* Döndrup Tsering, Kyongru Tulku

L

Ladakh, India, nuns in, 37–43

lama. *See* guru (teacher); guru devotion

The Lama Knows, 155

Lamdré (path and fruit), 204, 311n342

Lamrim Chenmo, 294–95n237, 307n324

Langmikpa, 202

Lapdrönma, Machik, 47, 54, 185, 274n48, 282n101

laukika siddhis (mundane powers), 163, 292–93n232

lay practitioners (*upasika*)

capacity for enlightenment, 28–29

dependence of monastics on, 23

enrobing of in Ladakh, 38

female, challenges to early monastics, 19–21, 26–28

inclusion in lineage of Tibetan women, 70

interrelationship with *religieux* in Tibet, 50–51

patronage, support for the Buddha, 35, 81–82, 84

Levi-Strauss, Claude, 290n207

lhakhas and *pawo* (spirit mediums), 47

Lhalungpa, Lobsang, 55, 57, 75, 282n104, 282n107

To Lhasa and Beyond (Tucci), 53

life history approach, 143

The Life of Marpa, 73

lineage-holders, 206–7, 210, 294n234, 312–13n352

Ling Derma lineage, origin story, 147–50

Ling Rinpoché, 56, 61, 65, 282n106

Lochen, Jetsun Ani (Shuksep Jetsun Lochen Rinpoché), 54–57, 70, 75–78, 282n107

Lopez, Donald Jr., 255, 322–23n434

Perfection of Wisdom literature, 25,
274n41
Pierce, Lori
background and practice, 107–8
Buddhist practice in Hawai'i, 95
experience in predominantly white
Buddhist centers, 115–16
on identifying as a Buddhist, 113–14
on implications of practicing diversity, 120–21
on racism and sexism in American
Buddhism, 120, 287, 287n184
pill retreats, 311n343
pithas (outer and inner pilgrimage
places/locations), 168–69, 189,
220–21
The Power-Places of Central Tibet
(Dowman), 72–73
Powers, John, 255
prajna (wisdom), 185–86
Prajnaparamita ("Perfection of
Women") texts, 25, 274n41
*Prayer, with Supplement, to the Lineage
Lamas of the Ganden Oral Tradi-
tion of Mahamudra*, 164–65,
205–6, 294n234, 311–12n346
Prebish, Charles, 258–59, 323n435
Prisoners of Shangri-La (Lopez), 255
Psychoanalytic Explorations in Art
(Kris), 143–44
Pure Land Buddhism, 124–25

R
racism. *See also* African Americans;
American (Western) Buddhism
in American Buddhism, efforts to
address, 106–7
changes to the Voting Rights Act,
318n387
educating *sanghas* about, 136–37

and the enduring legacy of slavery,
233
as a hateful term, 235
and the Jim Crow South, 233
manifestations in daily life, 233–35
sources and endurance of, 231–32
and white privilege, 235
raft parable, 127–28
Rahula, Walpola, 128, 251
Rank, Otto, 291n215
rddhi, 215–16
Rechungma, 69
Rechungpa, 73
Red Lotus School of Movement, Salt
Lake City, 110
refuge, Buddhist, 113–14, 209,
292n221, 313n353
rikma (wisdom being, mystic consort),
54, 184, 300n287
Rilu, Ani, 70
Rinzai Zen, 121
Rizong monastery, Ladakh, 38
Robinson, James, 178
Robinson, Leslie, 95
Robinson, Richard, 29–30, 273n34,
275n50
root guru, identifying, 211. *See also*
guru (teacher); guru devotion
Royce, Josiah, 319n402
ru (bone) lineage, 152, 291n214

S
sacred biography, 144, 162–64, 178,
191–92, 217. *See also* hagiography; *namthar*
saints, lives of, 162–64
Sakya order/tradition, 201, 204, 280,
311n342
Sakyadhita Conference of Buddhist
Women, Ladakh, 37–38, 40–41

and perfection of sexual union, 186
student interest in, 252–53
symbols for, 178
Siddhartha Gautama. *See* the Buddha
siddhas (perfected ones). *See also*
    namthar
  biographies, sources for, 303–4n312
  birth, magical symbols associated
      with, 291n216
  inspiration from, 211
  magical powers, 193, 215–17
  meditation practice, retreats, 204
  path taken by, 166, 217
  praying to, as inspirational, 206–7
  as proof of the effectiveness of tantric
      Buddhism, 163, 215, 304n313
  spiritual accomplishments, 213–16,
      302n307
  studies undertaken by, 204
  as subjects of *namthar*, 162, 191
  as successors to Tsongkhapa, 197
  supernatural powers, 192–93
siddhis (magical powers), 163, 193,
    213–17, 293–94n232
six perfections, 28, 83
six yogas system, 184. *See also* Niguma
*Sky Dancer: The Secret Life and Songs
    of the Lady Yeshe Tsogyel* (Dow-
    man), 72
"sky-dancer, sky-goer," dakini as, 174,
    177–78
slavery. *See also* African Americans;
    racism
  enduring trauma as legacy of,
      100–101, 232–33
  and evangelical Christianity, 133
  and white privilege, 235
smallpox epidemics, 202–3
Snellgrove, David

on the appeal of Tsongkhapa's teach-
    ings, 198
description of *dakini*, 175
on encountering living Tibetan Bud-
    dhists, 159
on *namthar*, 292n231, 296n241,
    305n315
on relationship between lay commu-
    nities and monasteries, 50–51
The Snow Lion's Turquoise Mane (Das),
    67–68
Soka Gakkai, 134
Sonam, Thubten, 145
Sönam Choklang (Second Panchen
    Lama), 202
Sönam Gyatso (Third Dalai Lama), 198
*Song of the Mystic Experiences of Lama
    Jé Rinpoché*, 316n373
Sorrow Mountain (Ani Pachen), 255
Srī-Mālā sutra, 33, 277n68
Stanner, W. E. H., 143, 290n203
Steele, Ralph, 111–12, 114–17, 136
stupas, 28, 83
suffering (*duhkha*)
  and the African American experi-
      ence, 126–27, 135–36, 232–233
  avoiding, as universal desire, 130–31
  types and meanings, 126
  understanding, as First Noble Truth,
      102
Suhita, Reverend, 95
Sukhasiddhi, 69
Sullā, 34, 89
Sunim, Venerable Samu, 97
Surya Das, Lama, 67–68

T
Takanashi, Master Ronald, 109
taknyi (two examinations), 204,
    311n342

About the Author

❧❧

Jan Willis (BA and MA in philosophy, Cornell University; PhD in Indic and Buddhist Studies, Columbia University) is Professor Emerita of Religious Studies at Wesleyan University in Middletown, Connecticut, and now Visiting Professor of Religious Studies at Agnes Scott College in Decatur, Georgia. She has studied with Tibetan Buddhists in India, Nepal, Switzerland, and the United States for five decades, and has taught courses in Buddhism for over forty-five years. She is the author of *The Diamond Light: An Introduction to Tibetan Buddhist Meditation* (1972), *On Knowing Reality: The Tattvartha Chapter of Asanga's Bodhisattvabhumi* (1979), *Enlightened Beings: Life Stories from the Ganden Oral Tradition* (1995), and the editor of *Feminine Ground: Essays on Women and Tibet* (1989). Additionally, Willis has published numerous articles and essays on various topics in Buddhism—Buddhist meditation, hagiography, women and Buddhism, and Buddhism and race. In 2001 her memoir *Dreaming Me: An African American Woman's Spiritual Journey* was published. It was reissued in 2008 by Wisdom Publications as *Dreaming Me: Black, Baptist, and Buddhist: One Woman's Spiritual Journey*. In December 2000 *TIME* magazine named Willis one of six "spiritual innovators for the new millennium." In 2003 she was a recipient of Wesleyan University's Binswanger Prize for Excellence in Teaching. *Newsweek* magazine's "Spirituality in America" issue in September 2005 included a profile of Willis, and in its May 2007 edition, *Ebony* magazine named Willis one of its "Power 150" most influential African Americans.

What to Read Next
from Wisdom Publications

⤴⤵

Dreaming Me
Black, Baptist, and Buddhist—One Woman's Spiritual Journey
By Jan Willis

One of *TIME* magazine's Top Religious Innovators for the New Millennium.

Enlightened Beings
Life Stories from the Ganden Oral Tradition
By Jan Willis

"The stories offer a dimension of understanding not seen in other literature. A fascinating addition to any library."—*Small Press*

The Way of Tenderness
Awakening through Race, Sexuality, and Gender
By Zenju Earthlyn Manuel

"Manuel's teaching is a thought-provoking, much-needed addition to contemporary Buddhist literature."—*Publishers Weekly*

Sanctuary
A Meditation on Home, Homelessness, and Belonging
By Zenju Earthlyn Manuel

"Zenju Earthlyn Manuel's *Sanctuary* offers us much-needed clarity and light in a time of increasing violence and confusion, daily assaults on our basic sense of belonging."—Acharya Gaylon Ferguson, PhD, core faculty, Naropa University

About the cover image:
Green Tara
Tibet; 19th century
Ground Mineral Pigment on Cotton
Rubin Museum of Art
Gift of Shelley and Donald Rubin
C2006.66.169 (HAR 176)

About Wisdom Publications

Wisdom Publications is the leading publisher of classic and contemporary Buddhist books and practical works on mindfulness. To learn more about us or to explore our other books, please visit our website at wisdomexperience.org or contact us at the address below.

Wisdom Publications
199 Elm Street
Somerville, MA 02144 USA

We are a 501(c)(3) organization, and donations in support of our mission are tax deductible.

Wisdom Publications is affiliated with the Foundation for the Preservation of the Mahayana Tradition (FPMT).